Lecture Notes in Computer Science 12246

More information about this series at http://www.springer.com/series/7409

Mark Hall · Tanja Merčun ·
Thomas Risse · Fabien Duchateau (Eds.)

Digital Libraries for Open Knowledge

24th International Conference on Theory and Practice of Digital Libraries, TPDL 2020
Lyon, France, August 25–27, 2020
Proceedings

Springer

Editors
Mark Hall
School of Computing and Communications
The Open University
Milton Keynes, UK

Tanja Merčun
Faculty of Arts
University of Ljubljana
Ljubljana, Slovenia

Thomas Risse
University Library J. C. Senckenberg
Goethe University Frankfurt
Frankfurt am Main, Germany

Fabien Duchateau
Université Claude Bernard Lyon 1
Villeurbanne, France

ISSN 0302-9743 ISSN 1611-3349 (electronic)
Lecture Notes in Computer Science
ISBN 978-3-030-54955-8 ISBN 978-3-030-54956-5 (eBook)
https://doi.org/10.1007/978-3-030-54956-5

LNCS Sublibrary: SL3 – Information Systems and Applications, incl. Internet/Web, and HCI

This Springer imprint is published by the registered company Springer Nature Switzerland AG
The registered company address is: Gewerbestrasse 11, 6330 Cham, Switzerland

Preface

We are happy and proud to present this volume of proceedings, which contains the accepted papers presented at the 24th International Conference on Theory and Practice of Digital Libraries (TPDL 2020), which should have taken place in Lyon, France, during August 25–28, 2020. TPDL 2020 was organized by the Université de Lyon and held conjointly with the 24th European Conference on Advances in Databases and Information Systems (ADBIS 2020) and the 16th French EDA days on Business Intelligence & Big Data. However, due to the COVID-19 pandemic, the joint conferences were held fully online for the first time during August 25–27, 2020.

The TPDL conference constitutes a leading scientific forum that brings together researchers, developers, content providers, and practitioners in the field of Digital Libraries. Digital libraries and repositories store, manage, represent, and disseminate rich and heterogeneous data that are often of enormous cultural, scientific, educational, artistic, and social value. Serving as digital ecosystems for empowering researchers and practitioners they provide unparalleled opportunities for novel knowledge extraction and discovery. New applications raise novel challenges that can only be addressed in an interdisciplinary community of researchers and practitioners from various disciplines including the Digital Humanities, Information Sciences, and others. Holding TPDL conjointly with ADBIS and EDA facilitated establishing connections and convergences between communities that could benefit from (and contribute to) the ecosystems offered by digital libraries and repositories.

TPDL 2020 received 53 submissions from more than 40 countries. These submissions were divided into 35 long papers, 10 short papers, and 8 poster and demo papers. Based on the reviews, meta-reviews, and discussion between reviewers, the Program Committee ensured that emerging topics, which could extend the field of Digital Libraries, were represented as well as more traditional areas in Digital Libraries. Of the long paper submissions, 14 were accepted (40%). Additionally, we accepted three short papers (30%) and one demo (12%). Due to the online nature of the conference, the demo was converted into a short paper. In total, 18 papers (34%) were accepted for these proceedings, which is below the acceptance rate of previous editions (typically around 45%), making this year's edition very selective.

The joint conferences welcomed five keynote speakers. Elaine Toms (University of Sheffield, UK) proposed "integrating Digital Libraries within work task systems," an inspiring talk on promoting effective knowledge work. Other keynotes from the Database and Information Systems fields were closely linked to Digital Libraries. Ioana Manolescu (Inria Saclay Île-de-France et École Polytechnique, France) focused on "rich data exploration at cloud scale" and Verónika Peralta (University of Tours, France) presented a talk about "data warehousing, exploratory analysis, OLAP." Johann Gamper (Free University of Bozen-Bolzano, Italy) introduced "processing and querying temporal data" and Amr El Abbadi (University of California, USA) spoke about "fault-tolerant distributed systems and databases."

In addition to the main conferences, the program included a common doctoral consortium track and six workshops: Modern Approaches in Data Engineering and Information System Design (MADEISD 2020), International Workshop on Intelligent Data – From Data to Knowledge (DOING 2020), the First Workshop on Assessing Impact and Merit in Science (AIMinScience 2020), Scientific Knowledge Graphs, the Second International Workshop on BI & Big Data Applications (BBIGAPP 2020), and the 10th International Symposium on Data-Driven Process Discovery and Analysis (SIMPDA 2020). These workshops allowed communities from Digital Libraries and Information Systems to discuss and share their experiences.

Finally, this conference would not have been successful without the help from many colleagues whose support and work was particularly appreciated during these difficult times. First, we thank all the researchers for submitting their papers to TPDL 2020, as well as our Program Committee members, both senior and regular, for their accurate and insightful discussions while reviewing submissions. A word of gratitude must be addressed to our workshop chairs: Mária Bieliková, Christos Papatheodorou, Guilaine Talens, and Ladjel Bellatreche, and to our doctoral consortium chairs: Elena Demidova, Maja Žumer, Barbara Catania, and Oscar Romero, for their efforts in managing their tracks. We acknowledge the excellent dissemination work of our publicity chairs, namely Sarantos Kapidakis, Jane Winters, George Buchanan, Adam Jatowt, Marc Spaniol, and Bernhard Wirth. We also express our gratitude to the Steering Committee members, who gave us complete confidence for organizing this edition of TPDL, and in particular to Trond Aalberg who coordinated the relationship between committees. We appreciate the work of our proceedings chairs Fadila Bentayeb, Nadia Kabachi, and Elöd Egyed-Zsigmond, as well as the local organizing team. Last but not least, we would like to thank our colleagues from the database and information systems community for this fruitful experience, with a special mention to Jérôme Darmont.

August 2020

Mark Hall
Tanja Merčun
Thomas Risse
Fabien Duchateau

Organization

General Chair

Fabien Duchateau	Université Lyon 1, France

Steering Committee Chair

Trond Aalberg	OsloMet, Norway

Steering Committee

Trond Aalberg	OsloMet, Norway
Bolette Ammitzboll	Jurik State and University Library, Denmark
George Buchanan	The University of Melbourne, Australia
Lazaros Iliadis	Democritus University of Thrace, Greece
Vittore Casarosa	ISTI-CNR, Italy
Milena Dobreva	University of Malta, Malta
Laszlo Kovacs	MTA SZTAKI, Hungary
Sarantos Kapidakis	Ionian University, Greece
Jaap Kamps	University of Amsterdam, The Netherlands
Wolfgang Neidl	L3S Research Center, Germany
Yannis Manolopoulos	Aristotle University of Thessaloniki, Greece
Cezary Mazurek	Poznań Supercomputing and Networking Center, Poland
Andreas Rauber	Technical University of Wien, Austria
Christos Papatheodorou	Ionian University, Greece
Edie Rasmussen	University of British Columbia, Canada
Ingeborg Solvberg	Norwegian University of Technology and Science, Norway
Marcin Werla	Qatar National Library, Qatar
Heiko Schuldt	University of Basel, Switzerland

Program Committee Chairs

Mark Hall	The Open University, UK
Tanja Merčun	University of Ljubljana, Slovenia
Thomas Risse	University Frankfurt, University Library J. C. Senckenberg, Germany

Program Committee

Trond Aalberg	OsloMet, Norway
Maristella Agosti	University of Padua, Italy
Hamed Alhoori	Northern Illinois University, USA
Robert Allen	Independent, USA
David Bainbridge	University of Waikato, New Zealand
Vangelis Banos	Aristotle University of Thessaloniki, Greece
José Borbinha	Universidade de Lisboa, Portugal
Maria Manuel Borges	University of Coimbra, Portugal
George Buchanan	The University of Melbourne, Australia
Ricardo Campos	Ci2 – Polytechnic Institute of Tomar, INESC TEC, Portugal
Vittore Casarosa	ISTI-CNR, Italy
Lillian Cassel	Villanova University, USA
Songphan Choemprayong	Chulalongkorn University, Thailand
Mickaël Coustaty	Laboratoire L3i, Université de La Rochelle, France
Theodore Dalamagas	ATHENA Research Center, Greece
Elena Demidova	L3S Research Center, Germany
Boris Dobrov	Research Computing Center of Moscow State University, Russia
Shyamala Doraisamy	University Putra Malaysia, Malaysia
Antoine Doucet	Université de La Rochelle, France
Fabien Duchateau	Université Claude Bernard Lyon 1, LIRIS, France
Ralph Ewerth	L3S Research Center, Leibniz Universität Hannover, Germany
Nicola Ferro	University of Padova, Italy
Edward Fox	Virginia Tech, USA
Nuno Freire	INESC-ID, Portugal
Richard Furuta	Texas A&M University, USA
Manolis Gergatsoulis	Department of Archives, Library Sciences and Museology, Greece
C. Lee Giles	Penn State University, USA
Koraljka Golub	Linnaeus University, Sweden
Marcos Goncalves	Federal University of Minas Gerais, Brazil
Paula Goodale	University of Sheffield, UK
Sergiu Gordea	AIT Austrian Institute of Technology, Austria
Jane Greenberg	Drexel University, USA
Mark Michael Hall	The Open University, UK
Andreas Henrich	University of Bamberg, Germany
Nikos Housos	IRI, Greece
Antoine Isaac	Europeana, VU University Amsterdam, The Netherlands
Adam Jatowt	Kyoto University, Japan
Robert Jäschke	Humboldt-Universität zu Berlin, Germany
Jaap Kamps	University of Amsterdam, The Netherlands

Sarantos Kapidakis	University of West Attica, Greece
Ioannis Karydis	Ionian University, Greece
Roman Kern	Graz University of Technology, Austria
Kimmo Kettunen	National Library of Finland, University of Helsinki, Finland
Martin Klein	Los Alamos National Laboratory, USA
Stefanos Kollias	National Technical University of Athens, Greece
Laszlo Kovacs	MTA SZTAKI, Computer and Automation Research Institute of the Hungarian Academy of Sciences, Hungary
Monica Landoni	Università della Svizzera italiana (USI), Switzerland
Suzanne Little	Dublin City University, Ireland
Ying-Hsang Liu	University of Southern Denmark, Denmark
Clifford Lynch	cni, USA
Yannis Manolopoulos	Open University of Cyprus, Cyprus
Zinaida Manžuch	Vilnius University, Lithuania
Bruno Martins	IST/INESC-ID – Instituto Superior Técnico, University of Lisbon, Portugal
Philipp Mayr	GESIS, Germany
Cezary Mazurek	Poznań Supercomputing and Networking Center, Poland
Robert H. Mcdonald	University of Colorado Boulder, USA
Tanja Merčun Kariž	University of Ljubljana, Slovenia
András Micsik	SZTAKI, Hungary
Jean-Philippe Moreux	Bibliothèque nationale de France, France
Agnieszka Mykowiecka	IPI PAN, Poland
Wolfgang Nejdl	L3S, University of Hannover, Germany
Michael Nelson	Old Dominion University, USA
Erich Neuhold	University of Vienna, Austria
Heike Neuroth	University of Applied Sciences Potsdam, Germany
David Nichols	University of Waikato, New Zealand
Kjetil Nørvåg	Norwegian University of Science and Technology, Norway
Christos Papatheodorou	Ionian University, Greece
Nils Pharo	OsloMet, Norway
Francesco Piccialli	University of Naples Federico II, Italy
Dimitris Plexousakis	Institute of Computer Science, FORTH, Greece
Edie Rasmussen	The University of British Columbia, Canada
Andreas Rauber	Vienna University of Technology, Austria
Cristina Ribeiro	INESC TEC, University of Porto, Portugal
Thomas Risse	University Frankfurt, University Library J. C. Senckenberg, Germany
João Rocha Da Silva	University of Porto, Portugal
Irene Rodrigues	Universidade de Evora, Portugal
Heiko Schuldt	University of Basel, Switzerland
Michalis Sfakakis	Ionian University, Greece

Frank Shipman	Texas A&M University, USA
Mário J. Silva	Universidade de Lisboa, Portugal
Marc Spaniol	Université de Caen Normandie, France
Shigeo Sugimoto	University of Tsukuba, Japan
Cyrille Suire	Université Paris-Saclay, UVSQ, France
Hussein Suleman	University of Cape Town, South Africa
Nina Tahmasebi	University of Gothenburg, Sweden
Atsuhiro Takasu	National Institute of Informatics, Japan
Diana Trandabat	Al.I.Cuza University of Iasi, Romania
Theodora Tsikrika	Information Technologies Institute, CERTH, Greece
Chrisa Tsinaraki	European Commission – Joint Research Center (EC – JRC), Italy
Douglas Tudhope	University of South Wales, UK
Yannis Tzitzikas	University of Crete and FORTH-ICS, Greece
Pertti Vakkari	Tampere University, Finland
Stefanos Vrochidis	Information Technologies Institute, Greece
David Walsh	Edge Hill University, UK
Michele Weigle	Old Dominion University, USA
Marcin Werla	Qatar National Library, Qatar
Jane Winters	School of Advanced Study, UK
Iris Xie	Universty of Wisconsin-Milwaukee, USA
Maja Žumer	University of Ljubljana, Slovenia

Additional Reviewers

Thorben Funke
Evangelos A. Stathopoulos
Prashant Chandrasekar
Eleftherios Kalogeros
Pavlos Fafalios
Maria-Evaggelia Papadaki
Michalis Mountantonakis
Michel Schwab
Alexandros Kokkalas
Yannis Marketakis
Brenda Santana
Sherzod Hakimov
Anett Hoppe
Xinyue Wang

Proceeding Chairs

Fadila Bentayeb	Université Lyon 2, France
Elöd Egyed-Zsigmond	INSA Lyon, France
Nadia Kabachi	Université Lyon 1, France

Workshop Chairs

Ladjel Bellatreche	ENSMA Poitiers, France
Mária Bieliková	Slovak University of Technology, Slovakia
Christos Papatheodorou	Ionian University, Greece
Guilaine Talens	Université Lyon 3, France

Doctoral Consortium Chairs

Barbara Catania	University of Genoa, Italy
Elena Demidova	L3S Research Center, Germany
Oscar Romero	Universitat Politécnica de Catalunya, Spain
Maja Žumer	University of Ljubljana, Slovenia

Publicity Chairs

Sarantos Kapidakis	Ionian University, Greece
George Buchanan	The University of Melbourne, Australia
Adam Jatowt	Kyoto University, Japan
Marc Spaniol	Université de Caen Basse-Normandie, France
Jane Winters	University of London, UK
Bernhard Wirth	University Frankfurt, University Library J. C. Senckenberg, Germany

Organizing Committee

Fadila Bentayeb	Université Lyon 2, France
Omar Boussaïd	Université Lyon 2, France
Jérôme Darmont	Université Lyon 2, France
Fabien Duchateau	Université Lyon 1, France
Elöd Egyed-Zsigmond	INSA Lyon, France
Mihaela Juganaru-Mathieu	École des Mines de Saint-Étienne, France
Nadia Kabachi	Université Lyon 1, France
Omar Larouk	ENSSIB Lyon, France
Fabrice Muhlenbach	Université de Saint-Étienne, France
Habiba Osman	Université Lyon 2, France
Muriel Perez	Université de Saint-Étienne, France
Pegdwendé Sawadogo	Université Lyon 2, France
Guilaine Talens	Université Lyon 3, France
Caroline Wintergerst	Université Lyon 3, France

Keynote Speakers' Bios

The 24th European Conference on Advances in Databases and Information Systems (ADBIS 2020), the 24th International Conference on Theory and Practice of Digital Libraries (TPDL 2020), and the 16th EDA days on Business Intelligence & Big Data (EDA 2020) were "colocated" online during August 25–27, 2020, because of the COVID-19 crisis. This joint event was set to be held originally in Lyon, France.

Keynotes were common to all three conferences. This chapter introduces the five keynote speakers of high scientific profile who honored us with an invited speech. We thank them very much. Extended abstracts of keynotes by: Amr El Abbadi, Johann Gamper, and Ioana Manolescu are included in this LNCS volume. Extended abstracts of keynotes by Veronika Peralta and Elaine Extended abstracts of keynotes by: Amr El Abbadi, Johann Gamper, and Ioana Manolescu are included in this LNCS volume. Extended abstracts of keynotes by Veronika Peralta and Elaine Toms are included in the EDA and TPDL proceedings, respectively.

Amr El Abbadi (University of California, USA)

Amr El Abbadi is a Professor of Computer Science at the University of California, Santa Barbara. He received his Bachelor in Engineering from Alexandria University, Egypt, and his PhD from Cornell University. His research interests are in the fields of fault-tolerant distributed systems and databases, focusing recently on Cloud data management and blockchain-based systems.

Prof. El Abbadi is an ACM Fellow, AAAS Fellow, and IEEE Fellow. He was Chair of the Computer Science Department at UCSB from 2007 to 2011. He has served as a journal editor for several database journals, including *The VLDB Journal and IEEE Transactions on Computers and The Computer Journal*. He has been Program Chair for multiple database and distributed systems conferences. He currently serves on the Executive Committee of the IEEE Technical Committee on Data Engineering (TCDE) and was a board member of the VLDB Endowment from 2002 to 2008.

In 2007, Prof. El Abbadi received the UCSB Senate Outstanding Mentorship Award for his excellence in mentoring graduate students. In 2013, his student, Sudipto Das received the SIGMOD Jim Gray Doctoral Dissertation Award. Prof. El Abbadi is also a co-recipient of the Test of Time Award at EDBT/ICDT 2015. He has published over 300 articles in databases and distributed systems and has supervised over 35 PhD students.

Johann Gamper (Free University of Bozen-Bolzano, Italy)

Professor Johann Gamper's main research areas are temporal databases, time series data, data warehousing and data analytics, approximate query answering, data summarization, and graph matching. His research concentrates on database technologies with a focus on processing and querying temporal data.

Johann Gamper is author of 120+ publications in international journals and conference proceedings, many of which are in the most prestigious outlets of database systems (TODS, VLDBJ, TKDE, SIGMOD, VLDB, ICDE). He regularly serves as reviewer for technical journals, PC member, and organizer of conferences.

Ioana Manolescu (Inria Saclay–Île-de-France et École Polytechnique, France)

Doctor Ioana Manolescu is a Senior Researcher who leads of the Inria/LIX CEDAR project-team, focused on Rich Data Exploration at Cloud Scale. She is also part-time professor at École Polytechnique, Paris.

Her research interests include models, tools, and algorithms for data journalism and journalistic fact-checking; efficient ontology-mediated query answering; and cloud-based management of web data.

Ioana Manolescu is also member of the PVLDB Endowment Board of Trustees.

Verónika Peralta (University of Tours, France)

Verónika Peralta is Associate Professor at the University of Tours, France, and a member of the Fundamental and Applied Computer Science Laboratory (LIFAT), since 2008. She received her PhD in Computer Science from the University of Versailles and the University of the Republic of Uruguay in 2006. Her research interests include data quality, data warehousing, exploratory analysis, OLAP, query recommendation, and query personalization.

Her teaching mainly concerns databases, data warehousing, and information systems. She has taught multiple courses since 1996, in several universities of France, Uruguay, and Argentina. She has also several years of professional experience as a data warehouse developer and consultant.

Elaine Toms (University of Sheffield, UK)

Elaine Toms is currently Professor of Information Innovation Management, Management School, University of Sheffield, UK. She previously held posts at the iSchool, University of Sheffield; the Faculty of Management and School of Information Studies, Dalhousie University, Canada; and the Faculty of Information, University of Toronto, Canada. She was the first information scientist to be appointed to a Canada Research Chair.

Over the course of her career, she has held multiple administration roles (e.g., Director of Teaching Quality Enhancement and of Research); been actively engaged in professional associations including ASIST (serving on the Board of Directors); has served as program chair for multiple conferences (e.g., ASIST, Hypertext, and JCDL); and currently serves on the editorial board of IPM and is an associate editor of JASIST.

She completed her PhD at Western University, Canada, from which she went on to examine multiple facets of the information interaction problem from interface issues to interruptions and task, with a particular focus on evaluation. Her work has been funded by multiple groups on both sides of the pond (e.g., both the science and social science research councils in Canada, OCLC, Heritage Canada, Canada Foundation for Innovation, Horizon 2020).

She has been an investigator with multiple research networks (e.g., NECTAR, Network for Effective Collaboration Through Advanced Research; PROMISE, Participative Research labOratory for Multimedia and Multilingual Information Systems Evaluation.

Integrating Digital Libraries within Work Task Systems (Abstract of Keynote)

Elaine G. Toms

The University of Sheffield, Sheffield, UK
e.toms@sheffield.ac.uk

Abstract. Has there ever been a time when integrated access to information has been more vital. Yet most (if not all) of our information systems that provide access to data and information remain silos, non-integrated with the primary work systems. Consider the variety of applications and centralised systems that one accesses in the performance of daily work. Even the simplest of tasks requires multiple discrete processes, procedures, tools and data sources. This keynote will discuss in particular the nature of work task highlighting the need for better tools – cognitive prostheses – to support knowledge work.

Keywords: Information retrieval · Digital libraries · Workplace systems · Knowledge work task

1 Introduction

For more than half a century, the information retrieval (IR) communities (including information interaction, database, digital libraries and human computer interaction) have worked to perfect the retrieval of information and data. As a result, our current capability to deliver topical relevance is quite simply, remarkable. Find a restaurant, the distance between cities, identify a bird, and how to remove glue from a surface are unassuming retrieval operations. But once the task becomes more complex requiring multiple retrieval operations as well as multiple types of analyses, then systems provide little assistance to the user about how to proceed. Consider the doctor who may need to revisit an IR system many times over the course of diagnosing an illness, building a knowledge base of the problem from multiple interactions with the data sources and her own knowledge and experience. An IR system may be somewhat tuned to the problem space, e.g., retrieval in medicine versus retrieval in law. But the system will have little understanding of the work task space in which the problem emerged. For much of knowledge work which dominates our economy today, IR systems may provide maximum support for retrieval but minimum support for task completion. With very few exceptions, even the digital libraries developed for particular contexts, e.g., universities, do not aid task completion which is left to the user to muddle through.

We are at an evolutionary stage in the development of IR systems that moves the 'goal post' a step beyond mere relevance to enabling enriched digital libraries that have extensive packages of tools to enable task completion. This keynote takes a top-down approach starting with the nature of knowledge work to make the case for better integration between what an IR system delivers and what the work task needs, highlighting the sorts of tools (essentially cognitive prostheses) that workers require.

2 About Work and Work Tasks

At the turn of the 20th century, work was mainly mechanistic – physical work subdivided into discrete and highly structured, assembly-line style tasks [6]. Over the course of the next few decades work evolved from this form to semi-automated (i.e., skilled), and now most work can be considered augmentation [4]. In the information-dominated 21st century, work is much more cognitively complex and intensive. The undertakings of today's worker centres almost solely on manipulating data and information.

Work activities which are defined within the scope of a person's job delineate the tasks that a worker will complete. Each of those activities are made up of individual tasks, for which there may be one or more sub-tasks, and sub-sub-tasks, etc. Finding, manipulating and using existing data and information is core to all activities and tasks. The simplest task – an "atomic unit" – could be doing one of the few mechanical tasks that remain – entering text using a keyboard, while the most complex may be making a multi-criterion based decision that takes many sub-tasks to complete. The process deployed by those activities and tasks will manipulate and transform data and information – data and information that flow from task initiation to task completion [7].

Consider as an example, the environmental manager who is currently assessing coastal setback in a local bay to assess how far from the crumbing shoreline can homes and other infrastructure be located. To accomplish this, manager needs to isolate many pieces of data and information, e.g., key geophysical parameters of the area (e.g., bathymetry, soil composition), and what is scientifically known about coastal erosion and how it might apply, and then model other parameters such as wind and waves. The manager needs to retrieve all of this before he can proceed. This will take many sources and need multiple tools before the job is accomplished. This is the nature of work in 21st century, and this is the sort of work for which we need more integrated tools.

The existing challenge for the information retrieval communities is the nature of the work. Various types of tasks have driven selected developments, e.g., question & answer. But to date there is no systematic description of various types of work that would enable the effective development of supporting systems, and in particular illustrate how best to integrate those pieces of information and the systems.

Even within the work research, there is a call for a better understanding of what workers actually do (see for example [1, 3]). The focus to date seems to be on the easily quantifiable jobs done by lower level occupational groups, or an analysis of work based on economic and social issues rather than the functional nature of the work [1] – the sort of information that can readily be interpreted as requirements for tool development. When technology is discussed, it is more likely going to be about automation and artificial intelligence rather than identifying the needs of work activities and tasks. This lack of detail from the work side has limited the development of tools to support the task.

3 About the Systems that Support Work

Some years ago, Brynjolfsson and MacAfee predicted the coming of the "second machine age." Indeed, in selected functions (e.g., manufacturing), technology has superseded humans in the conduct of many jobs. In knowledge work especially with tasks that still require significant human cognition and creativity to achieve objectives, technologies remain important supporting actors.

The challenge of today's worker is selecting from a myriad of independent tools. With the multiplicity of apps, the worker's toolbox may appear, analogically like a cluttered carpenter's tool cabinet. Yet most tasks completed by workers need technology interdependence so that the task completion is not disjointed [2]. That is, the tools need to interact with each other in the course of doing work. IR systems are one such tool that supports a very specific function, but operates independent of most work task systems, regardless of whether it is a student writing a paper, an executive deciding between two courses of action, a project manager finalizing a report of a project, a technologist producing help documentation, a trader assessing a course of action given a particular political statement, and a judge weighing the evidence in a particular case.

Take student tasks within the learning process as an example. Searching for information is but one very specific, but very important and prolific part of student work. Yet there is little integration of IR systems and the resulting digital libraries with the learning process. Students have to make those painstaking connections. The same can be said of most knowledge workers whose tasks depend on finding and using information and data.

When we think of tools and the integration of IR systems with work task, we forget that the tools required are more like 'cognitive prostheses' that support cognitive processing, rather that the physical tools that we associate with the word. Cognitive tools enable the worker to work more effectively with retrieved information. Tools of this sort can include a battery of things such as monitor, differentiate, extract, verify, stimulate, orientate re-find, keep track, opinion finding, make sense (see [7] for a more extensive set). Most of these tools are still simply ideas, but it is these mostly cognitive activities for which work needs significant support.

4 Conclusions

IR systems research have made remarkable strides in the past 50 years and digital libraries have built on those developments. Now is the time to integrate those accomplishments in the advancement of refined and purposeful tools that enable workers to actually work with the information and data that those systems supply. Work systems that enable more effective knowledge work remain rather amorphous and undefined. Clearly what is needed is a better understanding of what knowledge work tasks entail in order to support the work and the worker with a better suite of tools.

References

1. Ballieste, T., Elsheikhi, A.: The Future of Work: A Literature Review. International Labour Office, Research Department, Working Paper no. 29 (2018)
2. Bailey, D.E., Leonardi, P.M., Chong, J.: Minding the gaps: understanding technology interdependence and coordination in knowledge work. Organ. Sci. **21**(3), 713–730 (2010)
3. Committee on Techniques for the Enhancement of Human Performance, Commission on Behavioral and Social Sciences and Education, National Research Council. The Changing Nature of Work: Implications for Occupational Analysis. National Academy of Sciences (1999)
4. Davenport, T.H., Kirby, J.: Beyond automation. Harvard Business Review, June (2015)
5. Eurofound What do Europeans do at work? A task-based analysis: European Jobs Monitor 2016, Publications Office of the European Union, Luxembourg (2016)
6. Taylor, F.W.: Principles of Scientific Management. reprinted 1967, Scientific Management. Harper and Row (1912)
7. Toms, E.G.: Information activities and tasks in information at work. Facet Publishing (2019)

Contents

Knowledge Graphs and Linked Data

Requirements Analysis for an Open Research Knowledge Graph

Arthur Brack[1(✉)], Anett Hoppe[1(✉)], Markus Stocker[1(✉)], Sören Auer[1,2(✉)], and Ralph Ewerth[1,2(✉)]

[1] TIB – Leibniz Information Centre for Science and Technology, Hannover, Germany
{arthur.brack,anett.hoppe,markus.stocker,auer,ralph.ewerth}@tib.eu
[2] L3S Research Center, Leibniz University, Hannover, Germany

Abstract. Current science communication has a number of drawbacks and bottlenecks which have been subject of discussion lately: Among others, the rising number of published articles makes it nearly impossible to get a full overview of the state of the art in a certain field, or reproducibility is hampered by fixed-length, document-based publications which normally cannot cover all details of a research work. Recently, several initiatives have proposed knowledge graphs (KGs) for organising scientific information as a solution to many of the current issues. The focus of these proposals is, however, usually restricted to very specific use cases. In this paper, we aim to transcend this limited perspective by presenting a comprehensive analysis of requirements for an Open Research Knowledge Graph (ORKG) by (a) collecting daily core tasks of a scientist, (b) establishing their consequential requirements for a KG-based system, (c) identifying overlaps and specificities, and their coverage in current solutions. As a result, we map necessary and desirable requirements for successful KG-based science communication, derive implications and outline possible solutions.

Keywords: Scholarly communication · Research Knowledge Graph · Design science research · Requirements analysis

1 Introduction

Today's scholarly communication is a document-centred process and as such, rather inefficient. Scientists spend considerable time in finding, reading and reproducing research results from PDF files consisting of static text, tables, and figures. The explosion in the number of published articles [12] aggravates this situation further: It gets harder and harder to stay on top of current research, that is to find relevant works, compare and reproduce them and, later on, to make one's own contribution known for its quality.

M. Hall et al. (Eds.): TPDL 2020, LNCS 12246, pp. 3–18, 2020.
https://doi.org/10.1007/978-3-030-54956-5_1

Some of the available infrastructures in the research ecosystem already use *knowledge graphs* (KG)[1] to enhance their services. Academic search engines, for instance, such as *Microsoft Academic Knowledge Graph* [24] or *Literature Graph* [3] employ metadata-based graph structures which link research articles based on citations, shared authors, venues and keywords.

Recently, initiatives have promoted the usage of KGs in science communication, but on a deeper, semantic level [4,32,37,48,51,54]. They envision the transformation of the dominant document-centred knowledge exchange to knowledge-based information flows by representing and expressing knowledge through semantically rich, interlinked KGs. Indeed, they argue that a shared structured representation of scientific knowledge has the potential to alleviate some of the science communication's current issues: Relevant research could be easier to find, comparison tables automatically compiled, own insights rapidly placed in the current ecosystem. Such a powerful data structure could, more than the current document-based system, also encourage the interconnection of research artefacts such as datasets and source code much more than current approaches (like DOI references etc.); allowing for easier reproducibility and comparison. To come closer to the vision of knowledge-based information flows, research articles should be enriched and interconnected through machine-interpretable semantic content. Jaradeh et al.'s study [37] indicates that authors are also willing to contribute structured descriptions of their research articles.

The work of a researcher is manifold, but current proposals usually focus on a specific use case (e.g. the above-named examples focus on enhancing academic search). In this paper, we provide a detailed analysis of common work tasks in a scientist's daily life and analyse (a) how they could be supported by an ORKG, (b) what requirements result for the design of (b1) the KG and (b2) the surrounding system, (c) how different use cases overlap in their requirements and can benefit from each other. Our analysis is led by the following research questions:

1. What functionalities should be provided by ORKG interfaces?
   (a) Which user interfaces are necessary?
   (b) Which machine interfaces are necessary?
2. What requirements can be defined for the underlying ontologies?
   (a) Which granularity of information representation is needed?
   (b) To what degree is domain specialisation needed?
3. What requirements can be defined for the instance data?
   (a) Which approaches (human vs. machine) are suitable to populate the KG?
   (b) Which coverage of research artefacts is necessary for the instance data?
   (c) Which quality is necessary for the instance data?

[1] Acknowledging that knowledge graph is vaguely defined, we adopt the following definition: A *knowledge graph* (KG) consists of (1) an *ontology* describing a conceptual model, and (2) the corresponding *instance data* following the constraints posed by the ontology. The construction of a KG involves *ontology design* and *population* with instances.

We follow the design science research (DSR) methodology [33]. In this study, we focus on the first phase of DSR conducting a requirements analysis. The objective is to chart necessary (and desirable) requirements for successful KG-based science communication, and, consequently, provide a map for future research.

The remainder of the paper is organised as follows. Section 2 summarises related work on research knowledge graphs, scientific ontologies and methods for KG construction. The requirements analysis is presented in Sect. 3, while Sect. 4 discusses implications and possible approaches for ORKG construction. Finally, Sect. 5 concludes the requirements analysis and outlines areas of future work.

2 Related Work

This section provides a brief overview of (a) existing research KGs, (b) ontologies representing scholarly knowledge, and (c) approaches for KG construction.

2.1 Research Knowledge Graphs

Academic search engines (e.g. Google Scholar, Microsoft Academic, SemanticScholar) exploit graph structures such as the Microsoft Academic Knowledge Graph [24], SciGraph [68], or the Literature Graph [3]. These graphs interlink research articles through metadata, e.g. citations, authors, affiliations, grants, journals, or keywords.

To help reproducing research results, initiatives such as Research Graph [2], Research Objects [7] and OpenAIRE [48] interlink research articles with research artefacts such as datasets, source code, software, and presentation videos. Scholarly Link Exchange (Scholix) [16] aims to create a standardised ecosystem to collect and exchange links between research artefacts and literature.

Some approaches were proposed to interlink articles at a more semantic level: Paperswithcode.com is a community-driven effort to link machine learning articles with tasks, source code and evaluation results to construct leaderboards. Ammar et al. [3] interlink entity mentions in abstracts with DBpedia [43] and Unified Medical Language System (UMLS) [10], and Cohan et al. [17] extend the citation graph with semantic citation intents (e.g. cites as background or as used method).

Various scholarly applications benefit from semantic content representation, e.g. academic search engines by exploiting general-purpose KGs [67], and graph-based research paper recommendation systems [8] by utilising citation graphs and mentioned genes. However, the coverage of science-specific concepts in general-purpose KGs is rather low [3], e.g. the task "geolocation estimation of photos" from Computer Vision is neither present in Wikipedia nor in CSO (Computer Science Ontology) [59].

2.2 Scientific Ontologies

Various ontologies have been proposed to model metadata such as bibliographic resources and citations [53]. Iniesta and Corcho [58] reviewed ontologies to describe scholarly articles. In the following, we describe some ontologies that conceptualise the semantic content in research articles.

Several ontologies focus on rhetorical [19,30,66] (e.g. Background, Methods, Results, Conclusion), argumentative [45,63] (e.g. claims, contrastive and comparative statements about other work) or activity-based [54] (e.g. sequence of research activities) aspects and elements of research articles. Others describe scholarly knowledge with interlinked entities such as problem, method, theory, statement [15,32], or focus on the main research findings and characteristics of research articles described in surveys with concepts such as problems, approaches, implementations, and evaluations [25,64].

There are various domain-specific ontologies, for instance, mathematics [42] (e.g. definitions, assertions, proofs) and machine learning [40,49] (e.g. dataset, metric, model, experiment). The EXPeriments Ontology (EXPO) is a core ontology for scientific experiments conceptualising experimental design, methodology, and results [61].

Taxonomies for domain-specific research areas support the characterisation and exploration of a research field. Salatino et al. [59] provide an overview, e.g. Medical Subject Heading (MeSH), Physics Subject Headings (PhySH), Computer Science Ontology (CSO). Gene Ontology [1] and Chemical Entities of Biological Interest (CheBi) [21] are KGs for genes and molecular entities.

2.3 Construction of Knowledge Graphs

Automatic Construction from Text: Petasis et al. [55] provide a review on *ontology learning*, that is ontology creation from text, while Lubani et al.[47] review *ontology population systems*. Pajura and Singh [56] provide an overview of the involved tasks for *KG population*: (a) *knowledge extraction* to extract a graph from text with *entity extraction* and *relation extraction*, and (b) *graph construction* to clean and complete the extracted graph, as it is usually ambiguous, incomplete and inconsistent. *Coreference resolution* [46] clusters different mentions of the same entity and *entity linking* [41] maps them to entities in the KG. For *taxonomy population* Salatino et al. [59] provide an overview of methods based on rule-based natural language processing (NLP), clustering and statistical methods. In particular, the Computer Science Ontology (CSO) has been populated automatically from research articles [59].

Information Extraction from Scientific Text: Nasar et al. [50] provide a survey about scientific information extraction. Beltagy et al. [9] present benchmarks for several datasets.

There are datasets which are annotated at *sentence level* for several domains, e.g. biomedical [22,38], computer graphics [28], computer science [18], chemistry and computational linguistics [63]. They focus either on the rhetorical structure in abstracts [18,22,38] or full articles [28,45], or on the argumentative structure of full articles [63]. The datasets differentiate between five and twelve concept classes (e.g. Background, Objective, Results). On abstracts and full articles machine learning approaches achieve an F1 score of 83–92% [18] or 51–80% [28,44], respectively.

More recent corpora, annotated at *phrasal level*, aim at constructing a fine-grained KG from scholarly abstracts with the tasks of concept extraction [5,13,31,46], relation extraction [5,29,46], and coreference resolution [46]. They cover several domains, e.g. computational linguistics [29,31]; computer science, material sciences, and physics [5]; machine learning [46]; or a set of ten scientific, technical and medical domains [13]. The datasets differentiate between four to seven concept classes (like Task, Method, Tool) and between two to seven relation types (like used-for, part-of, evaluate-for). Concept extraction, coreference resolution and relation extraction achieve an F1 score of 45–89% [5,9,13], 48% [46] and 28–50% [5,29,46], respectively, and the inter-coder agreement is 60–76% [5,13,46], 68% [46] and 60%–90% [5,29,31,46], respectively. *This indicates, that these tasks are not only difficult for machines but also for humans.*

Manual Curation: WikiData [65] is one of the most popular KGs with semantically structured, encyclopaedic knowledge curated manually by a community. As of March 2020, WikiData comprises 80M entities curated by almost 25.000 active contributors. The community also maintains a taxonomy of categories and "infoboxes" which define common properties of certain entity types. Paperswithcode.com is a further community-driven effort to interlink machine learning articles with tasks, source code and evaluation results. KGs such as Gene Ontology [1] or Wordnet [26] are curated by domain experts. Research article submission portals such as easychair.org enforce the submitter to provide machine-readable metadata. Librarians and publishers tag new articles with keywords and subjects [68]. Virtual research environments enable the execution of data analysis on interoperable infrastructure and store the data and results in KGs [62].

3 Requirements Analysis

As the discussion of related work reveals, existing research KGs focus on specific use cases (e.g. improve search engines, help to reproduce research results) and mainly manage metadata and research artefacts about articles. We envision a KG in which research articles are interlinked through a deep semantic representation of their content to enable further use cases. In the following, we formulate the problem statement and describe our research method. This motivates our use case analysis in Sect. 3.1, from which we derive requirements for an ORKG.

Problem Statement: Scholarly knowledge is very heterogeneous and diverse. Therefore, an ontology that conceptualises scholarly knowledge comprehensively does not (and unlikely will) exist. Besides, due to the complexity of the task, the population of comprehensive ontologies requires domain and ontology experts. Current automatic approaches can only populate rather simple ontologies and achieve moderate accuracy (see Sect. 2.3). *On the one hand, we desire an ontology that can comprehensively capture scholarly knowledge and instance data with high quality and coverage. On the other hand, we are faced with a "knowledge acquisition bottleneck".*

Research Method: To illuminate the above problem statement we perform a *requirements analysis.* We follow the *design science research (DSR)* methodology [14,35]. The requirements analysis is a central phase in DSR, as it is the basis for design decisions and selection of methods to construct effective solutions systematically [14]. DSR's objective in general is the innovative, rigorous and relevant design of information systems for solving important business problems or the improvement of existing solutions [14,33]. To elicit requirements, we studied guidelines for systematic literature reviews [27,39,52] and interviewed members of the ORKG team at TIB (https://projects.tib.eu/orkg/project/team/), who are software engineers and researchers in the field of computer science and environmental sciences. Based on the requirements, we elaborate possible approaches to construct an ORKG, which were identified through a literature review (see Sect. 2.3). To verify our assumptions on the presented requirements and approaches, ORKG team members reviewed them.

3.1 Overview of the Use Cases

We define functional requirements with use cases [11]. A use case describes the interaction between a user and the system from the user's perspective to achieve a certain goal. As a motivating scenario it also guides the design of a supporting ontology [20].

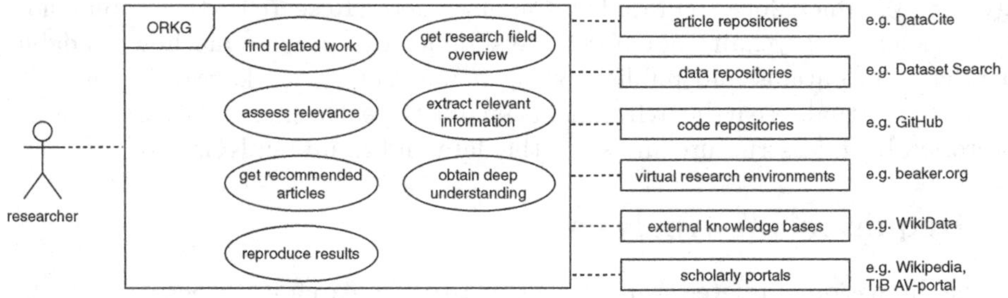

Fig. 1. UML use case diagram for the main use cases between the actor researcher, an Open Research Knowledge Graph (ORKG), and external systems.

There are many use cases (e.g. literature reviews, plagiarism detection, peer reviewer suggestion) and several stakeholders (e.g. researchers, librarians, peer reviewer, practitioners) that may benefit from an ORKG. In this study, we focus on use cases that support *researchers* (a) conducting literature reviews, (b) obtaining a deep understanding of a research article and (c) reproducing research results. A full discussion of all possible use cases of graph-based knowledge management systems in the research environment is far beyond the scope of this article. With the chosen focus, we hope to cover the most frequent, literature-oriented tasks of scientists. Figure 1 depicts the main identified use cases, which are described briefly in the following. Please note that we focus on how *semantic content* can improve these use cases and not further metadata.

Get Research Field Overview: Survey articles provide an overview of a particular research field, e.g. a certain research problem or a family of approaches. The results in such surveys are sometimes summarised in structured and comparative tables (an approach usually followed in domains such as computer science, but not as systematically practised in other fields). However, once survey articles are published they are no longer updated. Moreover, they usually represent only the perspective of the authors, i.e. very few researchers in the field. To support researchers to obtain an up-to-date overview of a research field, the system should maintain such surveys in a structured way, and allow for dynamics and evolution. A researcher interested in such an overview should be able to search or to browse the desired research field. Then, the system should provide related articles and available overviews, e.g. in a table or a leaderboard chart. While the user interface shows tabular, leaderboards, or other visual representations the backend should semantically represent information to allow for exploiting overlaps in conceptualisations between research problems or fields.

Find Related Work: Finding relevant research articles is a daily core activity of researchers. It should be possible to pose queries for related work, which can be fine-grained or broad search intents. Systems should preferably support natural language queries as approached by semantic search and question answering engines [6]. The system has to return a set of relevant articles.

Assess Relevance: Given a set of relevant articles the researcher has to assess whether the articles match the criteria of interest. Usually researchers skim through the title and abstract. Sometimes, the introduction and conclusions have to be considered. However, this is usually cumbersome and time-consuming. Presenting the researcher only the most important zones in the article in a structured way can boost this process. This includes, for instance, text passages that describe the problem tackled in the research work, the employed methods or materials, or the yielded results. Also, faceted drill-down methods based on the properties of semantic descriptions of research approaches will empower researchers to quickly filter and zoom into the most relevant literature.

Extract Relevant Information: To tackle a particular research question, the researcher has to extract relevant information from research articles. Such information is usually compiled in written text or comparison tables in a related work section or survey articles. For instance, for the question *Which datasets exist for scientific sentence classification?* a researcher who focuses on a new annotation study could be interested in (a) domains covered by the dataset and (b) the inter-coder agreement. Another researcher might follow the same question but with a focus on machine learning could be interested in (c) evaluation results and (d) feature types used. The system should support the researcher with tailored information extraction from a set of research articles: (1) the researcher defines a data extraction form as proposed in systematic literature reviews [39] (e.g. the above fields (a)–(d)) and (2) the system presents the extracted information for the corresponding data extraction form and articles in a table.

Get Recommended Articles: When the researcher focuses on a particular article, further related articles should be recommended by the system, for instance, articles that address the same research problem or apply similar methods.

Obtain Deep Understanding: The system should help the researcher to obtain a deep understanding of a research article (e.g. equations, algorithms, diagrams, datasets). For this purpose, the system should interlink the article with artefacts such as conference videos, presentations, source code, datasets, etc., and visualise the artefacts appropriately. Also text passages can be interlinked, e.g. method explanations in Wikipedia, source code snippets implementing algorithms or equations described in the article.

Reproduce Results: The system should provide the researcher links to all necessary artefacts to reproduce research results, e.g. datasets, source code, virtual research environments, materials describing the study, etc. Further, the system should maintain semantic descriptions of domain-specific and standardised evaluation protocols and guidelines.

3.2 Knowledge Graph Requirements

The non-functional requirements for the respective use cases are discussed in the light of the following dimensions.

1. *Domain specialisation of the ontology:* How domain-specific should the concepts be in the ontology? Various ontologies (e.g. [13,54]) propose domain independent concepts (e.g. Process, Method, Material). In contrast, Klampanos et al. [40] present a very domain-specific ontology for artificial neural networks.
2. *Granularity of the ontology:* Which granularity is required to conceptualise scholarly knowledge? For instance, the annotation schemes for scientific corpora (see Sect. 2.3) have a rather low granularity, as they do not have more than 10 classes and 10 relation types. In contrast, various ontologies (e.g [32,54]) with more than 20–35 classes and over 20–70 relations and properties are fine-grained and have a relatively high granularity.
3. *Coverage of the instance data:* Given an ontology, to which extent do *all* possible instances in *all* research articles have to be represented in the KG? For instance, given an ontology with a class "Task", the instance data for that ontology would have a high coverage if all tasks mentioned in all research articles are present.
4. *Quality of the instance data:* Given an ontology, which quality is necessary for the corresponding instances? In a KG with high quality all present instances must conform to the ontology and reflect the content of the research articles properly, e.g. an article is correctly assigned to the task addressed in the article, the F1 score in the evaluation results is correctly extracted, etc.

Next, we discuss the seven main use cases with regard to the required level of ontology domain specialisation and granularity, as well as coverage and quality

Table 1. Requirements and approaches for the main use cases. The upper part describes the minimum requirements for the ontology (domain specialisation and granularity) and the instance data (coverage and quality). The bottom part provides possible approaches for manual, automatic and semi-automatic curation of the KG for the respective use cases. "X" indicates that the approach is suitable for the use case while "(x)" means that the approach is only appropriate with human supervision. The left part (delimited by the vertical triple line) groups use cases suitable for manual, and the right side for automatic approaches. Vertical double lines group use cases with similar requirements.

		Extract relevant info	Research field overview	Deep under-standing	Reproduce results	Find related work	Recom-mend articles	Assess relevance
Ontology	Domain specialisation	high	high	med	med	low	low	med
	Granularity	high	high	med	med	low	low	low
Instance data	Coverage	low	low	low	med	high	high	med
	Quality	high	high	high	high	low	low	med
Manual curation	Maintain terminologies	-	X	-	-	X	X	-
	Define templates	X	X	-	-	-	-	-
	Fill in templates	X	X	X	X	-	-	-
	Maintain overviews	X	X	-	-	-	-	-
Automatic curation	Entity/relation extraction	(x)	(x)	(x)	(x)	X	X	X
	Entity linking	(x)	(x)	(x)	(x)	X	X	X
	Sentence classification	(x)	-	(x)	-	-	-	X
	Template-based extraction	(x)	(x)	(x)	(x)	-	-	-
	Cross-modal linking	-	-	(x)	(x)	-	-	-

of instance data. Table 1 summarises the requirements for the use cases along the four dimensions at ordinal scale. The use cases are grouped together, when they have (1) similar justifications for the requirements, and (2) a high overlap in ontology concepts and instances.

Extract Relevant Information and Get Research Field Overview: The information to be extracted from relevant research articles for a data extraction form is very heterogeneous and depends highly on the intent of the researcher and the research questions. Thus, the ontology has to be domain-specific and fine-grained to offer all possible kinds of desirable information. In addition, the provided information has to be of high quality, e.g. a provided F1 score of an evaluation result must not be wrong. However, missing information for certain questions in the KG may be tolerable for a researcher.

Obtain Deep Understanding and Reproduce Results: The provided information for these use cases has to be of high quality (e.g. accurate links to dataset, source code, videos, articles, research infrastructures). The ontology for representing default artefacts can be rather domain-independent (e.g. Scholix [16]). However, semantic representation of evaluation protocols require domain-dependent ontologies (e.g. EXPO [61]). Missing information is tolerable for these use cases.

Find Related Work and Get Recommended Articles: When searching for related work, it is essential not to miss relevant articles. Previous studies revealed that more than half of search queries in academic search engines refer to scientific entities [67] and the coverage of scientific entities in KGs is rather low [3]. Despite the low coverage, Xiong et al. [67] could improve the ranking of search results by exploiting KGs. Hence, the instance data for the "find related work" use case should have high coverage with fine-grained scientific entities. However, semantic search engines employ latent representations of KGs and text (e.g. graph and word embeddings) [6]. Since a non-perfect ranking of the search results is tolerable for a researcher, lower quality of the instance data is acceptable. Furthermore, due to latent feature representations, the ontology can be kept rather simple and domain-independent. For instance, the STM corpus [13] proposes four domain-independent concepts. Graph- and content-based research paper recommendation systems [8] have similar requirements since they also leverage latent feature representations, require fine-grained scientific entities, and non-perfect recommendations are tolerable.

Assess Relevance: To help the researcher to assess the relevance of an article according to her needs, the system should highlight the most essential zones in the article to get a quick overview. The coverage and quality of the presented information must not be too low, as otherwise the user acceptance may suffer. However, it can be suboptimal, since it is acceptable for a researcher when some of the highlighted information is not essential or when some important information is missing. The ontology to represent essential information should be rather domain-specific and quite simple (cf. ontologies for scientific sentence classification in Sect. 2.3).

4 Implications for ORKG Construction

In this section, we discuss the implications for the design and construction of an ORKG and outline possible approaches, which are mapped to the use cases in Table 1. Based on the discussion in the previous section, we can subdivide the use cases into two groups: (1) requiring high quality and high domain specialisation with only low requirements on the coverage (left side in Table 1), and (2) requiring high coverage with rather low requirements on the quality and domain specialisation (right side in Table 1). The first group requires manual approaches while the second group could be accomplished with fully automatic approaches. However, manually curated data can also support use cases with automatic approaches, and vice versa. Besides, automatic approaches can complement manual approaches by providing suggestions in user interfaces.

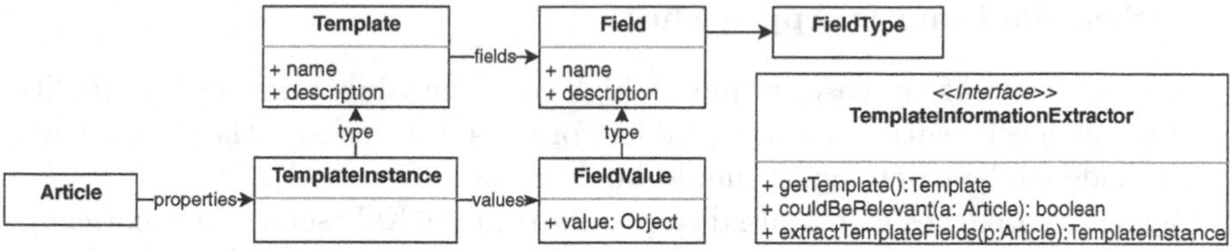

Fig. 2. Conceptual meta-model in UML for templates and interface design for an external template-based information extractor.

4.1 Manual Approaches

Ontology Design: The first group of use cases requires rather domain-specific and fine-grained ontologies. We suggest to develop novel or reuse ontologies that fit the respective use case and the specific domain (e.g. EXPO [61] for experiments). Moreover, appropriate and simple user interfaces are necessary for efficient and easy population.

However, such ontologies can evolve with the help of the community, as demonstrated by WikiData and Wikipedia with "infoboxes" (see Sect. 2.3). Therefore, the system should enable the maintenance of *templates*, which are pre-defined and very specific forms consisting of fields with certain types (see Fig. 2). For instance, to automatically generate leaderboards for machine learning tasks a template would have the fields Task, Model, Dataset and Score, which can then be filled in by a curator for articles providing such kind of results in a user interface generated from the template. Such an approach is also called *meta-modelling* [11], as the meta-model for templates enables the definition of concrete templates, which are then instantiated for articles.

Knowledge Graph Population: Several user interfaces are required to enable manual population: (1) populate semantic content for a research article by (1a) choosing relevant templates or ontologies and (1b) fill in the values; (2) terminology management (e.g. domain-specific research fields); (3) maintain research field overviews by (3a) assigning relevant research articles to the research field, (3b) define corresponding templates and (3c) fill in the templates for the relevant research articles.

Further, the system should also provide *APIs* to enable population by third-party applications, e.g. (i) submission portals such as easychair.org during submission of an article; (ii) authoring tools such as overleaf.com during writing; (iii) virtual research environments [62] to store evaluation results and links to datasets and source code during experimenting and data analysis.

To *encourage crowd-sourced content*, we see the following options: (a) *top-down enforcement* via submission portals and publishers; (b) *incentive models*: Researchers want their articles to be cited; semantic content helps other researchers to find, explore and understand an article; (c) provide *public acknowledgements* for curators.

4.2 (Semi-)automatic Approaches

The second group of use cases require a high coverage while a rather low quality and domain specialisation are acceptable. For these use cases, rather simple and domain-independent ontologies should be developed or reused.

Various approaches can be used to populate an ORKG (semi-)automatically. Methods for *entity and relation extraction* (see Sect. 2.3) can help to populate fine-grained KGs with high coverage and *entity linking* approaches can link mentions in text with entities. For cross-modal linking, Singh et al. [60] propose an approach to detect URLs to datasets in research articles automatically, while the Scientific Software Explorer [34] interlinks text passages in research articles with code fragments. To extract relevant information at sentence level, approaches for *sentence classification* in scientific text can be applied (see Sect. 2.3). To support the curator fill in templates semi-automatically, *template-based extraction* can (1) suggest relevant templates for a research article and (2) pre-fill fields of templates with appropriate values. For pre-filling, approaches such as for natural language inference used in leaderboard construction [36] or end-to-end question answering [23,57] can be employed.

Further, the system should enable to plugin *external information extractors*, developed for certain scientific domains to extract specific types of information. For instance, as depicted in Fig. 2, an external template information extractor has to implement an interface with three methods. This enables the system (1) to filter relevant template extractors for an article and (2) extract field values from an article.

5 Conclusions

In this paper, we have presented a requirements analysis for an Open Research Knowledge Graph (ORKG). An ORKG should represent the content of research articles in a semantic way to enhance or enable a wide range of use cases. We identified literature-related core tasks of a researcher that can be supported by an ORKG and formulated them as use cases. For each use case, we discussed specificities and requirements for the underlying ontology and the instance data. In particular, we identified two groups of use cases: (1) the first group requires high-quality instance data and rather fine-grained, domain-specific ontologies, but with moderate coverage; (2) the second group requires a high coverage, but the ontologies can be kept rather simple and domain-independent, and a moderate quality of the instance data is sufficient. Based on the requirements, we have described possible manual and semi-automatic approaches (necessary for the first group), and automatic approaches (appropriate for the second group) for KG construction. In particular, we propose a framework with lightweight ontologies that can evolve by community curation. Further, we have described the interdependence with external systems, user interfaces, and APIs for third-party applications to populate an ORKG.

The results of our work aim to provide a holistic view of the requirements for an ORKG and be a guideline for further research. The suggested approaches have to be refined, implemented and evaluated in an iterative and incremental process (see www.orkg.org for the current progress). Additionally, our paper can serve as a foundation for a discussion on ORKG requirements with other researchers and practitioners.

References

1. Harris, M.A.M.A., et al.: Gene ontology consortium: The gene ontology (GO) database and informatics resource. Nucleic Acids Res. **32**, D258–D261 (2004)
2. Amir, A., Jing-bo, W.: Research graph: building a distributed graph of scholarly works using research data switchboard. In: Open Repositories CONFERENCE (2017)
3. Ammar, W., et al.: Construction of the literature graph in semantic scholar. In: NAACL-HLT (2018)
4. Auer, S.: Towards an open research knowledge graph (2018). https://doi.org/10.5281/zenodo.1157185
5. Augenstein, I., Das, M., Riedel, S., Vikraman, L., McCallum, A.: Semeval 2017 task 10: scienceie - extracting keyphrases and relations from scientific publications. In: SemEval@ACL (2017)
6. Balog, K.: Entity-Oriented Search. The Information Retrieval Series. Springer, Heidelberg (2018). https://doi.org/10.1007/978-3-319-93935-3
7. Bechhofer, S., et al.: Why linked data is not enough for scientists. In: 2010 IEEE 6th International Conference on e-Science (2010)
8. Beel, J., Gipp, B., Langer, S., Breitinger, C.: Research-paper recommender systems: a literature survey. Int. J. Digit. Libr. **17**(4), 305–338 (2015). https://doi.org/10.1007/s00799-015-0156-0
9. Beltagy, I., Lo, K., Cohan, A.: Scibert: pretrained language model for scientific text. In: EMNLP (2019)
10. Bodenreider, O.: The unified medical language system (UMLS): integrating biomedical terminology. Nucleic Acids Res. **32**, D267–D270 (2004)
11. Vrandečić, D., Krötzsch, M.: Wikidata: a free collaborative knowledgebase. Commun. ACM **57**(10), 78–85 (2014)
12. Bornmann, L., Mutz, R.: Growth rates of modern science: a bibliometric analysis based on the number of publications and cited references. J. Assoc. Inf. Sci. Technol. **66**(11), 2215–2222 (2015)
13. Brack, A., D'Souza, J., Hoppe, A., Auer, S., Ewerth, R.: Domain-Independent extraction of scientific concepts from research articles. In: Jose, J.M., et al. (eds.) ECIR 2020. LNCS, vol. 12035, pp. 251–266. Springer, Cham (2020). https://doi.org/10.1007/978-3-030-45439-5_17
14. Braun, R., Benedict, M., Wendler, H., Esswein, W.: Proposal for requirements driven design science research. In: Donnellan, B., Helfert, M., Kenneally, J., VanderMeer, D., Rothenberger, M., Winter, R. (eds.) DESRIST 2015. LNCS, vol. 9073, pp. 135–151. Springer, Cham (2015). https://doi.org/10.1007/978-3-319-18714-3_9
15. Brodaric, B., Reitsma, F., Qiang, Y.: Skiing with DOLCE: toward an e-science knowledge infrastructure. In: FOIS (2008)

16. Burton, A., et al.: The scholix framework for interoperability in data-literature information exchange. D-Lib Mag. **23**(1/2) (2017)
17. Cohan, A., Ammar, W., van Zuylen, M., Cady, F.: Structural scaffolds for citation intent classification in scientific publications. In: NAACL-HLT (2019)
18. Cohan, A., Beltagy, I., King, D., Dalvi, B., Weld, D.S.: Pretrained language models for sequential sentence classification. In: EMNLP (2019)
19. Constantin, A., Peroni, S., Pettifer, S., Shotton, D.M., Vitali, F.: The document components ontology (DoCO). Seman. Web **7**(2), 167–181 (2016)
20. Degbelo, A.: A snapshot of ontology evaluation criteria and strategies. In: SEMANTICS, pp. 1–8. ACM (2017)
21. Degtyarenko, K., et al.: Chebi: a database and ontology for chemical entities of biological interest. Nucleic Acids Res. **36**, 344–350 (2008)
22. Dernoncourt, F., Lee, J.Y.: PubMed 200k RCT: a dataset for sequential sentence classification in medical abstracts. In: IJCNLP (2017)
23. Devlin, J., Chang, M., Lee, K., Toutanova, K.: BERT: pre-training of deep bidirectional transformers for language understanding. In: NAACL-HLT (2019)
24. Färber, M.: The microsoft academic knowledge graph: a linked data source with 8 billion triples of scholarly data. In: Ghidini, C. (ed.) ISWC 2019. LNCS, vol. 11779, pp. 113–129. Springer, Cham (2019). https://doi.org/10.1007/978-3-030-30796-7_8
25. Fathalla, S., Vahdati, S., Auer, S., Lange, C.: Towards a knowledge graph representing research findings by semantifying survey articles. In: Kamps, J., Tsakonas, G., Manolopoulos, Y., Iliadis, L., Karydis, I. (eds.) TPDL 2017. LNCS, vol. 10450, pp. 315–327. Springer, Cham (2017). https://doi.org/10.1007/978-3-319-67008-9_25
26. Fellbaum, C. (ed.): WordNet: An Electronic Lexical Database. Language, Speech, and Communication. MIT Press, Cambridge (1998)
27. Fink, A.: Conducting Research Literature Reviews. SAGE Publications, Thousand Oaks (2014)
28. Fisas, B., Saggion, H., Ronzano, F.: On the discoursive structure of computer graphics research papers. In: LAW@NAACL-HLT (2015)
29. Gábor, K., Buscaldi, D., Schumann, A.K., QasemiZadeh, B., Zargayouna, H., Charnois, T.: Semeval-2018 task 7: semantic relation extraction and classification in scientific papers. In: Proceedings of The 12th International Workshop on Semantic Evaluation (2018)
30. Groza, T., Kim, H., Handschuh, S.: Salt: semantically annotated latex. In: SAAW@ISWC (2006)
31. Handschuh, S., QasemiZadeh, B.: The ACL RD-TEC: a dataset for benchmarking terminology extraction and classification in computational linguistics. In: COLING 2014: 4th international workshop on computational terminology (2014)
32. Hars, A.: Structure of Scientific Knowledge. Springer, Heidelberg (2003)
33. Hevner, A.R., March, S.T., Park, J., Ram, S.: Design science in information systems research. MIS Q. **28**(1), 75–105 (2004)
34. Hoppe, A., Hagen, J., Holzmann, H., Kniesel, G., Ewerth, R.: An analytics tool for exploring scientific software and related publications. In: Méndez, E., Crestani, F., Ribeiro, C., David, G., Lopes, J.C. (eds.) TPDL 2018. LNCS, vol. 11057, pp. 299–303. Springer, Cham (2018). https://doi.org/10.1007/978-3-030-00066-0_27
35. Horváth, I.: Comparison of three methodological approaches of design research. In: ICED (2007)
36. Hou, Y., Jochim, C., Gleize, M., Bonin, F., Ganguly, D.: Identification of tasks, datasets, evaluation metrics, and numeric scores for scientific leaderboards construction. In: ACL (2019)

37. Jaradeh, M.Y., Oelen, A., Prinz, M., Stocker, M., Auer, S.: Open research knowledge graph: a system walkthrough. In: Doucet, A., Isaac, A., Golub, K., Aalberg, T., Jatowt, A. (eds.) TPDL 2019. LNCS, vol. 11799, pp. 348–351. Springer, Cham (2019). https://doi.org/10.1007/978-3-030-30760-8_31
38. Kim, S., Martínez, D., Cavedon, L., Yencken, L.: Automatic classification of sentences to support evidence based medicine. In: BMC Bioinformatics (2011)
39. Kitchenham, B., Charters, S.: Guidelines for performing systematic literature reviews in software engineering. Keele University and Durham University Joint Report, Technical report (2007)
40. Klampanos, I.A., Davvetas, A., Koukourikos, A., Karkaletsis, V.: Annett-o: an ontology for describing artificial neural network evaluation, topology and training. IJMSO **13**, 24–49 (2018)
41. Kolitsas, N., Ganea, O.E., Hofmann, T.: End-to-end neural entity linking. In: CoNLL (2018)
42. Lange, C.: Ontologies and languages for representing mathematical knowledge on the semantic web. Semant. Web **4**, 119–158 (2013)
43. Lehmann, J., et al.: Dbpedia - a large-scale, multilingual knowledge base extracted from wikipedia. Semant. Web **6**, 167–195 (2015)
44. Liakata, M., Saha, S., Dobnik, S., Batchelor, C., Rebholz-Schuhmann, D.: Automatic recognition of conceptualization zones in scientific articles and two life science applications. Bioinformatics **28**(7), 991–1000 (2012)
45. Liakata, M., Teufel, S., Siddharthan, A., Batchelor, C.R.: Corpora for the conceptualisation and zoning of scientific papers. In: LREC (2010)
46. Luan, Y., He, L., Ostendorf, M., Hajishirzi, H.: Multi-task identification of entities, relations, and coreference for scientific knowledge graph construction. In: EMNLP (2018)
47. Lubani, M., Noah, S.A.M., Mahmud, R.: Ontology population: Approaches and design aspects. J. Inf. Sci. **45**(4), 502–515 (2019)
48. Manghi, P., et al.: The OpenAIRE research graph data model (2019). https://doi.org/10.5281/zenodo.2643199
49. Mesbah, S., Fragkeskos, K., Lofi, C., Bozzon, A., Houben, G.J.: Semantic annotation of data processing pipelines in scientific publications. In: Blomqvist, E., Maynard, D., Gangemi, A., Hoekstra, R., Hitzler, P., Hartig, O. (eds.) ESWC 2017. LNCS, vol. 10249, pp. 321–336. Springer, Cham (2017). https://doi.org/10.1007/978-3-319-58068-5_20
50. Nasar, Z., Jaffry, S.W., Malik, M.K.: Information extraction from scientific articles: a survey. Scientometrics **117**(3), 1931–1990 (2018). https://doi.org/10.1007/s11192-018-2921-5
51. Oelen, A., Jaradeh, M.Y., Farfar, K.E., Stocker, M., Auer, S.: Comparing research contributions in a scholarly knowledge graph. In: SciKnow@K-CAP (2019)
52. Okoli, C.: A guide to conducting a standalone systematic literature review. CAIS **37**, 43 (2015)
53. Peroni, S., Shotton, D.M.: Fabio and cito: ontologies for describing bibliographic resources and citations. J. Web Semant. **17**, 33–43 (2012)
54. Pertsas, V., Constantopoulos, P.: Scholarly ontology: modelling scholarly practices. Int. J. Digit. Libr. **18**(3), 173–190 (2016). https://doi.org/10.1007/s00799-016-0169-3
55. Petasis, G., Karkaletsis, V., Paliouras, G., Krithara, A., Zavitsanos, E.: Ontology population and enrichment: state of the art. In: Paliouras, G., Spyropoulos, C.D., Tsatsaronis, G. (eds.) Knowledge-Driven Multimedia Information Extraction and

Ontology Evolution. LNCS (LNAI), vol. 6050, pp. 134–166. Springer, Heidelberg (2011). https://doi.org/10.1007/978-3-642-20795-2_6
56. Pujara, J., Singh, S.: Mining knowledge graphs from text. In: WSDM 2018 (2018)
57. Rajpurkar, P., Zhang, J., Lopyrev, K., Liang, P.: Squad: 100, 000+ questions for machine comprehension of text. In: EMNLP (2016)
58. Ruiz Iniesta, A., Corcho, O.: A review of ontologies for describing scholarly and scientific documents. In: 4th Workshop on Semantic Publishing (SePublica) (2014)
59. Salatino, A.A., Thanapalasingam, T., Mannocci, A., Birukou, A., Osborne, F., Motta, E.: The computer science ontology: a comprehensive automatically-generated taxonomy of research areas. In: Data Intelligent (2019)
60. Singh, M., et al.: Ocr++: a robust framework for information extraction from scholarly articles. In: COLING (2016)
61. Soldatova, L.N., King, R.D.: An ontology of scientific experiments. J. R. Soc. Interface **3**, 795–803 (2006)
62. Stocker, M., Prinz, M., Rostami, F., Kempf, T.: Towards research infrastructures that curate scientific information: a use case in life sciences. In: Auer, S., Vidal, M.E. (eds.) DILS 2018. LNCS, vol. 11371, pp. 61–74. Springer, Cham (2019). https://doi.org/10.1007/978-3-030-06016-9_6
63. Teufel, S., Siddharthan, A., Batchelor, C.: Towards discipline-independent argumentative zoning: evidence from chemistry and computational linguistics. In: EMNLP (2009)
64. Vahdati, S., Fathalla, S., Auer, S., Lange, C., Vidal, M.E.: Semantic representation of scientific publications. In: Doucet, A., Isaac, A., Golub, K., Aalberg, T., Jatowt, A. (eds.) TPDL 2019. LNCS, vol. 11799, pp. 375–379. Springer, Cham (2019). https://doi.org/10.1007/978-3-030-30760-8_37
65. Vrandečić, D., Krötzsch, M.: Wikidata: a free collaborative knowledgebase. Commun. ACM **57**(10) (2014)
66. de Waard, A., Tel, G.: The ABCDE format enabling semantic conference proceedings. In: SemWiki (2006)
67. Xiong, C., Power, R., Callan, J.P.: Explicit semantic ranking for academic search via knowledge graph embedding. In: WWW (2017)
68. Yaman, B., Pasin, M., Freudenberg, M.: Interlinking scigraph and dbpedia datasets using link discovery and named entity recognition techniques. In: LDK (2019)

Question Answering on Scholarly Knowledge Graphs

Mohamad Yaser Jaradeh[1(✉)], Markus Stocker[2], and Sören Auer[1,2]

[1] L3S Research Center, Leibniz University of Hannover, Hanover, Germany
jaradeh@l3s.de
[2] TIB Leibniz Information Centre for Science and Technology, Hanover, Germany
{markus.stocker,auer}@tib.eu

Abstract. Answering questions on scholarly knowledge comprising text and other artifacts is a vital part of any research life cycle. Querying scholarly knowledge and retrieving suitable answers is currently hardly possible due to the following primary reason: machine inactionable, ambiguous and unstructured content in publications. We present JarvisQA, a BERT based system to answer questions on tabular views of scholarly knowledge graphs. Such tables can be found in a variety of shapes in the scholarly literature (e.g., surveys, comparisons or results). Our system can retrieve direct answers to a variety of different questions asked on tabular data in articles. Furthermore, we present a preliminary dataset of related tables and a corresponding set of natural language questions. This dataset is used as a benchmark for our system and can be reused by others. Additionally, JarvisQA is evaluated on two datasets against other baselines and shows an improvement of two to three folds in performance compared to related methods.

Keywords: Digital Libraries · Information retrieval · Question Answering · Semantic web · Semantic search · Scholarly knowledge

1 Introduction

Question Answering (QA) systems, such as Apple's Siri, Amazon's Alexa, or Google Now, answer questions by mining the answers from unstructured text corpora or open domain Knowledge Graphs (KG) [14]. The direct applicability of these approaches to specialized domains such as scholarly knowledge is questionable. On the one hand, no extensive knowledge graph for scholarly knowledge exists that can be employed in a question answering system. On the other hand, scholarly knowledge is represented mainly as unstructured raw text in articles (in proceedings or journals) [3]. In unstructured artifacts, knowledge is not machine actionable, hardly processable, ambiguous [4], and particularly also not FAIR [32]. Still, amid unstructured information some semi-structured information exists, in particular in tabular representations (e.g., survey tables, literature overviews, and paper comparisons). The task of QA on tabular data has challenges [18], shared with other types of question answering systems. We propose

M. Hall et al. (Eds.): TPDL 2020, LNCS 12246, pp. 19–32, 2020.
https://doi.org/10.1007/978-3-030-54956-5_2

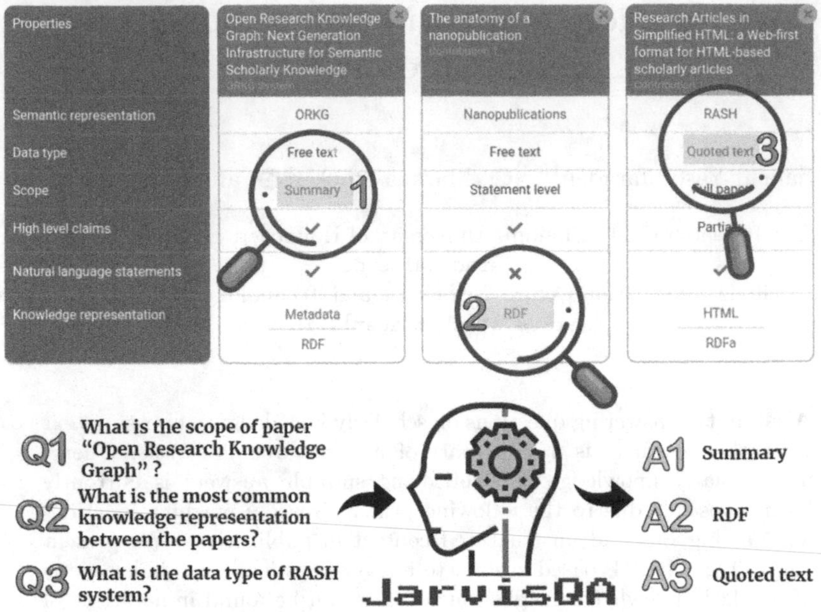

Fig. 1. Motivating Example. `JarvisQA` takes as input a table of semi-structured information and tries to answer questions. Three types of questions are depicted here. (**Q1**) Answer is directly correlated with the question. (**Q2**) Aggregation of information from candidate results. (**Q3**) Answer relates to another cell in the table.

a method to perform QA specifically on scholarly knowledge graphs representing tabular data. Moreover, we create a benchmark of tabular data retrieved from a scholarly knowledge graph and a set of related questions. This benchmark is collected using the Open Research Knowledge Graph (ORKG) [12].

The remainder of this article is structured as follows. Section 1 motivates the work with an example. Section 2 presents related work, which is supplemented by an analysis of the strengths and weaknesses of existing systems in the context of digital libraries. Section 3 describes the proposed approach. Section 4 presents the implementation and evaluation. Section 5 discusses results and future work. Finally, Sect. 6 concludes the paper.

Motivating Example. The research community has proposed many QA systems, but to the best of our knowledge none focus on scholarly knowledge. Leveraging the ORKG [12] and its structured scholarly knowledge, we propose a QA system specifically designed for this domain. Figure 1 illustrates a tabular comparison view[1] of structured scholarly contribution descriptions. Additionally, three questions related to the content of the comparison table are shown. The answers are implicitly or explicitly provided in the cells of the table. `JarvisQA`

[1] https://www.orkg.org/orkg/comparison/R8618.

can answer different types of questions. For Q1, the answer has a direct correlation with the question. For Q2, the system should first find the "knowledge representations" in the table and then find the most common value. For Q3, the answer is conditional upon finding another piece of information in the table first (i.e., JarvisQA has to find "RASH" in the table first), and then narrow its search to that column (or that paper) to find the correct answer.

We tackle the following research questions:

- **RQ1:** *Can a QA system retrieve answers from tabular representations of scholarly knowledge?*
- **RQ2:** *What type of questions can be posed on tabular scholarly knowledge?*

2 Related Work

Question answering is an important research problem frequently tackled by research communities in different variations, applications, and directions.

In open domain question answering, various systems and techniques have been proposed that rely on different forms of background knowledge. Pipeline-based systems, such as OpenQA [20], present a modular framework using standardized components for creating QA systems on structured knowledge graphs (e.g., DBpedia [1]). Frankenstein [28] creates the most suitable QA pipeline out of community created components based on the natural language input question. QAnswer [8] is a multilingual QA system that queries different linked open data datasets to fetch correct answers. Diefenbach et al. [7] discussed and compared other QA-over-KG systems (e.g., gAnswer [38], DEANNA [34], and SINA [27]) within the context of QALD "Question Answering over Linked Data" challanges [19].

Other types of QA systems rely on the raw unstructured text to produce the answers. Many of these systems are end-to-end systems that employ machine learning to mine the text and retrieve the answers. Deep learning models (e.g., Transformers) are trained and fine-tuned on certain QA datasets to find the answers from within the text. ALBERT [17] is a descendent of BERT [6] deep learning model. At the time of writing, ALBERT holds the third top position in answering the questions of SQuAD [24]. Such techniques model the linguistic knowledge from textual details and discard all the clutter in the text [37]. Other similar approaches include SG-Net [36], which uses syntax rules to guide the machine comprehension encoder-transformer models.

Tabular QA systems are also diverse and tackle the task with different techniques. TF-IDF [25] is used to extract features from the tables and the question, and to match them. Other models such as semantic parsers are used by Kwiatkowski et al. [16] and Krishnamurthy and Kollar [15]. Cheng et al. [5] propose a neural semantic parser that uses predicate-argument structures to convert natural language text into intermediate structured representations, which are then mapped to different target domains (e.g., SQL).

Another category of table QA systems is neural systems. TableQA [30] uses end-to-end memory networks to find a suitable cell in the table to choose.

Wang et al. [31] propose to use a directional self-attention network to find candidate tables and then use BiGRUs to score the answers. Other table oriented QA systems include HILDB [9] that converts natural language into SQL.

In the plethora of systems that the community has developed over the past decade, no system addresses the scholarly information domain, specifically. We propose a system to fill this gap and address the issues of QA on scholarly tabular data in the context of digital libraries (specifically with the ORKG[2]).

Though a variety of QA techniques exist, Digital Libraries (DL) primarily rely on standard information retrieval techniques [26]. We briefly analyze and show when and how QA techniques can be used to improve information retrieval and search capabilities in the context of DLs. Since DLs have different needs [11,26]; QA systems can improve information retrieval availability [2]. We argue that, Knowledge Graph based QA systems (or KG-QA) can work nicely within a DL context (i.e., aggregate information, list candidate answers). Nevertheless, the majority of the existing scholarly KGs (such as MAG [29], OC [23]) focus on metadata (e.g., authors, venues, and citations), not the scholarly knowledge content.

Another category of QA systems works on raw text, an important approach for DLs. However, such systems are not fine-tuned on scholarly data; rather, they are designed for open domain data. Furthermore, many of the end-to-end neural models have a built-in limitation [35] (i.e., model capacity) due to the architecture type, and as such cannot be used out of the box. Some systems circumvent the problem of capacity (i.e., the inability to feed the model large amounts of text) by having a component of indexing (e.g., inverted index, concept and entity recognition) that can narrow down the amount of text that the system needs to process as the context for questions.

3 Approach

We propose a system, called `JarvisQA`, that answers Natural Language (NL) questions on tabular views of scholarly knowledge graphs, specifically tabular views comprising research contribution information from scientific articles.

3.1 Data and Questions Collection

In order to evaluate our QA system we create the ORKG-QA benchmark, collected using the ORKG. The ORKG provides structured comparisons [21] of research contributions obtained from papers. The ORKG-QA benchmark comprises a dataset that integrates 13 tables, covering information spanning more than 100 academic publications. The data is collected through the ORKG API and the featured set of tables[3], which can be exported in CSV format.

Additionally, we created a set of questions that cover various types of information and facts that can be retrieved from those tables. The benchmark consists

[2] https://orkg.org/.

[3] https://www.orkg.org/orkg/featured-comparisons.

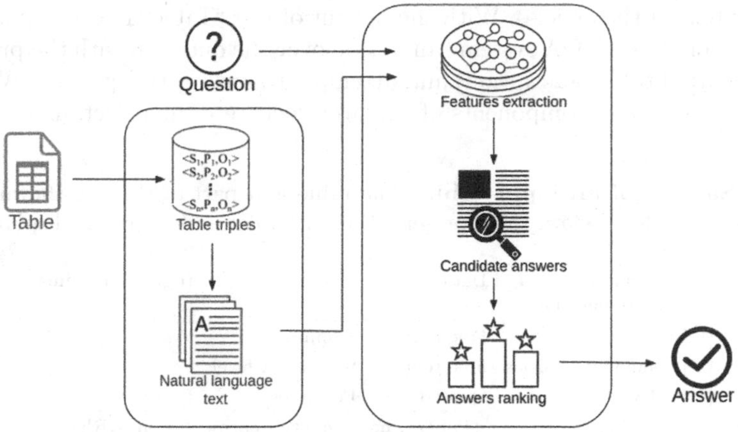

Fig. 2. System Architecture. JarvisQA was designed with modularity in mind. The system has two main components. (a) **Table 2Text (T2T)** component, which in turn has two functionalities: (1) to break the table into a set of triples $< s, p, o >$ and (2) to compile the triples into an NL sentence. Component (b) is the **engine of the QA system**, where an NL QA (BERT based) system is employed to answer the input question using the text, by extracting features, finding candidate answers, and ranking them.

of 80 questions in English. The questions cover a variety of question types that can be asked in the context of tables in the scholarly literature. These types of questions include aggregation questions (e.g., min, average and most common), ask questions (i.e., truc, false), answer listing questions, and questions that rely on combining information. In the ORKG-QA dataset[4], 39% are normal questions addressing individual cells in tables, 20% are aggregation questions, 11% are questions for which the answer relates to other parts of the table, and the rest are questions of different types (i.e., listings, ask queries, empty answers).

We also use the TabMCQ [13] QA dataset, specifically questions on the *regents* tables. TabMCQ was derived from multiple choice questions of 4th grade science exams and contains 39 tables and 3 745 related questions. While TabMCQ is not a scholarly dataset, but is to the best of our knowledge the closest one available. Since TabMCQ has only multiple-choice questions, we adapted the questions with only the correct choice.

3.2 JarvisQA System Architecture

`JarvisQA` is designed with modularity in mind. Hence, the core QA components are replaceable with newer or more fine-tuned versions. Figure 2 depicts the architecture in more detail. Since we used a natural language QA system, we need a pre-processing step that transforms the table information into the textual description (representing only the information contained in the table not the

[4] https://doi.org/10.25835/0038751.

entire raw text of the article). With the output of the "Table2Text" step and the input question, the NL QA system can reason over the question with the provided context (textual table description) and attempts to answer the question. We now discuss the individual components of the architecture in more detail.

Table 1. Sample of an input table. The table is a part of the one shown in the motivating example.[7] Below, the representation in triples and as text is displayed.

Title	Semantic representation	Data type	Scope	High level claims
Paper 1 [12]	ORKG	Free text	Summary	Yes
Paper 2 [10]	Nanopublications	Free text	Statement level	Yes
Paper 3 [22]	RASH	Quoted text	Full paper	Partially
Triples		<Paper1, hasSemanticRepresentation, ORKG>		
		<Paper1, hasDataType, FreeText>		
		<Paper1, hasScope, Summary>		
		...		
Text		Paper 1's semantic representation is "ORKG", its data type is "Free Text", and its scope is "Summary" ...		

Table2Text (T2T) Converter. Although `JarvisQA` operates on tabular data, the core QA engine processes textual contexts. To that end, tables have to be converted into coherent text snippets that represent the entirety of the information presented in the table. T2T component splits tables into its entries and converts entries into triples. Table 1 illustrates a sample table containing some information about three publications, along with their triples and textual representations compiled by the T2T component. Furthermore, the T2T component enriches the textual description with aggregated information (i.e., max value of certain rows, most common value used within some columns). This enables the system to answer aggregation-type questions such as "Which system has the maximum accuracy?" and "What is the most common method used among the papers?".

QA Core Engine. This component is the primary building block of `JarvisQA`. It is where reasoning over questions happens. The component uses a pre-trained natural language QA model. The model is a deep transformer, fine tuned on the SQuADv2 dataset to perform the QA task. The component is replaceable with any other similar transformer model (of different sizes and architectures). Our base implementation uses a fine tuned version of a BERT model and we evaluate our model using different model sizes and architectures. The model parameters are set: *maximum sequence length* to 512, *document stride* to 128, *top k answers* to 10, *maximum answer length* to 15, and the *maximum question length* to 64. As illustrated in Fig. 2, the QA engine extracts sets of features from the questions and the text (i.e., embeddings), then it finds a set of candidate answers and ranks them by confidence score. The benefits of such architecture

Table 2. Evaluation metrics used to experimentally benchmark JarvisQA against other baselines.

Metric	Definition
Global Precision	Ratio between correct answers retrieved in the top ranked position and the total number of questions
Global Recall	Ratio between the number of questions answered correctly at any position (here till the 10th retrieved answer) and the total number of questions
F1-Score	Harmonic mean of global precision and global recall
Execution Time	Elapsed time between asking a question and returning the answer
Inv. Time	$1 - \frac{average\ execution\ time\ for\ baseline}{maximum\ execution\ time\ for\ all\ systems}$
In-Memory Size	The total memory size used by system
Inv. Memory	$1 - \frac{memory\ size\ of\ baseline}{maximum\ memory\ size\ among\ all\ systems}$
Precision@K	Cumulative precision at position K
Recall@K	Ratio of correctly answered questions in the top K position and total number of questions
F1-Score@K	Harmonic mean of precision and recall at position K

are the flexibility in model choice, multilingualism, and reusability. Different transformer models can replace ours to support other languages, other datasets, and potentially other features. To accomplish these objectives, the system is built using the Transformers framework [33].

4 Experimental Study

We empirically study the behavior of `JarvisQA` in the context of scholarly tables against different baselines. The experimental setup consists of metrics and baselines. Table 2 lists the evaluation metrics for the performance measurements of the systems. Since a QA system can produce multiple answers and the correct answer can be any of the retrieved answers we use a metric that takes the position of the answer into account.
As baselines we use the following two methods for answer generation:

- *Random*: the answer is selected from all choices randomly.
- *Lucene*[8]: is a platform for indexing, retrieving unstructured information, and used as a search engine. We index the triple-generated sentences by Lucene. For each question, the top answer produced by Lucene is regarded as the final answer.

[8] https://lucene.apache.org/.

Table 3. JarvisQA performance on the ORKG-QA benchmark dataset of tabular data. The evaluation metrics are precision, recall, and F1-score at k position. JarvisQA is compared against two baselines on the overall dataset and specific question types. The symbol (-) indicates that the performance metric showed no difference than the reported value for higher K values. The results suggest that JarvisQA outperforms the baselines by 2–3 folds.

Questions type	Baseline	Precision @K				Recall @K				F1-Score @K			
		#1	#3	#5	#10	#1	#3	#5	#10	#1	#3	#5	#10
All	Random	0.02	0.06	0.08	0.16	0.02	0.07	0.09	0.18	0.02	0.06	0.08	0.17
All	Lucene	0.09	0.19	0.20	0.25	0.09	0.18	0.19	0.24	0.09	0.18	0.19	0.24
Normal	JarvisQA	0.41	0.47	0.55	0.61	0.41	0.47	0.53	0.61	0.41	0.47	0.54	0.61
Aggregation	JarvisQA	0.45	-	-	-	0.45	-	-	-	0.45	-	-	-
Related	JarvisQA	0.50	0.50	1.00	1.00	0.50	0.50	1.00	1.00	0.50	0.500	1.00	1.00
Similar	JarvisQA	0.11	0.25	0.67	-	0.11	0.25	0.67	-	0.11	0.25	0.67	-
All	JarvisQA	0.34	0.38	0.46	**0.47**	0.35	0.38	0.46	**0.48**	0.34	0.38	0.45	**0.47**

The evaluation was performed on an Ubuntu 18.04 machine with 128 GB RAM and a 12 core Xeon processor. The implementation is mostly based on HuggingFace Transformers[9], and is written in Python 3.7. The evaluation results for precision, recall, and F1-score are reproducible while other metrics such as time and memory depend on the evaluation system hardware. However, the ratio of the difference between the baselines should be similar or at least show a similar trend. The code to reproduce the evaluation results and the presented results are available online.[10]

Experiment 1 - JarvisQA Performance on the ORKG-QA Benchmark. In order to evaluate the performance of `JarvisQA`, we run the system and other baselines on the ORKG-QA dataset at various k values (k denotes the position of the correct answer among all retrieved answers). For this experiment we evaluate $k \in \{1, 3, 5, 10\}$. Moreover, the experiment was conducted on a specific subset of questions (based on types) to show the performance of the system for certain categories of questions. The tested question categories are: *Normal*: normal questions about a specific cell in the table with a direct answer; *Aggregation*: questions about aggregation tasks on top of the table; *Related*: questions that require retrieving the answer from another cell in the table; *Similar*: questions that address the table using similar properties (e.g., synonyms). Table 3 shows the performance of the baselines and our system on the ORKG-QA benchmark. The results show that `JarvisQA` performs better by 2–3 folds against Lucene, and Random baselines respectively.

[9] https://github.com/huggingface/transformers.
[10] https://doi.org/10.5281/zenodo.3738666.

Experiment 2 - Different Models of QA and Their Performance. We evaluate different types of QA models simultaneously to show the difference in performance metrics, execution time, and resource usage. Table 4 illustrates the difference in performance on the ORKG-QA benchmark dataset for different classes of questions and the overall dataset. `JarvisQA`'s QA engine employs the `BERT L/U/S2` model due to its execution time and overall higher accuracy at higher positions.

Table 4. Performance comparison of different deep learning models on the task of question answering with different model sizes and architectures using the ORKG-QA benchmark dataset. The results suggest that different models perform differently on various question types, and generally the bigger the model the better it performs. For each question type, the best results are highlighted.

	Questions type	Precision @K				Recall @K				F1-Score @K			
		#1	#3	#5	#10	#1	#3	#5	#10	#1	#3	#5	#10
BERT L/U/S1	Normal	0.35	0.49	0.53	**0.68**	0.34	0.47	0.51	**0.67**	0.34	0.48	0.52	**0.67**
	Aggregation	0.39	0.39	0.45	-	0.39	0.39	0.45	-	0.39	0.39	0.45	-
	Related	0.50	0.64	0.64	0.80	0.50	0.64	0.64	0.80	0.50	0.64	0.64	0.80
	Similar	0.11	0.25	**0.67**	-	0.11	0.25	**0.67**	-	0.11	0.25	**0.67**	-
	All	0.31	0.38	0.44	**0.50**	0.31	0.38	0.43	**0.49**	0.3	0.38	0.43	**0.50**
BERT L/C/S1	Normal	0.31	0.44	0.45	-	0.31	0.43	0.45	-	0.31	0.43	0.45	-
	Aggregation	0.27	0.39	0.39	0.45	0.29	0.39	0.39	0.45	0.27	0.39	0.39	0.45
	Related	0.65	**1.00**	-	-	0.70	**1.00**	-	-	0.67	**1.00**	-	-
	Similar	0.11	0.11	0.25	0.43	0.11	0.11	0.25	0.43	0.11	0.11	0.25	0.43
	All	0.27	0.35	0.37	0.39	0.29	0.37	0.39	0.41	0.27	0.36	0.37	0.40
BERT L/U/S2	Normal	0.41	0.47	0.55	0.61	0.41	0.47	0.54	0.61	0.41	0.47	0.54	0.61
	Aggregation	0.45	-	-	-	0.45	-	-	-	0.45	-	-	-
	Related	0.50	0.50	**1.00**	-	0.50	0.50	**1.00**	-	0.50	0.50	**1.00**	-
	Similar	0.11	0.25	**0.67**	-	0.11	0.25	**0.67**	-	0.11	0.25	**0.67**	-
	All	0.35	0.38	0.46	0.48	0.35	0.38	0.46	0.48	0.34	0.38	0.46	0.48
Distil BERT B/U/S1	Normal	0.14	0.27	0.36	0.46	0.16	0.29	0.36	0.46	0.15	0.27	0.35	0.45
	Aggregation	0.22	0.39	-	-	0.25	0.41	-	-	0.24	0.39	-	-
	Related	0.31	0.50	0.64	-	0.31	0.50	0.64	-	0.31	0.50	0.64	-
	Similar	0.00	-	-	-	0.00	-	-	-	0.00	-	-	-
	All	0.16	0.23	0.28	0.33	0.17	0.26	0.29	0.35	0.16	0.24	0.28	0.33
ALBERT XL/S2	Normal	0.34	0.47	0.51	-	0.34	0.47	0.51	-	0.34	0.47	0.51	-
	Aggregation	0.45	0.45	**0.52**	-	0.45	0.45	**0.52**	-	0.45	0.45	**0.52**	-
	Related	**1.00**	-	-	-	**1.00**	-	-	-	**1.00**	-	-	-
	Similar	0.43	0.43	**0.67**	-	0.43	0.43	**0.67**	-	0.43	0.43	**0.67**	-
	All	0.36	0.42	0.46	-	0.37	0.43	0.47	-	0.36	0.42	0.46	-

B = Base; L = Large; XL = X-Large; C = Cased; U = Uncased; S1 = Finetuned on SQuAD1; S2 = Finetuned on SQuAD2

Experiment 3 - Trade-Offs Between Different Performance Metrics. We illustrate trade-offs between different dimensions of performance metrics for the `JarvisQA` approach compared to the baselines. We choose global precision, global recall, F1-score, in-memory size, and execution time as five different dimensions. Figure 3 depicts the performance metrics trade-offs between our system and other baselines. `JarvisQA` achieves higher precision and recall while consuming considerably more time and memory than the other baselines.

Experiment 4 - Performance on TabMCQ. We also show the performance of our system on the TabMCQ dataset against the ORKG-QA dataset. We see the same trend in both datasets, that `JarvisQA` outperforms the baselines by many folds. TabMCQ is not directly related to scholarly knowledge. However, it shows that `JarvisQA` can generalize to related data and can answer questions about it. Table 5 presents the results of this experiment.

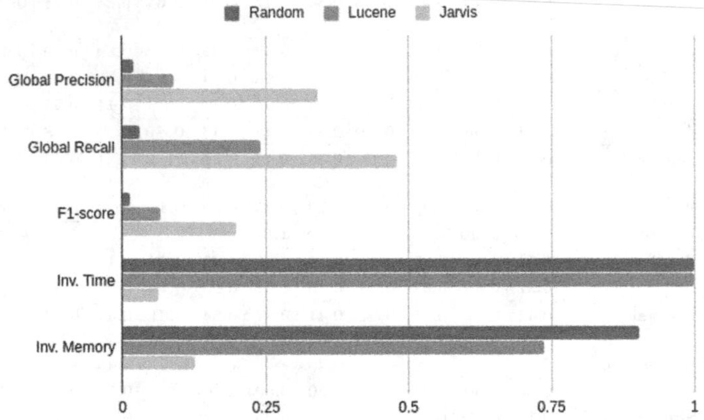

Fig. 3. Performance of the JarvisQA system. JarvisQA and the baselines are compared in terms of Global Precision, Global Recall, Global F1-Score, Inv.Time, Inv.Memory; higher values are better. JarvisQA improves Precision, Recall, and F1-Score by up to three times at the cost of execution time and memory consumption.

Table 5. Performance comparison using the two datasets TabMCQ and ORKG-QA against JarvisQA and the baselines. The results suggest that JarvisQA outperforms the baselines by substantially on both datasets. Best results are highlighted for both datasets.

System	Dataset	Precision @K				Recall @K				F1-Score @K			
		#1	#3	#5	#10	#1	#3	#5	#10	#1	#3	#5	#10
Random	TabMCQ	0.006	0.010	0.020	0.030	0.010	0.020	0.030	0.040	0.007	0.010	0.024	0.030
	ORKG	0.020	0.060	0.080	0.160	0.020	0.070	0.090	0.180	0.020	0.060	0.080	0.017
Lucene	TabMCQ	0.004	0.018	0.027	0.036	0.006	0.017	0.026	0.037	0.005	0.016	0.024	0.033
	ORKG	0.090	0.190	0.200	0.250	0.090	0.180	0.190	0.240	0.090	0.180	0.190	0.240
Jarvis	TabMCQ	0.060	0.090	0.100	**0.110**	0.070	0.090	0.110	**0.120**	0.060	0.080	0.100	**0.110**
	ORKG	0.340	0.380	0.460	**0.470**	0.350	0.380	0.460	**0.480**	0.340	0.380	0.450	**0.470**

5 Discussion and Future Work

The main objective of `JarvisQA` is to serve as a system that allows users to ask natural language questions on tablar views of scholarly knowledge. As such, the system addresses only a small part of the scholarly information corpus.

We performed several experimental evaluations to benchmark the performance of `JarvisQA` against other baselines using two different QA datasets. Different datasets showed different results based on the types of questions and the nature of the scholarly data encoded in the tables. Based on these extensive experiments, we conclude that usual information retrieval techniques used in search engines are failing to find specific answers for questions posed by a user. `JarvisQA` outperforms the other baselines in terms of precision, recall, and F1-score measure at the cost of higher execution time and memory requirements. Moreover, our system cannot yet answer all types of questions (e.g., non-answerable questions and listing questions).

Since `JarvisQA` utilizes a BERT based QA component, different components can perform differently, depending on the use case and scenario. Our system struggles with answers spanning across multiple cells of the table, and also in answering true/false questions. Furthermore, the answers are limited to information in the table (extractive method), since tables are not supplemented with further background information to improve the answers.

As indicated, the system can still be significantly improved. Future work will focus on improving answer selection techniques, and supporting more types of questions. Additionally, we will improve and enlarge the ORKG-QA dataset to become a better benchmark with more tables (content) and questions. `JarvisQA` currently selects the answer only from a single table, but use cases might require the combination of multiple tables or the identification of target table automatically (i.e., the system selects the table containing the correct answer from a pool of tables). Moreover, in the context of digital libraries, we want to integrate the system into the ORKG infrastructure so it can be used on live data directly.

6 Conclusion

Retrieving answers from scientific literature is a complicated task. Manually answering questions on scholarly data is cumbersome, time consuming. Thus, an automatic method of answering questions posed on scientific content is needed. `JarvisQA` is a question answering system addressing scholarly data that is encoded in tables or sub-graphs representing table content. It can answer several types of questions on table content. Furthermore, our ORKG-QA benchmark is a starting point to collaborate on adding more data to better train, evaluate, and test QA systems designed for tabular views of scholarly knowledge. To conclude, `JarvisQA` addresses several open questions in current information retrieval in the scholarly communication domain, and contributes towards improved information retrieval on scholarly knowledge. t can help researchers, librarians, and ordinary users to inquire for answers with higher accuracy than traditional information retrieval methods.

Acknowledgments. This work was co-funded by the European Research Council for the project ScienceGRAPH (Grant agreement ID: 819536) and the TIB Leibniz Information Centre for Science and Technology. The authors would like to thank our colleagues Kheir Eddine Farfar, Manuel Prinz, and especially Allard Oelen and Vitalis Wiens for their valuable input and comments.

References

1. Auer, S., Bizer, C., Kobilarov, G., Lehmann, J., Cyganiak, R., Ives, Z.: DBpedia: a nucleus for a web of open data. In: Aberer, K. (ed.) ASWC/ISWC -2007. LNCS, vol. 4825, pp. 722–735. Springer, Heidelberg (2007). https://doi.org/10.1007/978-3-540-76298-0_52
2. Bloehdorn, S.: Ontology-based question answering for digital libraries. In: Kovács, L., Fuhr, N., Meghini, C. (eds.) ECDL 2007. LNCS, vol. 4675, pp. 14–25. Springer, Heidelberg (2007). https://doi.org/10.1007/978-3-540-74851-9_2
3. Bornmann, L., Mutz, R.: Growth rates of modern science: a bibliometric analysis based on the number of publications and cited references. J. Assoc. Inf. Sci. Technol. **66**(11), 2215–2222 (2015). https://doi.org/10.1002/asi.23329
4. Bosman, J., et al.: The scholarly commons - principles and practices to guide research communication. https://doi.org/10.31219/OSF.IO/6C2XT
5. Cheng, J., Reddy, S., Saraswat, V., Lapata, M.: Learning structured natural language representations for semantic parsing. In: Proceedings of the 55th Annual Meeting of the Association for Computational Linguistics (Volume 1: Long Papers), pp. 44–55. Association for Computational Linguistics, Stroudsburg (2017). https://doi.org/10.18653/v1/P17-1005
6. Devlin, J., Chang, M.W., Lee, K., Toutanova, K.: Bert: pre-training of deep bidirectional transformers for language understanding. In: Proceedings of the 2019 Conference of the North American Chapter of the Association for Computational Linguistics: Human Language Technologies, pp. 4171–418. Association for Computational Linguistics, Stroudsburg (2019). https://doi.org/10.18653/v1/N19-1423
7. Diefenbach, D., Lopez, V., Singh, K., Maret, P.: Core techniques of question answering systems over knowledge bases: a survey. Knowl. Inf. Syst. **55**(3), 529–569 (2017). https://doi.org/10.1007/s10115-017-1100-y
8. Diefenbach, D., Lully, V., Migliatti, P.H., Singh, K., Qawasmeh, O., Maret, P.: QAnswer: a question answering prototype bridging the gap between a considerable part of the LOD cloud and end-users. In: The Web Conference 2019 - Proceedings of the World Wide Web Conference, WWW 2019, pp. 3507–3510. Association for Computing Machinery, Inc., May 2019. https://doi.org/10.1145/3308558.3314124
9. Dua, M., Kumar, S., Virk, Z.S.: Hindi language graphical user interface to database management system. In: Proceedings - 2013 12th International Conference on Machine Learning and Applications, ICMLA 2013, vol. 2, pp. 555–559. IEEE Computer Society (2013). https://doi.org/10.1109/ICMLA.2013.176
10. Groth, P., Gibson, A., Velterop, J.: The anatomy of a nanopublication. Inf. Serv. Use **30**(1–2), 51–56 (2010). https://doi.org/10.3233/ISU-2010-0613
11. Hersh, W.R.: Information Retrieval and Digital Libraries. In: Chen, H., Fuller, S.S., Friedman, C., Hersh, W. (eds.) Medical Informatics, Integrated Series in Information Systems, pp. 237–275. Springer, Boston (2005). https://doi.org/10.1007/0-387-25739-X_9

12. Jaradeh, M.Y., et al.: Open research knowledge graph: next generation infrastructure for semantic scholarly knowledge. Marina Del K-CAP**19** (2019). https://doi.org/10.1145/3360901.3364435
13. Jauhar, S.K., Turney, P., Hovy, E.: TabMCQ: a dataset of general knowledge tables and multiple-choice questions, February 2016. http://arxiv.org/abs/1602.03960
14. Karki, B., et al.: Question answering via web extracted tables and pipelined models, March 2019. http://arxiv.org/abs/1903.07113
15. Krishnamurthy, J., Kollar, T.: Jointly learning to parse and perceive: connecting natural language to the physical world. Trans. Assoc. Comput. Linguist. **1**, 193–206 (2013). https://doi.org/10.1162/tacl_a_00220
16. Kwiatkowski, T., Choi, E., Artzi, Y., Zettlemoyer, L.: Scaling semantic parsers with on-the-fly ontology matching. Technical report. www.wiktionary.com
17. Lan, Z., Chen, M., Goodman, S., Gimpel, K., Sharma, P., Soricut, R.: Albert: a lite Bert for self-supervised learning of language representations, September 2019. http://arxiv.org/abs/1909.11942
18. Lin, J.: The web as a resource for question answering: perspectives and challenges. In: LREC. Las Palmas (2002). https://www.aclweb.org/anthology/L02-1085/
19. Lopez, V., Unger, C., Cimiano, P., Motta, E.: Evaluating question answering over linked data. J. Web Semant. **21**, 3–13 (2013). https://doi.org/10.1016/j.websem.2013.05.006
20. Marx, E., Usbeck, R., Ngomo, A.C.N., Höffner, K., Lehmann, J., Auer, S.: Towards an open question answering architecture. In: ACM International Conference Proceeding Series, vol. 2014-September, pp. 57–60. Association for Computing Machinery, September 2014. https://doi.org/10.1145/2660517.2660519
21. Oelen, A., Jaradeh, M.Y., Stocker, M., Auer, S.: Generate fair literature surveys with scholarly knowledge graphs. In: JCDL 2020: The 20th ACM/IEEE Joint Conference on Digital Libraries (2020). https://doi.org/10.1145/3383583.3398520
22. Peroni, S., et al.: Research articles in simplified HTML: a web-first format for HTML-based scholarly articles. PeerJ Comput. Sci. **2017**(10) (2017). https://doi.org/10.7717/peerj-cs.132
23. Peroni, S., Shotton, D.: Opencitations, an infrastructure organization for open scholarship. Quant. Sci. Stud. **1**(1), 1–17 (2020). https://doi.org/10.1162/qss_a_00023
24. Rajpurkar, P., Zhang, J., Lopyrev, K., Liang, P.: Squad: 100,000+ questions for machine comprehension of text. In: EMNLP 2016 - Proceedings Conference on Empirical Methods in Natural Language Processing, pp. 2383–2392. Association for Computational Linguistics (ACL) (2016). https://doi.org/10.18653/v1/d16-1264
25. Ramos, J.: Using TF-IDF to determine word relevance in document queries. Technical report
26. Schatz, B.R.: Information retrieval in digital libraries: bringing search to the net. Science **275**(5298), 327–334 (1997). https://doi.org/10.1126/science.275.5298.327
27. Shekarpour, S., Marx, E., Ngonga Ngomo, A.C., Auer, S.: Sina: semantic interpretation of user queries for question answering on interlinked data. J. Web Semant. **30**, 39–51 (2015). https://doi.org/10.1016/j.websem.2014.06.002
28. Singh, K., et al.: Why reinvent the wheel: let's build question answering systems together. In: WWW 2018: Proceedings of the 2018 World Wide Web Conference, pp. 1247–1256. Association for Computing Machinery (ACM) (2018). https://doi.org/10.1145/3178876.3186023

29. Sinha, A., et al.: An overview of Microsoft Academic Service (MAS) and applications. In: WWW 2015 Companion - Proceedings of the 24th International Conference on World Wide Web, pp. 243–246. Association for Computing Machinery Inc., New York, May 2015. https://doi.org/10.1145/2740908.2742839
30. Vakulenko, S., Savenkov, V.: Tableqa: Question answering on tabular data, May 2017.http://arxiv.org/abs/1705.06504
31. Wang, H., Zhang, X., Ma, S., Sun, X., Wang, H., Wang, M.: A neural question answering model based on semi-structured tables. Technical report
32. Wilkinson, M.D., et al.: The FAIR guiding principles for scientific data management and stewardship. Sci. Data **3**(1), 1–9 (2016). https://doi.org/10.1038/sdata.2016.18
33. Wolf, T., et al.: Huggingface's transformers: state-of-the-art natural language processing, October 2019. http://arxiv.org/abs/1910.03771
34. Yahya, M., Berberich, K., Elbassuoni, S., Ramanath, M., Tresp, V., Weikum, G.: Natural language questions for the web of data. Technical report (2012)
35. Yin, J., Jiang, X., Lu, Z., Shang, L., Li, H., Li, X.: Neural generative question answering. In: IJCAI International Joint Conference on Artificial Intelligence 2016-January, pp. 2972–2978 , December 2015. http://arxiv.org/abs/1512.01337
36. Zhang, Z., Wu, Y., Zhou, J., Duan, S., Zhao, H., Wang, R.: SG-Net: syntax-guided machine reading comprehension, August 2019. http://arxiv.org/abs/1908.05147
37. Zinsser, W.: On Writing Well, 30th Anniversary Edition: An Informal Guide to Writing Nonfiction. HarperCollins (2012)
38. Zou, L., Huang, R., Wang, H., Yu, J.X., He, W., Zhao, D.: Natural language question answering over RDF - a graph data driven approach. In: Proceedings of the ACM SIGMOD International Conference on Management of Data, pp. 313–324. Association for Computing Machinery (2014). https://doi.org/10.1145/2588555.2610525

Context-Compatible Information Fusion for Scientific Knowledge Graphs

Hermann Kroll(✉), Jan-Christoph Kalo, Denis Nagel, Stephan Mennicke, and Wolf-Tilo Balke

Institute for Information Systems, TU Braunschweig, Braunschweig, Germany
{kroll,kalo,mennicke,nagel,balke}@ifis.cs.tu-bs.de

Abstract. Currently, a trend to augment document collections with entity-centric knowledge provided by knowledge graphs is clearly visible, especially in scientific digital libraries. Entity facts are either manually curated, or for higher scalability automatically harvested from large volumes of text documents. The often claimed benefit is that a collection-wide fact extraction combines information from huge numbers of documents into one single database. However, even if the extraction process would be 100% correct, the promise of pervasive information fusion within retrieval tasks poses serious threats with respect to the results' validity. This is because important contextual information provided by each document is often lost in the process and cannot be readily restored at retrieval time. In this paper, we quantify the consequences of uncontrolled knowledge graph evolution in real-world scientific libraries using NLM's PubMed corpus vs. the SemMedDB knowledge base. Moreover, we operationalise the notion of *implicit context* as a viable solution to gain a sense of *context compatibility* for all extracted facts based on the pair-wise coherence of all documents used for extraction: Our derived measures for context compatibility determine which facts are relatively safe to combine. Moreover, they allow to balance between precision and recall. Our practical experiments extensively evaluate context compatibility based on implicit contexts for typical digital library tasks. The results show that our implicit notion of context compatibility is superior to existing methods in terms of both, simplicity and retrieval quality.

Keywords: Implicit context · Knowledge graph · Digital libraries

1 Introduction

Knowledge graphs have revolutionised the access to entity-centric information on the Web, with *Google's knowledge graph*[1] and the *Wikidata knowledge base* [19] being prime examples. One reason is that the old 'Web of Documents' is more and more turning into a 'Web of Linked Data', which needs new access methods

[1] https://developers.google.com/knowledge-graph/.

M. Hall et al. (Eds.): TPDL 2020, LNCS 12246, pp. 33–47, 2020.
https://doi.org/10.1007/978-3-030-54956-5_3

beyond IR-style keyword search: entity-centric information needs to be structured, disambiguated, and semantically enriched by information from various sources. Thus, also in the well-curated domains of digital libraries, a trend to augment document collections to semantically enriched content bases is clearly visible. Especially in scientific libraries *Big Scholarly Data* in heterogeneous form (see [21] for a good overview) is exploited for value-adding services, such as related work recommendation, expert search, or information enhancement using specialised entity-centric databases, like *DrugBank*[2] or *UniProt*[3]. The ultimate vision currently is to extract facts from complete digital collections into one comprehensive knowledge graph for science, supporting complex information needs and offering a variety of additional services, see e. g. [1,7,18].

Yet, the question whether a document collection may still offer more than a collection of extracted facts was already raised at an early stage. An obvious problem concerns the *trustworthiness* of sources: there is a long-standing discussion about the actual truth or plausibility of extracted facts and how well they match with facts extracted from other sources [14]. Thus, keeping lineage or provenance information and respective reputation scores as metadata for each fact is vital [2]. A second class of problems is created by errors in the *algorithmic processes* necessary for fact extraction from natural language texts, covering entity recognition, disambiguation and linking, as well as reliable relation extraction, see e. g. [15]. In fact, all tasks in this process are still error-prone, and even small errors may quickly spoil the overall quality in knowledge graphs [10].

However, even if all these problems were solved, there would be still a major, yet rarely discussed issue: the general *validity* of facts. With respect to general fact validity, current knowledge graphs on the Web vastly differ from those used in scientific digital libraries. Whereas entity-centric data in typical Linked Open Data sources on the Web may or may not be correct, it still tends to be *generally* valid, as e. g. the *birthdate of a person* or *which actors played in some movie*. In contrast, entity-centric data reported in scientific digital collections is often more problematic. Consider for instance different medical treatment options with some active ingredient. They depend on many caveats: general concerns, unresolved discourses in the community, the specific disposition of an actual patient, etc. Another prime examples are clinical trials: even if they are methodically sound, their results can only be considered valid *within the limited context* investigated by each trial. Thus, given the problems to properly control studies currently the generalisability of facts extracted from clinical trials is difficult to assess.

Assume we extract the fact (`simvastatin`, `causes`, `rhabdomyolysis`) from some document reporting on a simultaneous treatment of patients with simvastatin and amiodarone. As the resulting interaction indeed may lead to rhabdomyolysis as a side effect, the information is correct. In the same fashion, we may correctly extract the fact (`simvastatin`, `treats`, `arteriosclerosis`) from some other document on treatment options for arteriosclerosis. But if we now use the combined knowledge graph to query the side effects of *simvastatin in*

[2] https://www.drugbank.ca.
[3] https://www.uniprot.org.

treating arteriosclerosis, we run into trouble: the fact that *simvastatin causes rhabdomyolysis* is not valid *in general.* It is only valid *within the context of simultaneous treatment with simvastatin and amiodarone.* Thus, without having facts restricted by their exact context, a free combination with other facts from the knowledge graph may at least be questionable, if not plain false. Yet, current extraction procedures do exactly this: after long years of standardisation, knowledge graphs typically store facts as simple RDF-triples [3]. This way, tearing facts out of documents and putting them into a knowledge graph means losing all contextual information. If such knowledge graphs are later used for tasks like knowledge discovery, question answering and querying, serious errors can be foreseen. The central question in designing knowledge graphs for digital libraries is thus: *How can knowledge graphs maintain a sense of context for their individual collection of facts?* And concerning later applications: *How can we combine individual facts or even completely merge fact collections while still maintaining their contexts?*

When working with RDF-triples, the *technical* solution for adding context information mostly relies on reification of triples. But how is the correct context for each fact determined? To overcome this problem, two approaches are common: 1. In the community project Wikidata, uploaders are also responsible for supplying all necessary contextual information as additional triples, called qualifiers [19]. 2. In cases where clear-cut contexts can a-priori be determined for some field, the direct modelling and extraction of n-ary relations from document collection are possible [6].

Yet, in both cases, the context needs to be modelled *explicitly.* In this paper, we harness valuable work in the digital library community on standardising provenance and bibliographic metadata (such as authors or keywords) to derive a novel *implicit*, i. e. document-based context model for knowledge graphs. Documents like scientific papers interweave facts in complex contexts and can be assumed to be intrinsically coherent, e. g. by describing all relevant assumptions, methods, observations and conclusions. Thus, for all facts our model takes advantage of the respective extraction documents' characteristics and uses them as an implicit context for facts. Such implicit contexts ensure that given a retrieval problem, only facts from a coherent group of documents can be combined to produce a valid result. Indeed, our experiments show that restricting the information fusion process of knowledge graphs to (restricted) document contexts has a high impact on the number and quality of possible candidates. In addition to structural requirements (graph matching), we consider the context approximated by documents sharing different characteristics to produce valid answers to a query. To improve the result quality for any given query, we operationalise and analyse metrics to find documents having **compatible** contexts. A context compatible set of documents can then be used to obtain better results in terms of validity for tasks like knowledge discovery and querying. We analyse our document-based implicit context model in Sect. 3 and provide a detailed experimental analysis in Sect. 4. Our contributions are:

1. We design and discuss a novel implicit context model suitable for digital libraries. We demonstrate the superiority of implicitly capturing contexts for a real-world knowledge graph in the medical domain.
2. Further, we introduce the concept of context compatibility, i. e. we extend strict document contexts to compatible contexts, increasing the recall for practical applications.
3. We publish all of our scripts as well as evaluation data and results in a publicly available GitHub repository[4] for reproducibility.

2 Related Work

Literature-based Discovery is a well-known and highly discussed topic, i. e. inferring new knowledge based on the current state of literature [16]. In this work, we focus on the application of scientific knowledge graphs for digital libraries. Contextualisation of data can be realised by adding additional contextual information to an individual statement or fact. Regarding RDF, this means to incorporate triples into the knowledge graphs that capture information about a specific triple already existent in the data. Ideas on how to represent contextual information in RDF are provided in [13]. This process is called reification of RDF data [8]. It is realised by introducing a new resource, referencing the reified triple in other statements.

Qualifiers for Contextualising Knowledge. Wikidata, the most extensive open knowledge base on the Web, tries to reify pure RDF facts by using so-called *qualifiers* [19]. Qualifiers add information to a fact by appending a property-value pair directly to it. An example fact (`simvastatin`, `causes`, `rhabdomyolysis`) may further be described by an additional qualifier, namely `when simultaneously used with` along with the respective value `amiodarone`. The qualifiers claim that *simvastatin causes rhabdomyolysis* only, in a simultaneous treatment with *simvastatin* and *amiodarone*. Thus, qualifiers may be used to add additional provenance and sometimes contextual information to simple RDF facts [9]. Even though Wikidata comprises around 30 million qualifier statements (10-2018), they are hardly used to express context for scientific facts, i. e. drug-disease treatments. Even more, only about 5% of all statements are qualifiers (573 million statements). Qualifiers are often restricting the statement they are referring to in a temporal manner, e. g. using the `start time` qualifier. Besides, they may add some provenance information such as references or citations to the statements. In other cases they state information that has no impact on the validity of the fact in question, e. g. the `determination method` is simply used with qualifier values like *chronometry* or *questionnaire* without affecting the validity of its fact. Using qualifiers in joining facts has no precise semantics, e.g. how can we decide whether two qualifiers describe the same context? The curation of explicit contexts is a huge task and moreover, working with explicit context models in practice is unclear.

[4] https://github.com/HermannKroll/ContextInformationFusion.

N-ary Fact Extraction. An extension of extracting binary facts is to harvest n-ary facts [6]. In a large-scale experiment, the authors prove that n-ary facts are more precise than just using binary facts [6]. Thereby, it is possible to explicitly extract and store the context of relations in a higher level relation. For our previous drug and side effect scenario, we may easily design a ternary relation capturing drug, the cause as well as the interacting drug: $causes \subseteq drug \times sideeffect \times interacting\ drug$. However, how good is n-ary fact extraction in practice? Ernst et al. extracted the relation *AthleteWonAward* from a news corpus consisting of 2.8 million documents with about 112 million sentences [6]. They mined 3804 binary, 1089 ternary, 224 4-ary, 23 5-ary and two 6-ary instances of this relation with their best configuration regarding precision. Even though n-ary facts are a promising idea to capture the context of facts, obtaining such n-ary facts is a difficult task, because it requires manually defining the context for every single relation by defining its arity, its domains and its semantics upfront. This is a very strong restriction because considering any possible context of some relation a priori is close to impossible.

Provenance. Another understanding of contexts is provenance, which mainly focuses on storing information attached to the actual fact [17]. The scope of provenance thereby ranges from storing only the explicit source document over additionally storing information related to its creation process such as the author or release date [20]. Provenance can then help to argue about the quality and trustworthiness of the statement in question. Provenance can be integrated into knowledge graphs by using Named Graphs [5]. These are linked to individual facts by extending RDF triples to form N-Quads [4]. In the last years, much work was spent on developing the so-called Prov-O Ontology Description [12]. Prov-O enables knowledge graph designers to encode and store arbitrary information, such as context, for knowledge graph facts. Unfortunately, Prov-O requires users to spend much work on manually providing this additional information, i. e. Prov-O comes with a similar problem as qualifiers in Wikidata. There is yet no solution to automatically reuse context information in the fusion process of knowledge graphs. As far as we know, there exists no practical evaluation of using contexts in typical knowledge graph tasks. With the introduction of our document-based implicit context model and evaluation on a real-world scenario, we extend the current state of literature by giving a practical solution to retain context for digital libraries. Therefore, already applied techniques like Prov-O, Named Graphs, as well as reification, may simply be used as an implementation providing the necessary context in the form of document references for our implicit context model.

3 Implicit Context

Instead of modelling contexts explicitly, textual documents (i. e. research papers) serve as contexts for knowledge graph facts. A scientific publication interweaves facts in assumptions, methods, observations and conclusions. Thus, the argumentative story of a scientific document provides all relevant context variables

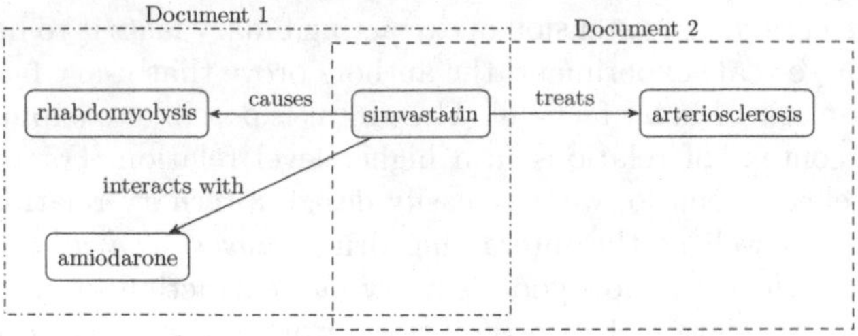

Fig. 1. Implicit context representation for a knowledge graph

implicitly, validating its contained facts. We assume scientific documents to come with a single context, e. g. clinical trials analyse drugs under stable conditions. Indeed, surveys and scientific papers might include several contexts, e. g. describing related work. For this paper, we assume that scientific knowledge graphs should be built by extracting facts out of the paper's main argumentation, i. e. skipping sections such as related work in the extraction process. For our running example, the document provides vital information that simvastatin only causes rhabdomyolysis, when the person is simultaneously treated with amiodarone. Here, the document itself implicitly defines and, thereby, determines the context of interest, because we assume the extracted facts to participate in the main argumentation of the paper. If we mine facts from a single document, then all extracted facts from this document naturally share the same context. The information fusion process by combining/joining facts from the same document to answer a query automatically leads to valid facts because they stem from the same context. In the scientific domain, this context often boils down to conclusions being observed under the same experimental conditions. Therefore, returning to our running example, we define the implicit context of a fact as the document it stems from, see Fig. 1 as an example.

When using a **strict implicit context**, we restrict the combination of facts to those facts within the same **context**, i. e. to facts extracted from the exact same document. Applied to our example, we obtain either that simvastatin treats arteriosclerosis, or that simvastatin causes rhabdomyolysis. We would not obtain the wrong side effect rhabdomyolysis in an arteriosclerosis treatment because there is not a single document validating it.

3.1 Context Compatibility

Obviously, restricting the fusion process of knowledge graphs to strict implicit context will have a substantial impact on the number of obtained results, because we combine facts stemming from the same document only. In addition to strict implicit contexts, we may assume that two scientific documents on simvastatin share the same context, e. g. they describe clinical trials analysing an arteriosclerosis treatment using simvastatin. Since both papers are clinical trials with the same experimental conditions, it seems promising that a combination of facts from both documents leads to valid query results. Hence, inferring new knowledge between different documents may also be possible. Our idea extends the restriction on pure document contexts to context compatibility ranging over sets of documents. This will lead to broader contexts and allows for a less restrictive combination of facts. Two documents d_1 and d_2, sharing the same context in the above-mentioned sense, will be denoted as **context compatible**: $d_1 \sim d_2$. Thereby, we require $\sim$ to be a reflexive binary relation over the document collection, i. e. one document is always compatible with itself. Combining facts from different but context compatible documents shall yield valid query results.

Comparing the contexts spanned by two or more documents directly is a tedious and time-consuming task that requires a deep understanding of documents' domains. Here, we use different metrics to approximate the context compatibility of documents. In digital libraries, a collection of documents typically provides valuable metadata information. Subsequently, we design two different kinds of similarity metrics to assess the context compatibility of documents: 1. metrics, which directly work on metadata information like authors and curated keywords, and 2. metrics, which build upon textual similarities for titles and abstracts. We choose a threshold-based classification approach to estimate whether two documents are context compatible or not. If the similarity value, computed by a metric, between two documents is above a threshold t, we assume the documents to have a compatible context. Thus, we can safely fuse the facts of two context compatible documents to form a valid answer.

Definition 1. *Let sim be a similarity metric between documents and* $t \in \mathcal{R}$ *a threshold value. Two documents* d_1 *and* d_2 *are context compatible, denoted by* $d_1 \sim d_2$, *if* $sim(d_1, d_2) \geq t$.

Metadata-Based Similarity Metrics. In scientific contexts, researchers typically work on a specific research field, e. g. a group of medical experts are researching *drug interactions with simvastatin.* They might write several publications about their findings based on similar assumptions like *experimental conditions.* Thus, we assume papers, written by the same authors, to have compatible contexts. We formulate the first metric sim_{author} to estimate context compatibility by using the Jaccard coefficient between the authors of documents. Since contexts of facts should be compatible, if they comprise similar assumptions or experimental designs, we try to capture this intuition by relying on the valuable manually curated metadata available for medical documents. In PubMed, documents are annotated with manual curated mesh headings and chemicals. A mesh heading is a mesh term describing medical entities, actors, processes and concepts like *humans*, *pain*, *trial* and *simvastatin.* The mesh headings, therefore, might capture the context that is given by a document. The second metric sim_{mesh} is defined as the Jaccard coefficient of the documents' mesh headings. Similarly to the mesh terms, we use the chemicals annotated to documents as an approximation for context compatibility. Therefore, $sim_{chemical}$ is defined as the Jaccard coefficient of the documents' chemicals.

Text-Based Similarity Metrics. In addition to the metadata-based approaches, we also try to capture the context compatibility by measuring textual similarities among the documents' texts. Here, sim_{title} is defined as the Jaccard coefficient between the titles of two documents to estimate the text-similarity between documents. The previous similarity metrics can only be applied to pairs of documents for determining context compatibility. To further extend fact fusions to more than a pair of documents, we suggest to also directly determine the compatibility between multiple documents by clustering documents into **context compatible sets** such that all documents inside such a set are pairwise context compatible. Given the respective documents the facts in the knowledge graph stem from, we use a clustering method to produce groups of documents with compatible contexts. Here, we use textual information, i. e. titles and abstracts of documents. We select a common method to cluster documents to understand whether compatible document sets are helpful: 1. We extract the titles and abstracts of documents. Thereby, we remove stop words and apply stemming. 2. We compute the TF-IDF matrix upon the texts. Words which occur very frequently or words which occur very rarely are removed. 3. Clustering documents with various texts requires much computational power. Thus, we use a principal component analysis (PCA) to reduce the number of dimensions to 300. 4. Finally, we apply a k-means++ clustering on the reduced matrix with different k values.

4 Analysis on SemMedDB

In the following experiments, we evaluate whether restricting fact combinations to their document contexts is capable of producing valid facts for typical medical queries. We perform a comparison to querying a knowledge graph without contextual information, allowing us to join arbitrary facts. In our expectations, using implicit context should increase the quality of query results substantially, while reducing the overall number of results. For the evaluation, we compare the number and quality of results for typical queries on a large medical knowledge graph called *SemMedDB* by using no context as a baseline and our implicit context models.

SemMedDB is a fact-based database consisting of medical entities and relations between them [11]. A fact mining process automatically extracted all facts from abstracts and titles of documents in PubMed. For each extracted fact in *SemMedDB*, a reference to its source document is retained. Hence, *SemMedDB* provides provenance information. We use *SemMedDB* 2019[5] in version *semmedVER40R*. This version comprises 20,124,700 distinct facts extracted 97,972,561 times. We design three experiments to compare the usage of *SemMedDB* as a knowledge graph without context on the one hand and with implicit context on the other. The experiments are built on three scientific queries, and are also depicted in Fig. 2: 1. Knowledge discovery via querying using the `causes` relation, 2. Predicting drug-drug interactions via a gene (like already performed by

[5] https://skr3.nlm.nih.gov/SemMedDB/.

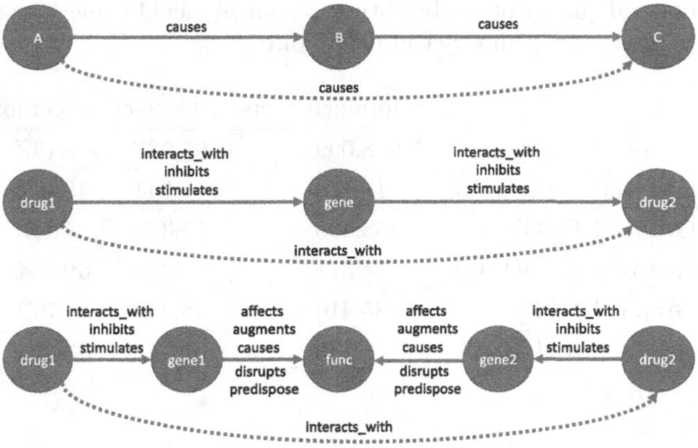

Fig. 2. Graph Patterns to derive new facts in SemMedDB. The dotted edge depicts the new derived fact

domain experts [22]) and 3. Predicting drug-drug interactions via a biological function (like already performed by domain experts [22]).

Transitive Causal Relation (Causes). `Causes` is used to express a relation between a cause and an effect of medical concepts, e. g. a drug and a disease. Since this relation is usually assumed to be transitive, the goal in this knowledge discovery task is to query for new facts by joining two existing causal facts from the knowledge graph. As an example, the facts (`simvastatin`, `causes`, `risk of heart disease`) and (`risk of heart disease`, `causes`, `heart failure`) may be joined to obtain the new fact (`simvastatin, causes, heart failure)`. To increase the quality of these facts, we select only facts appearing in at least three documents, yielding 153,024 distinct facts extracted 1,584,676 times from documents.

Predicting Drug-Drug Interactions (DDI). In a second experiment, we rely on a known approach for finding drug-drug interactions using *SemMedDB* [22]. Such an interaction may cause several side effects in a patient's treatment. Thus, finding these new interactions is a relevant task for medical experts that can be easily supported by knowledge graphs. Drug-drug interactions are discovered using two queries as described in [22]. We call these interactions *DDI-G*, a drug-drug interaction via a gene and DDI-F, a drug-drug interaction via a function.

Estimating the Result Quality. To be able to perform the evaluation, we take *SemMedDB* as the gold standard of medical knowledge and assume that it is 100% correct and also complete. As far as we know, there is no medical source comprising more medical domain knowledge than *SemMedDB*. *SemMedDB* contains a dedicated `causes` predicate and `interacts with` predicate between drugs. Thus, we count how many derived facts are contained in *SemMedDB* already and how many of them are correct. To estimate the recall, we take the

Table 1. Number and quality of newly distinct obtained facts by querying a knowledge graph without context and with strict implicit context

Graph	#Obtained facts	#Correct	Precision	Recall
Knowledge Graph (Causes)	7,978,099	95,037	1.19%	**100%**
Strict Implicit Context (Causes)	11,478	5,544	**48.3%**	5.83%
Knowledge Graph (DDI-G)	753,899	55,370	7.34%	**100%**
Strict Implicit Context (DDI-G)	1,311	909	**69.3%**	1.64%
Knowledge Graph (DDI-F)	18,685,416	148,346	0.79%	**100%**
Strict Implicit Context (DDI-F)	2,138	1,352	**63.2%**	0.9%

number of query answers on the knowledge graph without restricting fact combinations as an overestimation of the number of all correct results. Thereby, we overestimate the recall of the knowledge graph as being 100% and compare the remaining approach to that number. We underestimate the precision, because there may exist correctly derived facts, which are not included in our ground truth (the knowledge graph itself).

4.1 Strict Implicit Context

For the knowledge graph query experiments, we have no restrictions when joining facts and just perform a simple pattern matching from the query to the knowledge graph. In contrast, when using strict implicit context, we restrict fact combinations to the document contexts, i. e. combinations of facts are only possible within the context of a document. The number and quality of obtained results by using no context in comparison to using strict implicit context for all three tasks (causes, DDI-G and DDI-F) are listed in Table 1. The number of facts obtained from the baseline, a knowledge graph without context, differs by orders of magnitude compared to the knowledge graph with strict implicit context in all three experiments. However, the results only come with a precision of 1.19% (causes), 7.34% (DDI-G) and 0.79% (DDI-F) by using no context and 48.3% (causes), 69.3% (DDI-G) and 63.2% (DDI-F) by using strict implicit context. The recall decreases from 100% to 5.83% (causes), 1.64% (DDI-G) and 0.9% (DDI-F).

Discussion. In sum, using strict implicit document-based contexts outperforms the plain knowledge graph (no context) approach for all three experiments with regard to the precision. However, strict implicit context restricts the derivation process of facts to single document contexts, and thus a considerable amount of incorrect, but also some correct results are not returned. This leads to a lower recall in comparison to joining arbitrary facts. When querying a knowledge graph, a high degree of correctness is often needed. Particularly if medical experts need to verify drug-drug interactions in studies, high-quality results are desired.

4.2 Context Compatibility

We design context compatibility to increase the recall for different tasks in comparison to strict implicit context by allowing the fusion of facts stemming from compatible document contexts. Our evaluation comprises six different approaches for context compatibility on two different medical queries. Three of the approaches work purely on the metadata (i. e. chemical, mesh headings and authors) and three approaches work with textual measures (i. e. Jaccard coefficient between titles, clustering of titles and abstracts). The two queries are the causes query from Fig. 2 at the top and the DDI-G query depicted in Fig. 2 in the middle. Unfortunately, we have to skip the third experiment (DDI-F) here due to performance issues. In the DDI-F experiment, the knowledge graph produces around 18 million facts. Checking the context compatibility between documents, validating a fact derivation, leads to too many different combinations. For all our experiments, we evaluate different thresholds and k-values to report our findings as precision-recall curves. We check different thresholds (0 to 1.0 by a step size of 0.1) and 20 different k values ranging from 2 to 100,000. Additionally to the results presented in this paper, more experimental results can be found on our GitHub repository. To perform our experiments, we have accessed the metadata and texts of PubMed documents by downloading the latest version of the PubMed Medline 2019 as an XML dump[6], which provides title, abstracts and valuable metadata.

Causes Experiment. Figure 3 (a) depicts the precision-recall curve for the cause experiment using metadata similarity metrics. Note that selecting a threshold of 0.0 leads to the same result as using the knowledge graph approach without contextual restrictions and 1.0 leads to similar results as using strict implicit context. We achieve the best possible precision of about 48% with a recall of about 6% by using a threshold of 1.0 for sim_{mesh} and $sim_{authors}$. A higher recall is achieved when using $sim_{chemicals}$ because 53% of all documents provide curated chemicals, whereas the other metadata is less common. We obtain the best F1-Score of 25.5% (28.8% precision and 23% recall) for $sim_{authors}$ with a threshold of 0.1. Although sim_{author} outperforms the other metrics regarding precision and recall, sim_{author} provides only a small recall range. 9 of 10 thresholds for sim_{author} yield a recall below 23% and the last threshold yields 100% recall. Computing more fine-grained thresholds would not help here, because most of the papers have only a few authors yielding a small range of different Jaccard coefficients.

The results of our text-based approaches for context compatibility are depicted in Fig. 3 (c). Here, the clustering methods on titles and abstracts share a similar shape; hence they have a comparable performance. Variations of the number of clusters can cover a range of recall values between 0.6 and 1.0 while keeping an acceptable precision of around 10%. Hence, the methods can boost the precision of the knowledge graph 10-fold, while only sacrificing around 40%

[6] https://www.nlm.nih.gov/databases/download/pubmed_medline.html.

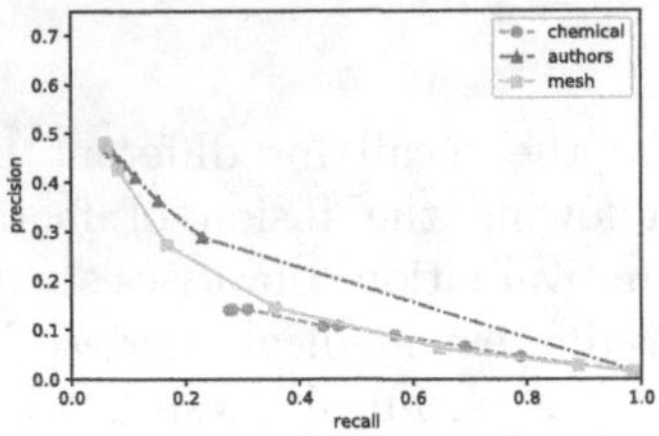

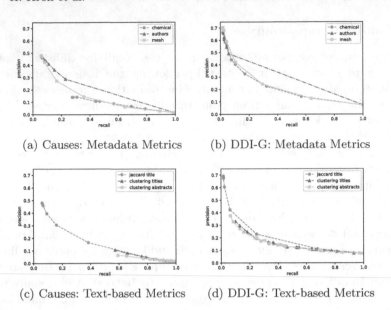

(a) Causes: Metadata Metrics

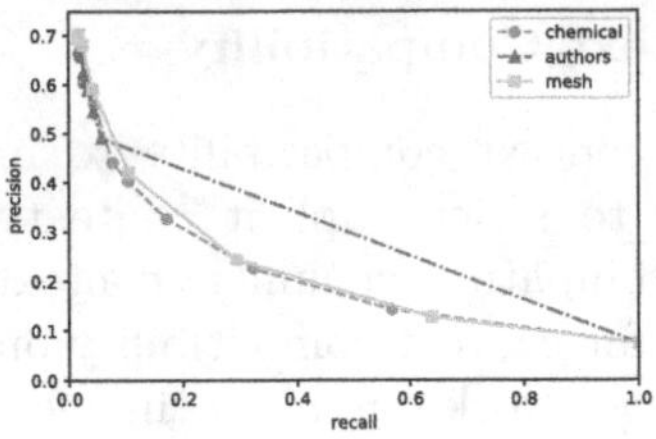

(b) DDI-G: Metadata Metrics

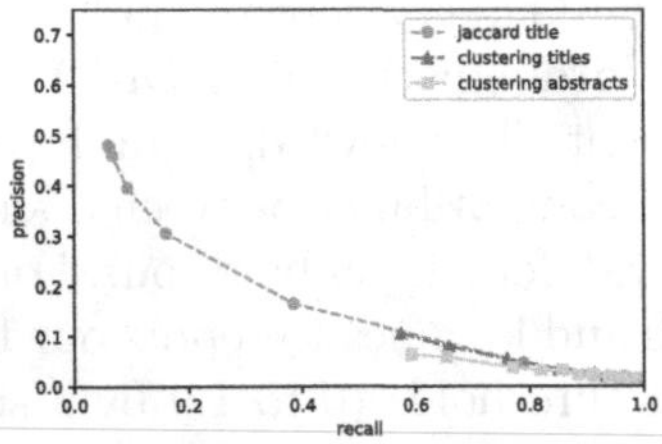

(c) Causes: Text-based Metrics

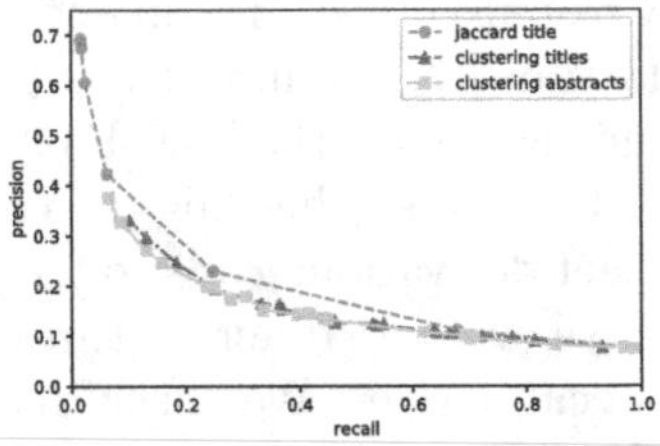

(d) DDI-G: Text-based Metrics

Fig. 3. Precision-recall curve of the experiments (Causes and DDI-G) by using different metrics to estimate the context compatibility between documents

of recall. In contrast, the Jaccard-based similarity sim_{title} outperforms the clustering methods (denoted as jaccard title in the plot). The approach achieves a comparable precision for high recall values. Besides, it is possible to achieve even higher precision, for sacrificing some correct results at lower recall values by achieving a precision of almost 50% at a recall of 10%.

Overall, we can summarise that sim_{author} and sim_{title} achieve the best results for the causes experiment. While sim_{author} performs better regarding precision, sim_{title} offers to select a broader range of recall values.

DDI Gene Experiment. Figure 3 (b) depicts the precision-recall curve for the DDI-G experiment using metadata similarity metrics. Again, $sim_{authors}$ outperforms the other metrics, e. g. selecting a threshold of 0.1 yields a precision of 49% and a recall of 6%. Compared to strict implicit context, the precision decreases from 69% to 49%, while the recall increases from 1.6% to 6%. Thereby, 9 of 10 thresholds for $sim_{authors}$ yield a recall below 6%. In this experiment, $sim_{chemical}$ performs better than in the causes experiment. We obtain the best F1-Score of 26.5% (22.6% precision and 32.1% recall) for $sim_{chemicals}$ with a threshold of 0.2. We assume that a chemical-based similarity fits best for a drug-based query.

We depict the precision-recall curve for the DDI-G experiment using text-based similarities in Fig. 3 (d). Again, the clustering methods on titles and abstracts share a similar shape. In comparison to the causes experiment, the clustering approaches provide a broader range of recall values with higher precision. The Jaccard-based similarity sim_{title} outperforms the clustering methods.

Similar to our previous experiments, all approaches boost the precision of the knowledge graph, which was around 7%, while keeping good recall values. Overall, for the DDI-G experiment, we can summarise that sim_{author} and sim_{title} achieve best results.

Discussion. All techniques for context compatibility can boost the poor quality of query answers on knowledge graphs by at least one order of magnitude while being able to retain high recall. Furthermore, the techniques offer much more flexibility than the knowledge graph without context and with strict implicit context alone by providing the possibility of choosing between precision and recall, depending on the application.

5 Conclusion

In this paper, we highlighted the importance of retaining document contexts for supporting typical knowledge graph tasks for digital libraries. Indeed, document context proves crucial for proving the validity of facts, especially, in scientific domains such as biomedicine or pharmacy. Moreover, we introduced *implicit contexts* using documents as an approximation of contexts and evaluated them in combination with compatible contexts for different tasks. Our experiments show the applicability and feasibility of document-driven contextualisation for tasks like knowledge discovery and querying in practice. Approximating contexts at the document-level offers an easy-to-use and, likewise, high-quality opportunity to maintain context in knowledge graphs. Storing techniques like Prov-O, Named Graphs and N-Quads are already ready-to-use and established fact mining processes may easily be extended by maintaining a reference for each fact to its source document, but nothing more. Providing context compatibility between documents might be as simple as designing metrics for already available metadata in digital libraries. This technique leads to an apparent increase of recall when using implicit contexts, but would not deny the valuable context given by librarian documents.

As future work, we would like to investigate measures for *story-based* similarity between documents and to evaluate their usefulness for context compatibility. The *story* of a document is related to its argumentation plus their contextual settings. We believe that a story-based similarity measure would improve the previously described similarity metrics in different tasks.

References

1. Auer, S., Kovtun, V., Prinz, M., Kasprzik, A., Stocker, M., Vidal, M.E.: Towards a knowledge graph for science. In: Proceedings of the 8th International Conference on Web Intelligence, Mining and Semantics. WIMS 2018. ACM (2018)
2. Bechhofer, S., et al.: Why linked data is not enough for scientists. Fut. Gener. Comput. Syst. **29**(2), 599–611 (2013)
3. Candan, K.S., Liu, H., Suvarna, R.: Resource description framework: metadata and its applications. SIGKDD Expl. **3**(1), 6–19 (2001)

4. Carothers, G.: RDF 1.1 N-Quads. https://www.w3.org/TR/n-quads/ (2014)
5. Carroll, J.J., Bizer, C., Hayes, P., Stickler, P.: Named graphs, provenance and trust. In: Proceedings of the 14th International Conference on WWW, WWW 2005, pp. 613–622. ACM (2005)
6. Ernst, P., Siu, A., Weikum, G.: Highlife: higher-arity fact harvesting. In: Proceedings of the 2018 World Wide Web Conference, WWW 2018, International World Wide Web Conference on Steering Committee, pp. 1013–1022 (2018)
7. Fathalla, S., Vahdati, S., Auer, S., Lange, C.: Towards a knowledge graph representing research findings by semantifying survey articles. In: Kamps, J., Tsakonas, G., Manolopoulos, Y., Iliadis, L., Karydis, I. (eds.) TPDL 2017. LNCS, vol. 10450, pp. 315–327. Springer, Cham (2017). https://doi.org/10.1007/978-3-319-67008-9_25
8. Hayes, P.J., Patel-Schneider, P.F.: RDF 1.1 Semantics. https://www.w3.org/TR/rdf11-mt/##whatnot (2014)
9. Hernández, D., Hogan, A., Krötzsch, M.: Reifying RDF: what works well with Wikidata? In: Proceedings of the 11th International Work. on Scalable Semantic Web Knowledge Base Systems. CEUR Working Proceedings, vol. 1457, pp. 32–47. CEUR-WS.org (2015)
10. Kalo, J.C., Homoceanu, S., Rose, J., Balke, W.T.: Avoiding Chinese Whispers: controlling end-to-end join quality in linked open data stores. In: Proceedings of the ACM Web Science Conference, WebSci 2015, pp. 5:1–5:10. ACM (2015)
11. Kilicoglu, H., Shin, D., Fiszman, M., Rosemblat, G., Rindflesch, T.C.: SemMedDB: a PubMed-scale repository of biomedical semantic predications. Bioinformatics **28**(23), 3158–3160 (2012)
12. Lebo, T., Sahoo, S., McGuinness, D.: PROV-O: The PROV Ontology. https://www.w3.org/TR/prov-o/ (2013)
13. Patel-Schneider, P.: Contextualization via qualifiers. In: Workshop on Contextualized Knowledge Graphs co-located with 17th International Semantic Web Conference on, CKG@ISWC 2018 (2018). http://wiki.knoesis.org/index.php/CKG2018
14. Pinto, J.M.G., Balke, W.-T.: Can plausibility help to support high quality content in digital libraries? In: Kamps, J., Tsakonas, G., Manolopoulos, Y., Iliadis, L., Karydis, I. (eds.) TPDL 2017. LNCS, vol. 10450, pp. 169–180. Springer, Cham (2017). https://doi.org/10.1007/978-3-319-67008-9_14
15. Shen, W., Wang, J., Han, J.: Entity linking with a knowledge base: issues, techniques, and solutions. IEEE Trans. Knowl. Data Eng. **27**(2), 443–460 (2015)
16. Swanson, D.R.: Complementary structures in disjoint science literatures. In: Proc. of the 14th Annual International ACM SIGIR Conference on Research and Development in Information Retrieval, pp. 280–289. SIGIR 1991, ACM (1991)
17. Tan, W.C.: Provenance in databases: past, current, and future. Bull. IEEE Comput. Soc. Techn. Committee Data Eng. **30**(4), 3–12 (2007)
18. Vahdati, S., Palma, G., Nath, R.J., Lange, C., Auer, S., Vidal, M.-E.: Unveiling scholarly communities over knowledge graphs. In: Méndez, E., Crestani, F., Ribeiro, C., David, G., Lopes, J.C. (eds.) TPDL 2018. LNCS, vol. 11057, pp. 103–115. Springer, Cham (2018). https://doi.org/10.1007/978-3-030-00066-0_9
19. Vrandečić, D., Krötzsch, M.: Wikidata: a free collaborative knowledgebase. Commun. ACM **57**(10), 78–85 (2014)

20. Wylot, M., Cudré-Mauroux, P., Hauswirth, M., Groth, P.: Storing, tracking, and querying provenance in linked data. IEEE Trans. Knowl. Data Eng. **29**(8), 1751–1764 (2017)
21. Xia, F., Wang, W., Bekele, T.M., Liu, H.: Big scholarly data: a survey. IEEE Trans. Big Data **3**(1), 18–35 (2017)
22. Zhang, R., et al.: Using semantic predications to uncover drug-drug interactions in clinical data. J. Biomed. Inform. **49**, 134–147 (2014)

VeTo: Expert Set Expansion in Academia

Thanasis Vergoulis[1(✉)], Serafeim Chatzopoulos[1,2], Theodore Dalamagas[1], and Christos Tryfonopoulos[2]

[1] IMSI, "Athena" Research Center, 15125 Athens, Greece
{vergoulis,schatz,dalamag}@athenarc.gr

[2] Department of Informatics and Telecommunications, University of the Peloponnese, 22100 Tripoli, Greece
trifon@uop.gr

Abstract. Expanding a set of known domain experts with new individuals, that have similar expertise, is a problem with many practical applications (e.g., adding new members to a conference program committee). In this work, we study this problem in the context of academic experts and we introduce VeTo, a novel method to effectively deal with it by exploiting scholarly knowledge graphs. In particular, VeTo expands the given set of experts by identifying researchers that share similar publishing habits with them, based on a graph analysis approach. Our experiments show that VeTo is more effective than existing techniques that can be applied to deal with the same problem.

Keywords: Expertise retrieval · Scholarly knowledge graphs

1 Introduction

Expanding a set of known domain experts with new individuals, that have similar expertise, is a problem that emerges in many real-life applications in academia and industry. For instance, consider a conference organiser that attempts to add new members to the program committee of the conference, since some old members have retired; or consider an officer in a funding agency that seeks new referees to review funding proposals, since some of the current ones are not available. Problems like these motivated the work in the broad area of *expert finding* [10].

Early works in this field assume that the person seeking for experts provides a set of keywords describing the desired topics of expertise. Thus, the proposed expert finding approaches (e.g., [3]) attempt to match these topics to experts by utilising the co-occurrences of topic keywords with person names in text corpora (e.g., websites, publications). However, in many cases it is difficult to explicitly define the desired topics as concrete sets of keywords. To overcome this issue various approaches (e.g., [4,8]) support querying by example: the seeker provides the name of a known expert of the desired field and the approach seeks individuals that seem to have a similar expertise profile. In most cases, the aforementioned profiles are constructed based on analysing the existing text corpora

M. Hall et al. (Eds.): TPDL 2020, LNCS 12246, pp. 48–61, 2020.
https://doi.org/10.1007/978-3-030-54956-5_4

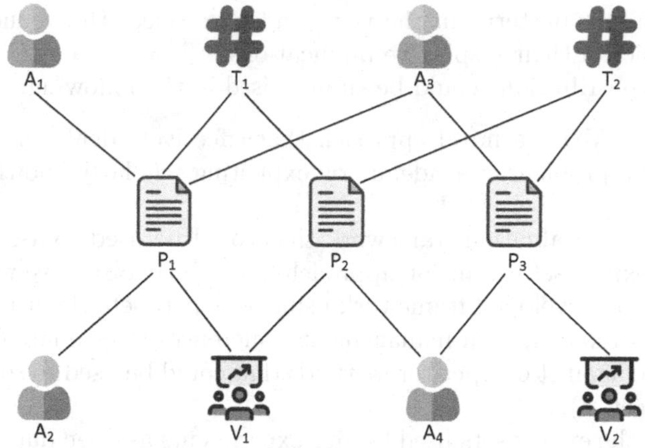

Fig. 1. An example scholarly knowledge graph including academics, papers, venues and topics.

(e.g., applying linguistic processing or topic modeling techniques). Although most such methods search for individuals that are similar to a single expert, some of them are also capable to identify similarities to groups of experts, as well [2].

As it is evident, the effectiveness of all previously described approaches depends on the availability of concrete text corpora that contain information about the expertise of the individuals. In the context of academia this means that these approaches require as input a large set of scientific publications. However, the full texts of publications are often restricted behind paywalls and, thus, it is practically impossible to construct a concrete set of the relevant texts. Moreover, even if it was possible to construct a corpus containing an adequate number of relevant publications, its size would be vast and, thus, gathering and preprocessing it in a regular basis would be a tedious and time-consuming task. This problem motivated the introduction of alternative methods that, instead, utilise *scholarly knowledge graphs* (e.g., [9]). In late years, due to the systematic effort of various developing teams, a variety of large scholarly knowledge graphs has been made available (e.g., the AMiner's DBPL-based datasets [20], the Open Research Knowledge Graph [11], the OpenAIRE Research Graph [12,13]). These heterogeneous graphs consist a very rich and relatively clean source of information about academics, their publications and relevant metadata. Figure 1 presents an illustrative example of such a graph comprising academics, papers, venues, and topics.

In this context, we introduce *VeTo*, a novel, knowledge graph-based approach to deal with the problem of expanding a set of known experts with new individuals with similar expertise. Our approach exploits recent developments in techniques to analyse heterogeneous graphs to identify similarities between researchers based on their publishing habits. In particular, VeTo takes advantage of latent patterns in the way academics select the venue to publish and in the topics of their respective publications.

Our main contributions could be summarised in the following:

- We introduce VeTo, a novel approach that effectively deals with the expert set expansion problem in academia by exploiting scholarly knowledge graphs (Sect. 3).
- We propose an evaluation framework that could be used to assess the effectiveness of expert set expansion approaches in a fairly objective way (Sect. 4).
- We exploit the developed framework using as expert sets the lists of program committees of known data management conferences to evaluate the effectiveness of VeTo against competitor methods that could be used to solve the same problem (Sect. 5).
- We provide the expert sets used for our experiments as open datasets so other researchers could use them as benchmarks following the same framework to evaluate the effectiveness of their own approaches (Sect. 5).

2 Background

The focus of this work is on a specific expert finding problem applied in the academic world: to reveal, among a set of candidate researchers C, the n most suitable of them, to extend a set of known experts E_{kn}. We refer to this problem as the *expert set expansion* problem, however it is also known as the *finding similar experts* problem (e.g., in [2]). This is a problem with various real-life applications like reviewer recommendation, collaborator seeking, new hire recommendation, etc.

In addition, for reasons elaborated in Sect. 1, we focus on approaches that exploit scholarly knowledge graphs to deal with the problem. *Knowledge graphs*, also known as *heterogeneous information networks* [19], are graphs that contain nodes and edges of multiple types capturing knowledge about entities (nodes) and the different types of relationships between them (edges). For instance, consider the scholarly knowledge graph illustrated in Fig. 1. This graph contains information about 3 papers (P_1, P_2, P_3), their venues (V_1, V_2), their topics (T_1, T_2), and the academics that have authored them ($A_1, \ldots, A_4$). Of course, real-life scholarly knowledge graphs contain a larger variety of entity types (e.g., academic institutions, funding organisations, research projects, as well).

Knowledge graphs capture rich information about their respective domains encoding not only direct relationships of the involved entities, but also more complex ones that correspond to larger paths in the graph. In particular, all paths that involve the same sequence of entity and edge types capture relationships of exactly the same semantics between their first and last nodes. These generalised path patterns are widely known as *metapaths* and we refer to the paths that follow these patterns as their *instances*. For example, in the graph of Fig. 1, the paths $A_1 - P_1 - T_1$ and $A_3 - P_3 - T_2$ both are instances of the metapath `Academic - Paper - Topic` (or `APT`, for brevity) and both have the same interpretation: they relate an academic with a topic through a paper authored by her.

In recent literature, the similarity of two entities (nodes) of the same type according to the semantics of a particular metapath is measured using the number of instances of this metapath that connect these nodes with nodes of the last node type of the metapath. For example, academics A_1 and A_2 seem similar based on the topics of their published papers (i.e., based on the semantics of the APT metapath) since they both have only one paper connecting them to the T_1 topic (i.e., 1 APT instance) and no paper connecting them to the T_2 topic (i.e., 0 APT instances).

A well-known metapath-based similarity measure that follows the previous intuition is JoinSim [21]. This measure calculates cosine similarity on node feature vectors based on the relationships indicated by a given metapath. For instance, given the metapath APT, JoinSim first constructs for each academic a feature vector with the topics related to the papers she has authored, and then calculates cosine similarity scores between the academics based on these vectors.

3 Our Approach

3.1 The Intuition

The main intuition behind VeTo, our approach, is that it deals with the expert set expansion problem by considering the similarities of academics to the experts based on a metapath-based similarity of academics, according to 2 particular metapaths, APT and APV, that capture interesting "publishing habits". In particular, the former considers the venues in which the compared academics select to publish their articles, while the latter the topics of their published articles.

3.2 Formal Description

Given a set of known experts E_{kn}, a set of candidates C, and the number of expansions that need to be performed n, VeTo performs the following steps:

1. For each expert $e \in E_{kn}$ its similarity scores to all candidates $c \in C$ according to the APV metapath are calculated and C^e_{APV}, the ranked list of all candidates based on these scores is produced.
2. A rank aggregation algorithm is applied on the C^e_{APV} for all $e \in E_{kn}$ to produce C_{APV}, the aggregated ranked list that ranks all candidates considering their similarities to all experts according to APV.
3. A procedure similar to the one performed in Steps 1 & 2 is followed to produce the ranked list C_{APT} that ranks all candidates according to their "aggregated" similarity based on the APV metapath.
4. A rank aggregation algorithm is applied on C_{APV} and C_{APV} to produce an aggregated ranked list C_{fin} that takes into account the similarities between experts and other academics based on both metapaths.
5. The n most similar items of C_{fin} as an answer to the given expert set expansion problem instance.

All metapath-based similarities required by our approach are calculated using the JoinSim [21] algorithm (see also Sect. 2). Regarding the rank aggregation algorithm, required in many steps of the approach, in this work, we select to use the *Borda Count* approach. Based on this approach, the aggregation of two ranked lists of size n is performed as follows: A score of n is assigned to the first element of each list, $n-1$ to the second, and so on. Then, for each of the n elements, the two scores (one for each list) are added to produce the final score for this element. Finally, the elements are being sorted in descending order based on the aggregated scores.

It should be noted that although the proposed approach is tailored to the problem of expert finding in academia, it could also be adapted and applied in other domains given the appropriate knowledge graphs and metapaths.

4 Proposed Evaluation Framework

A common issue in various expert finding problems is that it is not easy to evaluate the effectiveness of a given approach, since it is impossible to construct an objective ground truth. Luckily, in the context of expert set expansion, it was possible for us to develop an evaluation framework that can be used to assess the effectiveness of an approach based on a fairly objective ground truth. To the best of our knowledge, this is the first time that this evaluation framework is used for this problem.

The intuition behind this framework is to gather available expert lists from real-life applications (e.g., the PC members of a conference, editorial boards of journals) and, then, use each of them as dataset for a k-fold cross validation process. This means that, for each expert list E, a given approach is assessed as follows:

1. E is shuffled and, then, split in k disjoint sets $E_1, \ldots, E_k$, all of equal size[1] $n = \lfloor |E|/k \rfloor$.
2. For each E_i (with $i \in [1, k]$), a pair of training and testing set $\{E_i^{train}, E_i^{test}\}$ is constructed, where $E_i^{train} = \bigcup_{j \neq i} E_j$ and $E_i^{test} = E_i$.
3. For each $\{E_i^{train}, E_i^{test}\}$ pair:
   - we use E_i^{train} as the set of known experts (i.e., $E_{kn} = E_i^{train}$)
   - we apply the expert set expansion approach on E_i^{train} and get O_i, its output
   - we examine false & true positives and negatives in the top-x items of O_i based on E_i^{test} and we calculate proper information retrieval measures based on them, for $x \in [1, n]$ (where, $n = |O_i| = |E_i^{test}|$).

Regarding the information retrieval measures that are suitable to be used in Step 3 of the aforementioned process, we propose the use of top-x precision, recall, and F_1 score that can be defined as follows:

[1] The last one may be larger than the others, however it is easy to take this into consideration.

$$Precision = \frac{|O_i \cap E_i^{Test}|}{x}, \quad Recall = \frac{|O_i \cap E_i^{Test}|}{n},$$

$$F_1 = 2 \cdot \frac{Precision \cdot Recall}{Precision + Recall}$$

The larger the values of these measures are, the better the effectiveness of the method based on the given list E at the corresponding measuring point x is. The values of all measuring points could be used to construct a line plot.

Moreover, after completing the previous process for E, we propose to also calculate, for the same expert set, the mean reciprocal rank (MRR) based on all outputs O_i (for all $i \in [1, k]$) which can be calculated as follows:

$$MRR = \frac{1}{k} \sum_{i=1}^{k} \frac{1}{rank_i}$$

where, $rank_i$ refers to the rank position of the first true positive element in the output O_i.

The described evaluation framework was used for the experiments presented in Sect. 5. In particular, we gathered the list of program committee members for two well-known data management conferences (SIGMOD & VLDB) and applied the process of the framework on both of them using the aforementioned information retrieval measures. Gathering the program committee data was relatively easy by applying a semi-automatic approach that utlises Web page scrapping tools. In fact, our collected data could be used by third parties as benchmarks to evaluate the effectiveness of their own expert set expansion approaches. This is why we provide them as open datasets (more details in Sect. 5.1).

5 Evaluation

In this section we describe the experiments we have conducted to evaluate the effectiveness of our approach. In Sect. 5.1 we describe the experimental setup and in Sect. 5.2 we present our findings.

5.1 Setup

Approaches. The evaluation involves four different approaches to provide answer to the expert set expansion problem.

- *VeTo*, our proposed approach which exploits academics similarity according to the `APV` and `APT` metapaths (see also Sect. 3).
- *Baseline*, an approach that counts the number of papers an academic has published in the corresponding conference, ranks academics based on this number, and provides the top academics as the most suitable expansions.

- *ADT*, the best performing graph-based approach proposed in [9], that attempts to capture the association strength between two academics by considering the paths that relate them to topics (based on their papers) according to the ProductPaths technique.
- *WG*, a graph-based approach proposed in [2], which exploits working groups to capture similarity; in our context working groups correspond to co-authorship relations among academics[2].

The basic implementations of all approaches were written in Python, however, part of the preprocessing was implemented in C++ for improved efficiency. In addition, JoinSim [21] scores were calculated using the open entity similarity Java library HeySim[3].

Datasets. For our experiments, we used the following sets of data:

- *DBLP Scholarly Knowledge Graph (DSKG) dataset.* It contains data for approximately 1.5 M academics, their papers in the period 2000-2017, the corresponding venues and the involved topics. DSKG is based on the AMiner's DBLP citation network [20], enriched with topics assigned to papers by the CSO Classifier [15,16] (based on their abstracts). Finally, DSKG contains approximately 3.9 M and 34.1 M `APV` and `APT` metapath instances, respectively.
- *Program Committees (PC) dataset.* It contains program committee data from two well-known conferences from the field of data management: the ACM SIGMOD conference and the VLDB conference. The data were gathered by scrapping the official Web pages of these conferences for the years 2007–2017 and, then, applying a semi-automatic cleaning process to properly map the PC members to academics in the DSKG dataset.

The DSKG dataset was used as a knowledge base that the various approaches could take advantage of. The PC dataset, on the other hand, was used to create the required training and testing sets for the evaluation based on the framework described in Sect. 4). This latter dataset was also made openly available at Zenodo[4] so other researchers could use it as benchmark to assess the effectiveness of their own approaches.

5.2 Evaluation of VeToagainst Competitors

In this experiment, we compare the effectiveness of our approach against its rivals based on the framework discussed in Section 4 by using both expert sets in the PC dataset (SIGMOD and VLDB).

[2] We have also conducted experiments using *DOC*, the alternative graph-based approach proposed in the same paper, however it performed worse in all cases and its results were omitted from the experimental section for presentation reasons.
[3] https://github.com/schatzopoulos/HeySim.
[4] https://doi.org/10.5281/zenodo.3739316.

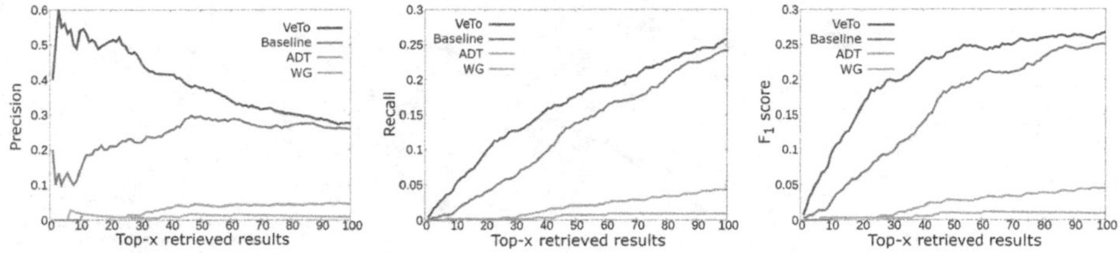

(a) Precision (b) Recall (c) F_1 score

Fig. 2. Evaluation against competitors for SIGMOD conference.

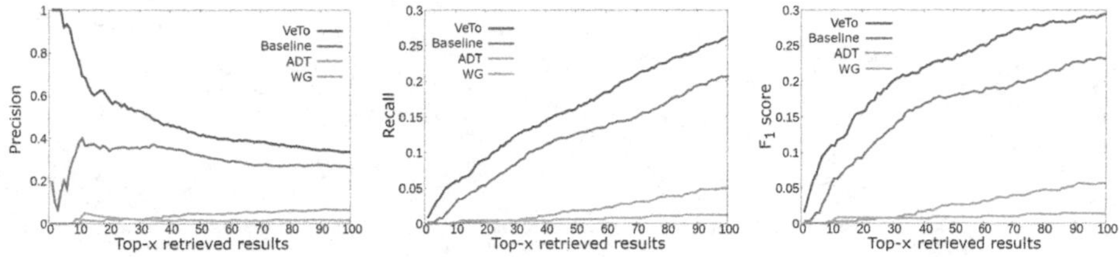

(a) Precision (b) Recall (c) F_1 score

Fig. 3. Evaluation against competitors for VLDB conference.

Top-*x* precision, recall & F_1-score. Figures 2 and 3 present the precision, recall and F_1 score of all compared approaches for SIGMOD and VLDB expert sets, respectively. Larger values for all measures indicate superior effectiveness. It is evident that VeTo clearly outperforms its competitors in all scenarios. More importantly, in both datasets, it achieves notably higher precision in comparison to all other approaches for at least the top-40 results. The latter fact is really important since, in practice, for most real-life applications of the expert set expansion problem, usually n is relatively small.

Furthermore, it should be noted that the baseline approach seems to work pretty well (but, at the same time, significantly worse than VeTo) in most cases. This result indicates that there is a correlation between the academics that publish articles in a conference and its program committee members. On the other hand, both ADT and WG do not perform well.

Table 1. MRR based on the folds of each dataset

	Baseline	ADT	WG	VeTo
SIGMOD	0.323	0.043	0.039	0.8
VLDB	0.357	0.046	0.061	1
Total	0.34	0.0445	0.05	0.9

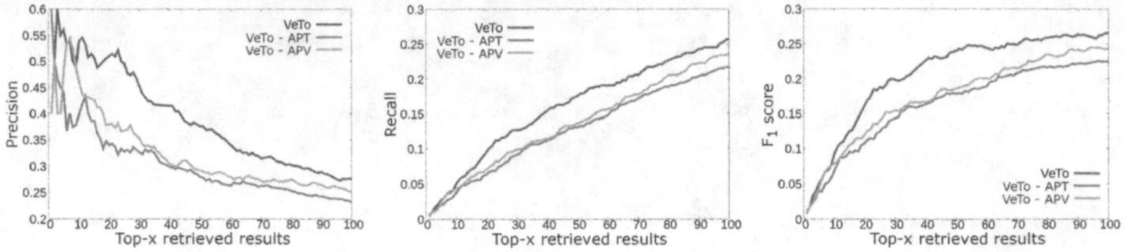

(a) Precision (b) Recall (c) F_1 score

Fig. 4. Comparison of different variants of our method for SIGMOD conference.

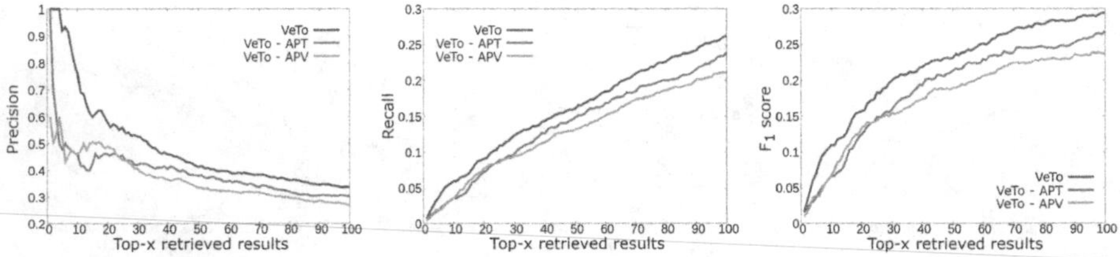

(a) Precision (b) Recall (c) F_1 score

Fig. 5. Comparison of different variants of our method for VLDB conference.

MRR per Conference. Table 1 includes the assessment of all approaches based on the mean reciprocal rank (MRR) for both expert sets (SIGMOD and VLDB) separately and in total (if we use simultaneously all their folds). Larger values of MRR indicate better approach effectiveness. The results are in compliance with the previous experiment: since VeTo achieves significantly larger precision for small values of x, it performs significantly better than its competitors in terms of MRR (see also MRR definition in Sect. 4). Again ADT and WG perform significantly worse than the baseline.

5.3 Studying and Configuring VeTo

In this section, we examine different configurations of our approach and we investigate the effect they have in its effectiveness.

Table 2. MRR of different variants based on the folds of each dataset

	VeTo-APT	VeTo-APV	VeTo
SIGMOD	0.766	0.766	0.8
VLDB	0.8	0.8	1
Total	0.783	0.783	0.9

Table 3. Top-10 recommendations per configuration (1st fold)

SIGMOD			
	VeTo-APT	VeTo-APV	VeTo
1	Jeffrey F. Naughton	Dong Deng	Jeffrey F. Naughton
2	Beng Chin Ooi*	Jeffrey F. Naughton	Beng Chin Ooi*
3	Neoklis Polyzotis*	Ihab F. Ilyas*	Ihab F. Ilyas*
4	Guoren Wang	Jennifer Widom	Neoklis Polyzotis*
5	Ihab F. Ilyas*	Beng Chin Ooi*	Jennifer Widom
6	Dongqing Yang	Philip Bohannon*	David J. DeWitt*
7	Wolfgang Lehner*	David J. DeWitt*	Volker Markl*
8	Stéphane Bressan	Michael J. Carey	Raghu Ramakrishnan
9	Ge Yu	Neoklis Polyzotis*	Michael J. Carey
10	Marios Hadjieleftheriou*	Lijun Chang	Ashraf Aboulnaga*
VLDB			
	VeTo-APT	VeTo-APV	VeTo
1	Dan Suciu*	Yannis Papakonstantinou*	Yannis Papakonstantinou*
2	Guoren Wang	Dong Deng	Christoph Koch*
3	Christoph Koch*	Jiannan Wang	Jennifer Widom*
4	Dongqing Yang	Jennifer Widom*	Volker Markl*
5	Timos K. Sellis*	Mourad Ouzzani*	Dan Suciu*
6	Ge Yu*	Renée J. Miller	Shivnath Babu*
7	Vassilis J. Tsotras	Philip Bohannon	Bolin Ding*
8	Xiaofeng Meng	Bolin Ding*	Renée J. Miller
9	Nikos Mamoulis*	Paolo Papotti*	Mourad Ouzzani*
10	Tengjiao Wang	Lu Qin	Marios Hadjieleftheriou

Studying the Effect of the Used Metapaths. VeTo's approach considers similarities of academics based on two criteria: their similarity based on the venues they prefer to publish (captured by the `APV` metapath) and on the topics of their published papers (captured by the `APT` metapath). In this experiment we examine the effect of each of these metapaths by implementing two VeTo's variants: one that considers only the `APV` metapath (called VeTo-APV) and a second one that considers only the `APT` metapath (called VeTo APT).

Figures 4 and 5 illustrate the measured top-x precision, recall and F_1 score of VeTo, VeTo-APV, and VeTo-APT for SIGMOD and VLDB, respectively, while Table 2 summarizes the corresponding MRR scores. It is evident that VeTo outperforms its two variants in all cases, however the variants usually achieve comparable (but always worse) effectiveness.

It should be noted that VeTo-APT achieves slightly higher precision and recall in most cases in the SIGMOD dataset, while the other variant is usually slightly better for VLDB. Moreover, in Table 3 we present the top-10 results provided by VeTo, VeTo-APV, and VeTo-APT based on the first fold of each

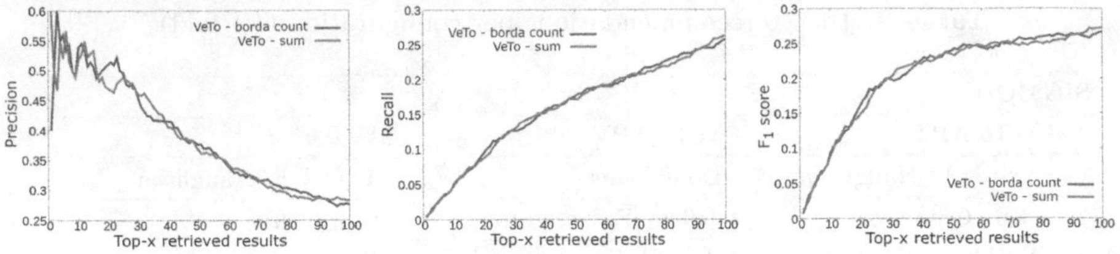

(a) Precision (b) Recall (c) F_1 score

Fig. 6. Comparison of different rank aggregation methods for SIGMOD conference.

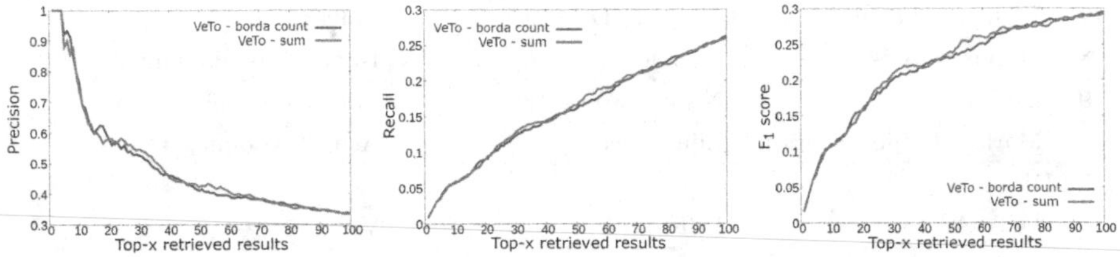

(a) Precision (b) Recall (c) F_1 score

Fig. 7. Comparison of different rank aggregation methods for VLDB conference.

expert set experiment. With asterisk we indicate all true positives. It is evident that, although both metapaths provide some common top suggestions (e.g., Ihab F. Ilyas in SIGMOD), they also identify some unique correct results (e.g., David J. DeWitt provided by VeTo-APV in SIGMOD) that the other metapath fails to bring. These findings indicate that both metapaths are capable to identify some unique good results, thus VeTo's approach to combine both of them has a potential to achieve improved performance (as is confirmed by our experiments).

Studying the Effect of Different Rank Aggregations. Part of VeTo's approach consists of using a rank aggregation algorithm. Our default selection in our implementation is Borda Count (see also Sect. 3). In this section, we examine the effect that the use of an alternative rank aggregation algorithm would have. We do so by implementing a variant that instead computes the similarity of a candidate as the sum of its similarities with the experts in the test set. This is a common rank aggregation algorithm used in various works (e.g., it is also used for JoinSim [2]). In Figs. 6 and 7 we present the top-x precision, recall, and F1-measure of this variant in comparison to the same measurements for the basic VeTo implementation that uses Borda Count. It is evident that no significant differences are observable.

6 Related Work

Expertise retrieval consists an interesting field of research in many disciplines like digital libraries, data management, information retrieval, and machine learning.

A wide range of problems, ranging from expert finding to expert profiling, belong in this field and there are many related real-time applications (e.g., collaboration recommendation, reviewer recommendation). A detailed review of the field is beyond the scope of the current work. The reader interested could refer to the excellent survey in [10]. In the next we will focus on the variations of the *expert finding* problem.

Finding experts for a given topic in the industry has been a relatively well-studied problem. Initial approaches relied on manually curated databases of skills and knowledge (e.g., [6]), however the interest quickly shifted to approaches that extract employee's expertise from document collections that could be found within corporate intranets or the Web [3,5]. A common platform to empirically assess such approaches has been developed by the TREC community[5] facilitating the development of various relevant methods [1,7,14,17]. Apart from details about the exact expert finding problems solved by each of the previous methods, VeTo significantly differs from these works in principle, since it is tailored for academic experts and since it does not rely on document collections because such collections are often available due to the existing paywalls.

Finding experts in academia, where the experts are researchers with knowledge and interests in a given topic, has also been an important field (e.g., [18,22]). However, most of these methods also rely on scientific text corpora which are often limited behind paywalls. Most relevant to VeTo are methods that try to exploit scholarly knowledge graphs to perform the same tasks (e.g., [9]). However, in contrast to them, VeTo takes advantage of recent developments in the field of heterogeneous information networks and knowledge graphs.

7 Conclusions

In this work, we study the expert set expansion problem for academic experts, i.e., given a set of known experts to find the n most suitable candidates to expand this set. In this context, we introduced VeTo, a set expert expansion approach for academic experts that exploits information from a given scholarly knowledge graph to estimate similarities between academics based on their publishing habits. Moreover, we introduce a new evaluation framework that can assess the effectiveness of such approaches in a fairly objective way. Finally, we utilise the developed framework to compare VeTo against a set of competitors showing that it is superior in terms of effectiveness.

Acknowledgments. We acknowledge support of this work by the project "Moving from Big Data Management to Data Science" (MIS 5002437/3) which is implemented under the Action "Re-inforcement of the Research and Innovation Infrastructure", funded by the Operational Programme "Competitiveness, Entrepreneurship and Innovation" (NSRF 2014–2020) and co-financed by Greece and the European Union (European Regional Development Fund).

Icons in Fig. 1 were collected from www.flaticon.com and were made by Freepik, Good Ware and Pixel perfect.

[5] https://trec.nist.gov/.

References

1. Balog, K., Azzopardi, L., de Rijke, M.: Formal models for expert finding in enterprise corpora. In: SIGIR 2006: Proceedings of the 29th Annual International ACM SIGIR Conference on Research and Development in Information Retrieval, Seattle, Washington, USA, August 6–11, 2006, pp. 43–50 (2006)
2. Balog, K., de Rijke, M.: Finding similar experts. In: Proceedings of the 30th Annual International ACM SIGIR Conference on Research and Development in Information Retrieval, SIGIR 2007, pp. 821–822. Association for Computing Machinery, New York (2007). https://doi.org/10.1145/1277741.1277926
3. Cao, Y., Liu, J., Bao, S., Li, H.: Research on expert search at enterprise track of TREC 2005. In: Proceedings of the Fourteenth Text Retrieval Conference, TREC 2005, Gaithersburg, Maryland, USA, November 15–18, 2005 (2005). http://trec.nist.gov/pubs/trec14/papers/microsoft-asia.ent.pdf
4. Chen, H.H., Gou, L., Zhang, X., Giles, C.L.: Collabseer: a search engine for collaboration discovery. In: Proceedings of the 11th Annual International ACM/IEEE Joint Conference on Digital Libraries, JCDL 2011, pp. 231–240. Association for Computing Machinery, New York (2011). https://doi.org/10.1145/1998076.1998121
5. Craswell, N., Hawking, D., Vercoustre, A.M., Wilkins, P.: P@noptic expert: searching for experts not just for documents. In: Ausweb Poster Proceedings, Queensland, Australia, vol. 15, p. 17 (2001)
6. Davenport, T.H., Prusak, L.: Working knowledge: how organizations manage what they know. Ubiquity **2000**(August), 6 (2000)
7. Fang, H., Zhai, C.X.: Probabilistic models for expert finding. In: Amati, G., Carpineto, C., Romano, G. (eds.) ECIR 2007. LNCS, vol. 4425, pp. 418–430. Springer, Heidelberg (2007). https://doi.org/10.1007/978-3-540-71496-5_38
8. Gollapalli, S.D., Mitra, P., Giles, C.L.: Similar researcher search in academic environments. In: Proceedings of the 12th ACM/IEEE-CS Joint Conference on Digital Libraries, JCDL 2012, pp. 167–170. Association for Computing Machinery, New York (2012). https://doi.org/10.1145/2232817.2232849
9. Gollapalli, S.D., Mitra, P., Giles, C.L.: Ranking experts using author-document-topic graphs. In: 13th ACM/IEEE-CS Joint Conference on Digital Libraries, JCDL 2013, Indianapolis, IN, USA, July 22–26, 2013, pp. 87–96 (2013). https://doi.org/10.1145/2467696.2467707
10. Gonçalves, R., Dorneles, C.F.: Automated expertise retrieval: a taxonomy-based survey and open issues. ACM Comput. Surv. **52**(5), 96:1–96:30 (2019)
11. Jaradeh, M.Y., et al.: Open research knowledge graph: Next generation infrastructure for semantic scholarly knowledge. In: Proceedings of the 10th International Conference on Knowledge Capture, K-CAP 2019, Marina Del Rey, CA, USA, November 19–21, 2019, pp. 243–246 (2019). https://doi.org/10.1145/3360901.3364435
12. Manghi, P., et al.: Openaire research graph dump, December 2019. https://doi.org/10.5281/zenodo.3516918
13. Manghi, P., et al.: The openaire research graph data model, April 2019. https://doi.org/10.5281/zenodo.2643199
14. Petkova, D., Croft, W.B.: Hierarchical language models for expert finding in enterprise corpora. Int. J. Artif. Intell. Tools **17**(1), 5–18 (2008)
15. Salatino, A., Osborne, F., Thanapalasingam, T., Motta, E.: The CSO classifier: ontology-driven detection of research topics in scholarly articles, pp. 296–311, August 2019

16. Salatino, A.A., Thanapalasingam, T., Mannocci, A., Osborne, F., Motta, E.: The computer science ontology: a large-scale taxonomy of research areas. In: Vrandečić, D., et al. (eds.) ISWC 2018. LNCS, vol. 11137, pp. 187–205. Springer, Cham (2018). https://doi.org/10.1007/978-3-030-00668-6_12
17. Serdyukov, P., Hiemstra, D.: Modeling documents as mixtures of persons for expert finding. In: Macdonald, C., Ounis, I., Plachouras, V., Ruthven, I., White, R.W. (eds.) ECIR 2008. LNCS, vol. 4956, pp. 309–320. Springer, Heidelberg (2008). https://doi.org/10.1007/978-3-540-78646-7_29
18. Sfyris, G.A., Fragkos, N., Doulkeridis, C.: Profile-based selection of expert groups. In: Fuhr, N., Kovács, L., Risse, T., Nejdl, W. (eds.) TPDL 2016. LNCS, vol. 9819, pp. 81–93. Springer, Cham (2016). https://doi.org/10.1007/978-3-319-43997-6_7
19. Shi, C., Li, Y., Zhang, J., Sun, Y., Yu, P.S.: A survey of heterogeneousinformation network analysis. IEEE Trans. Knowl. Data Eng. **29**(1), 17–37 (2017). https://doi.org/10.1109/TKDE.2016.2598561
20. Tang, J., Zhang, J., Yao, L., Li, J., Zhang, L., Su, Z.: ArnetMiner: extraction and mining of academic social networks. In: Proceedings of the 14th ACM SIGKDD, pp. 990–998. ACM (2008)
21. Xiong, Y., Zhu, Y., Yu, P.S.: Top-k similarity join in heterogeneous information networks. IEEE Trans. Knowl. Data En. **27**(6), 1710–1723 (2015)
22. Yang, K., Kuo, T., Lee, H., Ho, J.: A reviewer recommendation system based on collaborative intelligence. In: 2009 IEEE/WIC/ACM International Conference on Web Intelligence, WI 2009, Milan, Italy, 15–18 September 2009, Main Conference Proceedings, pp. 564–567 (2009). https://doi.org/10.1109/WI-IAT.2009.94

An Observational Study of Equivalence Links in Cultural Heritage Linked Data for *agents*

Nuno Freire[1(✉)], Hugo Manguinhas[2], and Antoine Isaac[2,3]

[1] INESC-ID, Lisbon, Portugal
nuno.freire@tecnico.ulisboa.pt
[2] Europeana Foundation, The Hague, The Netherlands
{hugo.manguinhas,antoine.isaac}@europeana.eu
[3] Vrije Universiteit Amsterdam, Amsterdam, The Netherlands

Abstract. This article presents an observational study of the virtual graph formed by equivalence links between *agent* entities across 8 knowledge bases. To evaluate the potential of this linked data graph, we measured the equivalences that it could provide for a real dataset. We crawled the virtual graph by starting from references to *agents* we found in descriptions of objects collected from data of cultural heritage institutions in Europeana. Our study characterizes the current virtual equivalence graph, presenting statistics about the links, their type and origin. Crawling the equivalences for *agent* URIs required several crawling iterations on the virtual equivalence graph. The amount of gathered equivalences grows steeply in the first 3 crawling iterations and stabilizes on the 4th iteration. VIAF was the KB with the highest number of equivalences, reaching 60.7%, and it was followed by Wikidata with 34.5%.

Keywords: Linked data · Agents · Equivalence links · Cultural heritage

1 Introduction

Nowadays, large knowledge bases (KBs) are available as linked data under open licenses, like DBpedia[1] and Wikidata[2]. Exploiting equivalences of entities across these KBs is crucial for data-driven application that require, e.g., to obtain additional data about an entity across several KBs, or to support disambiguation operations.

We conducted an observational study of the virtual graph formed by equivalence relations between entities of 8 open KBs for entities of type *agent* (persons, organizations) in cultural heritage (CH) data. In particular, we measured the quantity of equivalences that this graph could provide for a dataset from Europeana[3] containing references to *agents* in descriptions of CH objects.

This study provides insights about the equivalence links across KBs and the potential benefits of crawling this virtual equivalence graph for discovering equivalences of

[1] https://dbpedia.org/.
[2] https://www.wikidata.org/.
[3] https://pro.europeana.eu/our-mission.

M. Hall et al. (Eds.): TPDL 2020, LNCS 12246, pp. 62–70, 2020.
https://doi.org/10.1007/978-3-030-54956-5_5

agents referred to in datasets. It is informative for future research and for designing innovative applications, such as the case of Europeana who seeks to acquire *agent* name variants/translations or extra biographical information [1].

We follow, in Sect. 2, by describing related work on linked data and equivalence graphs. Section 3 presents how the study was conducted. Section 4 details the results and their analysis. Section 5 highlights our conclusions and presents future work.

2 Related Work

The exploitation of KB equivalence links for specific applications has been addressed earlier. Beek et al. (2018) have gathered the largest dataset of *owl:sameAs* statements from the web of data [2]. Similarly to us, Correndo et al. (2012) have conducted a statistical and qualitative analysis of the graph of instance level equivalences, and explored their use for computing alignments at conceptual level [3].

Research on the quality of linked data equivalence statements is relevant for us. It has especially reported (sometimes incorrect) uses of *owl:sameAs* to represent different degrees of equivalence [4–6]. Work on linked data aggregation and cleaning [7, 8] has also revealed data quality to be a challenge both at the level of semantics and the one of syntax [9, 10]. Especially relevant for us, an empirical study by Asprino et al. (2019) investigated the modelling style and the general structure of linked open data, including issues for the equivalence graphs formed by interlinking [11].

Regarding CH, the creation of KBs has been a long-term practice, and started much earlier than the emergence of the Semantic Web. In this domain however, the stated equivalences between major open KBs have not been studied recently.

3 Design of the Study

We have conducted an observational study gathering the existing equivalence relations between entities across 8 KBs:

- DBpedia - a multilingual KB created by extracting structured data from Wikipedia.
- data.bnf.fr (BnF) - a project by the French National Library that makes available data about bibliographic entities.
- datos.bne.es (BNE) - a KB of bibliographic data by the National Library of Spain.
- Library of Congress Names[4] (NAF) - a KB that provides authoritative data for names of persons, organizations, events, places, and titles.
- The Union List of Artist Names[5] (ULAN) - ULAN contains names, relationships, notes, sources, and biographical information for artists.
- Gemeinsame Normdatei[6] (GND) - an KB for personal names, subject headings and corporate bodies, managed mainly by the German National Library.

4 http://id.loc.gov/authorities/names.html.

5 https://www.getty.edu/research/tools/vocabularies/ulan/.

6 https://www.dnb.de/EN/Professionell/Standardisierung/GND/gnd_node.html.

- Virtual International Authority File[7] (VIAF) - a cooperation of OCLC with mainly national libraries, combining multiple KBs from libraries, archives and museums.
- Wikidata - a collaborative KB hosted by the Wikimedia Foundation.

By considering the transitive closure of the resulting compound set of equivalence statements, one obtains a virtual equivalence graph with entities from all the KBs as nodes. Our study was divided into two parts.

First, we measured the amount of stated equivalence relations between KBs by considering all the equivalences asserted by at least one KB, not using any additional external sources. The statements were collected preferably via SPARQL, or via a file-based RDF distribution of the KB. We collected all statements where the property was one of[8]: *owl:sameAs; skos:exactMatch; skos:closeMatch; or schema:sameAs.* This selection was based on a preliminary profiling of the KBs, where we found these standard properties to be the most often used for representing equivalence.

In the second part of the study, we focused on the entity type *agent*, and measured the quantity of equivalences that the joint equivalence graph could provide for a dataset containing references to *agents* in descriptions of CH objects.

The first task was to create a set of URIs referring to *agents*. For this purpose, we used the APIs[9] for accessing and querying the dataset aggregated by Europeana. We located 1,164,323 unique RDF resources about *agents* used by the Europeana data providers[10]. From these we excluded all anonymous (blank) nodes and all the URIs that contain a URI fragment appended to the URI of the CH object. These resources without a "real" identifier are likely to correspond to cases where the *agent* does not come from a pre-existing controlled, "authoritative" KB, but are just created ad-hoc for the description of the cultural object. The resulting set contains 286,090 unique *agent* URIs, and the majority of them belong to a KB in our study, as Table 1 shows.

The set of *agent* URIs was then used to initiate a series of crawling iterations of the equivalence graph. The crawler was instructed to crawl the statements with any of the properties mentioned in Sect. 3. It assumes that all properties are transitive, including *skos:closeMatch*, and that transitivity applies across all types of properties[11]. In the first iteration, we crawled directly the *agent* URIs and gathered all the equivalence relations their KB contained for them. From the second iteration and onwards, the crawler obtained equivalent *agent* URIs by searching in the KBs for any URI that was collected in previous crawling iterations and adding the URIs that these KBs declared to be equivalent to the original ones. At the end of each iteration, the crawler generated a report about the newly

7 https://viaf.org.

8 For readability purposes, in this article we abbreviate namespaces as follows: owl for http://www.w3.org/2002/07/owl#; skos for http://www.w3.org/2004/02/skos/core#; schema for http://schema.org/; wdt for http://www.wikidata.org/prop/direct/.

9 https://pro.europeana.eu/resources/apis.

10 We aim to provide insights that could be beneficial to providers and users of the original metadata, therefore, we have excluded the URIs used in automatic enrichment by Europeana (cf. https://pro.europeana.eu/page/europeana-semantic-enrichment).

11 This goes beyond the actual formal semantics of these properties, but we wanted to experiment with it nonetheless, to get an upper bound of the level of benefit obtainable from the equivalences - and experience shows that the biggest data quality issues actually lie elsewhere.

found equivalent URIs. We repeated the crawling process for newly found equivalences several times until the increase of URIs resulting from one iteration was negligible.

Table 1. Amounts of unique URIs in the set from Europeana that belong to a KB in the study

	DBpedia	BnF	BNE	NAF	ULAN	GND	VIAF	Wikidata	Other KBs (or none)
URI uses in Europeana	2	2,010	30,449	0	7,451	242,297	2,174	0	1707

4 Results

The study provided informative results on four aspects of the KBs and their virtual equivalence graph. Each aspect is presented in the following subsections.

4.1 Existing Equivalences Between Knowledge Bases

We did two measurements on the equivalence statements between the KBs. The first measurement considered all types of equivalences, and the second measurement was made considering solely *skos:closeMatch* equivalences. Our motivation for measuring separately the *skos:closeMatch* equivalences was because this property expresses equivalence with a degree of uncertainty, while the three others seek to capture exact equivalence, which may be an important aspect for many applications.

Table 2 presents the results considering the 4 properties for equivalence, showing the amounts of statements when a KB publishes an equivalence to another KB and when other KBs publish an equivalence to the KB being considered. The table also shows the number of KBs linked by equivalences to each KB. A total amount of 60,307,328 equivalences are stated in the 8 KBs.

The results show high interconnection between KBs. All KBs express equivalences to at least one other KB, and all KBs are the target of equivalences stated in at least one KB. An interesting observation is that 3 out of the 8 KBs are focused only on *agents* (VIAF, NAF and ULAN), and 2 of them, VIAF and NAF, are among the 3 most linked KBs. GND is the second most linked KB, and the most linked of the KBs that cover more than one entity type, followed by Wikidata and DBpedia.

skos:closeMatch equivalences are much less frequent than the exact equivalences and only two KBs use them: BnF and ULAN. They represent only 1.5% of the total amount of equivalences stated by BnF. ULAN applies *skos:closeMatch* more frequently, reaching nearly 50% of the equivalences published. Overall, 192,300 statements use the *skos:closeMatch* predicate, which represents only 0.3% of all the equivalences stated by the studied KBs (Table 3).

Table 2. The amounts of equivalence statements involving each knowledge base.

KB	As subject of equivalences		As object of equivalences		Total statements
	Statements	to KBs	Statements	from KBs	
VIAF	25,118,745	7	21,666,779	6	46,785,524
GND	11,313,935	4	9,454,213	5	20,768,148
NAF	6,101,051	1	14,216,491	6	20,317,542
Wikidata	4,624,309	6	9,785,342	4	14,409,651
DBpedia	7,396,520	3	977,907	5	8,374,427
BnF	4,505,773	5	3,124,674	3	7,630,447
BNE	997,183	5	698,329	2	1695,512
ULAN	249,812	2	383,593	2	633,405

Table 3. The amounts of *skos:closeMatch* statements involving each knowledge base.

KB	As subject of equivalences		As object of equivalences	
	Statements	to KBs	Statements	from KBs
GND			25,952	1
NAF			150,224	2
Wikidata			6	1
BnF	67,746	3		
BNE			16,118	1
ULAN	124,554	2		

4.2 Crawling of the Equivalences for *agent* URIs

The results of the crawling iterations on the URIs of Europeana are shown in Table 4. After the 1st iteration (i.e., crawling beginning from the URIs in the Europeana set alone) we found 50,112 equivalent URIs. The amount of gathered equivalences has increased steeply in the first 3 crawling iterations. From the 1st crawl to the 2nd, the number of equivalences increased by 588%, and it increased by 42% on the 3rd iteration. The number of newly acquired equivalences was 0.76% in the 4th iteration, and under 0.1% in the 5th, so we opted to analyse and report on the results up to the 4th iteration (included). Only 3 iterations were needed to collect 99% of the equivalences. Although not all KBs are directly connected by equivalences, this shows that equivalent *agent* instances are closely connected in the equivalence graph.

VIAF was the KB with the highest number of equivalent URIs found. After the 4th crawling iteration, 60.7% of the set had equivalent VIAF URIs. Wikidata had the 2nd highest number of equivalences, reaching 34.5%.

For 3 KBs, less than 10% of the set had equivalences: ULAN, BNE and GND. The lower result for ULAN was expected since it is focused on artists. GND was the KB with the most URIs in the Europeana set, therefore, this result can be explained by the fact that for all GND URIs in the set, only equivalences to other KBs could be found. The results of BNE may be also explained by its high presence in the Europeana set.

For researchers and practitioners designing innovative systems based on *agent* linked data, the choice for using one or more KBs will always be highly influenced by the specific domain of application. Nevertheless, the results of the study indicate VIAF as the most linked KB, and therefore, in future work we would like to further exploit its data and equivalences.

Table 4. The results of the 4 crawling iterations of the Europeana set of *agent* URIs.

KB	Initial Europeana set (a)	New equivalences found after each iteration (b)				% of the initial Europeana set with equivalences (c)
		1st crawl	2nd crawl	3rd crawl	4th crawl	
DBpedia	2	4,407	34,968	47,031	47,410	16.57%
BnF	2,010	6,282	9,803	53,280	54,554	19.07%
BNE	30,449	3,321	9,952	12,471	12,934	4.52%
NAF	0	11,935	15,554	77,702	78,207	27.34%
ULAN	7,451	1,737	3,439	12,137	12,701	4.44%
GND	242,297	7,684	8,596	14,939	15,100	5.28%
VIAF	2,174	13,095	170,057	173,608	173,613	60.68%
Wikidata	0	1,651	92,588	98,450	98,813	34.54%
Total	**284,383**	**50,112**	**344,957**	**489,618**	**493,332**	–
Δ from previous crawl	–	–	**588%**	**42%**	**0.76%**	–

a - number of URIs of each KB in the Europeana set
b - number of equivalences found after each iteration
c - percentage of the Europeana URIs that after the 4th iteration have an equivalence to the KB considered.

4.3 Compliance with Semantic Web Standards

One of our initial observations during the study was that Wikidata is the only KB which does not use the standard equivalence properties. In fact, in an earlier study on Wikidata's data about CH resources [12], we have observed that it uses a very limited number of the standard Semantic Web "meta-modeling" properties. During the current study, we observed that *owl:sameAs* is in use only for internal equivalences between Wikidata's entities. None of *skos:exactMatch*, *skos:closeMatch* nor *schema:sameAs* are used.

Instead, Wikidata uses its own *wdt:P2888* (exact match), and a set of properties categorized as *External identifiers*[12]. Each of these External identifier properties represents the local identifier for a Wikidata resource within the external information space of a particular institution or dataset. The values of statements with these properties are usually not URIs, and when a local identifier can be transformed into a URI, the definition of the property contains the formatting string for deriving the URI from the local identifier[13]. We have identified 159 properties of type *External Identifier* from which a URI could be derived.

We collected Wikidata's equivalences via its SPARQL endpoint, therefore we adapted our SPARQL queries to use the corresponding Wikidata properties. Another adaptation was done in the tools for analysis of the equivalence graph, so that the Wikidata properties would be considered as exact equivalences.

4.4 Data Quality of the Equivalence Statements

Our study did not have the objective to address the quality of equivalence statements, but we did come across a problem that blocked our crawling experiment, forcing us to find a solution. This problem was caused by four URIs used in 77,379 equivalence statements by VIAF, which seem plainly wrong[14]. Besides establishing wrong equivalences, this problem posed difficulties for crawling the equivalence graph. It would take several (probably many) additional iterations for the number of equivalent URIs to stabilize, and very large groups of equivalent URIs would be formed. To bypass the problem, we tried to filter out such incorrect URIs by detecting major outliers in terms of the mean of equivalences/URI. The mean of equivalences/URI in VIAF was of 1.006 and each of these four URIs were present in thousands of equivalence statements. The outlier URIs were discarded when we repeated the crawling process, therefore they were excluded from our study.

5 Conclusion and Future Work

The results obtained in our study confirm that the *agents* in KBs are highly interlinked. This high level of interlinking is in accordance with earlier studies of *owl:sameAs* general usage [3, 11] and the reports from the publishers of the CH KBs on the work they have carried out[15]. The study highlights also that the majority of equivalences are expressed with exact equivalence predicates (like *owl:sameAs*), while matches with uncertainty (*skos:closeMatch*) are a minority of 0.3%.

[12] The list of Wikidata properties for external identifiers is available at https://www.wikidata.org/wiki/Special:ListProperties/external-id.

[13] The properties will contain an attribute *wdt:P1921* (formatter URI for RDF resource).

[14] These 4 URIs are: http://data.bnf.fr/#foaf:Person; http://data.bnf.fr/#foaf:Organization; http://data.bnf.fr/#owl:Thing; and http://data.bnf.fr/#spatialThing. None correspond to an actual *agent* at BnF. We have mailed VIAF maintainers about it.

[15] For space reasons we cannot refer to all presentations and articles here. Some of them are accessible on the online documentation for the KB considered, given as earlier references.

Although each KB is not directly linked to all other KBs, all KBs are a source and a target of equivalence links. Crawling of the *agent* URIs used in Europeana shows that only a few crawling iterations of the equivalence graph are needed to acquire a nearly complete set of equivalences from all KBs. Three iterations were enough to collect 99% of the equivalences gathered after five iterations.

VIAF is the KB with the highest number of *agent* equivalences, followed by Wikidata. An equivalent VIAF URI was found for 60.7% of Europeana's *agent* URIs, and for Wikidata, equivalences were found in 34.5% of Europeana's *agent* URIs.

Future work includes the detection of possibly incorrect equivalences, since this study, like earlier research [4], has detected some quality issues in the (*owl:sameAs*) links. Conversely, it would be interesting to estimate recall issues, i.e. whether many new links could (and should) be created across KBs via automatic or manual alignment.

Acknowledgments. This work was partly supported by Portuguese national funds through Fundação para a Ciência e a Tecnologia (FCT) with reference UIDB/50021/2020 and by the European Commission under contract number 30-CE-0885387/00-80.

References

1. Charles, V., Manguinhas, H., Isaac, A., Freire, N., Gordea, S.: Designing a multilingual knowledge graph as a service for cultural heritage – some challenges and solutions. In: International Conference on Dublin Core and Metadata Applications, 2018 (2018)
2. Beek, W., Raad, J., Wielemaker, J., van Harmelen, F.: sameAs.cc: the closure of 500 M `owl:sameAs` statements. In: Gangemi, A., et al. (eds.) ESWC 2018. LNCS, vol. 10843, pp. 65–80. Springer, Cham (2018). https://doi.org/10.1007/978-3-319-93417-4_5
3. Correndo, G., Penta, A., Gibbins, N., Shadbolt, N.: Statistical analysis of the, network for aligning concepts in the linking open data cloud. In: Liddle, S.W., Schewe, K.-D., Tjoa, A.M., Zhou, X. (eds.) DEXA 2012. LNCS, vol. 7447, pp. 215–230. Springer, Heidelberg (2012). https://doi.org/10.1007/978-3-642-32597-7_20
4. Halpin, H., Hayes, P.J., McCusker, J.P., McGuinness, D.L., Thompson, H.S.: When owl:sameAs isn't the same: an analysis of identity in linked data. In: Patel-Schneider, P.F., et al. (eds.) ISWC 2010. LNCS, vol. 6496, pp. 305–320. Springer, Heidelberg (2010). https://doi.org/10.1007/978-3-642-17746-0_20
5. Ding, L., Shinavier, J., Shangguan, Z., McGuinness, Deborah L.: SameAs networks and beyond: analyzing deployment status and implications of owl:sameAs in linked data. In: Patel-Schneider, P.F., et al. (eds.) ISWC 2010. LNCS, vol. 6496, pp. 145–160. Springer, Heidelberg (2010). https://doi.org/10.1007/978-3-642-17746-0_10
6. Papaleo, L., Pernelle, N., Saïs, F., Dumont, C.: Logical detection of invalid SameAs statements in RDF data. In: Janowicz, K., Schlobach, S., Lambrix, P., Hyvönen, E. (eds.) EKAW 2014. LNCS (LNAI), vol. 8876, pp. 373–384. Springer, Cham (2014). https://doi.org/10.1007/978-3-319-13704-9_29
7. Beek, W., Rietveld, L., Schlobach, S., van Harmelen, F.: LOD Laundromat: why the semantic web needs centralization (even if we don't like it). IEEE Internet Comput. **20**(2), 78–81 (2016)
8. Fernández, J.D., Beek, W., Martínez-Prieto, M.A., Arias, M.: LOD-a-lot. In: d'Amato, C., et al. (eds.) ISWC 2017. LNCS, vol. 10588, pp. 75–83. Springer, Cham (2017). https://doi.org/10.1007/978-3-319-68204-4_7

9. Rietveld, L.: Publishing and consuming linked data: optimizing for the unknown. In: Studies on the Semantic Web, vol. 21. IOS Press (2016)
10. Radulovic, F., Mihindukulasooriya, N., García-Castro, R., Gomez-Pérez, A.: A comprehensive quality model for linked data. Seman. Web **9**(1), 3–24 (2018)
11. Asprino, L., Beek, W., Ciancarini, P., van Harmelen, F., Presutti, V.: Observing LOD using equivalent set graphs: it is mostly flat and sparsely linked. In: Ghidini, C., et al. (eds.) ISWC 2019. LNCS, vol. 11778, pp. 57–74. Springer, Cham (2019). https://doi.org/10.1007/978-3-030-30793-6_4
12. Freire, N., Isaac, A.: Technical usability of Wikidata's linked data: evaluation of machine interoperability and data interpretability. In: Abramowicz, W., Paschke, A. (eds.) Lecture Notes in Business Information Processing. Springer, Cham (2019). https://doi.org/10.1007/978-3-030-36691-9_47

Quality Assurance in Digital Libraries

Correspondence as the Primary Measure of Quality for Web Archives: A Grounded Theory Study

Brenda Reyes Ayala(✉)

University of Alberta, Edmonton, AB T6G 0T5, Canada
brenda.reyes@ualberta.ca

Abstract. Creating an archived website that is as close as possible to the original, live website remains one of the most difficult challenges in the field of web archiving. Failing to adequately capture a website might mean an incomplete historical record or, worse, no evidence that the site ever even existed. This paper presents a grounded theory of quality for web archives created using data from web archivists. In order to achieve this, I analysed support tickets submitted by clients of the Internet Archive's Archive-It (AIT), a subscription-based web archiving service that helps organisations build and manage their own web archives. Overall, 305 tickets were analysed, comprising 2544 interactions. The resulting theory is comprised of three dimensions of quality in a web archive: correspondence, relevance, and archivability. The dimension of correspondence, defined as the degree of similarity or resemblance between the original website and the archived website, is the most important facet of quality in web archives, and it is the main focus of this work. This paper's contribution is that it presents the first theory created specifically for web archives and lays the groundwork for future theoretical developments in the field. Furthermore, the theory is human-centred and grounded in how users and creators of web archives perceive their quality. By clarifying the notion of quality in a web archive, this research will be of benefit to web archivists and cultural heritage institutions.

Keywords: Web archiving · Information quality · Quality Assurance · Grounded theory

1 Introduction

In 1996, the Internet Archive was founded in San Francisco with the goal of building a universally accessible digital library. The Internet Archive began using a web crawler to periodically take snapshots of websites and store them as historical records. Internet users could then access these archived websites using the Wayback Machine, a special piece of software developed by the Internet Archive. As the World Wide Web evolved, the pace at which websites changed their content and appearance accelerated dramatically: websites were redesigned or disappeared altogether, additional materials such as video and audio were added, and

M. Hall et al. (Eds.): TPDL 2020, LNCS 12246, pp. 73–86, 2020.
https://doi.org/10.1007/978-3-030-54956-5_6

social media began to emerge. Often the Internet Archive's cache was the only record of how a website had evolved or that it had existed at all. By the dawn of the new millennium, the practice of "web archiving," as it became known, had spread beyond the Internet Archive. Organisations such as national libraries, governments, and universities began also to archive websites for the purpose of preserving their digital heritage.

Though enormous strides have been made, web archiving today remains a complicated and technically-challenging endeavour. New web technologies emerge constantly, and web archivists struggle to keep up. Creating an archived website that is as close as possible to the original, live website remains one of the most difficult challenges in the field. Failing to adequately capture a website might mean an incomplete historical record or, worse, no evidence that the site ever even existed. It is in the context of these challenges that this research takes place.

In the field of web archiving, there have been few comprehensive definitions of quality. One such definition was put forward by Masanès [13]. He defined quality in a web archive as having the following characteristics:

1. the completeness of material (linked files) archived within a target perimeter
2. the ability to render the original form of the site, particularly regarding navigation and interaction with the user [13]

This definition of quality, though useful, is centred on the technological tools needed to archive websites. Terms such as "target perimeter" refer to the configuration of web crawlers. If the web archive was created using alternative methods, or if crawlers were replaced in the future by newer, more efficient tools, then Masanés' definition would become obsolete. Another problem is that it lacks a human element; one never finds out what quality might mean to the users and creators of web archives. This definition ignores the context in which a web archive exists and whether or not it meets the needs of its users. A more robust definition of quality in web archives is needed, one that is independent of the technology currently in use to create web archives and that incorporates a human element. The lack of proper definitions of quality is indicative of a larger problem in the field of web archiving. The technical developments in the field have far outpaced the development of proper theoretical tools or models. Over two decades into its history, web archiving still lacks a theoretical underpinning. Essentially, we have technological tools to build web archives, but no conceptual tools to understand them.

The goal of this research is to build a theory of quality for web archives that is grounded in user-centred data. This goal leads to the following research question: What is the human-centred definition of quality for web archives? This paper presents the first theory created specifically for web archives and lays the groundwork for future theoretical developments in the field. Furthermore, the theory is human-centred and grounded in how users and creators of web archives perceive quality. It also marks the first application of grounded theory to the discipline of web archiving. By clarifying the notion of quality in a web archive, this research will be of benefit to web archivists and cultural heritage institutions who seek to improve the Quality Assurance processes for their organisations.

2 Previous Work

Over the last decade, researchers have begun to study the topic of quality for web archives. Some have also attempted to operationalize individual aspects of quality and to create metrics to effectively measure it. In their paper, Spaniol et al. (2009)[17] are primarily concerned with the quality of a crawl, not with replay of the archived website itself. The authors introduce the concept of (temporal) coherence for a web archive. The contents of a web archive are considered to be coherent if they appear to be "as of" time point x or interval *[x;y]*. In a web archive, coherence defects can occur during the crawl, a process which can take anywhere from a few minutes to weeks for large websites. The authors explored ways to visualize coherence defects in a web archive, so that crawl engineers could detect them and adjust their crawling strategies accordingly.

In a later paper, Denev, Mazeika, Spaniol, and Weikum [7] introduced the Sharp Archiving of Website Captures (SHARC) framework for data quality in web archiving. This framework included two measures of data quality for capturing websites: *blur* and *coherence*. Blur was defined as the expected number of page changes that a time-travel access to a site capture would accidentally see, instead of the ideal view of a instantaneously captured, "sharp" site. This value needed to be minimized in order to achieve a high-quality capture. The authors defined coherence as the number of unchanged and thus coherently captured pages in a site snapshot. Coherence needed to be maximized in order to achieve a high-quality capture.

The work of Ainsworth, Nelson, and Van de Sompel [2] further expanded the notion of temporal coherence in a web archive. They pointed out that archived web pages are composite objects and that, because of the constantly changing nature of the web, many elements and pages from the archived website will have been collected before or after the date presented by the Wayback Machine. The final, archived website presented to the user is often a patchwork collection of HTML pages, images, and scripts from different dates and is thus temporally incoherent. They defined the *temporal coherence* of an archived website (which they call a memento) in the following way: "an embedded memento [is] temporally coherent with respect to a root memento when it can be shown that the embedded memento's representation existed at the time the root memento was captured". Ainsworth, Nelson, and Van de Sompel [2] also specified an extension of their defined coherence states that involved calculating the similarity, or lack thereof, between two archived versions of the same website (or, as the authors put it, between two mementos). This comparison, which they called a "content pattern", takes into account not just the time of archival, but also the content of the two mementos in order to determine coherence. It is important to note that according to the authors, the additional computational cost of calculating these comparisons "may render content patterns unsuitable for casual archive use or in restricted bandwidth conditions".

Ainsworth and Nelson [1] were also concerned with defining quality as meeting measurable characteristics. Their work elaborates on the notion of coherence put forward by Denev, Mazeika, Spaniol, and Weikum [7]. They equate the completeness of a web archive to its coverage; in other words, a complete web archive does not have undesired or undocumented gaps.

Other researchers have addressed the notion of completeness in a web archive. Web archives do not contain complete and perfectly accurate copies of every single website they intend to capture; the dynamic nature of the web makes this almost technically impossible. However, not all missing elements are created equal. Many archived websites are missing elements but still retain most of their intellectual content, while other archived websites, such as maps, are rendered unusable due to missing elements. Brunelle, Kelly, SalahEldeen, Weigle, and Nelson [6] made precisely this point when they examined the importance of missing elements or resources and their impact on the quality of archived websites in their paper.

When deploying crawlers to capture a website, some crawl engineers pay special attention to embedded resources. Embedded resources are files, such as images, videos, or CSS stylesheets, that are present and referenced in a website. A user might not notice their presence, but embedded resources play a key role in ensuring the website looks and operates in the correct way. To this end, crawl engineers might calculate a percentage of missing embedded resources M_m in an archived website and use it to estimate the overall quality of the site. Brunelle, Kelly, SalahEldeen, Weigle, and Nelson [6] showed that M_m is not always consistent with human judgments of the quality of an archived website and was thus not a suitable metric for measuring the "damage" to an archived website caused by missing embedded resources. Instead, the authors proposed a new metric to assess this damage that is based on three factors: the MIME type, size, and location of the embedded resource [6].

AlNoamany, Weigle, and Nelson [3] also addressed quality problems that could affect the coherence of a web archive, such as off-topic web pages. Many web archives are topic-specific: they collect and preserve websites that cover a single topic or news event, such as Human Rights or the Arab Spring of 2010. Off-topic web pages are defined as those that have, over time, moved away from the initial scope of the page. This can occur because the page has been hacked, its domain has expired, or the service has been discontinued. The authors compiled three different Archive-It collections and experimented with several methods of detecting these off-topic webpages and with how to define threshold that separates the on-topic from the off-topic pages. According to their results, the cosine similarity method proved the best at detecting off-topic web pages. The authors also experimented with combining several similarity measures in an attempt to increase performance. The combination of the cosine similarity and word count methods yielded the best results, with an accuracy equal to 0.987, $F = 0.906$, and $AUC = 0.968$ [3].

Banos et al. [5] introduced the concept of website archivability, defined as the "sum of the attributes that make a website amenable to being archived". The more easily it was to archive a website, the greater its archivability. The authors introduced the CLEAR+ method to determine the archivability of a website. According to CLEAR+, an archivable website is accessible (a web crawler can traverse it easily); complies to common, accepted technical standards; cohesive (its components are not dispersed across different locations on the web); and uses descriptive metadata.

In their work, Poursardar and Shipman [15] conducted a user study to explore how users view the boundaries of web resources in institutional web archives, especially as compared to personal archives. Participants were recruited through Amazon's Mechanical Turk and presented with pairs of main/primary web pages. The authors found that, when accessing institutional web archives, users expect the main content to be preserved, as well as additional linked content, advertisements, and author information. In other words, users who access institutional web archives have expectations as to what content should be preserved that are similar to users accessing personal archives.

Kiesel, Kneist, Alshomary, Stein, Hagen, and Potthast [11] paper focused on the reproduction quality of archived websites. To this end, they introduced the Webis Web Archiver tool, which relied on emulating user interactions with a web page while recording all network traffic. In order to evaluate their tools, the researchers recruited human evaluators (recruited through Amazon's Mechanical Turk) to assess web pages in their dataset. The authors defined reproduction quality as thus: "the more individual users that scroll down a web page are affected in their perception or use of the web page by visual differences between the original web page and its reproduction, the smaller the reproduction quality for that web page." Reproduction quality was assessed on a 5-point Likert scale to account for different levels of perceived severity, ranked from no effect (score 1) to unusable reproduction (score 5). Some examples of the assessment scale used were:

- Score 1 (not affecting): Parts of the page are moved up and down a bit.
- Score 2 (small effect on a few visitors): Social media buttons, ads, or unimportant images or text are missing.
- Score 3 (small effect on many or all visitors): Comments on the main content are missing.
- Score 4 (affects, but page can still be used): Striking difference in colour, background, or layout.
- Score 5 (unusable page): Important/main content is missing and/or visitors can't use the right page due to differences.

As Kiesel et al.'s work acknowledges [11], many quality problems arise as a result of the replay process because current technologies such as the Wayback Machine are unable to adequately render the archived website as it originally appeared. The lack of adequate technologies to address quality problems in web archives was highlighted by Klein et al. [12] in their 2019 paper. The authors stated that current web archiving technologies were optimized to either: 1) operate at scale or 2) provide high-quality archival captures, but not both. To address this imbalance, they introduced the Memento Tracer framework, which aimed to achieve both quality and quantity, by allowing the curator to determine the desired components of a web resource that should be archived. Klein et al. acknowledged that quality in web archives is often subjective, and thus focused on the extent to which URIs that should be captured are actually captured. The authors "expect that a high-quality archival record to contain at least the same number of URIs as its live website version" [12]. In other words, a high-quality web archive is *complete*.

The recent focus on the issue of quality in web archives is significant and has resulted in a better understanding of what constitutes a high-quality archived website, and contributed to the emergence of tools designed to improve quality. However, these approaches have been somewhat piecemeal; some researchers focus on completeness, others on coherence, others on relevance, etc. Comprehensive notions of quality are still forthcoming. It is also important to note that assessments of quality obtained from Mechanical Turk users might differ from assessments of quality obtained from web archivists, who are experienced in the processes of creating web archives and might have different or higher standards for preserving web content due to institutional goals and mandates. The research presented here aims to address some of these gaps in the literature.

3 Methodology: Building a Theory of Quality in a Web Archive

In the 60s, Barney Glaser and Anselm Strauss created the methodology of Grounded Theory (GT), which they defined as "the discovery of theory from data - systematically obtained and analysed in social research" [8]. For the authors, theory was not a perfected product that explains all facets of a phenomenon, but a process, an ever-developing entity. GT is an inductive methodology; working closely from the data, the researcher begins the work of generating a theory. GT is optimal for this research problem for the following reasons:

1. There are no existing models or theories in the area of web archiving. GT is appropriate for situations such as these where a field is relatively unexplored and there is a need for theoretical explanations and models [10].
2. GT is user-centred. As its name implies, GT is heavily "grounded" in rich contextual data gathered from empirical research with actual persons [10].
3. GT is iterative. GT research involves the *constant comparison* method, which has the researcher constantly compare the emerging model/theory to the data. This allows the researcher to continually redefine a model and to become aware when no new information is emerging.

3.1 Data Gathering and Processing

The Internet Archive's Archive-It (AIT) is a subscription-based web archiving service that helps organisations build and manage their own web archives. Archive-It is currently the most popular web archiving service, with over 600 clients (called "partners") consisting of universities, state libraries and archives, museums, and national libraries in several countries [4]. The accounts of Archive-It clients are managed by a team of partner specialists. When a client encounters a problem with Archive-It, she first opens a support ticket using Zendesk, a popular customer-service platform. The ticket is received by a partner specialist, who is then responsible for addressing the issue. These initial tickets are part of the "Level 1" support. If the partner specialist determines that a problem is more serious or highly-technical in nature, the issue becomes a "Level 2" and a ticket is opened in JIRA, another issue-tracking platform. There is one support engineer who is responsible for addressing these Level 2 tickets. If he determines that the problem requires more extensive technical efforts, he will convert it to a "Level 3" ticket, which is then addressed by the software engineers at the Internet Archive.

AIT support tickets are a rich source of information regarding quality problems in web archives. They contain the opinions and views of individuals who are experienced creators of web archives, well-versed in web archiving processes, and familiar with institutional web preservation goals, whether they be clients or the partner specialists themselves. They contain rich descriptions of how quality problems are detected, analysed, and addressed, and are thus an ideal dataset for studying quality in all its dimensions.

The first step was to obtain Archive-It support tickets in order to analyse them. Since these tickets belonged to the Internet Archive, I negotiated a researcher agreement with the organisation to obtain support tickets from the years 2012 through 2016. The tickets received comprised a wide variety of institutions reflecting AIT's client base, from national libraries, to private organisations, to universities and museums from Europe, North America, and Asia. After the tickets were cleaned, I randomly selected the same amount of tickets for each year from 2013 through 2016. This randomisation approach was taken to minimise the selection bias that might have occurred if I had manually chosen which tickets to analyse. The final dataset of 645 tickets was then imported into the NVivo software package, a popular program for performing qualitative data analysis [16].

Among other conditions, the research agreement stipulates that the researcher anonymise any personal or institutional information present in the tickets, as well as any other potentially identifying information. In order to comply with the terms of this agreement, all the information presented in this paper has been anonymised: identifying elements such as personal names, names of institutions, and website addresses have been removed or changed.

Data Analysis. The tickets collected were Level 1 support tickets that had been submitted by AIT client. They included the initial question submitted by the client, the response given by the AIT partner specialist, and any subsequent communication between the two. As has been previously noted, Level 2 and Level 3 support tickets represent communication between the AIT support engineer and the team of software engineers. Because these tickets do not involve the AIT clients and are highly technical in nature, they do not contain the opinions of users and creators of web archives. Therefore, they were not considered relevant to the project and were not requested.

It is important to note that not all the AIT tickets deal with issues of quality in a web archive. Quite a few deal with collection management issues, such as how to manage user accounts for a collection of web archives, storage limitations, and questions about the privacy or public access to archived content. This research focuses on tickets in which the client discusses a perceived flaw in an individual archived website or an entire web archive. From prior experiences, I had seen that these types of tickets are the most likely to deal with issues of quality.

Support tickets not pertaining to quality issues were classified as such and separated from the main data of interest. Each ticket analysed consisted of the original ticket submitted by the client, the response sent by the AIT partner specialist, and any subsequent interactions between them. Tickets could be quite brief, consisting of three interactions (the original client ticket, the partner specialist's response, and the client's response), or they could have many interactions over time, spanning weeks or even months. Table 1 lists the number of tickets and interactions about quality that were analysed, which totalled 305 tickets and 2544 interactions.

Table 1. Number of tickets and interactions about quality analysed per year

Year	No. tickets about quality analysed	No. interactions analysed
2012	74	478
2013	65	492
2014	67	540
2015	58	528
2016	41	506
Total	305	2544

These support tickets were analysed using the GT techniques of open coding and theoretical memos to identify the main concepts and categories present in the data. According to the precepts of GT, after several rounds of coding, the researcher will reach *saturation*, a state when nothing new is being extracted from the data. Per the guidelines of Grounded Theory, only the core categories (that is, the ones that explain most of the variation in quality) are part of the final theory. In order to increase the quality and rigour of the study, I engaged in purposeful peer review. University professors were periodically invited to audit the entire research project, including the codebook, preliminary findings, and core categories. In addition to peers, employees of the Internet Archive were also invited to see the findings and comment on them.

4 Findings and Discussion

4.1 Core Categories

The grounded theory presented here consists of three dimensions (or core categories) that determine the quality of a web archive: correspondence, relevance, and archivability.

1. Correspondence: degree of similarity, or resemblance, between the original website and the archived website
   (a) Visual correspondence: similarity in appearance between the original website and the archived website
   (b) Interactional correspondence: the degree to which a user's interaction with the archived website is similar to that of the original
   (c) Completeness: the degree to which the archived website contains all of the components of the original
2. Relevance: pertinence of the contents of an archived website to the original website
   (a) Topic relevance: degree to which an archived website (or a web archive) includes only content that is closely related to that of the original website or the topic of the larger web archive
   (b) Size relevance: the similarity in size of the archived website to the original website
3. Archivability: degree to which the intrinsic properties of a website make it easier or more difficult to archive

Taken together, these three dimensions meet the requirements specified by Barney Glaser [9]. As core categories, they account for most of the behaviour of web archivists towards the quality of web archives that was seen in the data. Of all the three core categories examined, the dimension of correspondence was by far the most important, with 852 mentions across 226 tickets, much more than relevance (451 mentions across 127 tickets) and archivability (101 mentions across 78 tickets). **Due to its importance, the dimension of correspondence is the main focus of this work.**

4.2 Visual Correspondence

When describing a quality problem in the tickets, AIT clients will often compare the archived website to the original website. AIT clients have a strong idea of what the archived website should look or behave like and are quick to report any discrepancies. Table 2 displays some examples of problems with visual correspondence. In these, AIT clients point out how the visual appearance of the archived website does not match that of the original. Clients express these comparisons in a number of ways. One way is by including a direct link to the original website in their tickets. This allows the partner specialist to make quick comparisons between the live site and the archived website and note the differences. Table 2 shows some examples of tickets where the clients made these explicit comparisons. In ticket 103, the client tells the AIT partner specialist to check the live website for the "proper" version ("how it should look"). Many more tickets do not include the URL for the original website, but still explicitly compare it to the archived version. Some of these instances are also shown in Table 2. The clients describe the archived website as being problematic: it is "a bit off" (ticket 36), it "does not display properly" (ticket 302), or does not capture the "the look and feel" of the original (ticket 3420).

Table 2. Examples of problems with visual correspondence

Ticket Name	Text of the Ticket
ticket 103	I have done a crawl of the following: http://www.___.org/remembering/ and the YouTube video display is problematic in Wayback on the pages. While the host report has the YouTube videos captured, they are not showing up on the web pages. See http://wayback.archive-it.org/yyhttp://www. ___.org/remembering/life-work http://www.___.org/remembering/life-work for how it should look.
ticket 260	On the new http://www.stateu.edu/academics page we are not capturing the background images. I cannot figure out why since we are capturing other images from the same directory
ticket 33	(see http://___.uk/roman-scrolls compared to http://wayback.archive-it.org/http:// ___.uk/roman-scrolls) Poets - Text next to the portraits should change as you scroll over the navigation bar. (http:// ___.uk/ vs http://wayback.archive-it.org/http://poetry. ___.uk/)
ticket 36	I also noticed that the display for your www.nzlibrary.edu pages was a bit off
ticket 302	We're having some trouble with our Facebook site captures not displaying properly (or at all, really)
ticket 3420	One thing related though, the page is not capturing its look and feel well...Any suggestions? It's missing the background and objects are not in the right locations

Table 3. Examples of problems with interactional correspondence

Ticket name	Text of the ticket
ticket 114	The site renders fine and you can hover over the progress bar for the videos and see that the frames are captured, but the video won't play
ticket 27	Clicking "View all comments" under an update does not reveal the comments
ticket 33	the interactive floorplan isn't working as it should do - the text should appear over the map when you click on it, rather than in a list underneath
ticket 3276	I know I've captured the video but it doesn't play on the web page
ticket 3284	When i click on it, it briefly flashes to the homepage and then it displays a URL with the nationalscience URL in it twice
ticket 74	In some cases I hear audio but see no video

Table 4. Examples of problems with completeness

Ticket Name	Text of the Ticket
ticket 114	It looks like what is happening is that the video files themselves have not been captured
ticket 33	there should be a Google search bar at the top of both websites
ticket 296	on all most every blog that we have captured from blogspot the Way-back Machine does not include the subsequent pages beyond the first
ticket 311	We're still having some trouble capturing the JavaScript menu at the top of the main page. I know that JS can be wonky
ticket 3117	The News pages (which are located under each individual sport) are being captured, but the actual articles that are listed and linked out arc not
ticket 74	The issue with this seed is that for all previous crawls we were able to capture main text for individual ___ articles, but not comments

4.3 Interactional Correspondence

Interactional correspondence was defined as a sub-category of the correspondence dimension of quality. A problem with interactional correspondence occurs when a user's interaction with the archived website is different from that of the original, unexpected, or deficient. For example, on the live website, a web archivist clicks on a link and is taken to the corresponding target of that link, that is, another webpage. She expects the same thing to happen on the archived version of the original page. If it does not, and she is not taken to a different webpage, the archived website lacks interactional correspondence. Problems with interactional correspondence occur when there is a mismatch between a user's expectation of website behaviour and the actual behaviour displayed by the archived website.

Similarly, examples of problems with interactional correspondence are shown in Table 3. When the clients attempt to interact with the archived website as they would with the original, they report unexpected behaviours: the text in the interactive floor plans does not display in the correct location (ticket 33), a page displays only very briefly and then redirects to another location (ticket 3284), and clicking on a button does not display the comments (ticket 27). Video content in web archives is also difficult to replay (tickets 114, 3276, and 74).

It is important to note that these codes are not independent of each other. It is common for a low-quality archived website to have many problems, from missing pages to unexpected behaviours Some quality problems straddle several categories. For example, ticket 260 from Table 2 is presented as an instance of a visual correspondence problem, since the archived site does not include the background images as the original does. However, the same ticket can also be classified as a completeness problem, since the site is missing images (intellectual content) that it should contain. In fact, many (though not all) archived websites that exhibit mismatched appearance and behaviours do so because they are missing important files that provide needed visual elements or functionality. Though the categories are separate, they are often linked.

4.4 Completeness as a Type of Correspondence

Completeness has already been described as the completeness of an archived website as it relates to the original. A perfectly complete archived website contains all of the components of the original. A completeness problem occurs when the original website's content has not been captured or is not present in the archive. Lack of completeness is caused by the absence of needed content. Table 4 displays examples of completeness problems, where the clients note that an archived website is missing content that assumed to be present in the original. They report missing search boxes (ticket 33), articles (ticket 3117), menus (ticket 311), videos (ticket 114), comments (ticket 74), and in some cases, even archived websites that are missing many pages (ticket 296).

In the literature that was reviewed, completeness is often seen as a major aspect of quality, sometimes even equated with quality itself. It is present in the work of Masanés [13], Ainsworth and Nelson [1], Brunelle et al. [6], and Klein et al. [12]. It is therefore tempting to see completeness as its own separate dimension of quality in web archives, different from correspondence; however, this is a fallacy. An archived website can have a lack of correspondence with the original website yet still be perfectly complete. For example, it can have all the same components of the original, yet still look or behave differently from it. However, the reverse is not true: an archived website cannot be incomplete, yet still have 100% correspondence with the original. In logic, correspondence is known as a *necessary cause*:"If x is a necessary cause of y, then the presence of y necessarily implies the presence of x with a probability of 100%. The presence of x, however, does not imply that y will occur." [14]. The presence of a lack of completeness (y) always implies the presence of a lack of correspondence (x); however, the presence of correspondence does not imply a lack of completeness. Therefore, completeness is not a core category in the theory, but rather a subcategory.

The work presented in this paper is delimited because it is specific to small or medium-size web archives that are focused on covering a single topic or an event. It is not meant to describe larger web archives such as the *.gov* or *.fr*, which preserve an entire country's national domain. The theory of quality in web archives presented here makes an important assumption: that there exists a live version of a website to which the archived version can be compared. However, the correspondence of an archived webpage might not always be easily known. For example, if the original site has been lost, there is no way to compare it to the archived version, so a measure of correspondence cannot be calculated.

5 Conclusion and Future Work

This paper makes the following contributions:

1. The paper presents the first application of grounded theory to the discipline of web archiving.

2. It introduces the first theory of quality developed specifically about web archives, and lays the groundwork for future theoretical and practical developments in the field.
3. The theory is human-centred and grounded in how subject-matter experts in the field of web archiving perceive quality.
4. The theory is *comprehensive*, incorporating and unifying the work of previous researchers on web archives.
5. The theory is independent of the technology currently in use to create web archives, making it suitable to a wide variety of platforms, preservation contexts, and situations.

Taken together, the theory presented here represents the majority of quality problems seen in topic-centred or event-driven web archives today. According to Glaser and Strauss, a grounded theory must closely fit the data and also be clear and flexible [8]. This last requirement is especially important. A theory must be flexible enough that a user who applies the theory is able to adjust it and reformulate it as she encounters new data and situations. For example, if in the future, new technologies were developed to capture dynamic web content more successfully, the notions of visual correspondence, interactional correspondence, and completeness would still be relevant to quality in web archives. As Glaser and Strauss state "evidence and testing never destroy a theory (of any generality), they only modify it. A theory's only replacement is a better theory" [8].

Having clear concepts based on experts perceive the issue of quality can lead to the successful creation of metrics, methods, and tools that will enable web archivists to measure the quality of their web archives. For example, in order to measure the correspondence of a web archive, a program could be developed that would navigate to both the live website and its archived counterpart, and then calculate some measure of similarity between them in terms of visual correspondence, interactional correspondence, and completeness. Once the software to measure correspondence has been built, experiments could be carried out to determine which metrics perform best. Details such as these would need time and effort to be adequately worked out, but the results would ultimately lead to higher quality web archives, and thus, a better and more complete historical record.

References

1. Ainsworth, S.G., Nelson, M.L.: Evaluating sliding and sticky target policies by measuring temporal drift in acyclic walks through a web archive. Int. J. Dig. Libraries **16**(2), 129–144 (2014). https://doi.org/10.1007/s00799-014-0120-4
2. Ainsworth, S.G., Nelson, M.L., Van de Sompel, H.: A framework for evaluation of composite memento temporal coherence. Computing Research Respository (CoRR) abs/1402.0928 (2014), http://arxiv.org/abs/1402.0928
3. AlNoamany, Y., Weigle, M.C., Nelson, M.L.: Detecting off-topic pages in web archives. In: Kapidakis, S., Mazurek, C., Werla, M. (eds.) TPDL 2015. LNCS, vol. 9316, pp. 225–237. Springer, Cham (2015). https://doi.org/10.1007/978-3-319-24592-8_17

4. Archive-It: Learn more (2020). https://archive-it.org/learn-more
5. Banos, V., Manolopoulos, Y.: A quantitative approach to evaluate website archivability using the CLEAR+ method. Int. J. Dig. Libraries **17**(2), 119–141 (2015). https://doi.org/10.1007/s00799-015-0144-4
6. Brunelle, J., Kelly, M., SalahEldeen, H., Weigle, M.C., Nelson, M.L.: Not allmementos are created equal: measuring the impact of missing resources. Int. J. Dig. Libraries **1**, 1–19 (2015). https://doi.org/10.1007/s00799-015-0150-6
7. Denev, D., Mazeika, A., Spaniol, M., Weikum, G.: The SHARC framework for data quality in web archiving. VLDB J. **20**(2), 183–207 (2011). https://doi.org/10.1007/s00778-011-0219-9
8. Glaser, B., Strauss, A.: The Discovery of Grounded Theory: Strategies for Qualitative Research. Aldine Transaction (2009). http://amazon.com/o/ASIN/0202302601/
9. Glaser, B.: Theoretical Sensitivity: Advances in the Methodology of Grounded Theory. The Sociology Press, Mill Valley (1978)
10. Grbich, C.: Qualitative Data Analysis: An Introduction, 2nd edn. SAGE Publications Ltd, London (2012)
11. Kiesel, J., Kneist, F., Alshomary, M., Stein, B., Hagen, M., Potthast, M.: Reproducible web corpora: interactive archiving with automatic quality assessment. J. Data Inf. Qual. **10**(4), 10 (2018). https://doi.org/10.1145/3239574
12. Klein, M., Shankar, H., Balakireva, L., Van de Sompel, H.: The memento tracer framework: Balancing quality and scalability for web archiving. In: Doucet, A., Isaac, A., Golub, K., Aalberg, T., Jatowt, A. (eds.) Digital Libraries for Open Knowledge, pp. 163–176. Springer International Publishing, Cham (2019)
13. Masanès, J.: Web Archiving. Springer, Heidelberg (2006). https://doi.org/10.1007/978-3-540-46332-0
14. Ohio State University: Causal reasoning (2011). http://www.istarassessment.org/srdims/causal-reasoning-2/
15. Poursardar, F., Shipman, F.: How perceptions of web resource boundaries differ for institutional and personal archives. In: 2018 IEEE International Conference on Information Reuse and Integration (IRI). pp. 126–129 (2018). https://doi.org/10.1109/IRI.2018.00026
16. QSR International: Nvivo product range (2016). http://www.qsrinternational.com/nvivo-product
17. Spaniol, M., Mazeika, A., Denev, D., Weikum, G.: "Catch me if you can": Visual analysis of coherence defects in web archiving. In: Proceedings of the 9th International Web Archiving Workshop (IWAW), Corfu, Greece, September 30–October 1, 2009. pp. 27–37 (2009)

Assessing and Minimizing the Impact of OCR Quality on Named Entity Recognition

Ahmed Hamdi(✉), Axel Jean-Caurant, Nicolas Sidère, Mickaël Coustaty, and Antoine Doucet

University of La Rochelle, L3i Laboratory, La Rochelle, France
{ahmed.hamdi,axel.jean-caurant,nicolas.sidere, mickael.coustaty,antoine.doucet}@univ-lr.fr

Abstract. In digital libraries, the accessibility of digitized documents is directly related to the way they are indexed. Named entities are one of the main entry points used to search and retrieve digital documents. However, most digitized documents are indexed through their OCRed version and OCR errors may hinder their accessibility. This paper aims to quantitatively estimate the impact of OCR quality on the performance of named entity recognition (NER). We tested state-of-the-art NER techniques over several evaluation benchmarks, and experimented with various levels and types of synthesised OCR noise so as to estimate the impact of OCR noise on NER performance. We share all corresponding datasets. To the best of our knowledge, no other research work has systematically studied the impact of OCR on named entity recognition over datasets in multiple languages. The final outcome of this study is an evaluation over historical newspaper data of the national library of Finland, resulting in an increase of around 11% points in terms of F1-measure over the best-known results to this day.

Keywords: Digitized documents · Indexing · OCR · Named entity recognition

1 Introduction

Substantial amounts of printed documents are digitized and archived as images in digital libraries. This is notably the case of historical documents, which require an *Optical Character Recognition* (OCR) step to give access to their textual content. Unfortunately, while the performance of OCR systems has greatly improved, it remains imperfect. In addition, a great deal of documents were digitized in a time when storing high-quality images was difficult. Such documents cannot readily benefit from improvements in OCR quality. Several studies understandably suggest that the performance of natural language processing tools is harmed by the use of OCRed text, i.e., text resulting from an OCR process [18]. This naturally makes document access more difficult since simple keyword search

M. Hall et al. (Eds.): TPDL 2020, LNCS 12246, pp. 87–101, 2020.
https://doi.org/10.1007/978-3-030-54956-5_7

will for instance not match a query with the corresponding words if they suffer from OCR errors. The quality of the text generated using OCR engines depends on the algorithms used in OCR, on the parameter settings of the scanner used to digitize documents, on the quality of the original image and on the nature of the document. For instance, text generated from recent vs. historical newspapers or well-preserved vs. damaged manuscripts is usually not of the same quality. Even though a reasonable amount of OCR errors is known to have low impact on the readability of documents, the errors will be indexed as they are by search engines and other NLP tools. Subsequently, if some words are incorrectly recognized by the OCR process, they will be indexed with their errors. This causes a chain reaction for tools developed to analyze the resulting content.

A study has shown that named entities (NEs) are the first point of entry for users in a search system [10]. As an illustration, it has been observed that 4 out of 5 user queries on the Gallica digital library[1] contain at least one named entity [2]. For this reason, their quality is far more critical than that of most other words in OCRed documents. In order to improve the satisfaction of users' information needs, it is thus necessary to ensure their quality.

Named entity recognition (NER) is a task that emerged in the middle of the 1990*s* [12]. It aims to locate and categorize important concepts of a given text into a set of predefined classes. Three main labels are commonly used: persons, locations and organizations [22]. NER techniques can be gathered in two groups: rule-based and machine learning methods. For rule-based methods, the rules are mainly defined manually. They are related to linguistic descriptions, trigger words and lexica of proper names. These rules use patterns and regular expressions in order to locate and classify named entities. Machine learning approaches, on the other hand, aim to extract rules automatically based on learning systems trained on large corpora. Rule-based methods are clearly affected by OCR errors and are not able to deal with the degradation generated by the OCR, whereas, machine learning methods present a sufficient flexibility to be automatically adapted to process noisy texts. More recently, neural networks have been shown to outperform other supervised algorithms for NER. The first deep neural network based learning system has been developed in 2011 [4]. It reached very competitive results for NER in comparison to previous machine learning systems. Therefore, many NER systems using neural networks have been proposed and have shown their abilities to outperform all previous systems [25]. We present in this paper a comparative study of well-performing NER methods. We have chosen, in this work, to use four majors systems available: the well-known NER tool using Conditional Random Fields CoreNLP [8] and three neural network systems BLSTM-CRF [17], BLSTM-CNN [3] and BLSTM-CNN-CRF [20]. The reason being that processing degraded texts using rule based systems require substantial manual efforts to face all typical OCR degradations, unlike machine learning systems which are able to automatically overcome OCR degradations. Furthermore, most rule-based systems are domain-specific or language-dependent and cannot easily be extended to other domains or other languages [9]. Our goal is

[1] Gallica is the digital portal of the National Library of France.

to evaluate the impact of OCR error on NER accuracy when dealing with noisy text, a task strongly related to document indexing in digital libraries. To the best of our knowledge, no other research work has systematically studied the impact of OCR on named entity recognition over datasets in multiple languages.

In order to assess our work, we used three publicly available datasets which cover three languages (English, Dutch and Spanish). Given the lack of OCRed annotated data aligned with its ground truth, we have simulated test data by adding typical textual degradation given by an OCR engine. These data have been obtained by automatically adding many levels of degradation in those corpora. More specifically, we spread four types of common OCR degradation in the original clean text. As OCR error depends on the quality and the parameters of the digitization process, we also simulated typical scanning noises at two different levels: rare and reasonably frequent. We finally aligned clean and OCRed data in order to be able to use the same annotation data. Running NER systems through progressively noisy data allows us to draw a graph of NER results relative to OCR error rates. Results over our simulated OCRed resource show a general consistency with a real-life OCRed dataset extracted from Finnish historical newspaper provided by the national library of Finland, which confirms the relevance of our analysis.

The rest of the paper is organized as follows: Sect. 2 presents related work studying the impact of OCR. Section 3 consists in an overview of the datasets, followed by outlines of NER results over clean and OCRed texts in Sect. 4. Section 5 reports our experiments with real data and Sect. 6 concludes the paper.

2 Related Work

Despite decades of research, the output of OCR systems remains imperfect, especially when the original document is old, damaged or poorly digitized. OCR systems lie in the beginning of the digitalization pipeline and OCR errors tend to have a cumulative impact over the subsequent steps. For this reason, researchers have studied the impact of processing text data from noisy sources in order to understand the effects of OCR on text analysis tools.

Much research to process noisy data [32] has stemmed from the field of natural language processing (NLP). Lopresti Daniel [18] for instance considered a text analysis pipeline consisting of sentence boundary detection, followed by tokenization and POS tagging. They reported that among the errors generated by the OCR process, insertion errors were worse than character deletion errors on the sentence boundaries task, while OCR substitution errors were more impactful on POS tagging. The effects of noisy texts have been evaluated also on other NLP tasks such as document summarization [15] and machine translation [36].

Many other works focused on information retrieval from noisy data [5]. Chiron *et al.* [2] proposed a method to estimate the impact of OCR errors on the use of digital libraries. They built an OCR error model using a large corpus of OCRed documents aligned with their corresponding ground truth. Their model allowed the estimation of the risk that a user's query might fail to match with the targeted documents. Taghva *et al.* [33] showed that moderate OCR error rates have not desperate impact on the effectiveness of classical information retrieval measures. Other studies focused on the impact of OCR errors on the classification of pathology reports for cancer notification [37]. They concluded that OCR errors even with modest rates are not imperceptible for extracting cancer notification items.

For NER, several works have been done to extract NEs from diverse text types such as outputs of Automatic Speech Recognition (ASR) systems [7] informal SMS and noisy social network posts [29]. Palmerand Ostendorf [23] for example described an approach for improving named entity extraction from ASR systems outputs by explicitly modeling errors through the use of confidence scores. In a similar setting, Miller *et al.* [21] have studied the performance of named entity extraction under a variety of spoken and OCRed data. They trained the IdentiFinder system [1] on both clean and noisy input material, performance degraded linearly as a function of word error rates. They concluded that results may lose about 8 points of F-score with only 15% of word error rate. Rodriquez *et al.* [30] reported that manual correction of OCR output have not a very observable improvement on NER results. In [28], Riedl *et al.* presented a complete framework for named entity recognition for both contemporary clean and historical noisy German using transfer learning technique. They achieved state-of-the-art performance for historical datasets with less samples that contains noise. More recently, Hamdi *et al.* [13] and Pontes *et al.* [26] used synthetic OCRed English resources to respectively study the impact of OCR errors on named entity recognition and named entity linking.

In this paper, similarly to [30] and [21], we propose to study the evolution of the performance of named entity recognition systems over noisy OCR data. Unlike them we use more sophisticated NER systems relying on the most recent neural networks models. We also use larger corpora covering four languages, thanks to a technique that allows us to synthesize and test different types and levels of noise. They contain different types of degradation that correspond to the results of long storage and the impact of digitization processes. We defined two levels of degradation for each type in order to obtain a clearer view on OCR errors and their impact on the task of named entity recognition.

3 Dataset Overview

To the best of our knowledge, no publicly available corpus has been found with named entity annotations on both clean and noisy texts at the same time. In addition, there are corpora where text produced by an OCR process is aligned with the original text but NEs are not annotated. For this reason, we have taken advantage of three available NER corpora and simulated from them several OCRed versions with variable OCR error rates. We used the public corpora (CoNLL-02 and CoNLL-03) dealing with named entities and covering three languages: English [34], Spanish and Dutch [6]. English data consist of Reuters news stories between August 1996 and August 1997. The Spanish corpus is a collection of news wire articles made available by the Spanish EFE News Agency while the Dutch corpus consists of four editions of the Belgian newspaper "De Morgen". Those datasets are split into three subsets: a training set, a test set and a development set. The latter has been built in order to tune parameters of learning methods. All data files contain a single word per line with its associated named entity tag. Table 1 outlines details about each dataset used in this work.

Table 1. CoNLL-02 and CoNLL-03 datasets

		Sentences	Words		Named entities	
			Tokens	Terms	Tokens	Terms
Spanish	Train	8,323	264,715	26,099	32,795	6,821
	Dev	1,915	52,923	9,646	7,567	2,377
	Test	1,517	51,533	9,086	6,178	1,974
English	Train	14,987	204,567	23,624	29,450	6,955
	Dev	3,466	51,578	9,967	7,335	2,735
	Test	3,684	46,666	9,489	7,194	2,384
Dutch	Train	15,806	202,932	27,805	14,555	4,332
	Dev	2,895	37,762	8,151	2,751	1,033
	Test	5,195	68,995	11,803	4,170	1,567

The annotation of named entities follows the IOB-scheme (Inside, Outside, Beginning) where every token is labeled as B if the token is the beginning of a named entity, I if it is inside but not the first token within the named entity, or O otherwise [27]. Four classes have been used to label NEs: PER for persons, LOC for locations, ORG for organisations and MISC for other NEs.

From test data, we simulated several OCRed versions. To do so, we first extracted raw texts from test sets and converted them into images. These images have been contaminated by adding typical synthesised noise. We then extracted OCRed data using the Tesseract open source OCR engine v-3.04.01[2] which provides a language package covering many languages among them English, Dutch and Spanish. The subsequent noisy OCRed text and the original one were finally aligned and annotations of the original corpus were projected back on the noisy version. Figure 1 describes the main steps to simulate noisy corpora. We assume that the target text is similar to the indexed text in digital libraries.

In order to contaminate images, we used the DocCreator tool[3] developed by Journet *et al.* [16]. The tool provides many options to add degradation to document images such as blurring, ink degradation and adding phantom characters. In this work, we applied four types of degradation related to storage conditions or poor quality of printing materials that may be present in digital libraries material:

[2] https://github.com/tesseract-ocr/.
[3] http://doc-creator.labri.fr/.

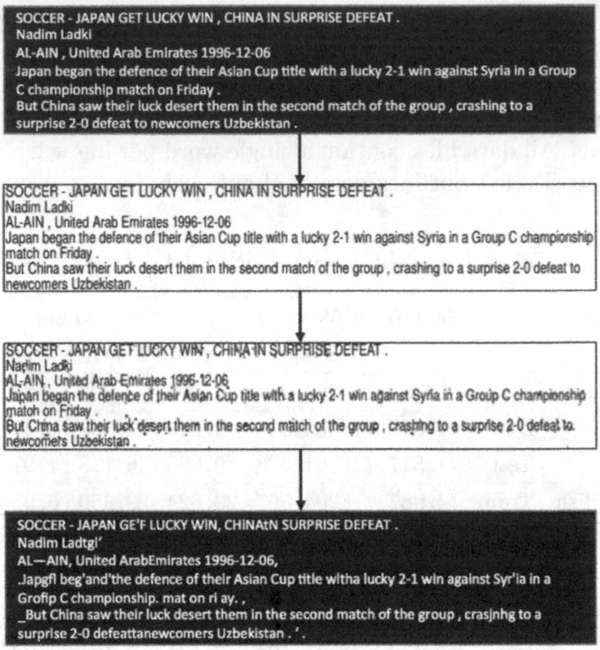

Fig. 1. Simulation of OCRed copora

- **character degradation** simulates degradation due to the age of the document or the use of a scanner incorrectly set. It consists in adding small ink spots on characters and can induce the partial obscuration of characters.
- **phantom degradation** simulates degradation in worn documents. Following successive uses, some characters can be progressively eroded. The digitization process generates phantom ink around characters.
- **bleed-through** simulates back side ink seeping through the front side of a page. This degradation only appears with double-sided pages.
- **blurring** simulates a blurring effect, as can be encountered during a typical digitization process with focus issue.

For each type of noise, we defined two levels of degradation: LEV-1 where noises are applied rarely and LEV-2 where degradation is reasonably more frequent. These levels allow generating noisy texts with an OCR error rate close to real cases [14]. These degradation levels and types allowed building eight versions for each test corpus. We additionally defined two versions that we call respectively LEV-0 and LEV-MIX. The LEV-0 version is the re-OCRred version of original images with no degradation added while the LEV-MIX version is the result of combining all the LEV-1 degradation types[4]. The LEV-0 degradation aims to evaluate the OCR engine through sharp images whereas the goal of using the

[4] We have not defined a level combining the LEV-2 degradations because it produces a very poor-quality images and provides unreadable documents.

LEV-MIX degradation is to be more similar to real-world documents. Degraded documents typically contain several OCR degradations simultaneously.

Following the text extraction by the OCR, the noisy text has been aligned to its original version using the tool RETAS [35]. An example of alignment made between the ground truth and its OCRed version is shown in Fig. 2. This alignment reflects the various errors made by the OCR engine. The difference between the two texts is denoted by the presence of the character '@'. Each '@' in the ground truth indicates the insertion of one character by the OCR while '@' in the noisy text indicates that one character has been deleted from the original text.

OCR : SOCCER - JAPAN GE'F@ LUCKY WI@N@, CHi@NAt@@N SURPRISE DEFEAT . Nadim Ladtg@i 'AL—@AIN@, United Arab@
GT : SOCCER - JAPAN GE@@T LUCKY W@IN , CH@INA@ IN SURPRISE DEFEAT . Nadim Lad@@ki @AL@-AIN , United Arab

OCR : Emirates 1996-12-06, . Japgfl@@ beg'and'@the defence of their Asian Cup title wl@th@a lucky 2-1 win a
GT : Emirates 1996-12-06@ @@Jap@@an beg@an@@ the defence of their Asian Cup title w@ith a lucky 2-1 win a

OCR : gainst Syr'ia in a Grofi@p C championship .mat@@ on @ri @ay@. , _ But China saw their luck desert the
GT : gainst Syr@ia in a Gro@up C championship @match on Fri@day . @@@@But China saw their luck desert the

Fig. 2. Original and noisy texts alignment

In order to evaluate the OCR quality, we used two measures: the Character Error Rate (CER) [14] which corresponds to the proportion of erroneous characters compared to the original text. and the Word Error Rate (WER) [19] which calculates the proportion of erroneous words compared to the total number of words in the original text. A word is considered as erroneous if it contains at least one character error. Table 2 details the OCR error rates at the character and the word levels in the different OCRed version of the three datasets.

As can be seen from Table 2, CER and WER considerably increase when noise is added, comparing to re-OCRed clean text (LEV-0). The table also shows that the noise distributed in the documents is homogeneous. The CER is quite low while the WER is relatively high. Except for Blurring LEV-2 degradation, the CER varies between ~1% and ~7% while the error rate at the word level always exceeds 8%. OCR error rates also show that blurring and character degradation are the most critical noise for digitized documents; they generated the highest error rate both at the character and word levels.

Despite applying the same degradation through all data, OCR is considerably more accurate through Spanish data, CER and WER rates respectively remain below 20% and 30%. On the other hand OCR error rates over English and Dutch data have more variable rates that can reach up to 50%. The bleed-through and phantom characters have a slight impact on the effectiveness of the OCR while

Table 2. Estimation of OCR errors rates

		English		Dutch		Spanish	
		CER	WER	CER	WER	CER	WER
LEV-0		1.7	8.5	1.6	7.8	0.7	4.8
Bleed-through	LEV-1	1.8	8.5	1.7	8.2	0.8	4.9
	LEV-2	1.8	8.6	1.8	8.9	0.8	5.4
Blurring	LEV-1	6.3	20.0	5.9	22.0	3.0	12.0
	LEV-2	41.3	54.0	27.0	44.7	19.5	29.9
Char deg.	LEV-1	3.6	21.8	4.5	25.1	2.1	14.2
	LEV-2	4.3	23.7	6.4	31.6	2.7	16.3
Phantom deg.	LEV-1	1.7	8.8	1.6	8.0	0.8	5.5
	LEV-2	1.8	10.0	1.7	8.4	0.9	5.9
LEV-MIX		6.9	22.8	5.8	22.2	3.5	11.9

ink degradation and blurring lead to the highest OCR error rates. Among these types of degradation, blurring is the most critical degradation that impacted the OCR outputs.

Concerning NEs, knowing their locations in the original text, we aligned them with corresponding words generated by the OCR. We identified then contaminated NEs and those well recognized by the OCR. A total of 3,623 English named entity tokens have been well recognized by the OCR which represents 63.33%. This rate achieves 72.14% for Spanish and 59.87% for Dutch. All the dataset used in this work are publicly available[5]. We provide for each test corpus (English, Dutch and Spanish) the degraded images and their noisy texts extracted by the OCR as well as the aligned version with clean data at the word and the character levels.

4 Evaluation and Results

Neural networks and the related training process require several hyper-parameters such as character embedding dimension, character-based token embedding, LSTM dimension, token embedding dimension, etc. The same parameters for training and testing have been applied on the different dataset: OCRed corpora and clean ones. English embedding has been done using Glove [24] while word2vec [11] was used for Dutch and Spanish word embeddings. Table 3 shows the results of NER on clean datasets. We used traditional metrics ([P]recision, [R]ecall and [F1]-score) to evaluate NER systems.

This first test shows that the results obtained with various methods are globally equivalent for the three languages. We can notice that neural network based approaches give slightly better results than CoreNLP. The same experiments

[5] https://zenodo.org/record/3877554.

Table 3. NER Results on clean data

		BLSTM-CRF	BLSTM-CNN	BLSTM-CRF-CNN	CoreNLP
English	P	89.54	90.57	91.05	86.35
	R	90.81	90.98	90.75	83.88
	F1	90.17	90.77	90.90	85.10
Dutch	P	79.68	78.61	81.22	74.61
	R	80.96	82.18	79.04	73.28
	F1	80.31	80.36	80.12	73.94
Spanish	P	87.23	87.05	87.54	75.06
	R	83.47	83.21	83.46	76.60
	F1	85.31	85.09	85.45	75.82

have been run on OCRed dataset. Unsurprisingly, NER accuracy drops proportionally to the rate of OCR errors which is related to the degradation type and level. Table 4 gives the F-score of each NER system on noisy data. Results show that compared to clean data, NER results may lose from 3 to 5 points for LEV-0 OCR-ed data. This proves that OCR has a negative impact for the NER task since LEV-0 represents OCR-ed data with no noise added. In other words, even with perfect storage and digitization, NER accuracy may be affected by the OCR quality. For other types of degradation, levels of OCR error rates vary from 8% to 50% at the word level and the NER F-score may drop from 90% to 50% for English. Compared to CoreNLP, deep-learning systems showed a better ability to overcome OCR errors. They achieved satisfactory results when the word error rate was less than 20%.

Results in Table 4 also indicate that the best NER F1-score (in **bold**) can be given by different NER systems according to the type and the level of degradation. For this reason, we calculated the δ measure which gives the minimum decrease rate between the best F1-score given in clean data and the best F1-scores given in noisy data for each type and level of degradation. This measure represents the perfect system that will give the best accuracy for all degradation levels. For the three languages, δ exceeds 40% in noisy data with WER and CER rates reaching more than 0.4 and 0.5 respectively. The Dutch F-score for example decreases under 50% using any one of the four systems through noisy texts extracted from blurred images with an OCR error rate of 44% at the word level.

Figure 3 shows the evolution of the δ measure with respect to degradation. Types of degradation have been sorted according to OCR rates. CER and WER curves are also given for comparison.

5 Experiments on Historical Dataset

An additional experiment was performed on real life OCRed data, based on Finnish-language historical newspapers from the National Library of Finland

Table 4. NER F1-score of noisy data

English	BLSTM-CRF	BLSTM-CNN	BLSTM-CRF-CNN	CoreNLP
Clean	90.17	90.77	**90.90**	85.10
LEV-0	86.77	86.93	87.45	79.61
Bleed_LEV-1	85.15	85.08	**86.11**	75.72
Bleed_LEV-2	84.63	**84.72**	83.96	75.27
Blur_LEV-1	**71.03**	70.99	**71.03**	63.39
Blur_LEV-2	59.77	58.98	**60.31**	49.15
DegChar_LEV-1	73.14	**74.22**	74.11	58.12
DegChar_LEV-2	**70.85**	69.43	68.77	55.06
PhantChar_LEV-1	85.59	85.67	**87.01**	74.21
PhantChar_LEV-2	84.58	85.03	**85.20**	73.66
LEV-MIX	**70.87**	70.11	70.82	63.35

Dutch	BLSTM-CRF	BLSTM-CNN	BLSTM-CRF-CNN	CoreNLP
Clean	80.31	**80.63**	80.12	73.94
LEV-0	73.96	73.66	**74.03**	68.36
Bleed_LEV-1	72.10	**73.49**	73.15	66.88
Bleed_LEV-2	72.06	**72.75**	**72.75**	65.45
Blur_LEV-1	63.55	63.56	**63.77**	50.88
Blur_LEV-2	42.78	42.18	**44.56**	30.50
DegChar_LEV-1	57.42	**57.89**	56.33	47.83
DegChar_LEV-2	**51.22**	50.98	50.78	39.16
PhantChar_LEV-1	72.23	**73.66**	73.18	67.12
PhantChar_LEV-2	70.12	**72.99**	72.97	64.15
LEV-MIX	64.33	64.17	**64.88**	53.78

Spanish	BLSTM-CRF	BLSTM-CNN	BLSTM-CRF-CNN	CoreNLP
Clean	85.31	85.09	**85.45**	75.82
LEV-0	85.11	84.25	**85.13**	74.44
Bleed_LEV-1	**84.08**	83.47	84.07	70.15
Bleed_LEV-2	**75.66**	74.99	75.12	68.77
Blur_LEV-1	68.77	66.14	**68.79**	62.41
Blur_LEV-2	60.12	56.73	**61.44**	51.32
DegChar_LEV-1	64.78	63.74	**64.93**	58.33
DegChar_LEV-2	63.01	62.09	**64.12**	52.67
PhantChar_LEV-1	77.12	74.59	**77.21**	68.99
PhantChar_LEV-2	67.77	74.15	**76.76**	67.37
LEV-MIX	72.75	71.17	**73.98**	61.14

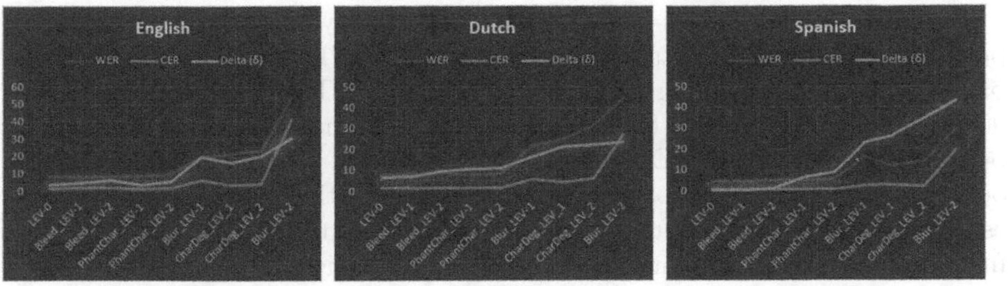

Fig. 3. NER F-score degradation according to OCR error rates

(NLF) [31]. The corpus contains around 450K tokens with more than 30K NEs. The NLF corpus distinguishes only two types of NEs: sPER and LOC. The CER and WER rates in the OCRed corpus are respectively 6.96% and 16.67% which is comparable to error rates given by the simulated bleed_LEV-2 degradation in the CoNLL corpora. Ruokolainen *et al.* [31] evaluated the NER annotation of the NLF corpus using CoreNLP. The system respectively yielded overall F1-scores of 71.92% and 78.79% for PER and LOC over OCRed texts which represents a loss of around 9–10% points compared to clean texts. This decrease is mostly equivalent to that obtained on the OCRed synthetic data using CoreNLP (see Table 4). With the same OCR error rates, NER F1-score on the English corpus presents a loss of 9.83% compared to results on clean corpus.

Using BLSTM-CRF, NER F1-score achieves 89.8% and 87.4% on clean and OCRed data respectively which represents a decrease rate of 2.4% points. The corresponding rates in the CoNLL corpora are between 4 and 8% points as shown in Fig. 3. Finnish results are slightly better than those obtained with synthetic data using BLSTM-CRF. This is not unexpected since the Finnish training set is larger than the CoNLL datasets. In addition the set of NEs in the NLF corpus is less refined than the set used in the CoNLL corpora. As we showed in Table 4, neural network based systems outperform CoreNLP, we have thus reported the same experiment on the NLF corpus using BLSTM-CRF. Results are shown in Table 5.

Table 5. Results on the NLF corpus

		LOC	PER	TOT
clean	P	93.39%	87.43%	90.82%
	R	91.86%	84.68%	88.74%
	F1	92.62%	86.03%	89.77%
OCRed	P	89.68%	83.31%	86.97%
	R	91.06%	83.54%	87.83%
	F1	90.36%	83.42%	87.40%

Results using the neural-network system are largely outperforming CoreNLP performances. For clean data, we obtained an overall F1-score of 89% (to be compared to 82%). More importantly, for OCRed data, the NER F1-score reaches 90.4% for PER and 83.4% for LOC, resulting in an improvement of around 11 points for both types of NEs. Despite the complexity of the NER task and the occurrence of several types of errors in the documents, the systems achieved interesting results. This proves that they can be used to distinguish named entities in degraded documents. Some word correction strategies, such as auto-encoders, language models, and so on, could be used to decrease the impact of OCR degradation on NER.

6 Conclusion

This paper is the most systematic evaluation of the impact of OCR errors on NER systems over multilingual datasets. We evaluated four machine-learning systems over three available datasets in English, Dutch and Spanish. We re-OCRed these collections and added four types of noises at two different levels in order to simulate various OCR output. All the noisy texts have been aligned with their corresponding ground truth in order to test the NER system through noisy data and to observe the evolution of their accuracy. This new dataset was made publicly available to the community. Such resources, combining OCRed data aligned with their clean version, are very useful for two reasons. First they can be used to train NLP algorithms over collections of documents that have been through an OCR process, as is notably the case of historical documents. Second, they can be used to estimate the impact of OCR over NLP applications and lead to recommendations, for instance on what application can reasonably be run over a document collection given its OCR quality.

We have studied the correlation between OCR error rates and NER accuracy using four effective systems. We showed that NER accuracy drops from 90% to 50% when the word error rate increases from 8% to 50%. These experiments were validated on a real OCR dataset in Finnish, where our systematic study allowed us to outperform the best-known results by $\sim$11% points.

This work showed that specific post OCR correction should be developed in order to improve NER results, and thus improve information access for end users.

Acknowledgements. This work has been supported by the European Union Horizon 2020 research and innovation programme under grant 770299 (NewsEye).

References

1. Bikel, D.M., Schwartz, R., Weischedel, R.M.: An algorithm that learns what's in a name. Mach. Learn. **34**(1–3), 211–231 (1999)

2. Chiron, G., Doucet, A., Coustaty, M., Visani, M., Moreux, J.P.: Impact of OCR errors on the use of digital libraries: towards a better access to information. In: Proceedings of the 17th ACM/IEEE Joint Conference on Digital Libraries, pp. 249–252. IEEE Press (2017)
3. Chiu, J.P., Nichols, E.: Named entity recognition with bidirectional lstm-cnns. arXiv preprint arXiv:1511.08308 (2015)
4. Collobert, R., Weston, J., Bottou, L., Karlen, M., Kavukcuoglu, K., Kuksa, P.: Natural language processing (almost) from scratch. J. Mach. Learn. Res. **12**, 2493–2537 (2011)
5. Croft, W., Harding, S., Taghva, K., Borsack, J.: An evaluation of information retrieval accuracy with simulated OCR output. In: Symposium on Document Analysis and Information Retrieval, pp. 115–126 (1994)
6. Erik, F., Sang, T.K.: Introduction to the CoNLL-2002 shared task: Language-independent named entity recognition. In: Proceedings of CoNLL-2002, pp. 155–158 (2002)
7. Favre, B., Béchet, F., Nocéra, P.: Robust named entity extraction from large spoken archives. In: Proceedings of the conference on Human Language Technology and Empirical Methods in Natural Language Processing, pp. 491–498. Association for Computational Linguistics (2005)
8. Finkel, J.R., Grenager, T., Manning, C.: Incorporating non-local information into information extraction systems by gibbs sampling. In: Proceedings of the 43rd Annual Meeting on Association for Computational Linguistics, pp. 363–370. Association for Computational Linguistics (2005)
9. Gali, K., Surana, H., Vaidya, A., Shishtla, P.M., Sharma, D.M.: Aggregating machine learning and rule based heuristics for named entity recognition. In: Proceedings of the IJCNLP-08 Workshop on Named Entity Recognition for South and South East Asian Languages (2008)
10. Gefen, A.: Les enjeux épistémologiques des humanités numériques. Socio-La nouvelle revue des sciences sociales, pp. 61–74 (2014)
11. Goldberg, Y., Levy, O.: word2vec explained: deriving mikolov et al'.s negative-sampling word-embedding method. arXiv preprint arXiv:1402.3722 (2014)
12. Grishman, R., Sundheim, B.: Message understanding conference-6: a brief history. In: The 16th International Conference on Computational Linguistics COLING 1996, vol. 1 (1996)
13. Hamdi, A., Jean-Caurant, A., Sidere, N., Coustaty, M., Doucet, A.: An analysis of the performance of named entity recognition over OCRED documents. In: 2019 ACM/IEEE Joint Conference on Digital Libraries (JCDL), pp. 333–334. IEEE (2019)
14. Holley, R.: How good can it get? analysing and improving OCR accuracy in largescale historic newspaper digitisation programs. D-Lib Magazine, **15**(3/4) (2009)
15. Jing, H., Lopresti, D., Shih, C.: Summarizing noisy documents. In: Proceedings of the Symposium on Document Image Understanding Technology, pp. 111–119 (2003)
16. Journet, N., Visani, M., Mansencal, B., Van-Cuong, K., Billy, A.: Doccreator: a new software for creating synthetic ground-truthed document images. J. Imag. **3**(4), 62 (2017)
17. Lample, G., Ballesteros, M., Subramanian, S., Kawakami, K., Dyer, C.: Neural architectures for named entity recognition. arXiv preprint arXiv:1603.01360 (2016)
18. Lopresti, D.: Optical character recognition errors and their effects on natural language processing. Int. J. Document Anal. Recogn. (IJDAR) **12**(3), 141–151 (2009)

19. Lund, W.B., Kennard, D.J., Ringger, E.K.: Combining multiple thresholding binarization values to improve OCR output. In: Document Recognition and Retrieval XX, vol. 8658, p. 86580R. International Society for Optics and Photonics (2013)
20. Ma, X., Hovy, E.: End-to-end sequence labeling via bi-directional LSTM-CNNS-CRF. arXiv preprint arXiv:1603.01354 (2016)
21. Miller, D., Boisen, S., Schwartz, R., Stone, R., Weischedel, R.: Named entity extraction from noisy input: speech and OCR. In: Proceedings of the Sixth Conference on Applied Natural Language Processing, pp. 316–324. Association for Computational Linguistics (2000)
22. Nadeau, D., Sekine, S.: A survey of named entity recognition and classification. Lingvisticae Investigationes **30**(1), 3–26 (2007)
23. Palmer, D.D., Ostendorf, M.: Improving information extraction by modeling errors in speech recognizer output. In: Proceedings of the First International Conference on Human Language Technology Research, pp. 1–5. Association for Computational Linguistics (2001)
24. Pennington, J., Socher, R., Manning, C.: Glove: global vectors for word representation. In: Proceedings of the 2014 Conference on Empirical Methods in Natural Language Processing (EMNLP), pp. 1532–1543 (2014)
25. Peters, M.E., Neumann, M., Iyyer, M., Gardner, M., Clark, C., Lee, K., Zettlemoyer, L.: Deep contextualized word representations. arXiv preprint arXiv:1802.05365 (2018)
26. Linhares Pontes, E., Hamdi, A., Sidere, N., Doucet, A.: Impact of OCR quality on named entity linking. In: Jatowt, A., Maeda, A., Syn, S.Y. (eds.) ICADL 2019. LNCS, vol. 11853, pp. 102–115. Springer, Cham (2019). https://doi.org/10.1007/978-3-030-34058-2_11
27. Ramshaw, L.A., Marcus, M.P.: Text chunking using transformation-based learning. In: Armstrong, S., Church, K., Isabelle, P., Manzi, S., Tzoukermann, E., Yarowsky, D. (eds.) Natural Language Processing Using Very Large Corpora, pp. 157–176. Springer, Dordrecht (1999) https://doi.org/10.1007/978-94-017-2390-9_10
28. Riedl, M., Padó, S.: A named entity recognition shootout for German. In: Proceedings of ACL, pp. 120–125. Melbourne, Australia (2018), http://aclweb.org/anthology/P18-2020.pdf
29. Ritter, A., Clark, S., Etzioni, O., et al.: Named entity recognition in tweets: an experimental study. In: Proceedings of the Conference on Empirical Methods in Natural Language Processing, pp. 1524–1534. Association for Computational Linguistics (2011)
30. Rodriquez, K.J., Bryant, M., Blanke, T., Luszczynska, M.: Comparison of named entity recognition tools for raw OCR text. In: KONVENS, pp. 410–414 (2012)
31. Ruokolainen, T., Kettunen, K.: À la recherche du nom perdu-searching for named entities with stanford ner in a finnish historical newspaper and journal collection. In: 13th IAPR International Workshop on Document Analysis Systems (2018)
32. van Strien, D., Beelen, K., Ardanuy, M.C., Hosseini, K., McGillivray, B., Colavizza, G.: Assessing the impact of OCR quality on downstream NLP tasks (2020)
33. Taghva, K., Borsack, J., Condit, A.: Effects of ocr errors on ranking and feedback using the vector space model. Inf. Process. Manage. **32**(3), 317–327 (1996)
34. Tjong Kim Sang, E.F., De Meulder, F.: Introduction to the CoNLL-2003 shared task: language-independent named entity recognition. In: Proceedings of the Seventh Conference on Natural Language Learning at HLT-NAACL 2003-vol. 4, pp. 142–147. Association for Computational Linguistics (2003)

35. Yalniz, I.Z., Manmatha, R.: A fast alignment scheme for automatic OCR evaluation of books. In: 2011 International Conference on Document Analysis and Recognition (ICDAR), pp. 754–758. IEEE (2011)
36. Yaser, A.O.: Effect of degraded input on statistical machine translation. In: 2005 Symposium on Document Image Understanding Technology, p. 103 (2005)
37. Zuccon, G., Nguyen, A.N., Bergheim, A., Wickman, S., Grayson, N.: The impact of OCR accuracy on automated cancer classification of pathology reports. In: HIC, pp. 250–256 (2012)

On the Persistence of Persistent Identifiers of the Scholarly Web

Martin Klein(✉) and Lyudmila Balakireva

Los Alamos National Laboratory, Los Alamos, NM 87545, USA
{mklein,ludab}@lanl.gov

Abstract. Scholarly resources, just like any other resources on the web, are subject to reference rot as they frequently disappear or significantly change over time. Digital Object Identifiers (DOIs) are commonplace to persistently identify scholarly resources and have become the de facto standard for citing them. We investigate the notion of persistence of DOIs by analyzing their resolution on the web. We derive confidence in the persistence of these identifiers in part from the assumption that dereferencing a DOI will consistently return the same response, regardless of which HTTP request method we use or from which network environment we send the requests. Our experiments show, however, that persistence, according to our interpretation, is not warranted. We find that scholarly content providers respond differently to varying request methods and network environments and even change their response to requests against the same DOI. In this paper we present the results of our quantitative analysis that is aimed at informing the scholarly communication community about this disconcerting lack of consistency.

Keywords: Digital object identifiers (DOIs) · HTTP resolution · Scholarly communication

1 Introduction

The web is a very dynamic medium where resources frequently are being created, deleted, and moved [2,5,6]. Scholars have realized that, due to this dynamic nature, reliably linking and citing scholarly web resources is not a trivial matter [13,14]. Persistent identifiers such as the Digital Object Identifier (DOI)[1] have been introduced to address this issue and have become the de facto standard to persistently identify scholarly resources on the web. The concept behind a DOI is that while the location of a resource on the web may change over time, its identifying DOI remains unchanged and, when dereferenced on the web, continues to resolve to the resource's current location. This concept is based on the underlying assumption that the resource's publisher updates the mapping between the

[1] https://www.doi.org/.

M. Hall et al. (Eds.): TPDL 2020, LNCS 12246, pp. 102–115, 2020.
https://doi.org/10.1007/978-3-030-54956-5_8

DOI and the resource's location if and when the location has changed. If this mapping is reliably maintained, DOIs indeed provide a more persistent way of linking and citing web resources.

While this system is not perfect [3] and we have previously shown that authors of scholarly articles often do not utilize DOIs where they should [17], DOIs have become an integral part of the scholarly communication landscape[2]. Our work is motivated by questions related to the consistency of resolving DOIs to scholarly content. From past experience crawling the scholarly web, for example in [9,12], we have noticed that publishers do not necessarily respond consistently to simple HTTP requests against DOIs. We have instead observed scenarios where their response changes depending on what HTTP client and method is used. If we can demonstrate at scale that this behavior is common place in the scholarly communication landscape, it would raise significant concerns about the persistence of such identifiers for the scholarly web. In other words, we are driven by the question that if we can not trust that requests against the same DOI return the same result, how can we trust in the identifier's persistence?

In our previous study [10] we reported the outcome of our initial investigation into the notion of persistence of DOIs from the perspective of their behavior on the web. We found early indicators for scholarly publishers responding differently to different kinds of HTTP requests against the same DOI. In this paper we expand on our previous work by:

- re-executing the previous experiments with an improved technical setup,
- adding additional experiments from a different network environment,
- adding additional experiments with different access levels to scholarly content, and
- adding a comparison corpus to help interpret our findings and put them into perspective.

Adding these dimensions to our previous work and applying various different yet simple HTTP request methods with different clients to a large and arguably representative corpus of DOIs, we address the following research questions:

1. What differences in dereferencing DOIs can we detect and highlight?
2. In what way (if at all) do scholarly content providers' responses change depending on network environments?
3. How do observed inconsistencies compare to responses by web servers providing popular (non-scholarly) web content?
4. What effect do Open Access and non Open Access content providers have on the overall picture?
5. What is the effect of subscription levels to the observed inconsistencies?

These five research questions (RQs) aim at a quantitative analysis of the consistency of HTTP responses. We do not claim that such consistency is the only factor that contributes to persistence of scholarly resource identifiers. We argue,

2 https://data.crossref.org/reports/statusReport.html.

however, that without a reassuring level of consistency, our trust in the persistence of an identifier and its resolution to a resource's current location is significantly diminished.

In the remainder of this paper we will briefly highlight previous related work (Sect. 2), outline the experiments' setup (Sect. 3), and address our research questions (Sect. 4) before drawing our conclusions (Sect. 5).

2 Related Work

DOIs are the de facto standard for identifying scholarly resources on the web, supported by traditional scholarly publishers as well as repository platforms such as Figshare and Zenodo, for example. When crawling the scholarly web for the purpose of aggregation, analysis, or archiving, DOIs are therefore often the starting point to access resources of interest. The use of DOIs for references in scholarly articles, however, is not as wide-spread as it should be. In previous work [17], we have presented evidence that authors often use the URL of a resource's landing page rather than its DOI when citing the resource. This situation is undesirable as it requires unnecessary deduplication for efforts such as metrics analysis or crawling. These findings were confirmed in a large scale study by Thompson and Jian [16] based on two samples of the web taken from Common Crawl[3] datasets. The authors were motivated to quantify the use of HTTP DOIs versus URLs of landing pages in these two samples generated from two snapshots in time. They found more than 5 million actionable HTTP DOIs in the first dataset from 2014 and about 10% of them in the second dataset from 2017 but identified as the corresponding landing page URL, not the DOI. It is worth noting that not all resources referenced in scholarly articles have a DOI assigned to them and are therefore subject to typical link rot scenarios on the web. In large-scale studies, we have previously investigated and quantified the "reference rot" phenomenon in scholarly communication [9,12] focusing on "web at large" resources that do not have an identifying DOI.

Any large-scale analysis of the persistence of scholarly resources requires machine access as human evaluations typically do not scale. Hence, making web servers that serve (scholarly) content more friendly to machines has been the focus of previous efforts by the digital library community with the agreement that providing accurate and machine-readable metadata is a core requirement [4,15]. To support these efforts, recently standardized frameworks are designed to help machines synchronize metadata and content between scholarly platforms and repositories [11].

The study by Alam et al. [1] is related to ours in the way that the authors investigate the support of various HTTP request methods by web servers serving popular web pages. The authors issue OPTIONS requests and analyze the values of the "Allow" response header to evaluate which HTTP methods are supported by a web server. The authors conclude that a sizable number of web servers inaccurately report supported HTTP request methods.

[3] http://commoncrawl.org/.

3 Experimental Setup

3.1 Dataset Generation

To the best of our knowledge, no dataset of DOIs that identify content representative of the diverse scholarly web is available to researchers. Part of the problem is the scale and diversity of the publishing industry landscape but also the fact that the Science, Technology, and Medicine (STM) market is dominated by a few large publishers [8]. We therefore reuse the dataset generated for our previous work [10] that consists of 10,000 randomly sampled DOIs from a set of more than 93 million DOIs crawled by the Internet Archive. We refer to [10] for a detailed description of the data gathering process, an analysis of the composition of the dataset, and a discussion of why we consider this dataset to be representative of the scholarly landscape. In addition, to be able to put our findings from the DOI-based dataset in perspective, we created a dataset of the top 10,000 most popular URIs on the web as extracted from the freely available "Majestic Million" index[4] on November 14, 2019.

3.2 HTTP Requests, Clients, and Environments

HTTP transactions on the web consists of a client request and a server response. As detailed in RFC 7231 [7] requests contain a request method and request headers and responses contain corresponding response headers. GET and HEAD are two of the most common HTTP request methods (also detailed in RFC 7231). The main difference between the two methods is that upon receiving a client request with the HEAD method, a server only responds with its response headers but does not return a content body to the client. Upon receiving a client request with the GET method, on the other hand, a server responds by sending the representation of the resource in the response body in addition to the response headers.

It is important to note that, according to RFC 7231, we should expect a server to send the same headers in response to requests against the same resource, regardless whether the request is of type HEAD or GET. RFC 7231 states: "The server SHOULD send the same header fields in response to a HEAD request as it would have sent if the request had been a GET...".

To address our research questions outlined earlier, we utilize the same four methods described in [10] to send HTTP requests:

- **HEAD**, a HEAD request with cURL[5]
- **GET**, a simple GET request with cURL

[4] https://blog.majestic.com/development/majestic-million-csv-daily/.
[5] A popular lightweight HTTP client for the command line interface https://curl.haxx.se/.

- **GET+** a GET request that includes typical browsing parameters such as user agent and accepted cookies with cURL
- **Chrome**, a GET request with Chrome[6]

We sent these four requests against the HTTPS-actionable format of a DOI, meaning the form of `https://doi.org/<DOI>`. This is an important difference to our previous work ([10]) where we did not adhere to the format recommended by the DOI Handbook[7]. For the first set of experiments and to address RQ1, we send these four HTTP requests against each of the 10,000 DOIs from an Amazon Web Services (AWS) virtual machine located at the U.S. East Coast. The clients sending the requests are therefore not affiliated with our home institution's network. Going forward, we refer to this external setup as the DOI_{ext} corpus. In addressing RQ2, we anticipate possible discrepancies in HTTP responses from servers depending on the network from which the request is sent. Hence, for the second set of experiments, we send the same four requests to the same 10,000 DOIs from a machine hosted within our institution's network. Given that the machine's IP address falls into a range that conveys certain institutional subscription and licensing levels to scholarly publishers, this internal setup, which we refer to going forward as DOI_{int}, should help surface possible differences. To address RQ3 we compare our findings to responses from servers providing non-scholarly content by sending the same four requests against each of the 10,000 URIs from our dataset of popular websites. From here on, we refer to this corpus as the Web dataset.

4 Experimental Results

In this section we report our observations when dereferencing HTTPS-actionable DOIs with our four methods. Each method automatically follows HTTP redirects and records information about each link in the redirect chain. For example, a HEAD request against https://doi.org/10.1007/978-3-030-30760-8_15 results in a redirect chain consisting of the following links:

1. http://link.springer.com/10.1007/978-3-030-30760-8_15
2. https://link.springer.com/10.1007/978-3-030-30760-8_15
3. https://link.springer.com/chapter/10.1007%2F978-3-030-30760-8_15

with the last one showing the 200 *OK* response code. Note that only the first redirect comes from the server at doi.org (operated by the Corporation for National Research Initiatives (CNRI)[8]) and it points to the appropriate location on the publisher's end. All consecutive redirects remain in the same domain and, unlike the HTTP DOI, are controlled by the publisher.

It is important to note that all four methods are sent with the default timeout of 30 s, meaning the request times out if a server does not respond within this time frame. In addition, all methods are configured to follow a maximum of 20 redirects.

[6] Web browser controlled via the Selenium WebDriver https://selenium.dev/projects/.
[7] https://www.doi.org/doi_handbook/3_Resolution.html.
[8] https://www.cnri.reston.va.us/.

4.1 Final Response Codes

The first aspect of consistency, as projected onto our notion of persistence, we investigate is the response code of the last accessible link in the redirect chain when dereferencing DOIs (or URIs in the case of the *Web* corpus). Intuitively and informed by our understanding of persistence, we expect DOIs as persistent identifiers return the same response code to all issued requests, regardless of the request method used.

Table 1 summarizes the response codes for our three different corpora and the four different methods for each of them. The frequency of response codes (in percent) is clustered into 200-, 300-, 400-, and 500-level columns, plus an error column. The latter represents requests that timed out and did not return any response or response code. The first main observation from Table 1 is that the ratio of response codes for all four methods and across all three corpora is inconsistent. Even within individual corpora, we notice significant differences. For example, for the DOI_{ext} corpus we see 40% and 24% of GET and GET+ requests respectively end in 300-level response codes. We consider this number particularly high as the vast majority of these responses have a 302 *Found* status code that indicates further action needs to be taken by the client to fulfill the request, for example, send a follow-up request against the URI provided in the Location header field (see RFC 7231 [7]). In other words, no HTTP request (and redirect chain) should end with such a response code. A different reason for these observations could be a server responding with too many consecutive 300-level responses, causing the client to stop making follow-up requests (the default for our methods was 20 requests). However, we only recorded this behavior a few times and it therefore can not explain these high numbers. Another observation for the same corpus is the fairly high ratios for 400-level responses, particularly for HEAD requests. The fact that this number (12.58%) is two to three times as high as for the other three requests for the same corpus is noteworthy.

Except for HEAD requests, the ratio of 300-level responses decreased for the DOI_{int} corpus. We do see more 301 *Moved Permanently* responses in this corpus compared to DOI_{ext} but given that this fact should not have a different impact for individual request methods, we can only speculate why the ratio for HEAD requests went up. The ratio of 400-level responses is not insignificant in both corpora and it is worth noting that this category is dominated by the 403 response code, which means a server indicates to a client that access to the requested URI is forbidden. This response would make sense for requests to resources for which we do not have institutional subscription rights or licensing agreements, for example, but then we would expect to see these numbers being consistent for all methods.

As a comparison, the requests for the *Web* corpus seem to mostly result in one of two columns. Either they return a 200-level response or an error (no response code at all). The ratios in the error category are particularly high for the GET and the GET+ methods at around 34%.

Table 1. Percentage of final HTTP response codes, aggregated into five levels, following the DOI/URI redirect chain

Corpus	Method	2xx	3xx	4xx	5xx	Err
DOI_{ext}	HEAD	75.4	9.93	12.58	2.09	0
	GET	53.07	40.49	6.06	0.06	0.32
	GET+	70.71	24.34	4.58	0.05	0.32
	Chrome	87.79	6.17	5.94	0.1	0
DOI_{int}	HEAD	70.64	16.98	8.85	3.52	0.01
	GET	76.13	16.66	5.71	1.48	0.02
	GET+	80.29	15.26	4.04	0.41	0
	Chrome	90.2	5.95	3.57	0.18	0.1
Web	HEAD	70.69	4.86	5.63	1.32	17.5
	GET	56.71	5.35	2.78	0.6	34.56
	GET+	57.43	5.54	1.87	0.52	34.64
	Chrome	74.8	4.56	2.66	0.65	17.33

4.2 Redirect Chain

The next aspect of persistence in our investigation is the overall length of the redirect chain when dereferencing DOIs. Intuitively speaking, we expect the chain length to be the same for persistent identifiers, regardless of the HTTP method used. Figure 1 shows histograms of chain lengths distinguished by corpora and request methods. Note that the reported lengths are independent of the final response code reported earlier and that DOIs/URIs that resulted in errors are excluded from this analysis. Figure 1a shows the observed chain lengths for the DOI_{ext} corpus. We note that the distribution of chain lengths is not equal among request methods. The GET and GET+ methods, for example, are much more strongly represented at length one than either of the other methods. Generally speaking however, lengths two, three, and four represent the majority for the requests in the DOI_{ext} corpus.

The same holds true for the DOI_{int} corpus (shown in Fig. 1b) but we notice the frequency of length one has almost disappeared. When comparing the two corpora, we observe that the Chrome method shows fairly consistent frequencies of redirect chain length and most often results in length three.

Figure 1c offers a comparison by showing the redirect chain lengths of dereferencing URIs from the Web corpus. We see a significant shift to shorter redirect chains with the majority being of length one or two. While we recorded chains of length four and beyond, these occurrences were much less frequent. The HEAD and Chrome methods appear to be well-aligned for all observed lengths.

It is worth mentioning that we recorded chain length beyond our set maximum of 20 (indicated as 21 in the figures). We question the reasoning for such responses but leave a closer analysis of these extensive redirect chains for future work.

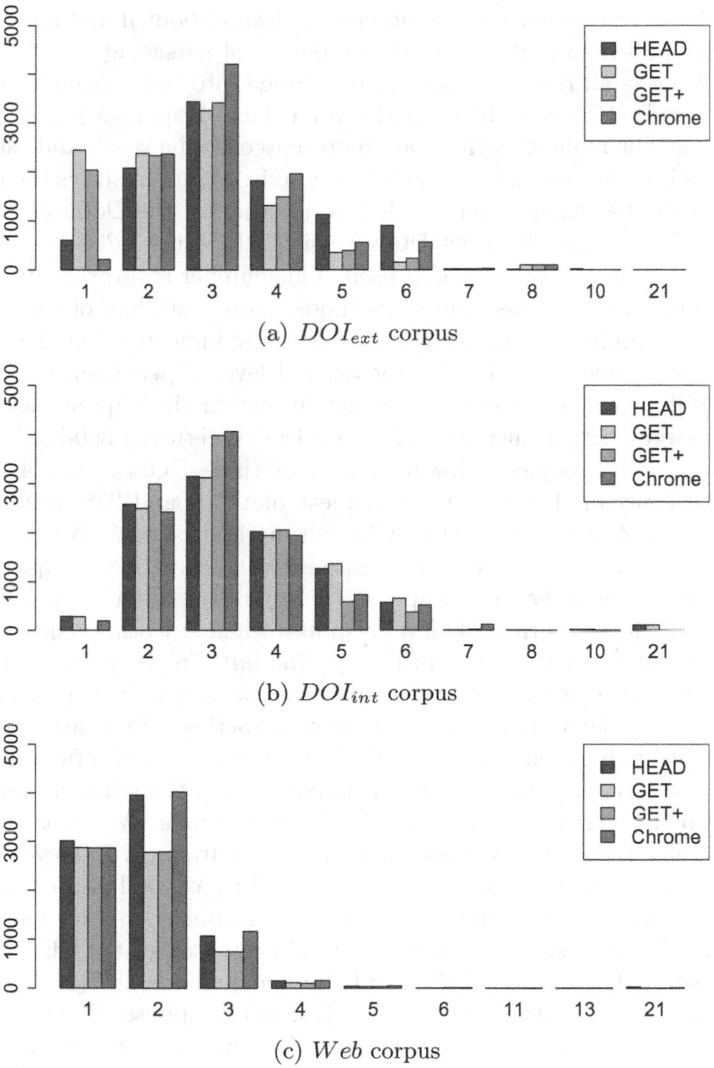

Fig. 1. Frequency (y-axes) of number of total links in DOI/URI redirect chains (x-axes) per corpus.

4.3 Changing Response Codes

The third aspect of our investigation centers around the question whether HTTP response codes change, depending on what HTTP request method is used. We have shown in Sect. 4.1 that dereferencing DOIs does not result in the same response codes but varies depending on what request method we used. In this section we analyze the nature of response code change per DOI and request method. This investigation aims at providing clarity about if and how response codes change and the ramifications for the notion of persistence.

Figure 2 shows all response codes again binned into 200- (green), 300- (light gray), 400- (red), 500-level (blue), and error (black) responses per DOI for all three corpora. The request methods are represented on the x-axis and each of the 10,000 DOIs is displayed on the (unlabeled) y-axis. Figure 2a shows the response codes and their changes from one method to another for the DOI_{ext} corpus. We see that merely 48.3% of all 10,000 DOIs consistently return a 200-level response, regardless of which request method is used. This number is surprisingly low. The fact that, consistently across request methods, more than half of our DOIs fail to successfully resolve to a target resource strongly indicates that the scholarly communication landscape is lacking the desired level of persistence. We further see major differences in response codes depending on the request method. For example, a large portion, just over 40%, of all DOIs return a 300-level response for the simple GET request. However, 12% of these DOIs return a 200-level response with any of the other three request methods and 25% return a 200-level response if only the HEAD or Chrome method is used. We further find 13% of DOIs resulting in a 400-level response with the HEAD request but of these only 30% return the same response for any of the other request methods. In fact, 25% of them return a 200-level response when any other request method is used. Without further analysis of the specific links in the redirect chain and their content, which we leave for future work, we can only hypothesize that web servers of scholarly content take the request method into consideration and respond accordingly when resolving DOIs. However, this lack of consistency is worrisome for everyone concerned about persistence of the scholarly record.

Figure 2b shows our findings from the DOI_{int} corpus. We see the numbers improved, most noticeably with 66.9% of DOIs returning a 200-level response across the board. However, we still find almost 14% of DOIs returning a 300-level response for the first three and a 200-level response only for our Chrome method. We also see a similar ratio of 400-level responses for the HEAD method that decreases with the GET, GET+, and Chrome methods, similar to our observation for the DOI_{ext} corpus. The ratio of 500-level responses slightly increased from 2% in the previous corpus to 3.5% here. However, here too the majority of those DOIs return a different response code when methods other than HEAD are used. The observations from Fig. 2b show that even requests sent from within a research institution network are treated differently by scholarly content providers and, depending on the request method used, the level of consistency suffers.

Figure 2c shows the numbers for the Web corpus and therefore offers a comparative picture to our above findings. For the Web corpus we see 53.6% of all 10,000 URIs returning a 200-level response code, which is ahead of the DOI_{ext} but well below the DOI_{int} corpus numbers. We further see 17% of URIs returning an error, regardless of the request. We can only speculate about the reasons for this high number of unsuccessful requests but our best guess is that web servers of these popular websites have sophisticated methods in place that detect HTTP requests sent from machines and simply do not send a response when detected.

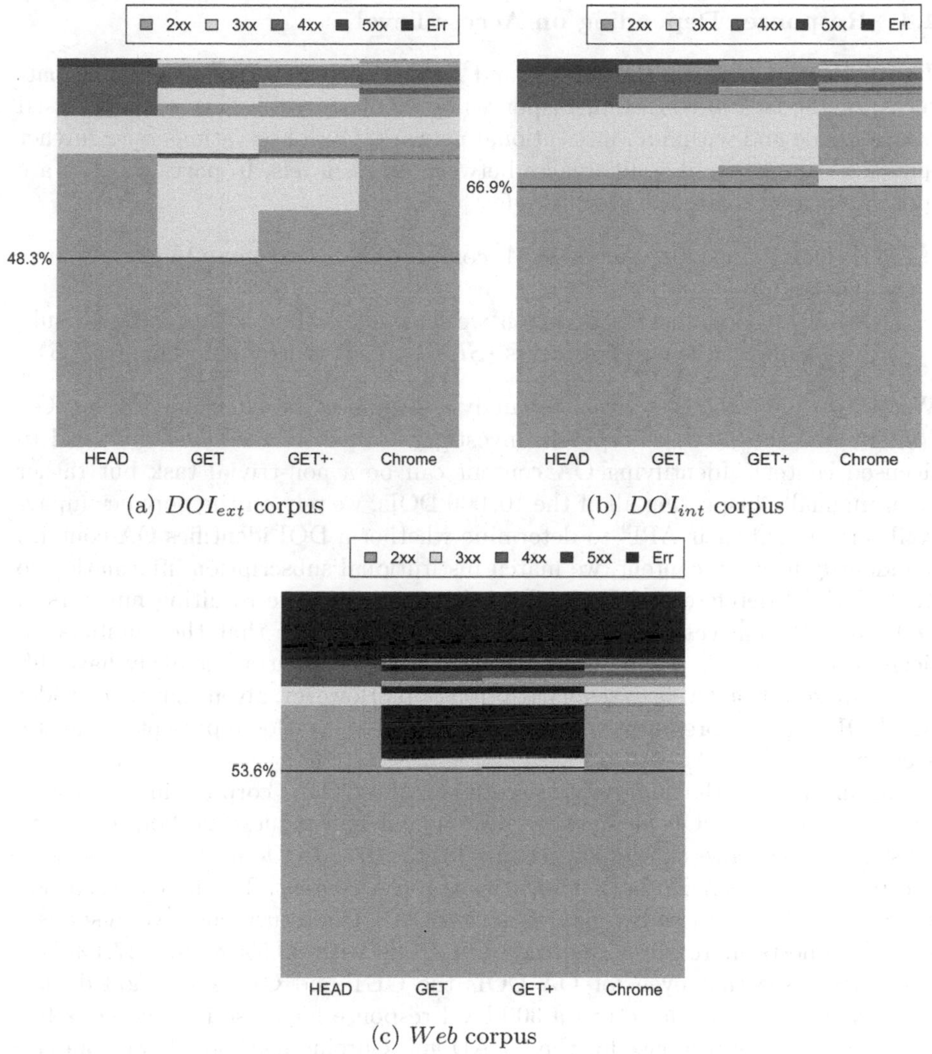

Fig. 2. Final HTTP response codes by DOI/URI per corpus (Color figure online)

This even holds true for our Chrome method, which closely resembles a human browsing the web. Not unlike what we have seen in the DOI_{ext} corpus the Web corpus shows 15% of requests not being successful with the GET and GET+ methods but being successful (200-level response) with the HEAD and Chrome methods. These findings indicate that popular but not necessarily scholarly content providers also send responses depending on the request method. However, we see fewer 300-, 400-, and 500-level responses for this corpus.

4.4 Responses Depending on Access Level

The distinction between the DOI_{ext} and DOI_{int} corpora serves to highlight patterns for the lack of consistent responses by scholarly publishers when accessed from outside and within an institutional network. Our observations raise further questions about possible differences between access levels. In particular, we are motivated to evaluate the responses for:

- DOIs identifying Open Access (OA) content versus their non-OA counterparts (nOA) and
- DOIs identifying content to which we have access due to institutional subscription and licensing agreements (SUB) versus those we do not ($nSUB$).

We utilize our DOI_{ext} corpus to analyze responses of DOIs identifying OA content and the DOI_{int} corpus to investigate responses for DOIs that lead to licensed content. Identifying OA content can be a non-trivial task but rather than manually inspecting all of the 10,000 DOIs, we rely on the popular unpaywall service and their API[9] to determine whether a DOI identifies OA content. To identify licensed content, we match institutional subscription information to base URIs of dereferenced DOIs. Table 2 summarizes the resulting numbers of DOIs and their access levels in our corpora. We realize that the numbers for licensed content may not be representative as other institutions likely have different subscription levels to scholarly publishers. However, given that we consider our DOI corpus representative, we are confident the ratios represent a realistic scenario.

Figure 3 shows the final response codes for the DOI_{ext} corpus, similar in style to Fig. 2, with the DOIs along the y-axis and our four request methods on the x-axis. Figure 3a shows the response codes for the 973 OA DOIs and Fig. 3b shows the remaining 9,027 DOIs that identify non-OA content. The first observation we can make from these two figures is that OA DOIs return 200-level responses for all requests more often than non-OA DOIs with 59.5% versus 47.1%. We can further see that even for OA DOIs the GET and GET+ method do not work well. 26% of DOIs return a 300-level response for these two methods but return a 200-level response for the HEAD and Chrome methods. If we compare Fig. 3 with 2a we can see a clear resemblance between Fig. 2a, the figure for the overall corpus, and Fig. 3b, the figure for non-OA DOIs. Given the fact that we have many more non-OA DOIs this may not be all that surprising but it is worth noting that by far the vast majority of 400- and 500-level responses come from non-OA DOIs. Given our dataset, this observation indicates that OA content providers show more consistency across the board compared to non-OA providers and their positive effect to the overall picture (Fig. 2a) is visible. A larger scale analysis of OA versus non-OA content providers is needed, however, to more reliably underline this observation. We leave such effort for future work.

[9] https://unpaywall.org/products/api.

Table 2. Distribution of DOIs leading to *OA* and *nOA* resources as well as to *SUB* and *nSUB* content in our dataset.

	OA	nOA		SUB	nSUB
DOI_{ext}	973	9,027	DOI_{int}	1,266	8,734

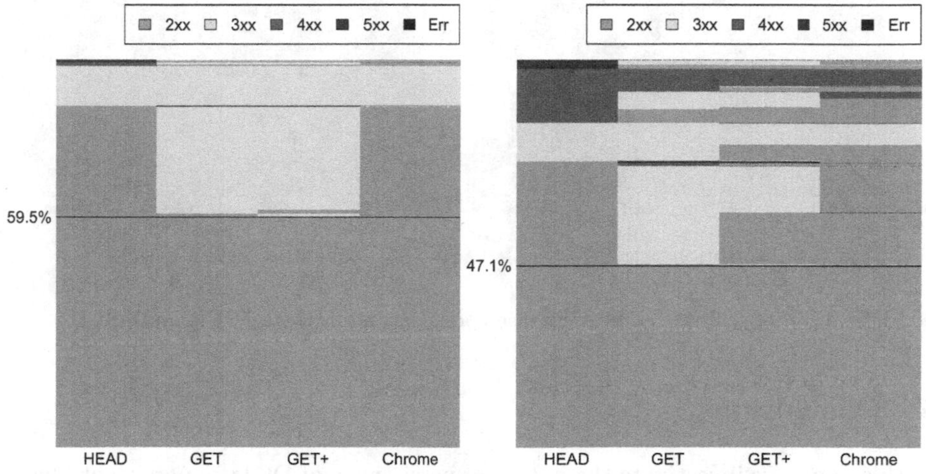

(a) OA articles (b) Non-OA articles

Fig. 3. DOI_{ext} final HTTP response codes distinguished by OA and nOA

Figure 4 shows the final response codes for DOIs that identify institutionally licensed content (Fig. 4a) and content not licensed by our institution (Fig. 4b). We see a much higher ratio of DOIs returning 200-level responses for all request methods for licensed content (84.3%) compared to not licensed content (64.4%). We also notice fewer 300-, 400-, and 500-level responses for licensed content and the Chrome method being almost perfect in returning 200-level responses (99%). When we again compare Fig. 4 to the overall picture for this corpus shown in Fig. 2b, we notice a strong resemblance between Figs. 4b and 2b. This leads us to conclude that providers, when serving licensed content, show more consistency and introduce fewer unsuccessful DOI resolutions.

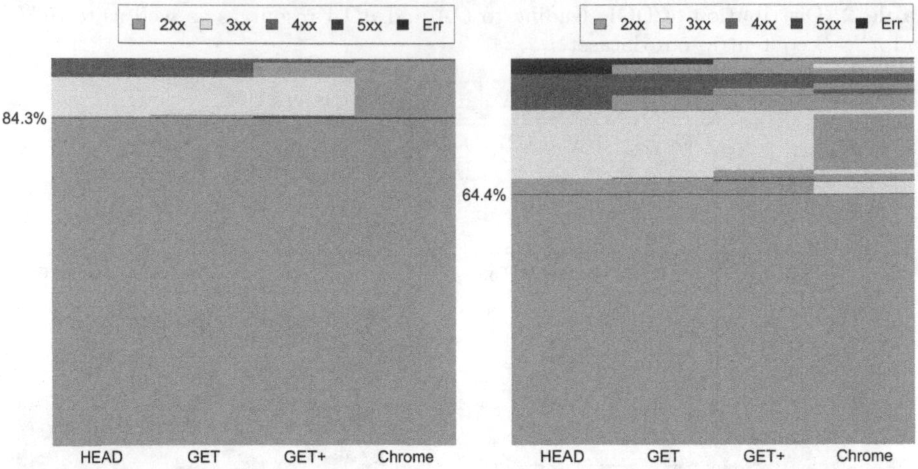

(a) Subscription articles (b) Non-subscription articles

Fig. 4. DOI_{int} final HTTP response codes distinguished by SUB and nSUB

5 Conclusions

In this paper we investigate the notion of persistence of DOIs as persistent identifiers from the perspective of their resolution on the web. Based on a previously generated corpus of DOIs and enhanced by an additional corpus of popular URIs, we present our results from dereferencing these resources with four very common but different HTTP request methods. We report on HTTP response codes, redirect chain length, and response code changes and highlight observed differences for requests originating from an external and internal network. We further analyze the effect of Open Access versus non-Open Access and licensed versus not licensed content. We expected the resolution of DOIs to be consistent but our findings do not show a consistent picture at all. More than half of all requests (51.7%) are unsuccessful from an external network compared to just over 33% from an institutional network. In addition, the success rate varies across request methods. We find that the method that most closely resembles the human browsing behavior (Chrome method) generally works best. We observed an alarming amount of changes in response code depending on the HTTP request method used. These findings provide strong indicators that scholarly content providers reply to DOI requests differently, depending on the request method, the originating network environment, and institutional subscription levels. Our scholarly record, to a large extend, relies on DOIs to persistently identify scholarly resources on the web. However, given our observed lack of consistency in DOI resolutions on the publishers' end, we raise serious concerns about the persistence of these persistent identifiers of the scholarly web.

References

1. Alam, S., Cartledge, C.L., Nelson, M.L.: Support for Various HTTP Methods on the Web (2014). http://arxiv.org/abs/1405.2330
2. Bar-Yossef, Z., Broder, A.Z., Kumar, R., Tomkins, A.: SIC transit gloria telae: towards an understanding of the web's decay. In: Proceedings of WWW 2004, pp. 328–337 (2004)
3. Bilder, G.: January 2015 DOI Outage: Followup Report (2015). https://www.crossref.org/blog/january-2015-doi-outage-followup-report/
4. Brandman, O., Cho, J., Garcia-Molina, H., Shivakumar, N.: Crawler-friendly web servers. SIGMETRICS Perform. Eval. Rev. **28**(2), 9–14 (2000). https://doi.org/10.1145/362883.362894
5. Cho, J., Garcia-Molina, H.: The evolution of the web and implications for an incremental crawler. In: Proceedings of VLDB 2000, pp. 200–209 (2000)
6. Cho, J., Garcia-Molina, H.: Estimating frequency of change. ACM Trans. Internet Technol. **3**, 256–290 (2003)
7. Fielding, R.T., Reschke, J.: Hypertext Transfer Protocol (HTTP/1.1): Semantics and Content (2014). https://tools.ietf.org/html/rfc7231
8. Johnson, R., Watkinson, A., Mabe, M.: The STM report - an overview of scientific and scholarly publishing. International Association of Scientific, Technical and Medical Publishers (2018). https://www.stm-assoc.org/2018_10_04_STM_Report_2018.pdf
9. Jones, S.M., Van de Sompel, H., Shankar, H., Klein, M., Tobin, R., Grover, C.: Scholarly context adrift: three out of four URI references lead to changed content. PLoS ONE **11**(12) e0171057 (2016). https://doi.org/10.1371/journal.pone.0167475
10. Klein, M., Balakireva, L., Shankar, H.: Who is Asking? Humans and Machines Experience a Different Scholarly Web (2019). https://doi.org/10.17605/OSF.IO/SMCY2
11. Klein, M., Sanderson, R., Van de Sompel, H., Warner, S., Haslhofer, B., Lagoze, C., Nelson, M.L.: A Technical framework for resource synchronization. D-Lib Magazine, **19**(1/2) (2013). https://doi.org/10.1045/january2013-klein
12. Klein, M., Van de Sompel, H., Sanderson, R., Shankar, H., Balakireva, L., Zhou, K., Tobin, R.: Scholarly context not found: one in five articles suffers from reference rot. PLoS ONE **9**(12), e115253 (2014). https://doi.org/10.1371/journal.pone.0115253
13. Lawrence, S., Pennock, D.M., Flake, G.W., Krovetz, R., Coetzee, F.M., Glover, E., Nielsen, F.A., Kruger, A., Giles, C.L.: Persistence of Web references in scientific research. Computer **34**(2), 26–31 (2001). https://doi.org/10.1109/2.901164
14. McCown, F., Chan, S., Nelson, M.L., Bollen, J.: The Availability and Persistence of Web References in D-Lib Magazine (2005). https://arxiv.org/abs/cs/0511077
15. Nelson, M.L., Smith, J.A., del Campo, I.G.: Efficient, automatic web resource harvesting. In: Proceedings of the 8th Annual ACM International Workshop on Web Information and Data Management, pp. 43–50. WIDM 2006 (2006). https://doi.org/10.1145/1183550.1183560
16. Thompson, H.S., Tong, J.: Can common crawl reliably track persistent identifier (PID) use over time? (2018). http://arxiv.org/abs/1802.01424
17. Van de Sompel, H., Klein, M., Jones, S.M.: Persistent URIS must be used to be persistent. In: Proceedings of WWW 2016, pp. 119–120 (2016). https://doi.org/10.1145/2872518.2889352

Ontology Design

Ontology Design for Pharmaceutical Research Outcomes

Zeynep Say[1(✉)], Said Fathalla[1,2], Sahar Vahdati[1,3], Jens Lehmann[1,4], and Sören Auer[5]

[1] Smart Data Analytics (SDA), University of Bonn, Bonn, Germany
s6zesayy@uni-bonn.de, {fathalla,jens.lehmann}@cs.uni-bonn.de
[2] Faculty of Science, University of Alexandria, Alexandria, Egypt
[3] Department of Computer Science, University of Oxford, Oxford, UK
sahar.vahdati@cs.ox.ac.uk
[4] Fraunhofer IAIS, Dresden, Germany
jens.lehmann@iais.fraunhofer.de
[5] TIB Leibniz Information Center for Science and Technology, Hannover, Germany
soeren.auer@tib.eu

Abstract. The network of scholarly publishing involves generating and exchanging ideas, certifying research, publishing in order to disseminate findings, and preserving outputs. Despite enormous efforts in providing support for each of those steps in scholarly communication, identifying knowledge fragments is still a big challenge. This is due to the heterogeneous nature of the scholarly data and the current paradigm of distribution by publishing (mostly document-based) over journal articles, numerous repositories, and libraries. Therefore, transforming this paradigm to knowledge-based representation is expected to reform the knowledge sharing in the scholarly world. Although many movements have been initiated in recent years, non-technical scientific communities suffer from transforming document-based publishing to knowledge-based publishing. In this paper, we present a model (PharmSci) for scholarly publishing in the pharmaceutical research domain with the goal of facilitating knowledge discovery through effective ontology-based data integration. PharmSci provides machine-interpretable information to the knowledge discovery process. The principles and guidelines of the ontological engineering have been followed. Reasoning-based techniques are also presented in the design of the ontology to improve the quality of targeted tasks for data integration. The developed ontology is evaluated with a validation process and also a quality verification method.

Keywords: Semantic web · Linked data · OWL Ontologies · Scholarly communication · Pharmaceutical research

1 Introduction

The expansion in the use of digital technologies has enabled recent developments in academia and consequently has shifted the way that scientists performing

M. Hall et al. (Eds.): TPDL 2020, LNCS 12246, pp. 119–132, 2020.
https://doi.org/10.1007/978-3-030-54956-5_9

research. Figure 1 presents the publication output percentages, grouped by field, in the world according to the National Science Foundation's (NSF) statistics. It shows that, in recent years, the medical and life science domains produced more publication output than other disciplines of science. Health research disciplines need advances in current big data management approaches [30], since there is a lack of fully Findable, Accessible, Interoperable, and Reusable (FAIR) [33] data resources in the health science domain, especially in pharmaceutical research. Pharmaceutical research has many rich and extensively available sources. However, searching and gaining insights from those resources is not an easy task for a pharmaceutical scientist. While structured and well-designed data is easier to be handled by human and also machines, research communities still lack support in providing facilities to produce structured knowledge. Thus, there is a need for developing such knowledge structure for pharmaceutical research data aiming at tackling these problems. The goal of Semantic Web is to structure and integrate unstructured data on the Web and transform this data into machine-readable formats [2].

In this paper, we propose an ontology (PharmSci) for modeling pharmaceutical research data. PharmSci ontology supports pharmaceutical research community by structuring data in order to make it easier to access, analysis, curate, and integrate from documented research towards providing services and unveiling hidden knowledge [28]. This work targets to answer research questions: *How can pharmaceutical research outcomes be supported with a machine-readable and interoperable domain model?* and *How can we increase the reusability and accessibility of pharmaceutical research data more effectively?* Our work helps researchers to find out reliable reference materials, sufficient details of experiments or procedures, and re-investigate experiment results. This work focuses on solving the challenges of large-scale scholarly data and maximize its usefulness. We followed best practices that provide a representation of scientific knowledge to enable interoperability and the principles of Methontology [13] to develop the ontology. The ontology coverage is defined with text analysis methods. Ontology reasoning techniques are presented to derive new facts. The developed ontology is evaluated with validation and verification methods. (PharmSci) is one of the Science Knowledge Graph Ontologies (SKGO) [9] Suite ontologies. The documentation of PharmSci can be found via its Persistent Uniform Resource Locators (https://w3id.org/skgo/pharmsci#) and its prefix has been registered at https://prefix.cc under the open CC-BY 3.0 license. RDF serializations can be found on SKGO's GitHub repository[1].

The remainder of the paper is organized as follows: In Sect. 2, the methodology and data retrieval technique are presented. The development in Sect. 3 presents the reuse of best practices and the developed conceptual model. Section 4 describes the evaluation with validation and verification methods. Related work is presented in Sect. 5 for life science and the scholarly domain. Section 6 provides the conclusion and directions for future research work.

[1] https://github.com/saidfathalla/Science-knowledge-graph-ontologies.

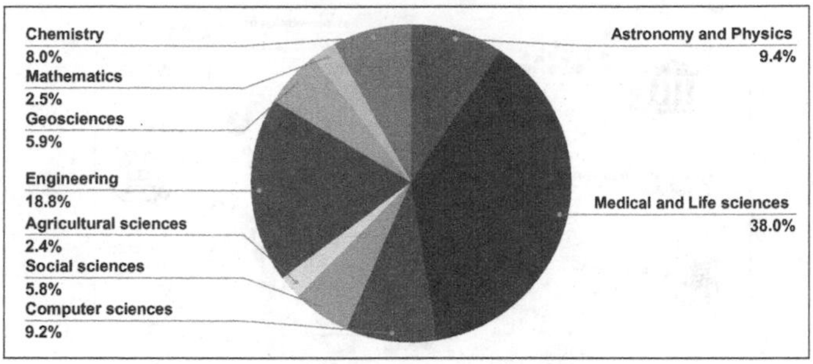

Fig. 1. Scientific publication output percentages by field in the world for the year 2017. (Source: National Science Foundation's (NSF) statistics [32])

2 Methodology

Knowledge Graphs bring enormous opportunities for improving the modern techniques of knowledge discovery. The use of Knowledge Graphs is on the rise due to they offer "smart data" which can be effortlessly understood by Artificial Intelligence (AI) technologies. The integration of Knowledge Graphs is a challenging task, and thereby ontologies are employed to build them since they formally represent concepts and their relations. The goal of PharmSci ontology is to respond to issues of a researcher by interlinking and sharing knowledge of a pharmaceutical research process. We followed the rules and principles of Methontology [13], which is an ontology development method to create domain models. The ontology development lifecycle composes development and supporting activities: specification, conceptualization, development, knowledge acquisition, and evaluation. In the specification phase, we define the domain, data coverage, and tools and techniques for the development of PharmSci. Knowledge acquisition and conceptualization are explained as follows.

Knowledge Acquisition. The necessary data to create the model can be revealed using text analysis techniques, non-structured or formal interviews with experts, or information acquisition tools. We use text analysis as a knowledge acquisition technique. A corpus[2] is defined with the topic 'multidrug resistance and ABC transporters in cancer'. 200 articles are chosen from pharmaceutical journals in Google Scholar[3] and ScienceDirect[4] related to corpus topic. We reduced 200 articles to 25 articles by means of a systematic review. We started to choose the most cited articles and eliminate articles that do not include clinical research. Then, we manually analyzed the most cited clinical research papers if they cover experimental research. Thus, clinical research papers with experimental research and the highest citation are chosen. First, we identify the common structures in the text. For example, the main parts of the research paper: the objective of the study, the main subjects and subtopics, and the study results.

[2] https://github.com/ZeynepSay/PharmSci/tree/master/CorpusData.
[3] https://scholar.google.com/.
[4] https://www.sciencedirect.com/.

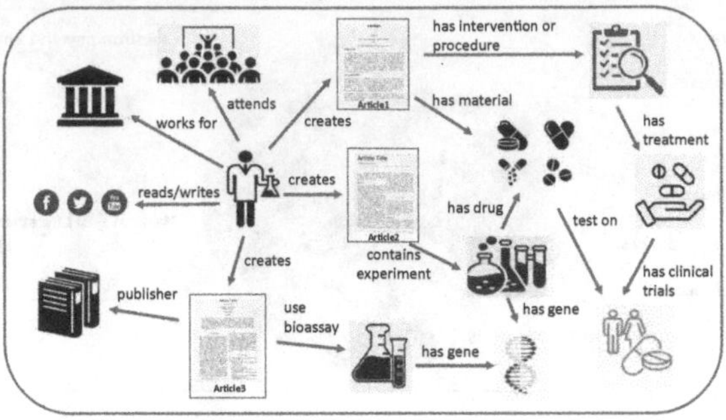

Fig. 2. A knowledge graph of the pharmaceutical research process. The content of the articles created by a scientist is transformed into entities and related to other entities with named relationships in a knowledge graph.

Afterward, we identify the most likely sentence patterns in the article by analyzing its content. For example, *"KB-8-5, which is three times as resistant to doxorubicin"* [15] sentence in the article, is transformed into "*cell line A resistant to drug B*". These patterns help us to shape the relations between concepts. Tables, graphs, and figures in articles are analyzed for ascertaining the values of the concept attributes and for identifying certain data regularities. Figure 2 illustrates how a pharmaceutical scientist investigatws the genes involved in multidrug resistance in lung cancer. It shows a knowledge graph of how the publication and research data on the Web can be linked and transformed into a structured domain model.
Conceptualization. The conceptual model is designed by organizing and structuring acquired knowledge and converts the informal view of a domain into a semiformal representation by using external representations from external schemas or terminologies. Besides, it includes the analysis of existing data models or ontologies from repositories and the determination of missing classes and properties for the successful formalization of the domain. We created a complete Glossary of Terms as a first thing for the pharmaceutical research domain. All classes and properties gathered in PharmSci glossary of terms to specify usable domain knowledge and its definitions. Figure 3 shows some of the captured classes and instances of the respective classes from pharmaceutical articles.

3 Development

FAIR Principles [33] guide us to increase the value of digital publishing by improving the infrastructure of scientific data. Our aim is to establish an interoperable system by reusing existing best practices. The result of the development is the ontology codified in a formal language. PharmSci is expressed in a W3C standard Web Ontology Language (OWL)[5] and developed by using Protégé

[5] https://www.w3.org/TR/owl2-overview/.

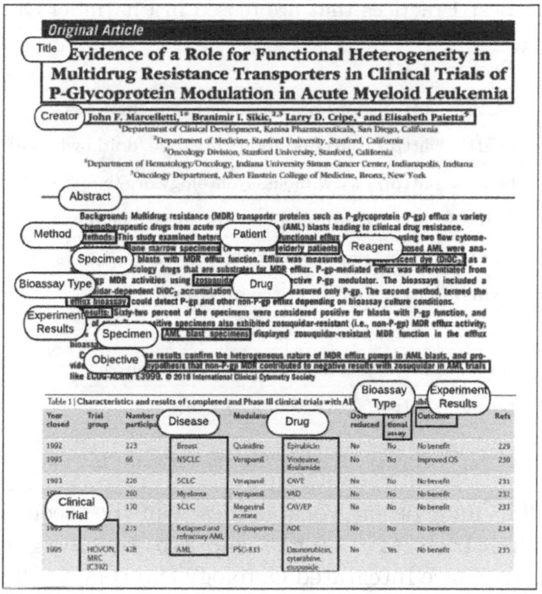

Fig. 3. Captured Entities of PharmSci from scientific publications.

v5.5.0 [23]. Classes are modeled to represent publication, research activity, clinical study (e.g., clinical trial), material (e.g., reagent), method (e.g., assay), patient, disease, specimen, and informational entities (e.g., objective). Figure 4 represents the main classes, object and data properties, and example instances of PharmSci Ontology. For example, a specific cell line or reagent name used in a particular study is represented as instances of classes in PharmSci ontology.

3.1 Reuse of Best Practices

In this phase, we consider integrating definitions from already existing semantic models instead of defining them from scratch. We use repositories and open libraries to find terms whose semantic and implementation are coherent with the terms identified in our conceptualization. The repositories and open libraries that we used are Bioportal[6], OntoBee[7], OBOFoundry[8] and Linked Open Vocabularies (LOV)[9] for finding terms in existing ontologies. Table 1 shows the prefixIRI and URL of all reused semantic models in this work.

PharmSci follows the National Cancer Institute (NCI) Thesaurus [16] for reusing classes such as `Method(NCIT:C71460)`, `Clinical Study(NCIT:C15206)`, `Material(NCIT:C48187)`, and `Clinical Trial(NCIT:C71104)`. Integrated

---

[6] https://bioportal.bioontology.org/.
[7] http://www.ontobee.org/.
[8] http://www.obofoundry.org/.
[9] https://lov.linkeddata.es/dataset/lov/.

Table 1. Best Practices that are reused in PharmSci Ontology

Prefix	URL
NCIT	http://purl.obolibrary.org/obo/ncit.owl
DOID	http://purl.obolibrary.org/obo/doid.owl
bao	http://www.bioassayontology.org/bao#
CHEBI	http://purl.obolibrary.org/obo/chebi.owl
CLO	http://www.ebi.ac.uk/cellline/
terms1	http://ns.nature.com/terms/
foaf	http://xmlns.com/foaf/0.1/
sio	http://semanticscience.org/resource/
terms	https://www.dublincore.org/

entities from NCIT and other vocabularies can be seen in Fig. 4. `sio:Experiment`, `sio:Specimen`, `sio:sample`, and `sio:investigation` entities are added from Semanticscience Integrated Ontology (SIO) [8] to PharmSci. Besides, PharmSci ontology uses entities that are related to assays, and they are taken from BioAssay Ontology (BAO) [29], such as `experimental setting(bao:BAO_0020005)`, `bioassay(bao:BAO_0000015)`, and `in vitro(bao:BAO_0020008)`. Terms related to chemical substances are imported from Chemical Entities of Biological Interest (ChEBI)[6], for example, `drug(CHEBI:23888)`, `reagent(CHEBI:33893)`, and `pharmaceutical(CHEBI:52217)`. We integrate disease definitions into PharmSci from Human Disease Ontology [22], for example, `disease of cellular proliferation(DOID:14566)` and `disease of infectious agent(DOID:0050117)`. Cell Line Ontology (CLO) is reused to define cell concepts used in the study. We employ nature publishing group ontologies [18] entities for describing metadata of scholarly domain, such as `terms1:Publication`, `terms1:Publisher`, and `terms1:Article`. DCMI [31] annotations and object properties are reused to link the classes of scholarly publishing domain (`dc:creator`, `terms:publisher`, `dc:title` etc.). `foaf:Person` from FOAF Vocabulary [3] is used to define authors of publications and `foaf:Organization` is used to define publishers in PharmSci. There are also subclass hierarchies in classes, for example, `cancer(DOID:162)` is subclass of `disease of cellular proliferation(DOID:14566)`.

3.2 Semantic Knowledge Representation in PharmSci

In this section, we attempt to identify distinct "triples" of a publication, clinical study, experiment, methods, and materials classes from the article's sentence structure and then normalize each component to standard terminology. OWL distinguishes properties into two main categories that are object properties and data properties. Object properties and data properties help us to relate entities and transforming data into knowledge. In PharmSci ontology, object

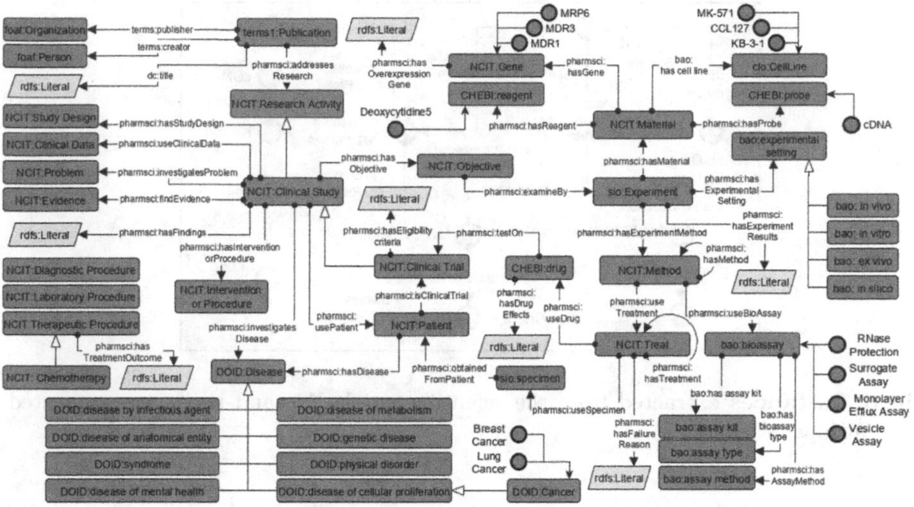

Fig. 4. PharmSci Ontological entities. The integration between the existing ontological entities in PharmSci ontology and relations. In addition, it shows the class Publication and its relation to other classes.

properties are used to link individuals to individuals, and datatype properties are used to link individuals to data values. We defined the `rdfs:domain` and `rdfs:range` of each property. For example, class `terms:Publication` describes the pharmaceutical research publications and it is the domain of the object property `pharmsci:addressesResearch` and the range of this property is `Research Activity(NCIT:C15429)` class. After specifying the domain and range of all properties, we set the object property relations between the instances. For example, the instance `pharmsci:ChemotherapyInLungCancer` of `Treat(NCIT:C70742)` class connected to instance `pharmsci:Vincristine` of class `drug(CHEBI:23888)` by the object property `pharmsci:useDrug`.

PharmSci also includes object properties with different characteristics such as reflexive, irreflexive, inverse, and asymmetric. The class `Material(NCIT: C48187)` is related to other classes with properties which are irreflexive and asymmetric such as `pharmsci:hasGene` and `pharmsci:hasReagent`. The object property `pharmsci:hasMethod` is reflexive property because a method can use the same method. The domain `Material(NCIT:C48187)` connects to class `cell line(CLO:0000031)` with object property `has_cell_line(bao:BAO_0002400)` which is inverse of `is_cell_line_of(bao:BAO_0002800)` object property.

Several data properties are defined to link instances to data values. Treatment or therapeutic procedures are an important part of a clinical study. Thus, `pharmsci:treatmentOutcome` and `pharmsci:treatmentFailureReason` are defined with the range `rdfs:Literal`. In addition, `pharmsci:hasDrug Effects` is another data property to define the effects of drug used in the treatment. PharmSci also contains data properties, such as `pharmsci:hasExperiemnt Results`, `pharmsci:hasEligibilityCriteria`, and `pharmsci:hasFindings`.

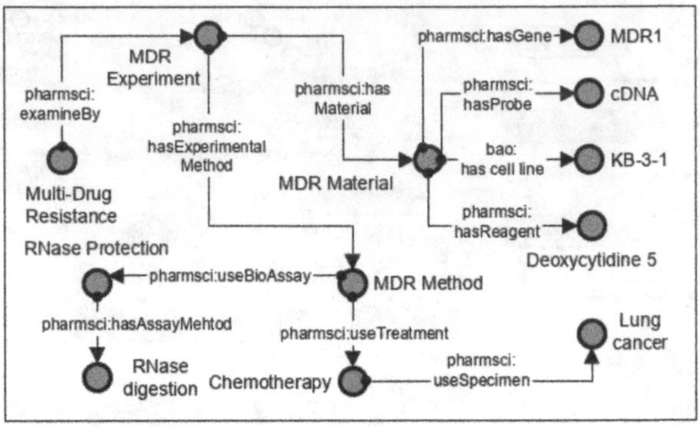

Fig. 5. Instances extracted from the scientific article [15] and their interconnected relationships in PharmSci.

In the knowledge acquisition step, instances are detected as members of the correct target classes and added as instances to the ontology with associated properties. PharmSci involves instances, such as the particular patient specimen, treatment types, reagents, genes, probes, assay types, or disease types in research. For example, `pharmsci:daunorubicin`, `pharmsci:vincristine`, `pharmsci:vinblastine`, and `pharmsci:etoposide` are drug types and defined as instances of `drug(CHEBI:23888)` class. Furthermore, `sio:specimen` class has instances, such as `pharmsci:poor_risk_acute_leukemia_samples` and `pharmsci:bone_marrow_aspirates`. Additionally, publication titles, publishers, authors, publication agents, and organizations are added as instances. Some of the instances extracted from the article [15] and their interconnected relations with each other are shown in Fig. 5.

3.3 Reasoning and Inference

Reasoning-based approaches are used to derive facts that are not expressed explicitly and make use of the expressive power of ontology. We define several SWRL [20] rules in order to infer new logical implicit axioms, and to discover inconsistencies among instances. The rules have been applied with Drools reasoner [25] in Protégé to export new axioms and declarations to instances inside the ontology. The following rule (Eq. 1) expresses the fact that clinical study has objective and objective examined by experiment; thus, we can infer that clinical study has an experiment. Drugs used in the treatment can also be part of an experiment material in the studies because treatment is an experimental method as in Eq. 2. Recursiveness of the properties is shown Eq. 3 and Eq. 4, `hasMethod` and `hasTreatment` are reflexive properties.

$$\begin{aligned} &ClinicalStudy(?x) \wedge hasObjective(?x, ?z) \wedge examinedBy(?z, ?y) \\ &\qquad \rightarrow hasExperiment(?x, ?y) \end{aligned} \tag{1}$$

$$Experiment(?x) \wedge hasExperimentMethod(?x, ?y) \wedge useDrug(?y, ?z) \rightarrow hasMaterial(?x, ?z) \quad (2)$$

$$hasMethod(?x, ?z) \wedge hasMethod(?z, ?y) \rightarrow hasMethod(?x, ?y) \quad (3)$$

$$hasTreatment(?x, ?z) \wedge hasTreatment(?z, ?y) \rightarrow hasTreatment(?x, ?y) \quad (4)$$

4 Evaluation

In the evaluation step, the developed ontology is assessed if it meets the requirements specifications and to ascertain the correctness and quality of our model. This phase includes validation as a first step that guarantees the correctness of an ontology. Verification is the second step to guarantee that the software environment and documentation represent the correct ontology.

4.1 Validation of Ontology

Query Execution of Competency Questions: Competency questions [17] are a list of questions that the knowledge base should be able to answer. We create these questions according to the content of the corpus of articles. The results of these questions confirm that the designed model contains enough detail of a particular area. 25 competency questions have been created in total, and Table 2 shows the 10 of the competency questions for PharmSci ontology. SPARQL queries have been implemented for each defined competency question. Listing 1.1 is the query for the question Q5 "What is the title of the Publications use the BioAssay 'Efflux Bioassay' as experiment method?" in the PharmSci competency question list.

Listing 1.1. SPARQL query for Q5 in Table 2.

```
SELECT  DISTINCT ?title
WHERE {
?publication   pharmsci:addressesResearch  ?study.
?publication   terms:title                 ?title.
?publication   terms:creator               ?creator.
?study         pharmsci:hasExperiment      ?experiment.
?experiment    pharmsci:hasMethod          ?method.
?method
pharmsci:useBisoassay pharmsci:Efflux_Bioassay.
}
```

The possible answer for Listing 1.1 is the publication with the title: *"Different Efflux Transporter Affinity and Metabolism of 99mTc-2-Methoxyisobutylisonitrile and 99mTc-Tetrofosmin for Multidrug Resistance Monitoring in Cancer"*. As a result of this validation phase, competency questions are answered and validated correctly with SPARQL queries.

Table 2. Predefined competency questions.

Query	Competency Question
Q1	Which Objective examined by Experiment Y for Clinical Study Z?
Q2	Which Clinical Study use the Experiment Method Y for Experimental Material X by using Gene as a material?
Q3	Which Cancer type X is studied by the Clinical Study Y?
Q4	Which Drugs are used in Therapeutic Procedure X and Clinical Study Y for Disease Z?
Q5	What is title of the Publications use the BioAssay Y as Experiment Method?

Comparative Analysis: This approach is used to compare the ontology with the content of a text corpus to check how far an ontology sufficiently covers the given domain. Our approach is to perform an automated term extraction with the latent semantic analysis [5] for the two different corpora. We analyzed the overlapped concepts and counted the number of these words separately for each corpus and ontologies. Then, Precision, Recall, and F1 values are calculated according to the total number of concepts (Keywords) defined in the ontology, most likely terms in analysis results (Class), and the number of matched concepts (Hits) with the corpus.

$$Precision = \frac{|N_{hits}|}{|N_{class}|} \;,\quad Recall = \frac{|N_{hits}|}{|L_{Keywords}|} \quad \text{and} \quad F1 = \frac{2 \times Precision \times Recall}{Precision + Recall}$$

Corpus 1 consists of search results of Google Scholar with the keywords 'multidrug resistance and ABC transporters in cancer'. Corpus 2 gathers 'in vitro evaluation in drug delivery' downloaded from ScienceDirect. Both corpora consist of 25 PDF files and converted to TSV files. (Details of analysis and corpora can be found as .tsv file on Github[10].) We used one of the current ontology in the pharmaceutical domain, which is Drug Interaction Knowledge Base (DIKB) [4], to evaluate how far it satisfies the pharmaceutical research and to compare with PharmSci. We selected 50 most likely words from the latent semantic analysis results (with high TF-IDF weight score) from two corpora, and then we compared these words for both ontologies. Table 3 shows how many words matched with corpora, and the calculations of precision, recall, and F1 value results. The F1 value of PharmSci is greater than DIKB, it is 0.16 for corpus 1 and 0.14 for corpus 2 (see Fig. 7). As a result, PharmSci ontology has more matched concepts than DIKB ontology.

4.2 Verification of Ontology

In this phase, we used the FOCA methodology [1], which has three main steps: Ontology type verification, questions verification, and quality verification. A

[10] https://github.com/ZeynepSay/PharmSci/tree/master/CorpusData.

total of 12 questions should be answered in the question verification step for their respective goal and metric. The expert should score the results of each question. After answering the questions, the expert establishes a grade for each question. Goal 1, 3 and 4 obtain 100% and Goal 2 is 50% for PharmSci (see Fig. 6). The result of this evaluation shows that PharmSci received high scores for adaptability, completeness, consistency, clarity, and computational efficiency metrics. However, it needs improvements for the conciseness metric because of moderate abstraction and some reused properties are not used in the model. The total quality of the ontology in the FOCA method is calculated by the beta regression models proposed by Ferrari [14]. The result of the total quality verification according to the beta regression model is 0.994 for PharmSci, which means it has high quality since its value close to 1.

Table 3. Precision, Recall, and F1 values for PharmSci and DIKB ontology [4]

Corpora	Ontology	Classes	Keywords	Hits	Precision	Recall	F1
Corpus-1	PharmSci	181	50	19	0.10	0.38	0.16
	DIKB	360	50	15	0.04	0.3	0.07
Corpus-2	PharmSci	181	50	16	0.09	0.32	0.14
	DIKB	360	50	12	0.03	0.24	0.06

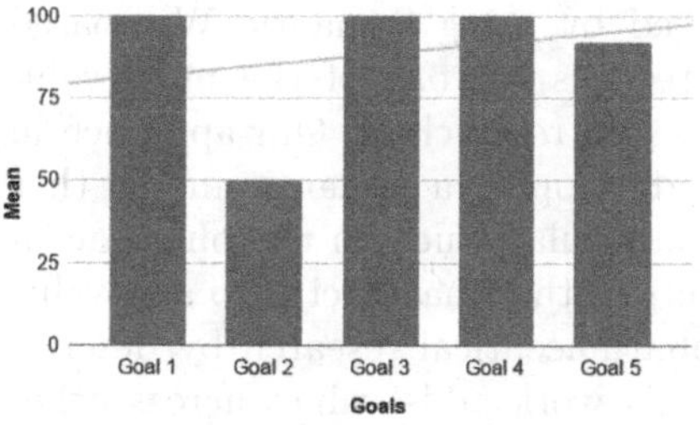

Fig. 6. Goal percentages for PharmSci

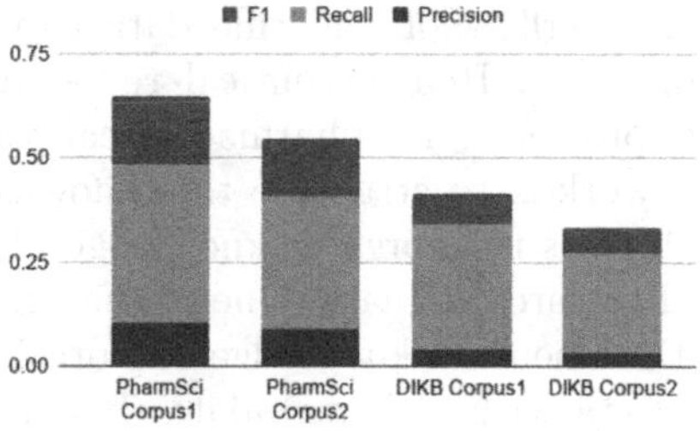

Fig. 7. Comparative Analysis Results

5 Related Work

Several available vocabularies, platforms, and schemas related to scholarly publishing and life science domain are presented. The Open Research Knowledge Graph [21] is an infrastructure for semantic scholarly knowledge acquisition, publication, processing, and curation. SN SciGraph[11] is the Springer Nature Linked Data platform that provides Linked Open Data as open research. In 2017, an initial step towards representing computer science research data was

11 https://scigraph.springernature.com/explorer.

taken by Fathalla et al. [10], also in other domains [11]. Subsequently, they developed the Semantic Survey Ontology (Semsur) [12], which semantically captures and represents the knowledge in review and survey articles. SPAR (Semantic Publishing and Referencing) [7,24] is a set of integral and orthogonal ontologies for defining metadata of the scholarly publication workflow. Another work that deals with information overload is the CSO classifier [26] automatically classifies research papers according to the metadata by using the Computer Science Ontology (CSO). The field of knowledge and data representation in the life science domain is vast. The Open Biomedical Ontologies (OBO) Foundry [27] was founded to address the problem of the proliferation of ontologies. OBO includes over 60 ontologies such as Gene Ontology and Cell Ontology. Medical Subject Headings (MeSH)[12] is a schema vocabulary developed in the field of Medicine. In the pharmaceutical research domain, there are also semantic models, for example, the Drug-Drug Interaction Ontology (DINTO) [19], and Drug Interaction Knowledge Base (DIKB) [4]. Also, the Drug-Drug Interaction Ontology (DINTO) [19] used the methontology [13] as an ontology development method. However, these models generally focused on drug-drug interaction or drug discovery topics. Thus, PharmSci ontology differs from these domain models and combines scholarly metadata with domain-specific metadata.

6 Conclusion

The results show that the issue of handling, accessing, and representing a constant overflow of scientific data can be solved by using Semantic Web-based approaches. Pharmaceutical research data records are one of the most valuable properties for pharmaceutical companies and researchers. Our approach in this work is to structure this knowledge by developing a semantic model that enables us to represent knowledge about a particular study in the pharmaceutical research domain. One of the core impacts of the PharmSci is to add value to the scientific knowledge exploration in pharmaceutical research by describing data with rich metadata. In addition, this work adds values across other research fields through its generalizability which enables to adapt it and extend it to a vast spectrum of science. Our evaluation results show that the developed ontology is ready to be re-used in services to be implemented for such applications. Thus, we envision community-supported semantic models that would enable automated exploration, analysis, understanding, and usage of metadata to gain worthy insights from scientific publications.

For future work, it is planned to develop a semantic model for other branches of science such as mathematics, physics, or earth science to allow knowledge extraction from unstructured and structured resources. Furthermore, PharmSci ontology will also be implemented and integrated into a semantic web-based platform Open Research Knowledge Graph (ORKG)[13], which is a TIB collaborative project that engages research communities in the development of technologies for open graphs about scientific knowledge.

[12] https://www.nlm.nih.gov/mesh/meshhome.html.
[13] https://projects.tib.eu/orkg/.

Acknowledgments. This work has been supported by ERC project ScienceGRAPH no. 819536, and the EPSRC grant EP/M025268/1, the WWTF grant VRG18-013, the EC Horizon 2020 grant LAMBDA (GA no. 809965), the CLEOPATRA project (GA no. 812997), and the German national funded BmBF project MLwin.

References

1. Bandeira, J., Bittencourt, I.I., Espinheira, P., Isotani, S.: Foca: a methodology for ontology evaluation. arXiv preprint arXiv:1612.03353 (2016)
2. Berners-Lee, T., Fischetti, M.: Weaving the Web: The original design and ultimate destiny of the World Wide Web by its inventor. DIANE Publishing Company (2001)
3. Brickley, D., Miller, L.: Foaf vocabulary specification, p. 91 (2007)
4. Brochhausen, M., Schneider, J., Malone, D., Empey, P.E., Hogan, W.R., Boyce, R.D.: Towards a foundational representation of potential drug-drug interaction knowledge. In: First International Workshop on Drug Interaction Knowledge Representation (DIKR-2014) at the International Conference on Biomedical Ontologies (ICBO 2014) (2014)
5. Deerwester, S., Dumais, S.T., Furnas, G.W., Landauer, T.K., Harshman, R.: Indexing by latent semantic analysis. J. Am. Soc. Inf. Sci. **41**(6), 391–407 (1990)
6. Degtyarenko, K., et al.: Chebi: a database and ontology for chemical entities of biological interest. Nucleic Acids Res. **36**, D344–D350 (2007)
7. Dimou, A., Vahdati, S., Di Iorio, A., Lange, C., Verborgh, R., Mannens, E.: Challenges as enablers for high quality linked data: insights from the semantic publishing challenge. PeerJ. Comput. Sci. **3**, e105 (2017)
8. Dumontier, M., et al.: The semanticscience integrated ontology (sio) for biomedical research and knowledge discovery. J. Biomed. Semant. **5**(1), 14 (2014)
9. Fathalla, S., Auer, S., Lange, C.: Towards the semantic formalization of science. In: Proceedings of the 35th Annual ACM Symposium on Applied Computing, pp. 2057–2059 (2020)
10. Fathalla, S., Vahdati, S., Auer, S., Lange, C.: Towards a knowledge graph representing research findings by semantifying survey articles. In: Kamps, J., Tsakonas, G., Manolopoulos, Y., Iliadis, L., Karydis, I. (eds.) TPDL 2017. LNCS, vol. 10450, pp. 315–327. Springer, Cham (2017). https://doi.org/10.1007/978-3-319-67008-9_25
11. Fathalla, S., Vahdati, S., Auer, S., Lange, C.: Metadata analysis of scholarly events of computer science, physics, engineering, and mathematics. In: Méndez, E., Crestani, F., Ribeiro, C., David, G., Lopes, J.C. (eds.) TPDL 2018. LNCS, vol. 11057, pp. 116–128. Springer, Cham (2018). https://doi.org/10.1007/978-3-030-00066-0_10
12. Fathalla, S., Vahdati, S., Auer, S., Lange, C.: Semsur: a core ontology for the semantic representation of research findings. Procedia Comput. Sci. **137**, 151–162 (2018)
13. Fernández-López, M., Gómez-Pérez, A., Juristo, N.: Methontology: from ontological art towards ontological engineering (1997)
14. Ferrari, S., Cribari-Neto, F.: Beta regression for modelling rates and proportions. J. Appl. Stat. **31**(7), 799–815 (2004)
15. Fojo, A.T., Ueda, K., Slamon, D.J., Poplack, D., Gottesman, M., Pastan, I.: Expression of a multidrug-resistance gene in human tumors and tissues. Proc. Nat. Acad. Sci. **84**(1), 265–269 (1987)

16. Golbeck, J., Fragoso, G., Hartel, F., Hendler, J., Oberthaler, J., Parsia, B.: The national cancer institute's thesaurus and ontology. J. Web Semant. First Look **1**(1), 4 (2003)
17. Grüninger, M., Fox, M.S.: Methodology for the design and evaluation of ontologies (1995)
18. Hammond, T., Pasin, M.: The nature. com ontologies portal. In: LISC@ ISWC, pp. 2–14 (2015)
19. Herrero-Zazo, M., Segura-Bedmar, I., Hastings, J., Martínez, P.: Dinto: using owl ontologies and SWRL rules to infer drug-drug interactions and their mechanisms. J. Chem. Inf. Model. **55**(8), 1698–1707 (2015)
20. Horrocks, I., Patel-Schneider, P.F., Boley, H., Tabet, S., Grosof, B., Dean, M., et al.: SWRL: a semantic web rule language combining owl and ruleml. W3C Member Submission **21**(79), 1–31 (2004)
21. Jaradeh, M.Y., et al.: Open research knowledge graph: next generation infrastructure for semantic scholarly knowledge. In: Proceedings of the 10th International Conference on Knowledge Capture, pp. 243–246 (2019)
22. Kibbe, W.A., et al.: Disease ontology 2015 update: an expanded and updated database of human diseases for linking biomedical knowledge through disease data. Nucleic Acids Res. **43**(D1), D1071–D1078 (2014)
23. Musen, M.A.: The protégé project: a look back and a look forward. AI Matters **1**(4), 4–12 (2015)
24. Peroni, S., Shotton, D.: The SPAR ontologies. In: Vrandečić, D., et al. (eds.) ISWC 2018. LNCS, vol. 11137, pp. 119–136. Springer, Cham (2018). https://doi.org/10.1007/978-3-030-00668-6_8
25. Proctor, M.: Drools: a rule engine for complex event processing. In: Schürr, A., Varró, D., Varró, G. (eds.) AGTIVE 2011. LNCS, vol. 7233, pp. 2–2. Springer, Heidelberg (2012). https://doi.org/10.1007/978-3-642-34176-2_2
26. Salatino, A.A., Osborne, F., Thanapalasingam, T., Motta, E.: The CSO classifier: ontology-driven detection of research topics in scholarly articles. In: Doucet, A., Isaac, A., Golub, K., Aalberg, T., Jatowt, A. (eds.) TPDL 2019. LNCS, vol. 11799, pp. 296–311. Springer, Cham (2019). https://doi.org/10.1007/978-3-030-30760-8_26
27. Smith, B., et al.: The obo foundry: coordinated evolution of ontologies to support biomedical data integration. Nat. Biotechnol. **25**(11), 1251 (2007)
28. Vahdati, S., Palma, G., Nath, R.J., Lange, C., Auer, S., Vidal, M.-E.: Unveiling scholarly communities over knowledge graphs. In: Méndez, E., Crestani, F., Ribeiro, C., David, G., Lopes, J.C. (eds.) TPDL 2018. LNCS, vol. 11057, pp. 103–115. Springer, Cham (2018). https://doi.org/10.1007/978-3-030-00066-0_9
29. Visser, U., Abeyruwan, S., Vempati, U., Smith, R.P., Lemmon, V., Schürer, S.C.: Bioassay ontology (BAO): a semantic description of bioassays and high-throughput screening results. BMC Bioinform. **12**(1), 257 (2011)
30. Wang, X., Williams, C., Liu, Z.H., Croghan, J.: Big data management challenges in health research–a literature review. Brief. Bioinform. **20**(1), 156–167 (2017)
31. Weibel, S., Kunze, J., Lagoze, C., Wolf, M.: Dublin core metadata for resource discovery. Internet Eng. Task Force RFC **2413**(222), 132 (1998)
32. White, K.: Science and engineering publication output trends: 2017 shows us output level slightly below that of china but the united states maintains lead with highly cited publications. National Science Foundation. Alexandria, VA, National Center for Science and Engineering Statistics (2019)
33. Wilkinson, M.D., et al.: The fair guiding principles for scientific data management and stewardship. Sci. Data **3**, 160018 (2016)

ArchOnto, a CIDOC-CRM-Based Linked Data Model for the Portuguese Archives

Inês Koch(✉), Cristina Ribeiro(✉), and Carla Teixeira Lopes(✉)

Faculty of Engineering of the University of Porto and INESC-TEC, Porto, Portugal
ines.koch@inesctec.pt, {mcr,ctl}@fe.up.pt

Abstract. Archives are faced with great challenges due to the vast amounts of data they have to curate. New data models are required, and work is underway. The International Council on Archives is creating the RiC-CM (Records in Context), and there is a long line of work in museums with the CIDOC-CRM (CIDOC Conceptual Reference Model). Both models are based on ontologies to represent cultural heritage data and link them to other information. The Portuguese National Archives hold a collection with over 3.5 million metadata records, described with the ISAD(G) standard. The archives are designing a new linked data model and a technological platform with applications for archive contributors, archivists, and the public. The current work extends CIDOC-CRM into ArchOnto, an ontology-based model for archives. The model defines the relevant archival entities and properties and will be used to migrate existing records. ArchOnto accommodates the existing ISAD(G) information and takes into account its implementation with current technologies. The model is evaluated with records from representative fonds. After the test on these samples, the model is ready to be populated with the semi-automatic transformation of the ISAD records. The evaluation of the model and the population strategies will proceed with experiments involving professional and lay users.

Keywords: EPISA · Linked data · Archival description · CIDOC-CRM · ArchOnto

1 Introduction

The Portuguese National Archives, Torre do Tombo (ANTT), one of the oldest institutions in Portugal, curates a unique collection of historical and contemporary objects that it has been accumulating since the 9th century. With a large number of documents in its custody, including large volumes of administrative data, organized in series and covering extended periods and the evolution of the institutions that create them, descriptive metadata is essential to the management of the archives. As the content of the documents is currently not searchable, metadata is the basis for browsing and querying the archives remotely, and

This work is financed by National Funds through the Portuguese funding agency, FCT—Fundação para a Ciência e a Tecnologia within project DSAIPA/DS/0023/2018.

M. Hall et al. (Eds.): TPDL 2020, LNCS 12246, pp. 133–146, 2020.
https://doi.org/10.1007/978-3-030-54956-5_10

remote access now exceeds the direct contact with the archives by several orders of magnitude. Considering the central role of metadata, it is essential that the information in the descriptive records is thoroughly explored and it is recognized that this is not always the case.

In a changing world where open information is supposed to be accessible to all, archives are also redefining their mission and considering the access to documents on a par with the preservation of the information therein. The ANTT is, therefore, concerned with the transformation of the archives, which involves the development of a new data model, a new information system, and new workflows and services to the public. A new data model is central to this transformation, as it stands at the core of the whole design and is instrumental in many aspects: in the expressiveness of the metadata created in the archives, in the ability to integrate existing records into the new model, in the fitness of the model to interoperate with other systems. The archives are no longer isolated, they need to link documents and their descriptions with external data that can provide context and enrich their contents.

The work described here is part of the EPISA project (Entity and Property Inference for Semantic Archives), a research project that brings together a team from Information and Computer Science and the archival experts from ANTT. EPISA intends to design and prototype an open-source knowledge platform representing archival information on a linked data model. Additionally, the project will work on the existing records to extract the relevant entities and their properties and take advantage of the wealth of information built by specialists over the years.

The project will assist the ANTT in moving from the ISAD(G) multilevel description model to a graph data model based on state-of-the-art technologies that can provide data for Artificial Intelligence algorithms to extract resources and infer relationships between those resources, having the current textual descriptions as a starting point.

The ArchOnto model is presented here and evaluated based on a selection of archival records. These records include fonds with a large volume of data, like parochial records, and fonds of unique objects, the so-called treasures.

2 Standards for Cultural Heritage

Considering the initiative of creating a new data model for archives, it is essential to have a knowledge of the standards that are currently used for cultural heritage.

The General International Standard for Archival Description, ISAD(G), and its associated standards issued by the International Council on Archives (ICA) is widely adopted and has been the basis for DigitArq [9], the platform currently used for archival description by the ANTT. The ISAD(G) [6] is an archival description standard that is characterized by a multilevel structure that allows the archival description to be made from general to specific, representing the context and hierarchical structure of the fonds and its components.

It is also necessary to consider data models that include the atomization of cultural heritage records, i.e. the transformation of flat textual fields into structured subgraphs with meaningful entities, and their connection to external information as Linked Open Data. In what follows, we will have a sense of what already exists and how it can contribute to our goals.

2.1 CIDOC-CRM

The CIDOC-CRM (Conceptual Reference Model) [4], a formal ontology, was developed by the International Committee for Documentation (CIDOC) of the International Council of Museums (ICOM). This model, which aims to exchange, mediate, and integrate heterogeneous sources of information related to cultural heritage, is being actively developed by the CRM-SIG (CRM - Special Interest Group). After several changes over a period of over 10 years, it was considered an ISO standard in 2006 (ISO 21127), and a 2014 version is under review (ISO 21127: 2014). Building on the concept of the event, CIDOC-CRM is quite complete with regard to the representation of people, places, and time periods, concepts that are also central to the archival description.

Due to its origin in the museum community, it is in this domain that examples of institutions that applied the model are found. These include the British Museum[1] and the Museo del Prado[2]. Although CIDOC-CRM is recognized as the base model for the implementation of linked data in these institutions, it is articulated with other models, as in the case of Museo del Prado, where FRBR (Functional Requirements for Bibliographic Records, a model that originated in the library community) [5] is applied, among some more specific vocabularies.

In addition to museums, CIDOC-CRM has already been applied in other areas, namely in Archaeological Heritage, where it has been promoted in the context of the Ariadne Project [1]. Within the archives, work has been carried out mapping the EAD (Encoded Archival Description) standard to CIDOC-CRM. EAD is an XML language that represents the ISAD(G) standard. The mapping of EAD to CIDOC-CRM [2] took into account concepts that are extremely relevant for the transformation of the data model currently used by the Portuguese National Archives. Among these is the level of description, central to ISAD(G). These first experiments were focused on archival requirements but did not evolve to the proposal of a more substantial model.

2.2 RiC-CM

A new data model is currently under development in the area of archives that incorporates the existing archival standards, following their principles in a conceptual data model, the RiC-CM [7]. In addition to the data model, an ontology, called RiC-O (Records in Context Ontology), is being defined by the Expert Group on Archival Description (EGAD) from the ICA. This model aims to represent all archival concepts, taking into account the main descriptive entities.

[1] https://www.britishmuseum.org/.

[2] https://www.museodelprado.es/modelo-semantico-digital/modelo-ontologico.

Thus, properties, classes, and attributes that represent the essential relationships present in the archives are considered. This opens the ground for the cooperation between our project and the RiC-CM initiative, in the same spirit we have adopted with regard to CIDOC-CRM, and more so given the fact that this proposal is aimed specifically at archives.

2.3 Comparison

A comparison of standards is summarized in Table 1 that highlights several commonalities and differences. The models originating in the archives take into account the hierarchical structure intrinsic to the domain. CIDOC-CRM and RiC-CM are both based on semantic web concepts and therefore aim to represent cultural heritage data as linked data. While the ISAD(G) standard has a limited number of elements for which values typically have a rich structure, the more recent models have a number of properties an order of magnitude larger, attesting to their more atomized representation of knowledge. The number of properties presented for RiC is taken from the RiC-O ontology. All models have institutional support in the corresponding working groups under well-established cultural heritage institutions, and while ISAD(G) currently supports the implementation of archival information systems, the other still lack the test of actual deployment.

Table 1. Comparison of ISAD(G), CIDOC-CRM and RiC-CM.

	ISAD(G)	CIDOC-CRM	RiC-CM
Hierarchical	✔	✖	✔
LOD	✖	✔	✔
Ontology	✖	✔	✔
Number of properties	26 elements	285 properties	449 properties
Institutional support	ICA (+25 years)	ICOM (+15 years)	ICA (5 years)
Implementation on archives	Custom	(none known)	None
Most recent version	2000	2020	2020
Support	ICA	CIDOC-CRM SIG	ICA (EGAD)

3 ArchOnto, a Modular Ontology for Archives

The Portuguese National Archives were early adopters of the ISAD(G) standard. They created a set of rules and recommendations for consistent use of the standard at national and regional level [3]. Moreover, a custom-designed information system was developed in close collaboration with the archives experts and deployed in all archives, enforcing the aggregation of records at national level.

After almost two decades and several system updates, the system no longer supports the requirements of the archives, in more than one aspect: the data model that embodies the ISAD(G) is limited, the technologies that support the information system are too rigid, expensive and difficult to maintain, the mission of the archives has extended into new processes, and more user profiles have to be considered. In the sequel, we focus on the choice of the data model.

It was clear from the requirements of the archives that the new model has to be more fine-grained and able to identify documents but also events, people, and their roles and connections. This is in line with recent work in knowledge graphs and linked open data, where bits and pieces of information from various sources are linked using properties defined in many different contexts. The information in the archives is no longer regarded as isolated, but rather able to connect to information created by other instances.

Looking for existing models in this line, we considered the RiC-CM. However, as this model was still in a preliminary phase in 2018 when this work started, it was necessary to find a more mature model, and the CIDOC-CRM stood as a strong candidate.

Although CIDOC-CRM has evolved over more than a decade and is now a stable model, it is in steady development, and the EPISA project team has been following its evolution. The ArchOnto model proposed here takes into account the current version of CIDOC-CRM, version 6.2.7 [4].

3.1 The Process of Adapting CIDOC-CRM for Archival Use

With CIDOC-CRM as the foundation, we began to structure the ArchOnto model, considering the information present in the ISAD(G) descriptors and how it might be mapped to CIDOC-CRM. Due to the expressiveness of CIDOC-CRM, we concluded that most of the information present in the ISAD(G) elements would be easily represented there. However, we also found that not all information from ISAD(G) would turn into CIDOC-CRM.

A data model for archives began to be composed based on the CIDOC-CRM, following the general principle that the elements of the model should be implemented as a knowledge graph via a graph database. The model is represented in the ArchOnto ontology, which aims to include information from all the records in the Portuguese National Archives and is being embedded in ArchGraph [8], a knowledge graph that will support the archival information system. We will focus here on ArchOnto and its evolution, but the operational concerns raised by ArchGraph have been essential in the design of ArchOnto.

The first approach to ArchOnto [8] aimed at using just CIDOC-CRM, including its recommendations for the representation of non-binary relationships, and some extensions already validated by the CIDOC-CRM. As CIDOC-CRM was created for museums, there are core concepts for the archives that are not present in this model, such as the level of description. The process of adapting CIDOC-CRM for archival use took several steps, detailed as follows.

CIDOC-CRM Extensions. Our first approach was to create Data Property extensions to cope with the limited number of data properties in CIDOC-CRM, using them to capture the semantics of the elements from the descriptions associated to the various archival objects [8]. Note that most of CIDOC-CRM properties are Object Property, used to relate individuals.

Most of these data properties were created to accommodate information from the text fields of the ISAD(G) elements.

From CIDOC-CRM Extensions to Separate Ontologies. The CIDOC-CRM extension approach required a large number of data properties, so we evolved to create the ISAD Ontology to put them together, rather than including them as CIDOC-CRM extensions. This separate ontology is then imported into the ArchOnto model. Besides these properties, subproperties of *P3 has note*, the ISAD Ontology contains all elements of ISAD(G), which will be atomized with CIDOC-CRM in order to have finer-grained descriptions. Table 2 shows some examples of data properties that were captured first as CIDOC-CRM extensions and then as part of the ISAD Ontology.

Table 2. CIDOC-CRM data properties extensions to ISAD Ontology.

CIDOC-CRM extension	ISAD Ontology
ARP1 has administrative history	ISAD7 has administrative history
ARP2 has archival history	ISAD8 has archival history
ARP3 has scope	ISAD9 has scope

Classes and object properties that existed as CIDOC-CRM extensions in the preliminary ontology were also moved to the N-ary ontology (presented below). This organization in separate ontologies is more flexible in the sense that, if CIDOC-CRM changes and these ontologies are no longer necessary, they can be dropped.

Remaining CIDOC-CRM Extensions. Despite the move of properties and classes to other ontologies, there were cases of Classes and Object Properties that remained as extensions of the CIDOC-CRM model. These include the ones considered essential to archives, such as the level of description, which is represented by the *ARE1 Level of Description* class and the *ARP12 has level of description*, *ARP8 upper level* and *ARP9 lower level* properties (see Fig. 1). The basic principles of the archival organization require that each *Unit of Description* be assigned a description level and that levels be organized hierarchically. This takes into account organization principles that are well established in the archives, but can also be considered an enduring principle for large collections, in that description can be performed for more or less vast collections of documents and then inherited if their organization is maintained.

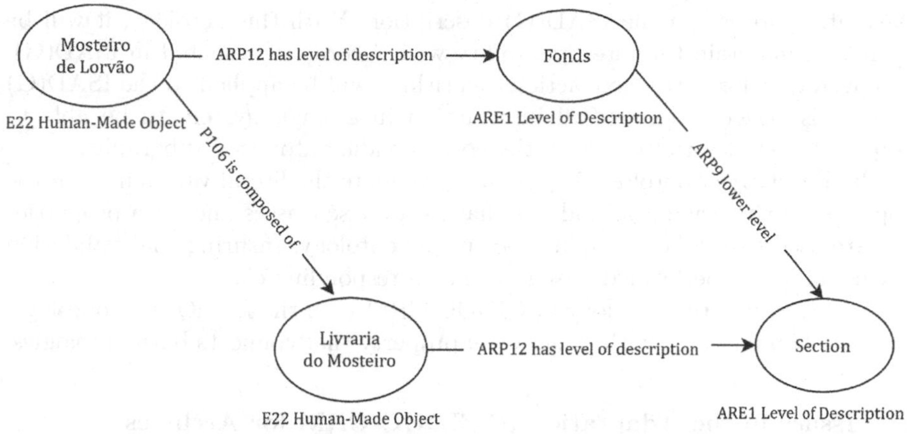

Fig. 1. Levels of description in CIDOC-CRM. Original record at https://digitarq.arquivos.pt/details?id=4381091.

3.2 The Ontologies in ArchOnto

With a better knowledge of CIDOC-CRM and archival standards, some decisions made the model for the archives more complete and, therefore, more able to represent the universe of archives. As such, ArchOnto went from an ontology where CIDOC-CRM was imported and extended to an ontology where more ontologies are imported to represent more accurately the existing archival records. This is quite in line with the semantic web principles of reusing existing ontologies whenever they are available and working on the additional concepts for our domain.

ArchOnto[3] currently has five ontologies at its base, which complement each other. Besides the CIDOC-CRM (base ontology), we will briefly summarize N-ary, the ISAD Ontology, DataObject, and an ontology for the connection between CIDOC-CRM and DataObject.

The N-ary ontology was created taking into account the CIDOC-CRM recommendations[4] for the representation of tuples with an arity higher than two. With this ontology, it is possible to represent all instances in which it is necessary to build associations that are not binary, i.e., that connect more than two individuals.

The ISAD Ontology is in place to represent the elements of the ISAD(G) standard without atomization. It is based on data properties that capture each of the ISAD(G) elements, thus maintaining the information from the original records, making sure that what was previously described with ISAD(G) is not lost when atomized for ArchOnto. It also allows, whenever necessary, the validation of the contents that have been atomized, checking if they comply with the

[3] OWL version available on GitHub - ArchOnto2020: https://github.com/feup-infolab/archontology.

[4] http://www.cidoc-crm.org/sites/default/files/Roles.pdf.

information present in the ISAD(G) description. With this ontology, it will be possible to maintain the interoperability with records represented in ISAD(G). Moreover, as information extraction algorithms will be applied to the ISAD(G) fields, it is easier to expose all information in a single system to be able to compare legacy descriptions with the corresponding atomized subgraphs.

The DataObject ontology is present to validate the literal values used in the properties of the new data model. It has as its base classes and data properties that are used to validate simple types in the ontology, ensuring that validation for each object is performed based on the corresponding class.

Finally, to link the ontology of CIDOC-CRM with the DataObject ontology, we created an ontology with a *hasValue* property that connects both ontologies.

3.3 Issues in the Adaptation of CIDOC-CRM for Archives

In the adaptation of CIDOC-CRM to the archives, we had to make sure that ISAD(G) descriptions were mapped to the new model. In this mapping process, we tried, as much as possible, to use CIDOC-CRM features. However, when this model was unable to satisfy our requirements, we created classes and properties to represent the ISAD(G) attributes, making their semantics explicit in the new model.

Types. As we explored the mapping between ISAD(G) and CIDOC-CRM, we became aware that the CIDOC-CRM *E55 Type* class was extensively used. This class is very versatile and is used with many of the concepts that are present in ISAD(G) and not in CIDOC-CRM. The broad use of this class did not contribute to separate the specific semantics of each concept that was being represented. Naturally, if used in a large number of concepts, they would no longer be differentiated.

To face this challenge, we decided to create subclasses of *E55 Type*, to have specific types to distinguish identifiers from personal names, date from language or legal status, while considering the concepts present in the records. Many of these concepts already correspond to controlled vocabularies in the archives, and some are listed in Table 3, as well as the subclasses that represent them.

Table 3. Proposal of CIDOC-CRM extensions - some subclasses of *E55 Type*.

Proposal of CIDOC-CRM extension	Examples
ARE5 identifier type	Reference code, physical location
ARE6 date type	Predominant date
ARE7 name type	First name, surname, nickname
ARE8 role type	Material author, bride, godfather

Conceptual Object vs Physical Object. While applying CIDOC-CRM, we noticed the existence of concepts that are not central to ISAD(G) and archival practice. The distinction between the physical object and the conceptual object is an example of this. The two concepts emerged with the need to identify the language of a document.

Initially, all the ISAD(G) elements were mapped as related to the physical object. However, when considering the language of a document, we found that in CIDOC-CRM it should not be associated with a physical object, but rather to a conceptual object. The language should be related to the expression of a work, an abstract concept distinct from the material object that embodies such an abstraction. The language should, therefore, appear as a property of a conceptual object.

According to CIDOC-CRM, objects that do not have a physical dimension, but transmit information about the physical world, are considered conceptual objects. These objects cannot be destroyed, they exist as long as an individual can conceive them through their memory.

In the mapping process, a substantial effort went into exploring the possibilities of turning extensive textual elements in ISAD(G) into their atomized versions, namely in the association of entities mentioned in the ISAD(G) records with conceptual objects. Among these elements are, in addition to the language, the scope and content, the notes, the publication notes and the access conditions.

As for the physical object, CIDOC-CRM considers it an item of a material nature with clear boundaries that can be independently documented. The physical object, unlike the conceptual object, has a physical dimension and, therefore, can be moved, if its weight allows it. As with the Conceptual Object, there are also ISAD(G) elements that are sources of information to atomize and associate with a physical object. Among these attributes are the titles, the support, the dimension and the location of the documents (in the sense of physical location).

Considering that in the ISAD(G) standard the distinction between the physical and the conceptual object is not explicit, in the ISAD Ontology it was decided to relate all attributes to physical objects.

Validation of Data Types. Data types have a careful treatment in ArchOnto as they stand at the interface between the higher-level concepts of the domain and the implementation and validation that applications are supposed to perform in order to enforce the validity of the knowledge graph. A set of basic data types have therefore been represented in the DataObject ontology and articulated with CIDOC-CRM for the properties that range over objects such as strings, dates, or identifiers.

We can take dates as an example, as they are ubiquitous in archival records, appear under different formats, and require strong validation. CIDOC-CRM provides classes and properties to deal with dates that go as far as considering them as individuals. DataObject handles the transition to the actual representation as values with validated formats. Like the dates, the titles also need validation, going through a similar validation process.

In the case of dates, the adopted format is intended to be uniform. For that, all mapped dates will have a format that specifies the date and time when a given event happens, according to the *dateTime* data type — xsd:dateTime, which has the format "YYYY-MM-DDThh:mm:ss".

To validate dates, it is necessary to use the CIDOC-CRM, the DataObject, and the ontology that links these two ontologies, and it is the DataObject that supports validation of the date format. All dates, according to CIDOC-CRM, must be related to an event, which is the starting point for its validation. Figure 2 illustrates the validation of a date using CIDOC-CRM classes and properties complemented with those from DataObject.

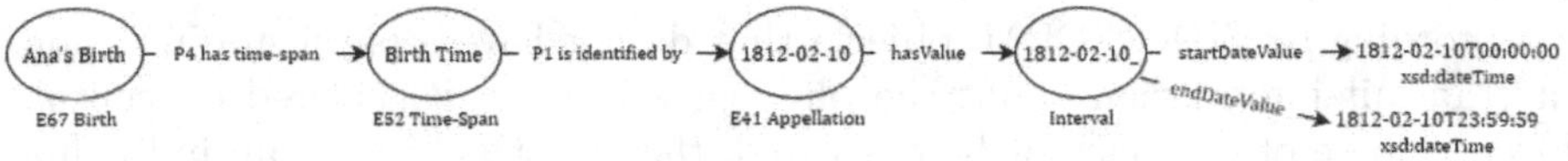

Fig. 2. Validation of a date in CIDOC-CRM. Original record at https://pesquisa.adporto.arquivos.pt/details?id=1374655.

4 Evaluation of CIDOC-CRM for Archives

Following the design of the ArchOnto model, the team that is developing the model tested it with several pilot cases extracted from the DigitArq database of archival records. As DigitArq has a great diversity of records, we used records of different kinds of fonds present in this database. Three examples are used in this evaluation - one from a parish fonds, one from judicial records and a unique object, classified as a treasure.

Among the parish fonds, a series of documents related to baptism records[5], where homogeneity of information was observed, were selected. In the judicial records, a document related to an orphan record[6] was chosen, which proved to be quite rich in information. Finally, a treasure[7] was selected, which has a wide variety of information present, making it a very extensive record.

Throughout the ArchOnto mapping, some of the concepts used in the archives, the ones also present in CIDOC-CRM, were mapped directly to the new model. These were the first elements to be mapped, and therefore, to be evaluated, and include the reference code, title, dates, dimension and support, language, and physical location.

From the ISAD(G) elements available, the reference code and the physical location can be considered identifiers of the document, and are therefore mapped through the class *E42 Identifier*. On the other hand, the dimension is mapped

[5] Sample baptism record: https://pesquisa.adporto.arquivos.pt/details?id=1374655.
[6] https://digitarq.adevr.arquivos.pt/details?id=1174365.
[7] https://digitarq.arquivos.pt/details?id=4381091.

through the *E54 Dimension* class, support by *E57 Material*, titles by *E35 Title*, dates by *E52 Time-Span*, and the language by *E56 Language*. In Fig. 3, the different ISAD(G) elements can be observed, with the title of the document being portrayed having a formal type, and, therefore, a subclass of *E35 Title* is used to indicate its type, in this case *ARE2 Formal Title*. The dates, as they need validation, are not represented in Fig. 3. Dates give rise to more detailed mini graphs, such as the one already illustrated in Fig. 2.

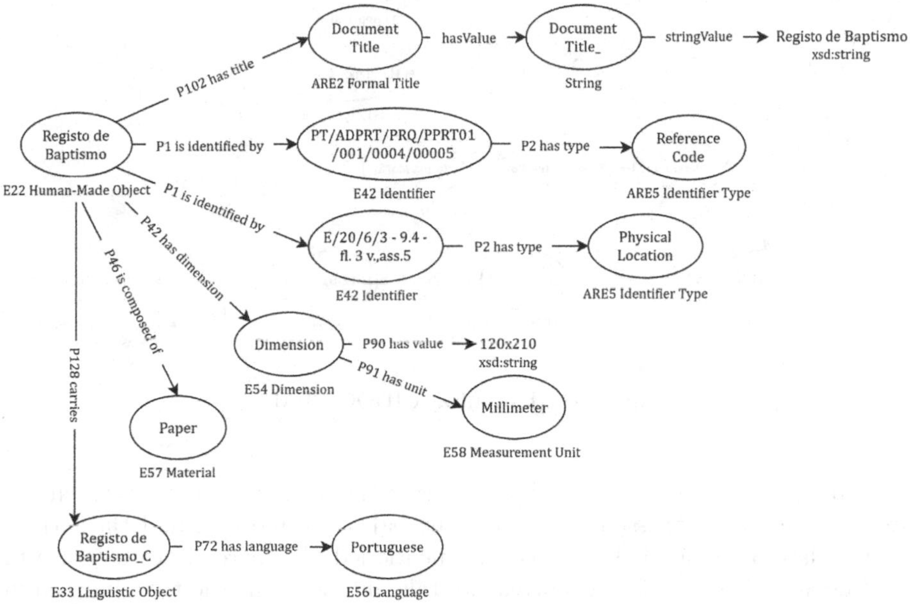

Fig. 3. Evaluation of ISAD(G) concepts in CIDOC-CRM. Original record at https://pesquisa.adporto.arquivos.pt/details?id=1374655.

As the representation of events is central to the CIDOC-CRM, it is essential to evaluate if these can capture some of the concepts that are present in the ISAD(G) standard. The elements where events appear frequently are those that capture the Archival History, Biographical History, and Scope and content.

Several records that mention events in their contents were analyzed. In these records, there are events such as birth, death, and marriage. The CIDOC-CRM provides an explicit representation for the first two events through specific classes and properties, but not to the third (marriage).

In the documents used here, the events come from the textual content of the ISAD(G) elements, since they are not identified separately in this standard. It is, therefore, essential to extract these contents, so that they can be represented through CIDOC-CRM. For this preliminary evaluation, the events were manually identified with the analysis of the records, and their mapping into CIDOC-CRM used the ArchOnto ontology.

As ISAD(G) has descriptive attributes as its base, it is necessary to bear in mind that the events represented may not be the main point of the description, but rather additional information with respect to the document being described. For example, the *Registo de Baptismo*[8], where the goal is to describe Ana's baptism registry, also mentions the event of her birth, as a secondary event.

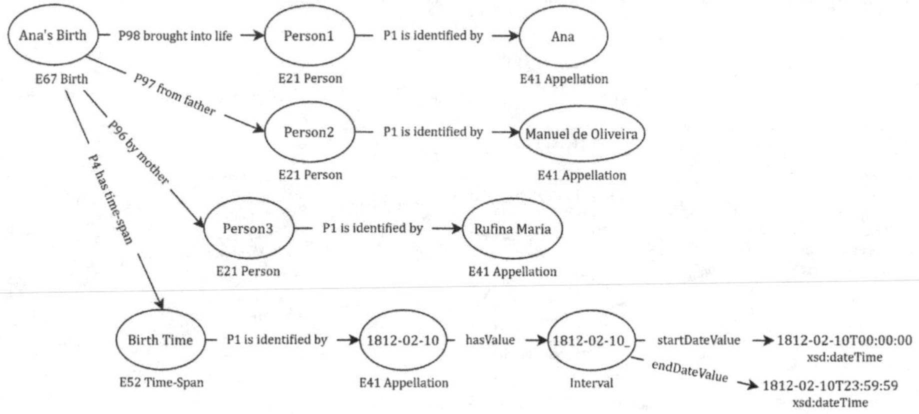

Fig. 4. Birth event at CIDOC-CRM.

Figure 4 shows part of a graph with the event of Ana's birth, in which the three people who witnessed the event (the baby, the mother, and the father) and the date on which it happened are mentioned. As there is no reference to the time at which the birth occurred, we take into account the time interval in which it may have occurred on the indicated day.

Looking at the description of the document "Processo de inventário orfanológico por óbito de Maria Henriqueta Fragoso Barahona Carvalho e Mira", a record describing the assets related to orphaned children, the events of death and marriage are present. Unlike the death event, which bears the date on which it occurred, the wedding event has to be inferred through the description, since this only refers to Maria Henriqueta as being married to José Paulo.

In Fig. 5, the marriage event is represented, but the fact that the event is marriage has to come from the event object itself, as CIDOC-CRM provides no specific class for this kind of event, unlike the birth and death events. With this in mind, the wedding event was mapped based on a ternary relationship, where two people had specific roles in the event. In this case, Person 1 is in the role of bride and Person 2 in the role of fiancé. This graph excerpt makes use of the N-ary pattern twice, linking people with events and the roles they play therein.

[8] Original record at: https://pesquisa.adporto.arquivos.pt/details?id=1374655.

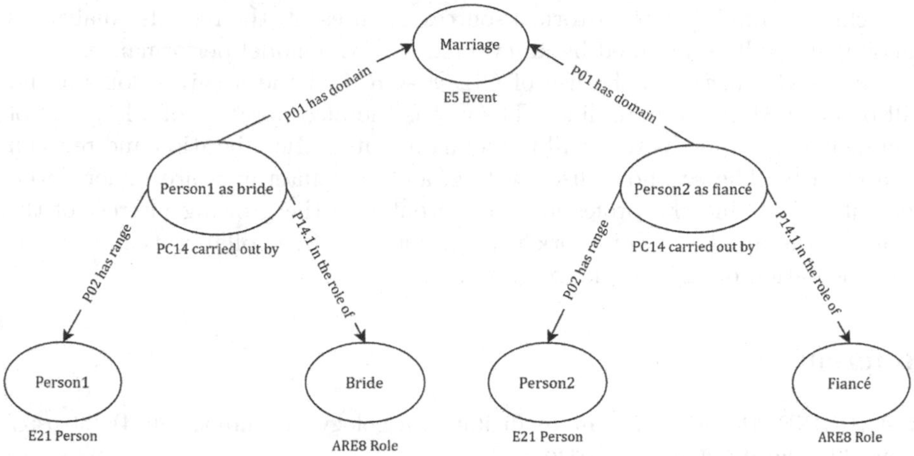

Fig. 5. Marriage event at CIDOC-CRM. Original record at https://digitarq.adevr.arquivos.pt/details?id=1174365.

5 Conclusions

This work has shown that the CIDOC Conceptual Reference Model can be extended and used as a model for archives. We presented a data model, ArchOnto, represented as an ontology and based on the CIDOC-CRM. Special attention was given to entities and properties that are essential for archives and for the applications that manage and provide access to their information.

Two principles were followed in this first approach to an archival model. The first is to accommodate existing information. The records created by archival specialists are a wealth of information with high standards. It is essential to turn this information into its Linked Data counterpart without losing its integrity. Moreover, archivists will continue to generate such records, and therefore the new model should be intelligible to them. The second principle is to favour implementation. The model has been developed alongside the selection of the technology stack that is expected to support the new archival information system. Choices took into account the ease of implementation and the extent to which validation of information added to the records can be done at various points: when migrating information from existing records, when archivists create new records, when records are imported into the archives from the public administration sources.

Given the large number and diversity of available records, the first step to validate the model has used samples of records from different fonds, having in common the fact that they are frequently accessed. The first is a set of parish records, for which there is a large number in series that span centuries. This illustrates records with a common format and that provide well-known relations for the individuals involved. The second is a judicial record and the third a record from a Portuguese national treasure, for which detailed metadata was created by archivists, linking it to historical sources. At present, the records' analysis is ongoing and will be followed by an evaluation of the model performance.

This work illustrates the use of CIDOC-CRM in the archival domain and will be pursued in two main lines. The first is the incorporation of a large set of documents, in a process that will use a mix of automatic migration and revision by archivists. The second is user testing, and user interfaces are under development considering the professional users but also the growing interest of the public in the archives. This work will continue in close collaboration with the implementation of the knowledge graph.

References

1. ARIADNE: the way forward to digital archaeology in Europe (2014). https://arachne.dainst.org/project/ariadne
2. Bountouri, L., Gergatsoulis, M.: The semantic mapping of archival metadata to the CIDOC CRM ontology. J. Arch. Organ. **9**(3–4), 174–207 (2011)
3. Direcção Geral de Arquivos: Grupo de Trabalho de Normalização da Descrição em Arquivo: Orientações para a Descrição Arquivística, 2nd edn. Direção Geral de Arquivos, Lisboa (2007)
4. ICOM/CIDOC CRM Special Interest Group: Definition of the CIDOC Conceptual Reference Model. ICOM, 6.2.7 edn. (2019)
5. IFLA Study Group: Functional Requirements for Bibliographic Records. K.G. Saur Verlag, Munich (2009)
6. International Council on Archives: ISAD(G) Second Edition. International Council on Archives (2000)
7. International Council on Archives: Records in context: a conceptual model for archival description. International Council on Archives (2016)
8. Koch, I., Freitas, N., Ribeiro, C., Lopes, C.T., da Silva, J.R.: Knowledge graph implementation of archival descriptions through CIDOC-CRM. In: Doucet, A., Isaac, A., Golub, K., Aalberg, T., Jatowt, A. (eds.) TPDL 2019. LNCS, vol. 11799, pp. 99–106. Springer, Cham (2019). https://doi.org/10.1007/978-3-030-30760-8_8
9. Ramalho, J.C., Ferreira, J.C.: DigitArq: creating and managing a digital archive. In: Engelen, J., de Souza Costa, S.M., Moreira, A.C.S. (eds.) Building Digital Bridges: Linking Cultures, Commerce and Science: 8th ICCC/IFIP International Conference on Electronic Publishing (2004)

Knowledge-Based Categorization of Scientific Articles for Similarity Predictions

Nolwenn Bernard[1(✉)], Jonathan Weber[2], Germain Forestier[2], Michel Hassenforder[2], and Bastien Latard[1,2]

[1] MDPI, Basel, Switzerland
{bernard,latard}@mdpi.com
[2] IRIMAS, Université de Haute-Alsace, Mulhouse, France

Abstract. Staying aware of new approaches emerging within specific areas can be challenging for researchers who have to follow many feeds such as journals articles, authors' papers, and other basic keyword-based matching algorithms. Hence, this paper proposes an information retrieval process for scientific articles aiming to suggest semantically related articles using exclusively a knowledge base. The first step categorizes articles by the disambiguation of their keywords by identifying common categories within the knowledge base. Then, similar articles are identified using the information extracted from the categorization, such as synonyms. The experimental evaluation shows that the proposed approach significantly outperforms the well known cosine similarity measure of vectors angles inherited from word2vec embeddings. Indeed, there is a difference of 30% for P@k ($k \in [1, 100]$) in favor of the proposed approach.

Keywords: Information retrieval · Categorization · Scientific literature · Document similarity

1 Introduction

Nowadays, the number of scientific articles available in digital format has exploded. Their processing is time-consuming and hence, automatic tools are widely used by researchers to stay up-to-date, as stated by Pain [25]. Improving bibliographic searches could have a positive impact on the scientific literature [30]. The major challenge of this process is its scalability; indeed, these days, databases such as arXiv[1] and Scilit[2] freely propose millions of articles. Thus, text mining is necessary for suggesting relevant documents regarding a topic. Text mining is commonly defined as the process of extracting interesting

[1] https://arxiv.org/.
[2] https://www.scilit.net/.

M. Hall et al. (Eds.): TPDL 2020, LNCS 12246, pp. 147–160, 2020.
https://doi.org/10.1007/978-3-030-54956-5_11

and nontrivial patterns or knowledge from unstructured text documents. This process involves different fields, such as information retrieval, text analysis, and categorization.

The purpose here is to suggest semantically related scientific articles based on a categorization method and similarity measure. The approach proposed in this article aims to improve and extend upon the previous work presented by Latard et al. [18], henceforth referred to as the original approach. They stated an approach which categorizes articles using keyword disambiguation, which provides good results in terms of precision, yet with the drawback of low coverage (i.e., less than 50% of articles are categorized). Therefore, the objective of the proposed approach is to have a higher coverage than the original one in terms of categorized articles in order to compete with the probabilistic approaches broadly used in text mining. To achieve this, category assignation was transformed to be more permissive than the original approach and lemmatization was included in the categorization process.

As far as we know, a fully automated cross-domain information retrieval process for scientific articles exclusively based on an knowledge base does not exist. Using semantics in this type of process permits extension beyond the scope of possibilities [1,17] and the introduction of word sense disambiguation. Indeed, the use of synonyms, hypernyms, etc. is able to complete the query in comparison to the use of only keywords.

This paper starts by a brief overview of related works (Sect. 2). Then, the proposed method is explained (Sect. 3). Next, Sect. 4 presents a comparison with an approach using word embeddings and cosine similarity measure. Finally, the results will be discussed (Sect. 5).

2 Related Works

In 2018, the number of new scientific papers published per year was estimated to be over 3 million [11]; therefore, providing the most relevant suggestions has become a challenge. This has led to a growing interest in information retrieval and information extraction. Information retrieval aims to retrieve the most relevant documents from a corpus based on a given query. Therefore, it often combines text mining techniques [8] and similarity measures in order to retrieve the closest documents. Text mining also embraces information extraction whose purpose is to extract meaningful information from unstructured documents.

Word embedding covers techniques in natural language processing, where words of the vocabulary are mapped to real-valued vectors. Semantic similarities are identified based on the usage of a word in the corpus and its neighbors, as stated by Firth [2]: *"You shall know a word by the company it keeps!"*. In the literature, word embedding is generally associated with word2vec [21], which is a tool based on a multi-layer neural network. For example, word2vec generated models have been used by the Microsoft Academic search engine [12] and by the Computer Science Ontology classifier [27].

Vector space model is described by Salton et al. [28] as the representation of the corpus into a $m * n$, matrix where columns represent the corpus documents and rows embrace all terms of the entire corpus vocabulary. This vector representation is widely used because it provides a practical way to manipulate and compare documents. Indeed, common similarity measures [9], such as Euclidean distance and cosine similarity, take advantage of this vector representation.

Word sense disambiguation [23] is the capacity to identify the sense of an ambiguous word regarding its usage context. In many text mining applications [20,29], this step of disambiguation is crucial. Knowledge sources are essential for word sense disambiguation; they can be structured, such as thesauri and ontologies, or unstructured, like sense-annotated corpora.

The categorization workflow [18] used as a base for this work takes advantage of keywords' metadata to find semantic relations between an article's keywords. In another work, Latard [16] uses these metadata to define a similarity metric to retrieve similar articles in a corpus.

3 Proposed Approach

3.1 Categorization

The categorization of scientific articles is the first step of the proposed approach. Word sense disambiguation is important knowing that an article's keywords can be ambiguous; for example, *synthesis* can be understood as a logical reasoning in a mathematics context or as chemical compound production in chemistry. Therefore, the knowledge base BabelNet [24] is used to select the most consistent keyword's meanings depending on the article's context. It is a multilingual encyclopedic dictionary and a semantic network based on the integration of several semantic lexicons (WordNet [22], VerbNet) together with collaborative databases (Wikipedia[3] and other Wiki data). It can be seen as a dictionary where a single word has different meanings called synsets in the rest of this paper with different senses. Synsets contain several elements of information and for this system, only three of them are kept: categories (C), domains (D), and neighbor synsets (N). A synset s is defined as follows:

$$s = \{C, D, N\} \tag{1}$$

Categorization Workflow. From their research work, Gil-Leiva and Alonso-Arroyo [5] highlighted that the keywords provided by authors bring relevant and meaningful information. In *Web Of Science*[4], keywords are provided by the authors or by the algorithm "KeyWords Plus" [4] or both. Given that we assume that an article's keywords are legitimate, they are used as the only input in this step of the process.

Figure 1 represents the categorization's step workflow [16]. An article's keywords without any preprocessing are used as input to search for an exact match

[3] https://www.wikipedia.org/.

[4] https://www.webofknowledge.com/.

in BabelNet, but many keywords composed of several words are not indexed in BabelNet. Hence, in the case of a first stage without results, a second stage, in which keywords are split, is proposed. Then connected synsets are identified (e.g., Fig. 2) and their related data, such as categories and domains, are extracted and considered as contextually related to this article.

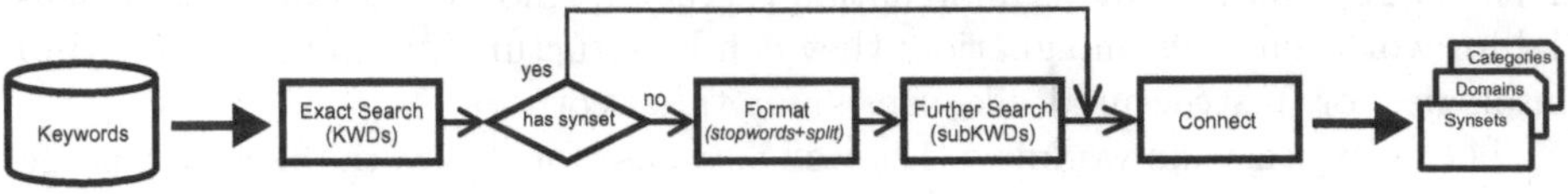

Fig. 1. Simplified workflow of the categorization stage

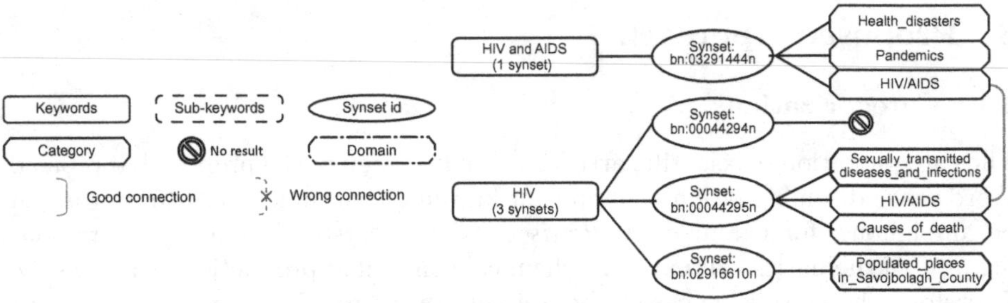

Fig. 2. Simple connection by categories

Improvement. In order to categorize more articles than the original approach, in other words, increasing the article coverage, less restrictions are applied during the synset connections. For this part, three points are taken into consideration: lemmatization, synsets connections by domains, and an article's categories.

Lemmatization is the process of reducing the different forms of a word to one single form, commonly called a lemma. For example, play is the lemma of "playing, played, plays". Obtaining generic keywords which may have a greater chance of being indexed in BabelNet is a good solution. Qazanfari et al. [26] showed that using lemmas improved the precision and accuracy of their recommendation system. That is why lemmatization is included in both search approaches (i.e., exact and further). Indeed, the initial keyword set has the first chance to give results and lemmatization is attempted in a second chance in the case of an empty result set. Let us focus on the keyword "Software development processes" to demonstrate the benefit of this feature, as it is not indexed in BabelNet and therefore, nothing is returned using the exact search. At the this point, the original method launches the further search with the sub-keywords "Software development", "Software processes" and "development processes" and gives the set of categories C_O. This approach lemmatizes the input before trying the exact search again with "Software development process" which retrieves the categories C_L. Even if the retrieved categories are close, a deviation is noticeable with the ones from C_O and, indeed, *Marketing* digresses from the main topic.

$$C_O = \{Software\_project\_management, Software\_development, Project\_management, Product\_development, Marketing, Computer\_occupations\}$$
$$C_L = \{Software\_development\_process, Formal\_methods, Methodology, Software\_engineering\}$$

In the original method, only categories were involved in the synset connection process because the focus was on precision. Yet, the generality of the domains[5] can be used as an advantage because it is more probable that articles share common domains. This implies that there are more potential articles with data. Let us focus on an example, an article with the keywords *"kerosene reforming, novel combustion technologies, hydrogen assisted combustion"* does not have connected synsets by categories. If domains are taken in consideration (Fig. 3), there are

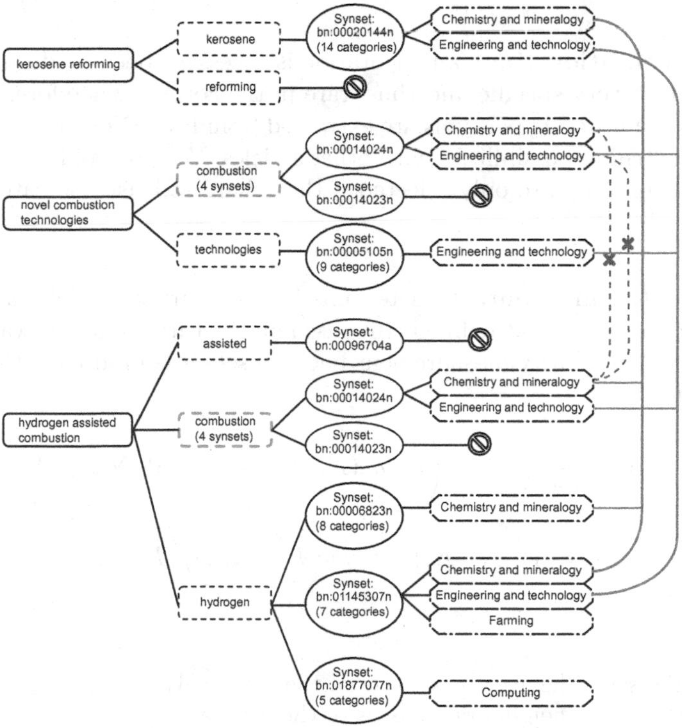

Fig. 3. Domains connection

[5] BabelNet has 34 domains (e.g., "Computing", "Astronomy") and many categories that are mostly inherited from Wikipedia.

connections, thus, some synsets are validated (e.g., bn:00020144n, bn:00014024n) and added to the set A_S, which regroups all the synsets of the article A.

The last transformation of the original method concerns the category attribution. An article's categories have an important impact on the data augmentation phase. For the purpose of increasing an article's coverage, it was decided to assign all categories from connected synsets to the article (Eq. 2). For example, the categories "Sexually_transmitted_diseases_and_infections", "Health_disasters", "Pandemics", "Causes_of_death" will be added to "HIV/AIDS" for the article in Fig. 2.

$$\begin{gathered} \text{Let } s_1,\, s_2 \in A_S \\ A_C = \{c \mid c \in (s_1.C \cup s_2.C)\} \end{gathered} \tag{2}$$

where A_C is all the categories of the article A.

3.2 Related Articles

Finding related articles is the second step of the proposed process, where data inherited from categorization are exploited. It is divided into two steps: 1) data augmentation and 2) similarity measurement.

Data Augmentation. Data augmentation is necessary because disambiguated words might be very specific and thus, rare in the corpus. Therefore, neighbors such as synonyms and hypernyms are extracted from BabelNet's knowledge base to expand matching possibilities with other articles. Yet, to avoid bringing unrelated neighbors, they are only selected if they share at least one category with the article.

Similarity Measurement. To determine how similar two articles are, a similarity equation (Eq. 3) was defined [16] based on the three different ways to connect articles. A similarity measurement between sets is computed with weighted Jaccard indexes.

$$\begin{aligned} sim(A_i, A_j) = \frac{1}{\alpha+\beta+\gamma} * \Bigg(& \alpha\, jac(K_i, K_j) + \frac{\beta}{2}\, jacKN(K_i, N_j, K_j) \\ & + \frac{\beta}{2}\, jacKN(K_j, N_i, K_i) + \gamma\, jacNN(N_i, N_j, K_i, K_j) \Bigg) \end{aligned} \tag{3}$$

where:

- K_x is the set of keywords' synsets of the article A_x
- N_x is the set of neighbors' synsets of the article A_x
- $jac()$, $jacKN()$ and $jacNN()$ are three Jaccard index variants, respectively defined in Eq. 4, Eq. 5 and Eq. 6.

There are three different ways to connect articles together which use keywords' synsets extracted from both categorization and data augmentation:

1. *Keyword intersection*: Articles share the same keywords' synsets, and this is the obvious and most reliable connection.

$$jac(K_i, K_j) = \frac{|K_i \cap K_j|}{|K_i \cup K_j|} \quad (4)$$

2. *Keyword-Neighbor intersection*: Keywords' synsets of the first article belong to neighbors of the second article and vice-versa. This connection is considered as moderately reliable.

$$jacKN(K_i, N_j, K_j) = \frac{|K_i \cap N_j|}{|K_i \cup N_j| - |K_i \cap K_j|} \quad (5)$$

3. *Neighbor intersection*: Articles share the same neighbors; this is the farthest and least reliable connection.

$$jacNN(N_i, N_j, K_i, K_j) = \frac{|N_i \cap N_j|}{|N_i \cup N_j| - (|K_i \cap N_j| + |N_i \cap K_j|)} \quad (6)$$

An heuristic analysis of the Eq. 3 was realized to evaluate the impact of the coefficients α, β, and γ. This showed that as the three ways to connect articles together do not have the same confidence, maximizing α will provide more accurate results than the maximization of β and γ because the keyword intersection is the most reliable. Knowing that, the values of 4, 2 and 1 were, respectively, chosen for α, β, and γ for the rest of this article [16].

4 Evaluation

4.1 Dataset

The analysis presented in this article was performed using *Web of Science Dataset WOS-46985* from Kowsari et al. [14], which has been specifically used for text classification [7,15]. This dataset contains 46,985 articles from *Web of Science* divided into seven domains and 134 categories. For the rest of the evaluation, only domains were taken into consideration because the proximity of the dataset's categories might lead to high overlapping.

4.2 Metric

Eye tracking studies on user behavior regarding ranked results of a web search [6,10] showed that the higher the rank, the less attention is paid by the user to consult this suggestion. Hence, given the number of scientific articles in the literature, precision at k (P@k) is a suitable metric to evaluate this method, as the focus is on the first k elements which are considered as the most similar. Indeed, it is improbable that a user wants to read all similar articles retrieved in the literature. P@k is defined as follows:

$$\text{P@k} = \frac{\#Relevant\ articles\ in\ top_k}{k} \quad (7)$$

Articles sharing the same domain were called relevant articles; the maximum value of k was experimentally set to 100. Yet, this metric has a weak point: the dependency on k [19]. Let us say that k equals 10 and the method proposes only six related articles even if these six articles are relevant, the precision would not be 1 but 0.6. In order to minimize this, a customized top_k, called "linked top$_k$" was created. The aim is to increase the number of relevant articles retrieved using their top_k (Fig. 4).

$$top_k = \{w_i, ..., w_k\} \quad 1 \leq i \leq k \tag{8}$$

where w_i is the weight of the ith related article.

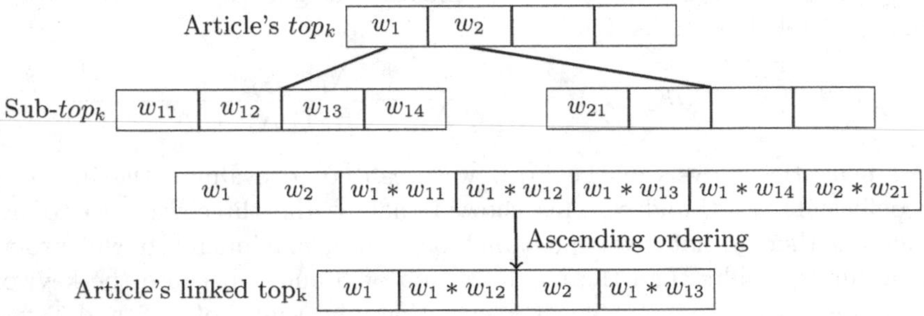

Fig. 4. Article's linked top$_k$, with $k = 4$

4.3 Word2vec and Cosine Similarity (w2v-Cos)

Mikolov et al. [21] introduced word2vec as a machine learning approach using a multi-layer neural network to learn semantic word proximity. The models trained by word2vec learning techniques represent the syntactic probabilities of words' co-occurrence and can be used to predict the next words in a sequence. For the experiment, the model trained[6] on a part of Google News dataset (100 billion words) was employed. It contains 300-dimensional vectors for 3 million words and phrases. These vectors are exploited to compute the similarity between two words.

In this case, each split keyword is passed to the network and the 300-dimension vectors, in return, are averaged to obtain a mean vector and then stored. To determine the similarity between two articles the cosine similarity measure (Eq. 9) was chosen.

$$sim_c = \frac{V_i \cdot V_j}{|V_i| \times |V_j|} \tag{9}$$

where V_x is the mean vector of the article A_x.

[6] https://code.google.com/archive/p/word2vec/.

The cosine is defined in the interval $[-1, 1]$ but only the positive space $[0, 1]$ is used in this experiment because all components of article vectors are non-negative [13]. Two articles with a cosine similarity of 1 are considered as the same while a similarity of 0 means no correlation between them.

4.4 Analysis

The first notable point is that w2v-cos is largely outperformed by the other approaches. Indeed, it stagnates around a precision of 19% for k between 1 and 100 (Fig. 5a) while the original approach has an average precision of 25% and the proposed approach reaches 49%. The article coverage as well as the permissiveness of the approach during the categorization step can justify the wide difference between the original and proposed approaches.

As explained earlier, P@k has limits, especially its dependency on the k value, and thus, the original approach is penalized more than the proposed approach due to the coverage (46.8% against 88.2% for the proposed approach). The w2v-cos approach is less impacted; indeed, there are only 11 articles without vector representation. In order to minimize this dependency, a second version of P@k was created (Eq. 10), which permits the precision to be evaluated on real proposed articles. With this new metric, the precision is not biased by the difference between k and the number of articles in top_k, as is the case with P@k.

$$\text{P'@k} = \frac{\#\textit{Relevant articles in top}_k}{\text{Number of articles in } top_k} \tag{10}$$

Figure 5b illustrates that the usage of this new metric, the w2v-cos curve (i.e., green) is the same as in Fig. 5a because this approach always proposes the maximum number of articles, except for the 11 articles without vector representation. Concerning the two others, Fig. 5b shows a slightly advantage for the original approach; yet, it is necessary to nuance with the total number of pairs retrieved (Table 1). In fact, P'@100 is nearly the same but the proposed approach retrieved 4,108,432 pairs, which is more than twice the number retrieved by the original approach.

Table 1. Comparison of retrieved pairs with $k = 100$, best values are in bold

Approach	P@100	P'@100	#proposed pairs	#correct pairs	#missing pairs
w2v-cos	0.185	0.185	**4,697,400**	867,377	**1,100**
Original	0.222	**0.553**	1,831,027	1,041,567	2,867,473
Original-linked	0.259	0.541	2,248,478	1,215,297	2,450,022
Proposed	0.475	0.543	4,108,432	2,234,326	590,068
Proposed-linked	**0.478**	0.542	4,142,957	**2,246,657**	555,543

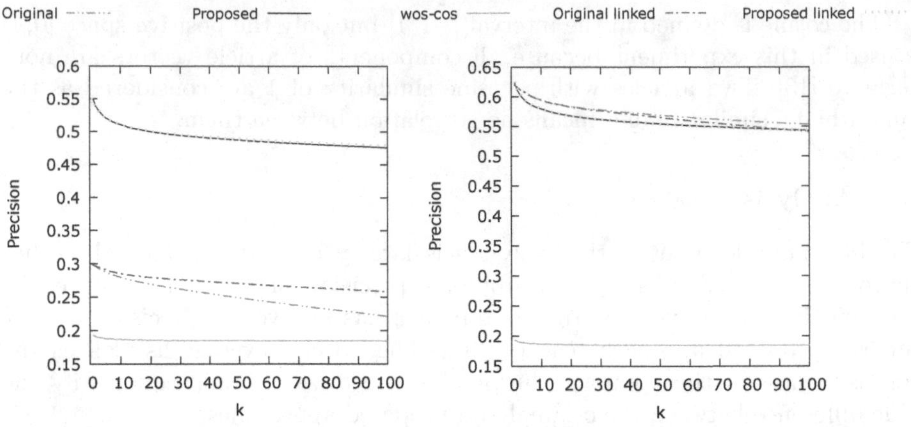

(a) P@k (b) P'@k

Fig. 5. Curves comparing the different approaches, suffix linked for the approaches using linked top_k (Color figure online)

As expected, using linked top_k increases the number of proposed pairs and slightly increases P@k (Fig. 5a). The influence of linked top_k is more remarkable for the original approach; indeed, it lowered the number of missing pairs by 14.6 points. Missing pairs represent the difference between the expected number of pairs (i.e., #articles * k) and the number of pairs the approach is able to propose. Yet, this linking tends to bring more wrong pairs than good ones, as demonstrated with a subtle decrease of P'@100: 1.2 points for the original approach and 0.2 points for the proposed one. In fact, using top_k of the relevant articles as an intermediary for the construction of linked top_k (Fig. 4) introduces a loss of confidence in the proposed articles. Therefore, if the focus is on quantity, applying this linking can be a good compromise because the loss of precision is negligible.

As presented in Fig. 5b, the precision of the different approaches can be improved. The first thing to notice is the proximity of certain domains, such as *Medical* and *Psychology*. This proximity is reflected in Table 2, which presents the first seven combinations most found for k between 1 and 100. Indeed, for each approach, the combination Medical/Psychology appeared in the first three positions. Let us exemplify this with a concrete case using the original approach, where K_i is in the *Medical* domain and K_j is in *Psychology*:

- $K_i = \{$***Alzheimer's disease***, *cerebrovascular disease*, ***dementia***, *estrogen, menopause, prevention*$\}$
- $K_j = \{$***Alzheimer's disease***, *nonverbal communication, emotional prosody, behavioral and psychological symptoms of* ***dementia*** *(BPSD)*$\}$.

Despite the fact that these articles have distinct domains, their keywords (K_i, K_j) are quite similar. Hence, after the categorization step, they have the same synsets and are considered as similar, which makes sense in reality. On the contrary, certain associations seem illogical, like the first set of keywords K_i in *Psychology* and the second one K_j in *MAE*:

- K_i = {*Facial*, ***Emotion***, *Lateralisation, Stroke*, ***Perception***}
- K_j = {*Battery electrical vehicles, Repertory grid technique, Comparison of modes of transport, Subjective* ***perception***, ***Emotions***}.

The categorization step for these sets in the original approach finds the same synsets coming from perception and emotions and thus, the similarity is 1. In that case, using the proposed approach, or w2v-cos, which is more permissive, does not assign a similarity of 1; indeed, more keywords have data and so the disambiguation is better. Hence, the notion of dissimilarity between these sets is introduced, which makes sense.

Moreover, the domain overlapping of w2v-cos shows that this approach has trouble distinguishing *Medical* from all other domains. This can explain such a gap in terms of the precision between this approach and the other two. For example, the two following sets of keywords (K_i, K_j) related to the fields of medicine and electrical engineering are considered as being highly similar even though there is no obvious relation. Moreover, no relation is found using the other two approaches, thus qualifying these sets as uncorrelated.

- K_i = {*HCV, Flaviviridae, epidemiology, Saudi Arabia*}
- K_j = {*Electric machines, Machine control, Magnetic losses, Multilevel systems, Physics-based modeling, Power system simulation, System analysis*}.

This example highlights a limit of the w2v-cos approach; indeed, the model assigns at least one vector for 99.9% of the articles using a probabilistic method [21]. This type of method can be seen as a black box; thus, the method to build vectors is unclear, which complicates the understanding of such incongruous associations.

Table 2. Most found domain combinations with the number of occurrences for each approach

Original		Proposed		w2v-cos	
Medical/Medical	20,074,800	Medical/Medical	46,084,918	Medical/Medical	22,149,123
Psychology/Psychology	11,383,939	Psychology/Medical	18,407,072	CS/Medical	19,929,028
Psychology/Medical	9,754,968	Psychology/Psychology	17,936,117	Medical/Psychology	19,578,757
Biochemistry/Medical	7,119,827	Medical/Biochemistry	16,363,304	Medical/ECE	18,017,840
ECE/ECE	6,368,952	CS/CS	15,058,490	Biochemistry/Medical	17,761,059
Biochemistry/Biochemistry	6,173,909	ECE/ECE	12,009,851	Medical/Civil	13,602,961
CS/CS	5,639,581	Biochemistry/Biochemistry	11,268,296	Medical/MAE	10,052,781

5 Discussion

As stated previously in Sect. 4.4, the proposed approach outperforms w2v-cos used as a baseline; yet, the precision can be improved. A possible solution to increase the precision would be to introduce a threshold. The similarity is defined as between 0 and 1, with 0 corresponding to no correlation. Knowing that, the study of the distance[7] distribution of top_k (Fig. 6) can bring relevant information towards finding a critical distance. As shown in Fig. 6, as the distance increases, the proportion of wrong pairs increases while the precision decreases. Thus, finding the distance where the wrong predictions start to represent more than 50% of the proposed pairs and filtering the pairs with a higher distance in articles' top_k might improve the precision. However, this solution implies a loss of proposed articles.

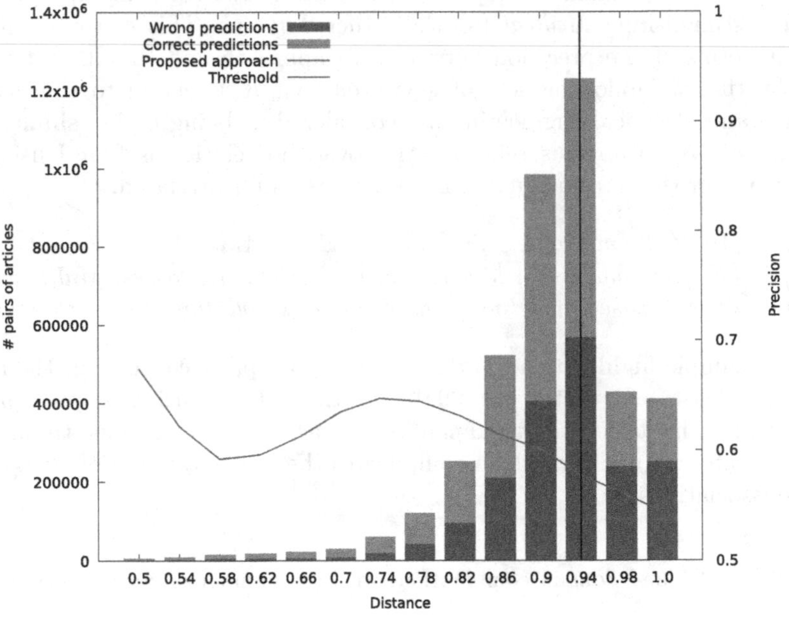

Fig. 6. Distance distribution and precision of top_k using the proposed approach.

In this case, the proposed approach has an average of 55.8% for P'@k ($k \in [1, 100]$). The critical distance is reached at 0.94, where good predictions represent 51.4% of the proposed pairs. At this point, filtering will decrease the number of proposed pairs by 20.4 points. This drop goes along with an augmentation of P'@k average to 56.6%. In this context, the difference between the proposed approach and its filtered version is marginal and it shows that introducing a threshold impacts the precision. Given this, more variants of the threshold

[7] distance = 1 − similarity.

selection need to be tested such that there will be more information regarding its influence and the user can choose whether to accept this compromise.

6 Conclusion

The aim of this paper was to present a process of suggesting related scientific articles. This process is composed of two major steps: the categorization and the suggestion using a similarity measure. The objective of increasing the coverage compared to the original approach was completed. Indeed, the coverage reaches 88.2% compared to 48.6% for the original approach. However, on this point, w2v-cos is still superior but it is outperformed by the proposed approach in terms of precision.

The experiments permitted us to establish that the proposed approach can compete against probabilistic methods such as baseline w2v-cos. The analysis highlights that word sense disambiguation is more efficient in the proposed approach, leading to a much better precision than w2v-cos.

The proposed approach provides promising results and improves upon the original one. In the future, the reproducibility of this approach could be evaluated using another dataset. Moreover, to support the previous assumption, a comparison with other probabilistic approaches such as the binary independence retrieval model [3] will be done in future work.

References

1. Ensan, F., Bagheri, E.: Document retrieval model through semantic linking. In: WSDM, pp. 181–190. ACM (2017)
2. Firth, J.G.: A synopsis of linguistic theory 1930–1955 in studies in linguistic analysis, Oxford (1962)
3. Fuhr, N.: Probabilistic models in information retrieval. Comput. J. **35**(3), 243–255 (1992)
4. Garfield, E.: Current eamments. Curr. Contents **32**, 3–7 (1990)
5. Gil-Leiva, I., Alonso-Arroyo, A.: Keywords given by authors of scientific articles in database descriptors. J. Am. Soc. Inf. Sci. Technol. **58**(8), 1175–1187 (2007)
6. Guan, Z., Cutrell, E.: An eye tracking study of the effect of target rank on web search. In: SIGCHI, pp. 417–420. ACM (2007)
7. Heidarysafa, M., Kowsari, K., Brown, D.E., Meimandi, K.J., Barnes, L.E.: An improvement of data classification using random multimodel deep learning (RMDL). Int. J. Mach. Learn. Comput. **8**(4), 298–310 (2018)
8. Hotho, A., Nürnberger, A., Paass, G.: A brief survey of text mining. In: LDV Forum, vol. 20, pp. 19–62 (2005)
9. Huang, A.: Similarity measures for text document clustering. In: NZCSRSC, vol. 4, pp. 9–56 (2008)
10. Joachims, T., Granka, L.A., Pan, B., Hembrooke, H., Gay, G.: Accurately interpreting clickthrough data as implicit feedback. In: SIGIR, vol. 5, pp. 154–161 (2005)
11. Johnson, R., Watkinson, A., Mabe, M.: The STM report: an overview of scientific and scholarly publishing (2018). https://www.stm-assoc.org/2018_10_04_STM_Report_2018.pdf

12. Kanakia, A., Shen, Z., Eide, D., Wang, K.: A scalable hybrid research paper recommender system for Microsoft academic. In: The World Wide Web Conference, pp. 2893–2899. ACM (2019)
13. Korenius, T., Laurikkala, J., Juhola, M.: On principal component analysis, cosine and euclidean measures in information retrieval. Inf. Sci. **177**(22), 4893–4905 (2007)
14. Kowsari, K., Brown, D.E., Heidarysafa, M., Meimandi, K.J., Gerber, M.S., Barnes, L.E.: HDLTex: hierarchical deep learning for text classification. In: ICMLA, pp. 364–371. IEEE (2017)
15. Kowsari, K., Heidarysafa, M., Brown, D.E., Meimandi, K.J., Barnes, L.E.: RMDL: random multimodel deep learning for classification. In: ICISDM, pp. 19–28. ACM (2018)
16. Latard, B.: Scientific search engines: from the categorization to the information retrieval. Ph.D. thesis, Université de Haute-Alsace (2019)
17. Latard, B., Weber, J., Forestier, G., Hassenforder, M.: Towards a semantic search engine for scientific articles. In: Kamps, J., Tsakonas, G., Manolopoulos, Y., Iliadis, L., Karydis, I. (eds.) TPDL 2017. LNCS, vol. 10450, pp. 608–611. Springer, Cham (2017). https://doi.org/10.1007/978-3-319-67008-9_54
18. Latard, B., Weber, J., Forestier, G., Hassenforder, M.: Using semantic relations between keywords to categorize articles from scientific literature. In: ICTAI, pp. 260–264. IEEE (2017)
19. Manning, C., Raghavan, P., Schütze, H.: Introduction to information retrieval. Nat. Lang. Eng. **16**(1), 100–103 (2010)
20. Menaka, S., Radha, N.: Text classification using keyword extraction technique. Int. J. Adv. Res. Comput. Sci. Softw. Eng. **3**(12), 734–740 (2013)
21. Mikolov, T., Chen, K., Corrado, G.S., Dean, J.: Efficient estimation of word representations in vector space. arXiv preprint arXiv:1301.3781 (2013)
22. Miller, G.A.: WordNet: a lexical database for English. Commun. ACM **38**(11), 39–41 (1995)
23. Navigli, R.: Word sense disambiguation: a survey. ACM Comput. Surv. **41**, 10:1–10:69 (2009)
24. Navigli, R., Ponzetto, S.P.: BabelNet: the automatic construction, evaluation and application of a wide-coverage multilingual semantic network. Artif. Intell. **193**, 217–250 (2012)
25. Pain, E.: How to keep up with the scientific literature (2016). https://www.sciencemag.org/careers/2016/11/how-keep-scientific-literature
26. Qazanfari, K., Youssef, A., Keane, K., Nelson, J.: A novel recommendation system to match college events and groups to students. IOP Conf. Ser.: Mater. Sci. Eng. **261**(1), 1–15 (2017)
27. Salatino, A.A., Osborne, F., Thanapalasingam, T., Motta, E.: The CSO classifier: ontology-driven detection of research topics in scholarly articles. In: Doucet, A., Isaac, A., Golub, K., Aalberg, T., Jatowt, A. (eds.) TPDL 2019. LNCS, vol. 11799, pp. 296–311. Springer, Cham (2019). https://doi.org/10.1007/978-3-030-30760-8_26
28. Salton, G., Wong, A., Yang, C.S.: A vector space model for automatic indexing. Commun. ACM **18**, 613–620 (1975)
29. Shehata, S.: A wordnet-based semantic model for enhancing text clustering. In: ICDM, pp. 477–482. IEEE (2009)
30. Shemilt, I., et al.: Pinpointing needles in giant haystacks: use of text mining to reduce impractical screening workload in extremely large scoping reviews. Res. Synth. Methods **5**(1), 31–49 (2014)

User Requirements and Behaviour

Participatory Indexing in the Eyes of Its Potential Users: An Example of a Co-design of Participatory Services in an Academic Digital Library

Elina Leblanc(✉)

Laboratoire TEMOS, Université Bretagne-Sud, Lorient, France
elina.leblanc@univ-ubs.fr

Abstract. Participatory indexing allows users of a digital library to add descriptors based on controlled vocabularies to digital content. Similar to participatory tagging, tested by several cultural websites such as digital museums or libraries, it could help users better understand the way librarians organize their collections, improve their searches and harmonize the keywords of all the library. In this paper, we present the experiments made by *Fonte Gaia Bib* (*FG Bib*), a French-Italian academic digital library, in the elaboration of a participatory indexing tool. To design such a tool, the project chose a participatory design by organizing two-days workshops with potential users. This method provided several ideas to implement a participatory tool that meets users' needs. These workshops also provided preliminary data on the way users conceptualize participatory services in the context of a cultural heritage and academic project.

Keywords: Indexing · Participatory services · Academic digital libraries · Digital humanities · Participatory design · Controlled vocabularies

1 Introduction: Towards a Participatory Indexing Service

In participatory digital libraries, which allow their users to contribute to the enrichment of their collections, the addition of keywords or tagging is one of the most widespread forms of contribution. Users are invited to associate a descriptor of their choice with a resource, without referring to a controlled vocabulary and without *a posteriori* validation. These keywords do not replace the classifications and controlled vocabularies used by librarians but complement them [3]. They are the very expression of the needs and interests of the users. They constitute thus important information for the further development of a digital library [5].

However, this service has limitations in terms of harmonization of contributions (duplicates, multiple spellings, personal keywords), tools and presentation of the service to other users [3]. It brings no enrichment to the user, except the personal satisfaction of sharing knowledge with others. Tagging then seems to be participation for participation's sake, as having no other purpose than to follow the codes of the social web.

M. Hall et al. (Eds.): TPDL 2020, LNCS 12246, pp. 163–170, 2020.
https://doi.org/10.1007/978-3-030-54956-5_12

In this paper, we propose to explore another solution to allow users to add keywords: participative indexing. Here we mean indexing in a librarian sense, i.e. adding keywords to works from pre-existing controlled vocabularies, such as RAMEAU [22] for French or the *Library of Congress Subject Headings* [19] for English. These controlled vocabularies are based on very precise rules that indicate the order in which the keywords must be placed. Thus, in the case of RAMEAU, the indexing of a work must follow the model below:

Initial access (Heading) - subject subdivision - geographical subdivision - chronological subdivision - form subdivision.

A work on pastries in Alsace will therefore have the following RAMEAU description: Pâtisseries – France – Alsace (France).

However, indexing faces several obstacles. On the user's side, the form and organization of keywords is opaque, since the user does not understand the rules behind those vocabularies. On the library side, indexing requires encyclopedic knowledge, which is no longer possible with the current evolution of the profession towards greater versatility of activities. Participatory indexing would then come to alleviate these difficulties. Indeed, our hypothesis is that an indexing tool based on standardized vocabularies would introduce users to library indexing methods, placing them in a librarianship perspective, and disseminating good practices. Users would thus acquire indexing skills, as well as a better understanding of the classification system and the thinking of librarians. They would thus improve the quality of their searches.

On the librarian side, participatory indexing would have the advantage of harmonizing keywords and unifying searches. It would also allow to test another solution for validating user contributions, as controlled vocabularies would ensure indirect control by the librarians.

This article proposes a reflection on the development of such a participatory indexing service and on the way the public of a digital library sees it, by using the example of the *Fonte Gaia* project and its academic digital library *Fonte Gaia Bib* (*FG Bib*), currently under development at the Grenoble Alpes University Library [15]. *FG Bib* is a French-Italian multi-partner library for Italian studies, which follows digital humanities methods for its elaboration [4]. It offers a variety of contents (manuscripts and prints from the 15th to the 19th century) in French and Italian, for a mixed audience of researchers and lay users. *FG Bib* is characterized by its participatory vocation, inviting users to contribute to the enrichment of its contents either by adding keywords or comments, or by producing digital scholarly editions or scientific descriptions[1]. *Fonte Gaia* views participation as a form of knowledge mediation, where the user transmits knowledge to the library and to other users, while acquiring knowledge and skills in return. In the model of citizen sciences, the aim is to introduce users to scientific and library skills [1, 10]. In the case of indexing, which is a librarian skill, more than creating citizen scientists, it would be a matter of creating citizen librarians. Indeed, the participatory indexing service will be aimed at students, PhD students, or lay users, and could be used by librarians of the Grenoble University Library during training courses on searching for documents in digital libraries.

---

[1] These services are currently being implemented. The digital library currently online is a beta version. A preview of the new version is available on the project's blog [8].

To develop such a participatory indexing service, we have chosen to use a method that is itself participatory, by organizing participatory design workshops based on a hackathon model. In the field of digital humanities, only a few projects used participatory design methods, such as the *Infinite Ulysses*, *VERA* (*Virtual Environments for Research in Archaeology*) or *Digipal* projects [11, 12, 14, 17]. While these projects only involve end-users, we choose to involve the entire public of a digital library. In our case, this means involving not only end-users, but also librarians who are traditionally in charge of the indexing of library's digital content. In this way, our aim is to build a tool that do not replace librarians' work, but fit in with their professional practices.

With the support of the *Collex-Persée* program[2], we had the opportunity to organize participatory modeling workshops that looked like a hackathon, since they took place over several days and involved several teams of participants. Called "Hacke ta bibliothèque! (Hack your library!)" [16], this event offered participants the following challenge: to prefigure a participatory and multilingual indexing tool based on three controlled vocabularies in French (RAMEAU), Italian (*Nuovo Soggetario* [21]) and English (*Library of Congress Subject Headings*). By choosing such a method, we wished not only to involve our potential users in the design of the digital library and to design a service that meets their needs, but also to obtain preliminary data on the way users conceptualize participatory services in the context of a cultural heritage project.

This paper is organized as follows: Sect. 2 presents the participatory workshop process. Section 3 describes the participatory indexing tools devised by our participants. Section 4 offers an analysis of these tools and what they tell us about the perception of our participants of indexing and user participation in digital libraries.

2 Course of the Event

The event "Hack your library!" took place from 10 to 12 April 2019, at the Grenoble Alpes University Library. The first day was dedicated to a seminar on the place of participatory services in digital libraries. This seminar presented the issues that participants were confronted with during the hackathon. The next two days were devoted to workshops on the development of the indexing service.

Of the twelve participants who responded to the call for participation, eight came on the day of the event, allowing us to form two teams of equal size. Each team consisted of two librarians and two students in Italian studies or in digital humanities. To help carry out the challenge, the two teams benefited from the expertise of several resource persons in the field of controlled vocabularies, natural language processing, semantic web or digital libraries. At the end of these two days, the participants presented their ideas to a jury, which was responsible for selecting a winning project.

---

[2] The *Collex-Persée* program is a scientific interest group dedicated to the valorisation of documentary and scientific information, and to linking documentation professionals with researchers within the framework of projects centred on the digitisation of corpora and the creation of services [13].

During our hackathon, we emphasized the presence of resource persons, experts in their field, who were able to exchange with users and pass on their knowledge. The aim was that at the end participants would have a different view of digital libraries and service design.

Our event is characterized by a challenge restricted to an issue specific to the librarian's profession. As a result, we did not attract the same audience as other events of this type: it was not developers, but potential users of the service they were going to design. It was a privileged opportunity to gain insight into users' needs and perceptions of the services of a digital library. We thus propose another way of reusing all of the data produced, rather than simply putting the winning project into production.

3 Presentation of the Results

3.1 The First Project: A Simplified Indexing Tool

The first team designed a participatory indexing tool that does not require a user account. The tool has an easy to use and intuitive interface aimed at students, enlightened amateurs or young researchers.

In this scenario, the user first selects a type of keywords (subject, place, date, document type), then chooses one or more keywords by browsing the tree structure of the selected controlled vocabulary (see Fig. 1). The tool is based on a lighter version of the controlled vocabulary (here RAMEAU), displaying only the families of keywords that have a meaning in relation to the *Fonte Gaia* collections. The indexing process is also simplified: the user does not create RAMEAU headings, as presented above, but only selects terms that he believes describe the work.

Fig. 1. Mock-up of the indexing tool imagined by the first team (CC-BY)

When the user validates his contribution, the tool suggests equivalents in Italian, thanks to an alignment between RAMEAU and the *Nuovo Soggetario*. If no equivalent is found, the user can suggest a translation. The keywords are then subjected to a double evaluation: a validation by the other users, in the form of a vote for or against, and a final validation by an expert of the project.

The added keywords improve the searches of other users, allowing them to extend their searches to keywords close to the one they are looking for. The tool exploits here another facet of controlled vocabularies. Indeed, these latter are based both on a hierarchical structure, from the broadest term to the most precise term, and on a horizontal structure, i.e. linking together terms expressing the same idea, but belonging to different trees in the vocabulary. For example, in RAMEAU, *drame* is related to *dramaturge* or *tragédie*. These associations of ideas allow the user to encounter other themes or works and thus promote serendipity.

3.2 The Second Project: A Platform for Initiation to Digital Humanities

The second team chose a different orientation, by imagining "a participative training device for digital humanities". This system is mainly aimed at students, supervised by researchers or librarians.

This content co-creation platform offers several types of activities (see Fig. 2): 1) metadata enrichment, 2) addition of keywords to portions of images of pages using the IIIF (*International Image Interoperability Framework*) [18] technology and the *Mirador* visualization tool [20], 3) transcription and encoding of text with the TEI (*Text Encoding Initiative*) markup language [23]. Each activity is accompanied and validated by specialists, whether professors supervising students or librarians. Participatory indexing appears here at an image level: *Mirador* allows to annotate portions of images and add keywords to them. This team therefore envisaged that users select these keywords from controlled vocabularies.

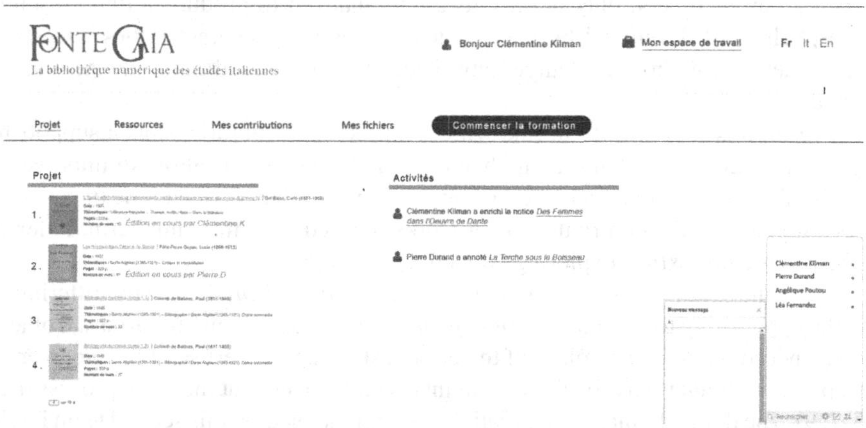

Fig. 2. Mock-up of the participative training device in digital humanities imagined by the second team (CC-BY)

3.3 Towards Two Levels of Indexation for *Fonte Gaia Bib*

At the end of the two days of workshops, we chose to reward the second project. Although more ambitious and more complex, it is in line with *Fonte Gaia*'s pedagogical objectives and proposes an original use of controlled vocabularies, not at the level of the book, but at the level of the text.

The philosophy of the first project, on the contrary, faces ethical obstacles, embodied in the participants' proposal to "do indexing without knowing it". Proposing to index unknowingly and without benefit to the user is in the end equivalent to making the user work for the library without knowing it. While the tool can be commended for its ease of use, it lacks transparency: no mention of the controlled vocabularies and their role is envisaged on the mock-ups made by the participants (see Fig. 1). The user adds keywords without knowing where they come from and why.

However, due to the conceptual quality of this project, it will also be integrated into *Fonte Gaia Bib*, after a phase of adjustment and discussion with the participants. The digital library will thus offer two levels of indexing: one indexing at the level of the work and another at the text level.

4 Discussion: What Can We Learn for the Design of Future Digital Libraries?

4.1 One Service, Several Ways to Participate

Despite similar profiles composing them, the two teams showed very different visions of participation. The first team envisioned participation as a *cooperative* activity. Indeed, cooperation is based on the principle of division of work. Each member of a group works individually on a task assigned to him or her. It does not involve exchanges between group members: only the results are mutualized to produce a finite resource [2, 7, 9]. The tool developed by the first team takes these characteristics, proposing a one-off activity, without exchange with other users and based on a juxtaposition of knowledge.

However, this tool is fully in line with the missions of librarians, as a support for research and serendipity. On the one hand, the added keywords allow to improve the searches of others through query expansion. On the other hand, when indexing a work, the tool suggests to the contributor other works indexed with the same term. Indexing thus becomes a pretext for exploring collections (see Fig. 1).

The second team envisioned participation as a *collaborative* activity, offering its users the opportunity to co-create content *with* scientific experts and librarians. Collaboration is indeed based on a pooling of the efforts, skills and expertise of the members of a group. It is no longer only the final result that is mutualized, but the work process itself [2, 6, 7, 9]. The digital humanities initiation system imagined by this second team implements these characteristics by making students, scholars and librarians work together. This system is part of the library's mission to train users but is also in line with scientific practices in digital textual scholarship, of which it disseminates good practices.

4.2 Participatory Indexing as an Introduction to Librarians' Practices

Although different, these two projects have a similar vision of the indexing activity, which is considered too complex to be carried out by lay users. In both cases, a simplified indexing was envisaged: the user adds keywords from predefined vocabularies, which allows to overcome the shortcomings of tagging. A limitation of these imagined tools is that they do not take into account the principles of use and combination of keywords of each vocabulary, that librarians must follow, described in Sect. 1.

The influence of the library profile of half of the participants is evident here. Indeed, indexing from controlled vocabularies is at the heart of the librarian's profession and follows precise rules. If the librarians do not reject the idea of a participatory indexing service, the development of a participatory indexing service can be seen as a challenge to their skills. By developing simplified indexing tools, the aim would be to highlight their expertise and authority, emphasizing that indexing cannot be improvised or made available to everyone. Both projects thus offer users an enriching indexing experience, which introduced them to a lightened version of librarians' practices.

Another common point between these projects is the care taken in monitoring and validating the results. In both cases, the contributions are ultimately validated by experts. Both projects propose validation systems that meet the requirements of accuracy and scientific rigour expected not only by users of an academic digital library, but also by librarians who share part of their professional activities with the library public. The aim is thus to guarantee the scientificity and quality of the data by applying the "seal of the institution" to them.

5 Conclusions and Future Works

In this paper, we proposed another way of thinking about adding keywords with participatory indexing. Through this example, we also presented a case study of participatory design of digital services in the context of an academic digital library. The use of participatory design allowed us to enrich *Fonte Gaia Bib*'s service offering by directly involving its potential users in the development of the library.

These workshops also highlighted different ways of conceiving a participatory service among our participants, that can be of use for future digital libraries with participatory services: participation of a cooperative nature and in line with the missions of librarians (project 1) and participation of a collaborative nature that is part of scientific activities (project 2). In both cases, participants envisioned a participatory service that has an impact on the entire audience of a digital library, i.e. on its users, the librarians and the contributors themselves.

Based on this preliminary data, we wish to repeat this experience in future work, extending it to a larger number of participants and offering a challenge not focused on a particular participatory service, but on participatory services in general. These new workshops will allow us to continue our reflections on how users conceptualize participatory services in a cultural heritage context, and thus improve the design of our digital library services.

References

1. Blaser, L.: Old weather: approaching collections from a different angle. In: Ridge, M. (ed.) Crowdsourcing our Cultural Heritage, pp. 45–56. Ashgate, Farnham (2014)
2. Choi, B.C.K., Pak, A.W.P.: Multidisciplinary, interdisciplinary and transdisciplinary in health research, services, education and policy: 1. Definitions, objectives, and evidence of effectiveness. Clin. Invest. Med. **29**(6), 351–364 (2006)
3. Durieux, V.: Collaborative tagging et folksonomies. L'organisation du web par les internautes. Les Cahiers du numérique **6**(1), 69–80 (2010)
4. Fonio, F., Mouraby, C.: La Fonte Gaia: bibliothèque numérique et blogue scientifique. In: Expérimenter les humanités numériques. Des outils individuels aux projets collectifs. Les Presses de l'Université de Montréal, Montréal (2017)
5. Holley, R.: Tagging full text searchable articles: an overview of social tagging activity in historic Australian Newspapers August 2008 - August 2009. D-Lib Mag. **16**(1/2) (2010). https://www.dlib.org/dlib/january10/holley/01holley.html
6. Hord, S.M.: Working together: cooperation or collaboration? (1981)
7. Kozar, O.: Towards better group work: seeing the difference between cooperation and collaboration. English Teach. Forum **48**(2), 16–23 (2010)
8. Mézard, F.: Présentation de la Nouvelle Version de la Bibliothèque numérique. https://fontegaia.hypotheses.org/2714. Accessed 02 Apr 2020
9. Misanchuk, M., Anderson, T.: Building community in an online learning environment: communication, cooperation and collaboration (2001)
10. Romeo, F., Blaser, L.: Bringing citizen scientists and historians together. In: Trant, J., Bearman, D. (eds.) Proceedings of the Museums and the Web 2011: Archives and Museums Informatics, Toronto (2011)
11. Visconti, A.: "How can you love a work, if you don't know it?": critical code and design toward participatory digital editions (2015)
12. Warwick, C.: Studying users in digital humanities. In: Warwick, C., Terras, M., Nyhan, J. (eds.) Digital Humanities in Practice. Facet Publishing, London (2012)
13. Collex-Persée. https://www.collexpersee.eu/. Accessed 04 June 2020
14. DigiPal. http://www.digipal.eu/. Accessed 04 June 2020
15. Fonte Gaia Bib (FG Bib). http://www.fontegaia.eu. Accessed 04 June 2020
16. Hacke ta bibliothèque. https://hackathonfg.sciencesconf.org/. Accessed 04 June 2020
17. Infinite Ulysses. http://www.infiniteulysses.com. Accessed 04 June 2020
18. International Image Interoperability Framework (IIIF). https://iiif.io/. Accessed 04 June 2020
19. Library of Congress Subject Headings. https://id.loc.gov/authorities/subjects.html. Accessed 04 June 2020
20. Mirador. https://projectmirador.org/. Accessed 04 June 2020
21. Nuovo Soggettario. https://thes.bncf.firenze.sbn.it/index_eng.html. Accessed 04 June 2020
22. RAMEAU. https://rameau.bnf.fr/. Accessed 04 June 2020
23. Text Encoding Initiative (TEI). https://tei-c.org/guidelines/. Accessed 04 June 2020

Understanding User Behavior in Digital Libraries Using the MAGUS Session Visualization Tool

Tessel Bogaard[1(✉)], Jan Wielemaker[1,2], Laura Hollink[1], Lynda Hardman[1,3], and Jacco van Ossenbruggen[1,2]

[1] Centrum Wiskunde & Informatica, Amsterdam, The Netherlands
{tessel.bogaard,jan.wielemaker,laura.hollink,laura.hollink, lynda.hardman,jacco.van.ossenbruggen}@cwi.nl
[2] Vrije Universiteit Amsterdam, Amsterdam, The Netherlands
[3] Universiteit Utrecht, Utrecht, The Netherlands

Abstract. Manual inspection of individual user sessions provides valuable information on how users search within a collection. To support this inspection we present a session visualization tool, Metadata Augmented Graphs for User Sessions (MAGUS), representing sessions in a digital library. We evaluate MAGUS by comparing it with the more widely used table visualization in three representative tasks of increasing complexity performed by 12 professional participants. The perceived workload was a little higher for MAGUS than for the table. However, the answers provided during the tasks using MAGUS were generally more detailed using different types of arguments. These answers focused more on specific search behaviors and the parts of the collection users are interested in, using MAGUS's visualization of the (bibliographic) metadata of clicked documents and selected facets. MAGUS allows professionals to extract more, valuable information on how users search within a collection.

Keywords: Information visualization · Search behavior · Digital libraries · Metadata · Log analysis · User study

1 Introduction

Many studies on large-scale analyses of search logs in digital libraries [2,10,12,19] provide a high-level view of user behavior through methods that report descriptive statistics over groups of sessions, such as demographics, average session duration or number of clicks. Less is known, however, about how search logs can be presented to a researcher or library professional to understand the behavior of individual users. Manual inspection of user sessions (coherent sequences of interactions of an individual user within the search system) provides valuable information on how a user searches within a collection. System developers, for example, inspect sessions to assess whether user behavior on their platform conforms to the system's design. And library professionals are interested in understanding how users search in different parts of the collection to improve search features.

M. Hall et al. (Eds.): TPDL 2020, LNCS 12246, pp. 171–184, 2020.
https://doi.org/10.1007/978-3-030-54956-5_13

In our research we inspect and interpret user behavior within a historical collection, for instance how users search within different time periods. In the context of a digital library, the documents in the collection are frequently described with rich, professionally curated bibliographic metadata, which can be used to identify users with specific interests [2].

Frequently, a table visualization is used to inspect individual sessions [8]. A table is uncomplicated, typically consisting of a list of queries and URLs of corresponding clicked documents. This, however, has some disadvantages. As an example, in a table it is not directly visible in which part of the collection a user searched; if this is within a specific period, such as World War II (WWII), or for a specific type of document, such as newspaper adverts or family announcements. Also, it can be difficult to recognize specific interaction patterns, such as a user returning to an earlier query, especially in longer sessions.

We present MAGUS (Metadata Augmented Graphs for User Sessions), a tool for visualizing a session in a meaningful way. We describe the design of MAGUS, and discuss in what ways it can overcome the limitations of a table visualization. For example, MAGUS visualizes the facets selected during search and the metadata of clicked documents, providing a visualization of the specific parts of the collection a user is interested in. We evaluate the MAGUS visualization by comparing it with a table representation in three representative tasks completed by 12 participants from diverse professional backgrounds. The questions we address in the evaluation are: (i) *Is session inspection easier in terms of time and effort spent when using MAGUS?*; and (ii) *Are the answers provided better in terms of accuracy and level of detail when using MAGUS?* For transparency, we report all measurements taken, including those that gave negative or inconclusive results, such as agreement between participants or the perceived workload.

2 Related Work

Log Analysis in Digital Libraries. Search logs collected from digital libraries and archives has been studied frequently [2,3,6,10,12,15,16,19]. In some cases, studies focus on the detection and analysis of (topical) user interests, for example to categorize search topics [10,15], or to identify usage patterns in different parts of the collection [2,3]. These studies focus on a statistical analysis of search logs. However, manual inspection of individual sessions can also provide valuable information on how users search in a search system. For example, in [8], individual search behavior is studied to train and develop machine learning algorithms to be able to predict whether a user is demonstrating struggling or exploring search.

Visualization of User Behavior. Frequently used visualisations such as the Behavior Flow in Google Analytics show results aggregated over all users, providing a bird's eye view of search behavior. Similarly aggregated graph visualizations have been used in earlier work, e.g. [4,9]. To visualize a single session, a simple table format is frequently used, e.g. [8]. Alternatively, single sessions have been represented as linear sequences of colored blocks, with the colors denoting the type of interaction or page visited [13,14,20,21]. In [17], this idea is applied to the search logs of a digital library, with the colors also denoting typical interactions such as adding or removing facets during the search. In this work, we aim to gain more insights into individual user behavior by visualizing single user sessions. We use a directed graph to represent a complete session, and use color and shape of the graph nodes to represent the search and click interactions. The directed graph representation allows the visualization of both the complete navigational path of a user and the repeated user interactions in a single node.

User Studies. In a meta-review of empirical studies focusing on user experience, Pettersson et al., [18], report that in 26% of the studies standardized questionnaires are used, and in 31% user activity is logged, often in combination with other methods, with most studies combining quantitative and qualitative data. In our user study, we similarly combine methods, using activity logging and standardized questionnaires, the NASA-TLX [7] and the System Usability Scale [5], combined with open questions and analysis of answers provided to the tasks.

3 Session Visualization

To visualize a session, we need to specify the start and end of the session, record the queries, facets, and search options submitted during the session and collect information about the documents clicked by the user. For our study, we identify sessions from search logs based on the concept of a clickstream, following the navigational path of a user. The queries, facets, and search options represent the user's search interactions on the platform, and are logged by the search system. Documents in a digital library are frequently described using bibliographic metadata. Clicked documents can be annotated with this metadata, providing insights into the parts of the collection the user searched [3].

3.1 Session as a Table

Table 1. Example table format used by Hassan et al. adapted from [8]

5:55:48 PM	**Query**		Employment issues articles
5:55:52 PM		**-Click**	http://jobseekeradvice.com/category/employment...
6:01:02 PM	**Query**		Professional career advice
6:01:05 PM		**-Click**	http://ezinearticles.com/?Career-Advice-and-Pro...
6:03:09 PM		**-Click**	http://askville.amazon.com/buy-version-Tax-soft...
6:03:35 PM	**Query**		What is a resume
6:04:21 PM		**-Click**	http://en.wikipedia.org/wiki/R%C3%A9sum%C3%A9...
6:07:15 PM			**END OF SESSION**

Sessions are frequently visualized using a table format, typically containing the user queries and URLs of clicked results sequentially, Table 1 and [8]. The format

Date	Query	Info	URL	
"Wed Oct 21 09:11:13 2015"	↳	'click_id=ddd:011108016:mpeg21:a0262'	https://resolver.kb.nl/resolve?urn=ddd:0 ...	1
"Wed Oct 21 09:11:23 2015"	↳	'download_id=ddd:011108016:mpeg21:a0262'	http://www.delpher.nl/nl/pres/view/ocr?l ...	2
"Wed Oct 21 09:11:23 2015"	↳	'download_id=ddd:011108016:mpeg21:a0262'	http://www.delpher.nl/nl/pres/view/cite? ...	3
"Wed Oct 21 09:19:33 2015"	"amersfoort 5 mei 1945"	[]	(-)	4
"Wed Oct 21 09:20:38 2015"	"nsb amersfoort mei 1945"	[]	(-)	5
"Wed Oct 21 09:21:30 2015"	"nsb verzet mei 1945"	[]	(-)	6
"Wed Oct 21 09:21:31 2015"	"nsb verzet mei 1945"	[]	(-)	7
"Wed Oct 21 09:21:55 2015"	↳	'click_id=ddd:010593367:mpeg21:a0288'	https://resolver.kb.nl/resolve?urn=ddd:0 ...	8
"Wed Oct 21 09:50:31 2015"	"nsb verzet mei 1945"	[]	(-)	9
"Wed Oct 21 09:50:46 2015"	↳	'click_id=ddd:010593367:mpeg21:a0288'	https://resolver.kb.nl/resolve?urn=ddd:0 ...	10
"Wed Oct 21 09:51:41 2015"	"nsb 1945"	[]	(-)	11
"Wed Oct 21 09:51:43 2015"	"nsb 1945"	[]	(-)	12
"Wed Oct 21 09:52:49 2015"	"nsb 1945"	"[type=artikel]"	(-)	13
"Wed Oct 21 09:53:16 2015"	"nsb 1945"	"[type=artikel]"	(-)	14
"Wed Oct 21 09:53:34 2015"	"nsb 1945"	"[type=artikel]"	(-)	15
"Wed Oct 21 09:53:44 2015"	"nsb 1945"	"[type=artikel]"	(-)	16
"Wed Oct 21 09:53:59 2015"	↳	'click_id=ddd:010622618:mpeg21:a0311'	https://resolver.kb.nl/resolve?urn=ddd:0 ...	17

Fig. 1. Session from Fig. 2 visualized as a table

is uncomplicated, providing an overview of user queries and clicked results. For our table visualization, we adapt the example for the open web, [8], to the context of a digital library. Our table consists of four columns (see Fig. 1): (i) the timestamps of the interactions; (ii) the user query, or in the case of a click or download, an arrow; (iii) additional information on the search interactions, such as selected facets or search options, or a document identifier for clicks and downloads; and (iv) a link to a clicked or downloaded document.

A table visualization suffers from a number of disadvantages. *Issue 1:* it is difficult to see the connection among interactions other than their time sequence. *Issue 2:* it is not easy to recognize repeated interactions, for example, it is not directly visible when a user returns to an earlier query, for example rows 9 and 10 are equal to rows 7 and 8, Fig. 1. *Issue 3:* it can be hard to view all interactions in a session at once, to see how often each type of interaction occurs, especially for longer sessions. In the context of a digital library, it is difficult to see *issue 4*: which facets users selected during the search; and *issue 5:* the (bibliographic) metadata of the clicked results which can provide meaningful information about the different parts of the collection users are interested in. To address these disadvantages we have developed a session visualization tool, the Metadata Augmented Graphs for User Sessions (MAGUS).

3.2 Introducing MAGUS

In MAGUS[1], a session is visualized as a directed graph where the nodes represent the user interactions, and the arrows the navigational path of the user (addressing *issue 1*). MAGUS is built in the SWISH DataLab environment[1], where Graphviz[2] was used for graph visualization. Figure 2 visualizes a relatively small user session. The session starts at the top, where the gray shape indicates that the user arrived by following a link from an external website, in this case a link from a Facebook post. Through the link, the user arrives directly on a specific article (rectangle). From here, the user performed three interactions, temporally ordered from left to right. The user downloads the OCR text of the

[1] Demo and source code available at https://swish.swi-prolog.org/p/magus.swinb.
[2] http://www.graphviz.org/.

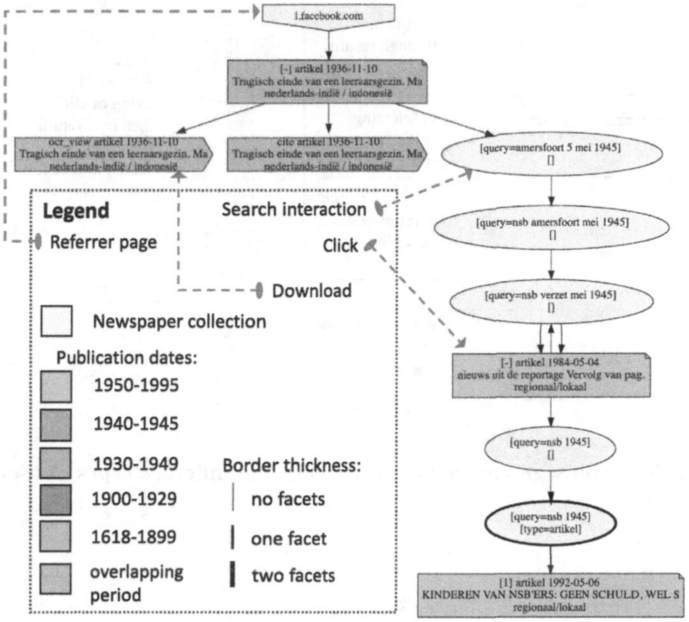

Fig. 2. Session from Fig. 1 visualized with MAGUS (Color figure online)

article, followed by its citation (both indicated by a block arrow shape), then leaves the entry page by initiating a new query and navigating to the search results page (indicated by the yellow ellipse, addressing *issue 3*).

From there, a series of interactions follows: two searches with query refinements (ellipses) and a click on an article (rectangle) are followed by a brief return to the previous page, and back to the article (indicated by the back and forth arrows above the first green rectangle, *issue 2*). To understand the user's search intent it is useful to, in addition to the query, also know which facets were selected (*issue 4*). The user initially used no facets (indicated by the empty square brackets [] in the ellipses), but later added a [type=article] facet, constraining the document type to article (indicated by the thicker line for the last ellipse).

In the historical collection where the example is taken from, it helps library professionals and historians to understand in which period the user is interested. MAGUS allows specific metadata fields to be used to color the nodes in the graph. In this example, we use the publication date from the library's metadata records to color the click nodes. The light red used on the top left indicates documents published in the period around WWII, while the green on the bottom right indicates documents published after 1950 (addressing *issue 5*).

Users exhibit many different interaction patterns, Fig. 3, some of which can be more easily distinguished in MAGUS than in a table. For example, a user clicking from one results page to another using the "next button", or a user selecting

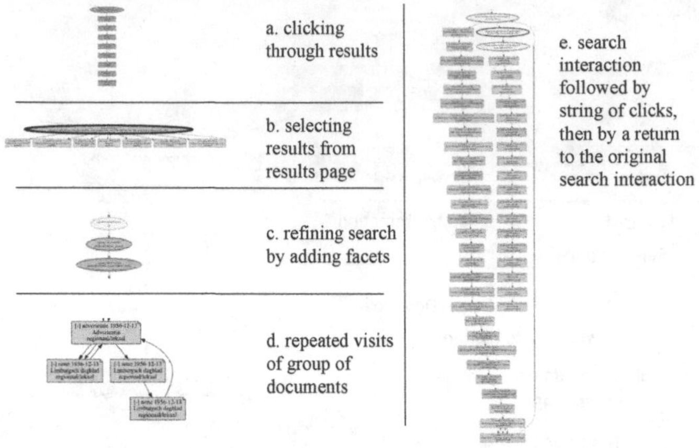

Fig. 3. Multiple graph segments in small size showing different types of user behavior.

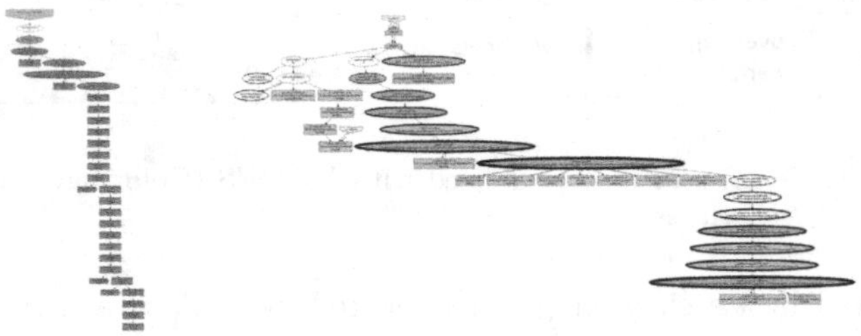

Fig. 4. Two small session graphs. The user on the left was browsing through documents published in the 1900-29 period (succession of blue rectangles). The user on the right was using faceted (thick borders) search interactions (ellipses) after 1950 (green). (Color figure online)

multiple results from the results page and opening them in a new tab, result in deep vertical versus broad horizontal graphs respectively, Fig. 4. Even when the graphs have been reduced in size to a small scale, the difference between the typical "click" behavior of the user on the left can be easily distinguished from the more search-oriented behavior of the user on the right (*issue 3*): the session on the left is dominated by clicks (rectangles) while the session on the right has alternates searches (ellipses) with clicks (*issue 3*). The use of facets is easy to recognize (*issue 4*) in the session on the right by the thick lines used to draw the ellipses of the search nodes, while their color indicates the use of time facets in the post–1950 period (green). The use of the publication dates from the metadata records (*issue 5*) to color the click nodes also immediately conveys that the user on the left is focusing on the 1900–29 period (blue) while the user on the right is more interested in the post–1950 period (green). Additional information about the interaction is displayed in each node. The click and download interactions

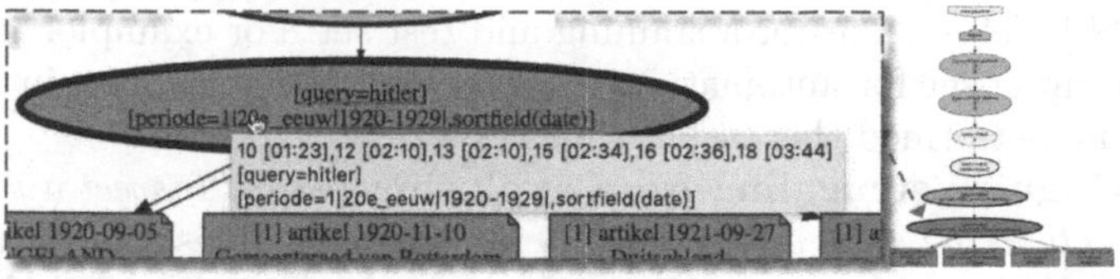

Fig. 5. Hovering over a node displays timestamps with a counter relative to the start of the session, clicking on the node links to the visited web page.

include the document metadata values, the document title, and the page number of the results page of the click. The search interactions include the query, selected facets, and search options used. In addition to the visualizations, hovering over a node will display timestamps relative to the start of the session, and a link to the web page visited (see Fig. 5).

4 Evaluation Setup

In a small-scale experiment we evaluate MAGUS and compare it with a table visualization, Fig. 1. We recruited 12 participants (of which 5 men) among historians, computer scientists, library collection specialists and data scientists. We asked them to perform three tasks and measured the time spent, perceived workload, usability scores (widely used for user studies, [18]). In addition, we measured the certainty of and agreement among the answers given, and performed an analysis of their free-text answers. The experiments were performed on HTTP server logs from the National Library of the Netherlands[3]. The search platform provides access to historical newspaper documents using a faceted interface, with the facets based on the (bibliographic) metadata describing the documents within the collection (such as the publication date). We cleaned and split the logs into sessions as described in [3].

Tasks. The study includes three tasks of increasing complexity. The sessions we selected to be visualized in the tasks all relate to one specific subject–WWII–in the sense that they contain queries and/or clicks on documents about topics related to WWII. This choice is inspired by an ongoing collaboration with the NIOD Institute for War, Holocaust and Genocide Studies[4].

Task 1: identify information needs: *Inspect a session and assess if one of the information needs of the user is to find documents about a topic directly related to WWII.* This task is relevant, for example, to historians who are interested in users searching for WWII-related documents, to understand how users search and which topics they search for. Such a task can also be relevant

[3] Logs collected from the search platform https://www.delpher.nl/, access granted under a strict confidentiality agreement.

[4] https://www.niod.nl/en.

to manual label sessions for a training and test set. For example, [11] created such a training set for automatic segmentation of search topics in logs. Each participant performed this task 4 times (subtasks 1.1–1.4).

Task 2 distinguish struggling from exploring users: *Inspect a session and assess whether the user was struggling or exploring.* This kind of task could be performed by a library professional who seeks to understand if users find what they are looking for in the library collection. It is also relevant when building a training set for a classifier, as was done by crowd workers in [8]. Disambiguation between struggling and exploring sessions is important both for understanding search success and when providing real-time user support [8]. Participants performed this task 4 times (subtasks 2.1–2.4).

Task 3 describe a cluster of sessions: *Provide fitting labels and descriptions for four clusters of sessions, by inspecting four sessions per cluster.* In this task, we study to what extent inspection of a few (in this case four) individual sessions allows a professional to see shared, high-level usage patterns and distinguish different types of uses.

For tasks 1 and 2, we manually selected sessions that we judged to be suitable for the tasks and that demonstrate a user interest in WWII topics, based on a list of WWII-related terms provided by the NIOD. For task 3, we clustered sessions including WWII topics using a k-medoids algorithm as described in [2]. This resulted in four distinct clusters. Table 2 provides median values of the clustering features, serving as a high-level overview of the sessions in each cluster. Cluster 1 contains sessions with mainly clicked documents and little search interactions; cluster 2 sessions with clicked documents followed by downloads; cluster 3 sessions with faceted search, focusing on the 1930–49 period; and cluster 4 faceted search with the focus outside the 1930–49 period. In task 3, participants of the study were not shown the session statistics, but were presented with the four most typical sessions of each cluster, i.e. the sessions with the shortest Manhattan distance to the set of medians of the session features in a cluster.

Table 2. Median values of all clustering features for the four clusters.

Cluster	Clicks	Downloads	Search	Search facets	Search WWII facets	Search 1930–49 facets	Search time ranking	Clicks WWII	Clicks 1930–49
1	**88%**	0%	11%	0%	0%	0%	0%	1%	20%
2	33%	**64%**	0%	0%	0%	0%	0%	0%	0%
3	22%	0%	**76%**	**46%**	0%	**11%**	0%	**50%**	**91%**
4	23%	0%	**74%**	**44%**	0%	0%	6%	3%	18%

Two Visualizations. We use a within-subjects design where each participant is exposed to both visualizations. We always present tasks and sessions in the same order. However, we present the visualizations in different orders to avoid measuring a learning effect for either visualization. One group uses MAGUS for subtasks 1.1 and 1.2, the table for subtasks 1.3, 1.4, 2.1 and 2.2, and then

MAGUS for subtasks 2.3, 2.4 and task 3, the other group swaps the visualization tools. Participants are randomly spread over the groups.

Procedure, Data Collection and Data Preparation. First, each participant receives a short training in the use of both visualizations. Then, the participant performs the three tasks. Finally, the participant fills out the System Usability Scale (SUS) questionnaire [5] for both visualizations, and provides further written comments on the use of both visualizations. For the sessions in tasks 1 and 2, the participants select an answer (yes/no on task 1; struggling/exploring on task 2) and provide a free-text justification of their answer. For the clusters in task 3, they provide a free-text label and description. After each session or cluster, we ask participants to assign a measure of their certainty on a five-point Likert scale. After each task and for each visualization method, the participants fill out a NASA TLX questionnaire [7]. All tasks were timed.

We manually annotate the free-text answers to record whether the participants' arguments contain one or more of eight categories of information about a session: (1) queries (for example, a participant writes "hitler as search term"); (2) clicks (for example, "left [...] without clicking"); (3) downloads ("the user didn't download"); (4) links ("possibly saved links"); (5) specific content or metadata values in documents or search facets ("all post-war phenomena" or "time range around ww2 (30–49)"); (6) search behavior ("doesn't use facets", or "click through the results"); (7) blacklist notice, a warning page shown before accessing Nazi-propaganda ("he/she clicked on the blacklist consent"); (8) time ("he/she spent not too much time"). Subjective arguments are left out, such as "he/she seems knowledgeable", "I wonder if they can find it", "couldn't find what he/she was looking for", or "feels more frustrated".

5 Evaluation Results

Table 3. Argument analysis of participants' free-text explanations and descriptions.

Task	Visualization	Mean word count	Arg. count	Query	Click	Downl.	Link	Spec. content/ metadata	Search techn./ behavior	Blackl.	Time
1	MAGUS	14	57	25	3	0	0	25	1	3	0
	Table	13	54	37	0	0	0	16	1	0	0
2	MAGUS	26	75	26	16	6	2	6	16	2	1
	Table	25	59	25	12	4	0	2	12	0	4
3	MAGUS	20	55	2	12	7	5	10	19	0	0
	Table	22	58	7	16	10	6	4	15	0	0
Combi	MAGUS	20	**187**	53	31	13	7	**41**	**36**	5	1
	Table	20	171	**69**	28	14	6	22	28	0	4

Free-Text Answers. We analyze the manually annotated free-text answers by counting how many times each argument-category was used by participants. Table 3 shows the number of arguments in total and of each category separately, for the three tasks as well as overall. It also lists the mean word count of the free-text answers. We notice that only slightly more arguments were used with MAGUS than with the table visualization (187 for MAGUS vs. 171 for the table), and on average the same number of words (20). Only in task 2 participants clearly use more arguments when using MAGUS. However, the type of arguments used is different between the two visualizations. When using the table, participants use the query more frequently as an argument (53 times with MAGUS vs. 69 with the table). With MAGUS, the focus is more strongly on specific content and metadata (41 times with MAGUS vs. 22 with the table), and on search behavior (36 vs. 28). This suggests that MAGUS indeed focuses participants' attention not only on the query but also on other aspects present in the sessions, such as the metadata and the search techniques used.

The free-text cluster descriptions given by participants in task 3, show a difference between MAGUS and the table. As discussed in Sect. 4, cluster 3 focuses on WWII, while cluster 4 does not. Five out of six participants who used MAGUS for task 3 mention this in their description of cluster 3 and/or cluster 4. Only one of the participants that used the table does, labeling cluster 4 as "advanced search after WWII". This demonstrates how MAGUS can improve the quality of answers for tasks where it is important to understand how users search in different parts of the collection.

Agreement Between the Participants. For tasks 1 and 2, we do not consider answers as correct or incorrect, but rather check whether participants agreed on their answers. The number of participants that agreed with each other is exactly the same among participants that used MAGUS and among those that used the table, showing that the visualization method does not impact the agreement. Agreement is different for the different tasks, with almost perfect agreement on task 1 and moderate disagreement on task 2.

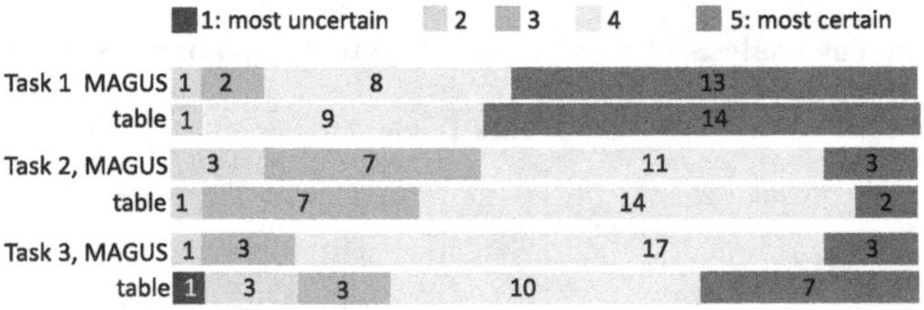

Fig. 6. Certainty: number of times each point on a Likert scale from uncertain to certain was selected.

Certainty of the Answers. We find no differences between MAGUS and the table with respect to how certain participants are of their answers (Fig. 6).

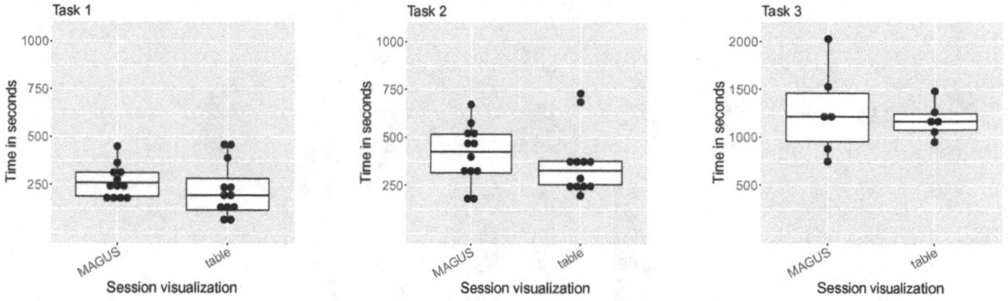

Fig. 7. Time spent per task. Dots represent participants. (Different scale on Task 3.)

Time Spent. The participants need, on average, more time when using MAGUS than when using the table for task 1 and especially task 2. There is no clear difference on task 3. The observed difference in time spent between the two visualizations is small compared with the variation among participants and the difference between tasks, with task 3 requiring considerably more time (Fig. 7).

Workload. Table 4 presents the perceived workload for both session visualizations. Workload is measured through the NASA TLX questionnaire on six dimensions. For task 1, the perceived workload is lower for MAGUS than for the table on all dimensions. For task 2, on the other hand, all workload dimensions are scored slightly higher for MAGUS, and for task 3 the workload is even considerably higher for MAGUS. However, again, standard deviations are high on all questions; variation among participants is generally higher than the difference between the table and MAGUS.

Table 4. Perceived workload measure, on a scale from 0 to 100, lower is better.

	Task 1				Task 2				Task 3			
	MAGUS		Table		MAGUS		Table		MAGUS		Table	
	Mean	Sd	Mean	Sd	Mean	Sd	Mean	Sd	Mean	Sd	Mean	Sd
Mental demand	20	37	34	36	51	17	47	22	67	14	52	21
Physical demand	8	9	10	18	11	6	10	5	19	23	13	6
Temporal demand	15	19	21	26	31	18	26	16	41	24	32	23
Performance	20	30	27	28	45	17	40	18	53	12	40	13
Effort	17	32	31	33	43	16	41	18	62	13	34	14
Frustration	14	23	14	18	27	23	23	18	27	18	26	10

Usability. In terms of the reported usability (Fig. 8), the differences are small. MAGUS is liked a bit more than the table. Some participants find the table cumbersome. On the other hand, the participants feel that MAGUS is a bit more difficult to use, as can be seen from the slightly better scores of the table visualization on complexity, ease of use, and the need for support. While the

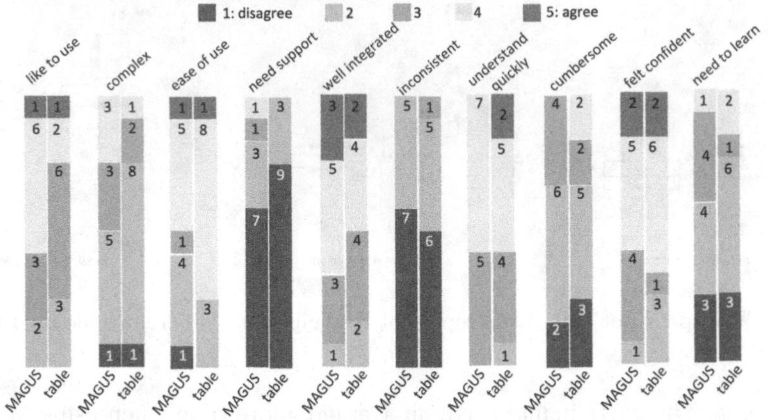

Fig. 8. Usability: number of times each point on a Likert scale from uncertain to certain was selected in the System Usability Scale (SUS) questionnaire.

majority of participants reported that there was little need to learn how to use the two visualizations, multiple participants comment on this. For example, participant 1, an information professional, writes: "You need to learn how to read a graph and understand what is happening in it. But if you inspect it (more) carefully with a legend, then it provides a wealth of information!" We find no conclusive differences with respect to the usability aspects "well integrated", "inconsistant", "understand quickly" and "felt confident."

6 Conclusion

We have developed MAGUS, a tool for visualizing individual user sessions. MAGUS visualizes a user's navigational path as a directed graph, mapping repeated interactions onto a single node. Our tool highlights the different types of user interactions such as searches, clicks and downloads, the use of search facets, and relevant metadata of the clicked documents. In this way, MAGUS allows researchers and library professionals to recognize different interaction patterns and provides insights into the parts of the collection a user is interested in.

We have evaluated our tool on three tasks performed by 12 professionals in a comparison with a standard table visualization. An analysis of the free-text answers demonstrated that MAGUS indeed enabled participants to identify the part of the collection a user is interested in, and that it helps to distinguish different types of search behavior. Further empirical research into specific aspects of the session visualization separately, such as the metadata coloring, could provide more insights into the benefits of each aspect. The results of the workload questionnaire and activity logging suggest that participants find MAGUS more difficult to use than the table, even though the participants do like the tool. MAGUS may be perceived as more difficult due to the steeper learning curve associated with our tool, and it would be interesting to do a follow-up study to confirm this. A larger follow-up study could also include an investigation of the different professional backgrounds of participants, for example, to compare whether data professionals and domain experts use the tool differently. Furthermore, we would like to investigate which types of tasks specifically benefit from MAGUS, and for which types of sessions the tool works best, as several participants mentioned the benefit of MAGUS for long, complicated sessions.

Acknowledgements. We would like to thank the National Library of the Netherlands, the NIOD Institute for War, Holocaust and Genocide Studies, and BNNVARA (public broadcasting company) for their support. This research is partially supported by the VRE4EIC project, a project that has received funding from the European Union's Horizon 2020 research and innovation program under grant agreement No. 676247.

References

1. Bogaard, T., Wielemaker, J., Hollink, L., van Ossenbruggen, J.: SWISH DataLab: a web interface for data exploration and analysis. In: Bosse, T., Bredeweg, B. (eds.) BNAIC 2016. CCIS, vol. 765, pp. 181–187. Springer, Cham (2017). https://doi.org/10.1007/978-3-319-67468-1_13
2. Bogaard, T., Hollink, L., Wielemaker, J., Hardman, L., van Ossenbruggen, J.: Searching for old news: user interests and behavior within a national collection. In: Proceedings of the 2019 Conference on Human Information Interaction and Retrieval CHIIR 2019, pp. 113–121. ACM, New York (2019). https://doi.org/10.1145/3295750.3298925
3. Bogaard, T., Hollink, L., Wielemaker, J., van Ossenbruggen, J., Hardman, L.: Metadata categorization for identifying search patterns in a digital library. J. Doc. **75**(2), 270–286 (2019). https://doi.org/10.1108/JD-06-2018-0087
4. Brainerd, J., Becker, B.: Case study: e-commerce clickstream visualization. In: Andrews, K., Roth, S.F., Wong, P.C. (eds.) IEEE Symposium on Information Visualization 2001 (INFOVIS'01), SanDiego, CA, USA, 22–23 October 2001, pp. 153–156. IEEE Computer Society (2001). https://doi.org/10.1109/INFVIS.2001.963293
5. Brooke, J., et al.: SUS-A quick and dirty usability scale. Usability Eval. Ind. **189**(194), 4–7 (1996)
6. Clough, P., Hill, T., Paramita, M.L., Goodale, P.: Europeana: what users search for and why. In: Kamps, J., Tsakonas, G., Manolopoulos, Y., Iliadis, L., Karydis, I. (eds.) TPDL 2017. LNCS, vol. 10450, pp. 207–219. Springer, Cham (2017). https://doi.org/10.1007/978-3-319-67008-9_17
7. Hart, S.G., Staveland, L.E.: Development of NASA-TLX (Task Load Index): results of empirical and theoretical research. In: Advances in Psychology, vol. 52, pp. 139–183. Elsevier (1988)
8. Hassan, A., White, R.W., Dumais, S.T., Wang, Y.M.: Struggling or exploring? Disambiguating long search sessions. In: Seventh ACM WSDM (2014). https://doi.org/10.1145/2556195.2556221
9. Hong, J.I., Landay, J.A.: WebQuilt: a framework for capturing and visualizing the web experience. In: Proceedings of the 10th International Conference on World Wide Web WWW 2001, pp. 717–724. ACM, New York (2001). https://doi.org/10.1145/371920.372188

10. Huurnink, B., Hollink, L., Van Heuvel, W.D., De Rijke, M.: Search behavior of media professionals at an audiovisual archive: a transaction log analysis. J. Am. Soc. Inform. Sci. Technol. (2010). https://doi.org/10.1002/asi.21327
11. Jones, R., Klinkner, K.L.: Beyond the session timeout: automatic hierarchical segmentation of search topics in query logs. In: Proceedings of the 17th ACM Conference on Information and Knowledge Management CIKM 2008, pp. 699–708. ACM, New York (2008). https://doi.org/10.1145/1458082.1458176
12. Jones, S., Cunningham, S.J., Mcnab, R., Boddie, S.: A transaction log analysis of a digital library. Int. J. Digit. Libr. **3**(2), 152–169 (2000). https://doi.org/10.1007/s007999900022
13. Lam, H., Russell, D.M., Tang, D., Munzner, T.: Session viewer: visual exploratory analysis of web session logs. In: Proceedings of the IEEE Symposium on Visual Analytics Science and Technology, IEEE VAST 2007, Sacramento, California, USA, 30 October–1 November 2007, pp. 147–154. IEEE Computer Society (2007). https://doi.org/10.1109/VAST.2007.4389008
14. Liu, Z., Wang, Y., Dontcheva, M., Hoffman, M., Walker, S., Wilson, A.: Patterns and sequences: interactive exploration of clickstreams to understand common visitor paths. IEEE Trans. Vis. Comput. Graph. **23**(1), 321–330 (2017). https://doi.org/10.1109/TVCG.2016.2598797
15. Meij, E., Bron, M., Hollink, L., Huurnink, B., de Rijke, M.: Mapping queries to the linking open data cloud: a case study using DBpedia. J. Web Semant. **9**(4), 418–433 (2011). https://doi.org/10.1016/j.websem.2011.04.001
16. Niu, X., Hemminger, B.: Analyzing the interaction patterns in a faceted search interface. J. Assoc. Inf. Sci. Technol. (2015). https://doi.org/10.1002/asi.23227
17. Niu, X., Hemminger, B.M.: A method for visualizing transaction logs of a faceted OPAC. Code4Lib J. **66**(5), 1030–1047 (2010)
18. Pettersson, I., Lachner, F., Frison, A.K., Riener, A., Butz, A.: A Bermuda Triangle?: a review of method application and triangulation in user experience evaluation. In: Proceedings of the 2018 CHI Conference on Human Factors in Computing Systems CHI 2018, pp. 461:1–461:16. ACM, New York (2018). https://doi.org/10.1145/3173574.3174035
19. Walsh, D., Clough, P., Hall, M.M., Hopfgartner, F., Foster, J., Kontonatsios, G.: Analysis of transaction logs from national museums Liverpool. In: Doucet, A., Isaac, A., Golub, K., Aalberg, T., Jatowt, A. (eds.) TPDL 2019. LNCS, vol. 11799, pp. 84–98. Springer, Cham (2019). https://doi.org/10.1007/978-3-030-30760-8_7
20. Wei, J., Shen, Z., Sundaresan, N., Ma, K.L.: Visual cluster exploration of web clickstream data. In: 2012 IEEE Conference on Visual Analytics Science and Technology, VAST 2012, Seattle, WA, USA, 14–19 October 2012, pp. 3–12. IEEE Computer Society (2012). https://doi.org/10.1109/VAST.2012.6400494
21. Zhao, J., Liu, Z., Dontcheva, M., Hertzmann, A., Wilson, A.: MatrixWave: visual comparison of event sequence data. In: Begole, B., Kim, J., Inkpen, K., Woo, W. (eds.) Proceedings of the 33rd Annual ACM Conference on Human Factors in Computing Systems, CHI 2015, Seoul, Republic of Korea, 18–23 April 2015, pp. 259–268. ACM (2015). https://doi.org/10.1145/2702123.2702419

Characteristics of Dataset Retrieval Sessions: Experiences from a Real-Life Digital Library

Zeljko Carevic(✉), Dwaipayan Roy, and Philipp Mayr

GESIS – Leibniz Institute for the Social Sciences, Cologne, Germany
Zeljko.Carevic@gesis.org

Abstract. Secondary analysis or the reuse of existing survey data is a common practice among social scientists. Searching for relevant datasets in Digital Libraries is a somehow unfamiliar behaviour for this community. Dataset retrieval, especially in the social sciences, incorporates additional material such as codebooks, questionnaires, raw data files and more. Our assumption is that due to the diverse nature of datasets, document retrieval models often do not work as efficiently for retrieving datasets. One way of enhancing these types of searches is to incorporate the users' interaction context in order to personalise dataset retrieval sessions. As a first step towards this long term goal, we study characteristics of dataset retrieval sessions from a real-life Digital Library for the social sciences that incorporates both: research data and publications. Previous studies reported a way of discerning queries between *document search* and *dataset search* by query length. In this paper, we argue the claim and report our findings of an indistinguishability of queries, whether aiming for a dataset or a document. Amongst others, we report our findings of dataset retrieval sessions with respect to query characteristics, interaction sequences and topical drift within 65,000 unique sessions.

1 Introduction

With the vast availability of research data on the Web within the Open Data initiatives, searching for it becomes an increasingly important and timely topic. The Web hosts a whole range of new data species, published in structured, unstructured and semi-structured formats – from web tables to open government data portals, knowledge bases such as Wikidata and scientific data repositories. This data fuels many novel applications, for example, fact checkers and question answering systems, and enables advances in machine learning, artificial intelligence and information retrieval.

Dataset retrieval has emerged as an independent field of study from the text retrieval domain. The latter is well-known in information retrieval (IR) with research leading to significant improvements. Dataset retrieval, on the other hand, represents a challenging sub-discipline of information retrieval with substantial differences in comparison to traditional document retrieval [4,11].

M. Hall et al. (Eds.): TPDL 2020, LNCS 12246, pp. 185–193, 2020.
https://doi.org/10.1007/978-3-030-54956-5_14

Datasets, especially in disciplines such as the social sciences, often encompass complex additional material such as codebooks (incl. variable descriptions), questionnaires, raw data files and more. Due to the higher complexity of datasets, the applicability of IR models build mainly for document retrieval is questionable. In addition, the motivations and information needs of researchers seeking for datasets are too manifold to be supported by out-of-the-box retrieval technologies. Disciplines that encourage the re-use of datasets or secondary analysis, such as, the social sciences might thus not be supported sufficiently during dataset retrieval. One way of supporting users during dataset retrieval is the development of an integrated dataset retrieval system that employs advances from established document retrieval systems and adopts these techniques to the field of dataset retrieval. Our long term goal in the project ConData[1] is to develop an effective dataset retrieval system, that incorporates personalised searching by employing contextualised ranking features which aim at tailoring search results towards the users' information needs. In order to develop a contextualised dataset retrieval approach, it is necessary to first gain a better understanding of different characteristics during dataset retrieval. Obtaining these kinds of behavioural data is usually hard. We address this shortcoming by analysing real-life user behaviour within a Digital Library for research data and related information for the social sciences [6]. As an initial outcome of this study, we report our findings on comparing dataset retrieval with document retrieval sessions corresponding to query characteristics, interaction sequences and topical drift within 65,000 unique search sessions.

2 Related Work and Motivation

Although started as a fundamental database task, the diverse nature of searched entities (which can be images, graphs, tables etc.) establishes dataset retrieval as a research domain for itself. The distinctive aspects of dataset retrieval regarding complex information needs (and in turn, query formulations) make it a difficult process in comparison to document search [3,10,11]. However, traditional keyword-based retrieval approaches are still in use in the domain of dataset retrieval although they are observed to be less effective for the task [4]. In order to exploit the additional information available for datasets, researches have been going on [2,5] to achieve further improvement.

An important sub-task during a retrieval session is to characterise the query to understand whether the search intent is of document or dataset. Considering the diversity in nature between dataset retrieval and document retrieval, an integrated search system (having both, datasets as well as documents as a repository) would benefit in selecting appropriate searching mechanism if the query intent is recognized. However, in [9], Kacprzak et al. reported the difficulty in understanding the users' intent when performing dataset search. They have subtly drawn a co-relation between query length and the type of query, and

[1] http://bit.ly/Condata.

concluded with a suggestion to use longer queries for dataset retrieval. Experimented in an artificial setting without a naturalistic information need, however, they concluded that their observation could be considered as an approximation of the user behaviour for comparing dataset and document search.

Few of the works on studying user behaviour in dataset search have been done examining queries submitted to open data portals and online communities [5,9]. However, in [8], Jansen and Spink concluded that it is not possible to directly compare the results of a transaction log analysis across different search engines.

In this work, we focus on characterising the users' intent when performing publication (document) search and research data (dataset) search[2].

3 Experimental Materials

We conduct our experiment in a real-life Digital Library for the social sciences[3]. This integrated search system (ISS) allows users to search across different data collections: research datasets, publications, survey variables, questions from questionnaires, survey instruments and tools for creating surveys. The focus of the following study is on datasets and publications. The collection covering research datasets comprises 6,267 studies that are collected within our institution and 107,595 studies coming from other institutes. The collection covering publications comprises 48,234 records mainly as open accessible articles from the social sciences. Information items are interlinked whenever possible to allow a better findability and reuse of the data. The ISS uses category facets which enable a user to switch between data types. Furthermore, category facets ensure that result lists contain exactly one data type at a time. The ISS is mainly used by social scientists. A thorough report about the technical system, the content and its users can be found in [6].

The user interactions within the ISS are anonymously logged, which makes it possible to study user behaviour on a larger scale. Amongst others, the log covers user actions such as *queries submitted, record views, browse/filter operations*. For this study, we considered all search sessions from January 2018 to December 2019. Sessions and their corresponding identifiers are not bound to a timeout. Instead, a session expires in ISS on termination of the Web browser. In order to determine a realistic session timeout, we decided to consider sessions exceeding an inactivity of 30 min as a new session. After this operation, we identified 30,695 dataset retrieval sessions and 34,550 sessions that were focused on publications.

Given a query `Q`, ISS returns a list of distinct categories such as **"research data"**, **"publications"** along with *"variables & questions"*, *"instruments & tools"* from which a user can choose to retrieve a corresponding result set. For this study, we are interested in those sessions containing queries that led to record views either in the category *research data* or in *publication*. We discriminate the *research data search* and *publication search* from the log based on the

[2] The words (*document, publication*) and (*dataset, research data*) are used interchangeably in the rest of the paper to imply the same concept.

[3] Accessible via: https://search.gesis.org. See details in [6].

type of the succeeding record viewed by the user. We categorise a query as a publication search (or, dataset search) if the user has viewed a record of type publication (or research data) immediately after submitting the query to ISS. Finally, we extract only those sessions that are either of type *research data* or *publication*. In total, our preprocessed log file consists of 142,028 rows. The rows in the log represent queries submitted by users (identified by a session fingerprint) and corresponding record views which are either of type publication or research data. The former type accounts for 79,931 records and the later for 62,097 records. Certain preprocessing steps are necessary before analysing the transaction log: we remove sessions having queries that are either empty or contain unrecognisable characters (which might result from erroneous encoding).

4 Results and Observations

In this section, we present the results of our transaction log analysis. First, we summarize the results of our query characterisation in Sect. 4.1. We compare and contrast dataset search and publication search on the basis of session-level information and sequential interaction information, respectively in Sect. 4.2 and Sect. 4.3.

4.1 Query Characterization

In this study, we try to differentiate queries on the basis of their search intent (publication or research data search). In Table 1, we present the basic statistics of queries with respect to publications and datasets.

Table 1. Average statistics comparing queries for dataset and publication search.

	Datasets	Publications
Total query count	62,097	79,931
Unique query count	18,706 (30.12%)	33,228 (41.57%)
Avg. query length (char)	15.93	19.67
Avg. query length (terms)	1.89	2.07
Queries with digits (%)	21.57%	3.22%

The following observations can be drawn from Table 1.

- Publication search is more common than dataset search, with almost 28% more submitted queries, in the ISS. This is in line with the observations already made in [6].
- Dataset search queries are much more repetitive than publication search queries with 69.88% queries getting re-issued to the search system; in contrast, the queries are less repeated (58.43%) for publication searches. We can interpret this observation by the variety of forms in representing the information need for publication searches (as compared to dataset search).

- On average, the length of a dataset search query (measured by the number of characters[4] as well as the number of terms in the query) is less as compared to publication search. This observation is in conflict with the notion presented in [9], where the authors suggested issuing longer queries for dataset search. The reason can be a difference in the experimental settings of our study and [9] where the authors acknowledge the artificial, crowd-sourced nature of their study.
- Queries for dataset search significantly more often contain numerical digits as compared to queries for publication search. Research data includes a significant number of periodic records which are titled mentioning the periods (e.g. `allbus 2014, allbus 2016` etc. which refer to a biennial survey conducted since 1980).

4.2 Analyzing Sessions

In Table 2, we report the average number of record views for dataset search and publication search in a session. From the table, we can see that the number of record views per session is higher for publication search than for dataset search. This implies that users having a publication search intent are expected to view more items than for a dataset search intent. In other words, we assume that the information need for a dataset search can be addressed by a comparatively less number of record views than publication search.

Table 2. Number of record views per session with different search intent.

	Datasets	Publications
Avg. record views per session	2.02	2.31
Avg. record views per session (unique)	1.61	2.06

Session Diversity

In a single session, a user could have multiple information needs and might have issued multiple queries to ISS. In order to identify the diversity of the information need, an elementary way would be to observe the similarity of the issued queries. However, being keyword queries, term overlap based similarity measurements, like IR-based TF-IDF model or a set-based Jaccard similarity model, would perform poorly when computing similarities among queries.

To have a better understanding of the diversity in information needs, an appropriate approach would be to inspect the similarity of viewed records: *intra-record similarity is inversely proportional to the underlying diversity of a session* [1]. We hypothesise that a heterogeneous set of viewed records indicates high diversity.

[4] Character count is used considering the linguistics of German language; the queries submitted to the ISS are mixed, some in German and others in English.

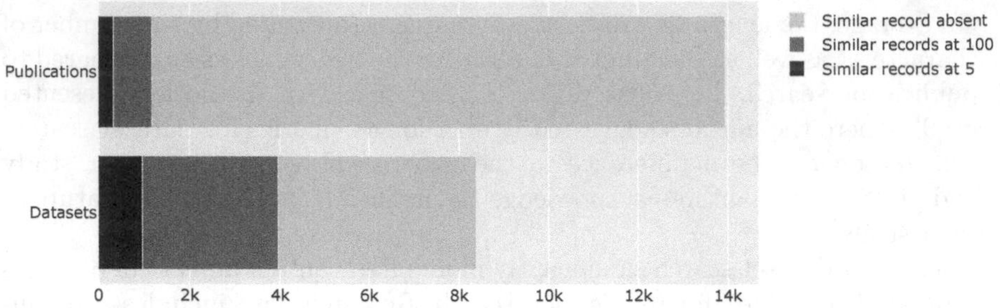

Fig. 1. Session diversity at the top 100 and the top 5 similar records. (Color figure online)

In a single session S, let a user has viewed a set of records $\{r_f, \cdots, r_l\}$ ($r_i \in$ {publication, research data}). To determine whether a session can be considered as homogeneous, we measure the similarity between the first (r_f) and last (r_l) encountered record. In order to do this, however, a similarity threshold value is needed to be fixed with annotated training data. Instead, we apply the *More Like This (MLT)*[5] module that is readily available in Elasticsearch. In the MLT module, similarity is computed using BM25 similarity between a given document (*seed* document) and all the documents in the collection; it returns a list of documents which are similar in content with the seed document. This approach, in comparison to query similarity, enables us to utilise the set of descriptive metadata to determine the similarity between documents while at the same time, being more robust to query modifications.

For a session S, we define a tuple (r_f, r_l) consisting of the first and last viewed record. We consider r_f to be the seed document for the *MLT* module. For both, publications and datasets we retrieve top k similar items for the seed (r_f) using *MLT* module. If the last viewed record r_l is present within the top k more-like-this records, we consider the session as topically homogeneous. However, choosing an appropriate k is crucial in understanding the diversity of the session. For this study, we experiment with setting k to 100 for a lenient understanding, and to 5 for a more rigorous and restricted understanding of diversity.

The result of this analysis is presented graphically in Fig. 1. In the figure, the light grey shade corresponds to sessions for which the last record r_l is not found within the top 100 more-like-this records. The blue and dark blue shades indicate the number of sessions for which the last record r_l has been located respectively within the top 100 and the top 5 records as returned by *MLT* module. Note that this analysis is not applicable to those sessions having only one record view.

For dataset search (presented at the bottom of Fig. 1), we note that approximately 11% sessions (particularly 964) are seen to be very focused to a particular topic (dark blue) for which the last viewed record (r_l) has been found within the top 5 more-like-this items. The last record is found within top 100 more-

[5] https://bit.ly/MLT-elastic.

like-this items for 2993 sessions (blue) which accounts for 35.7%. However, the publication search sessions seem much more diverse: we found only 846 sessions (6.1%) having a last record contained in the top 100 more-like-this items and only 329 sessions (2.3%) for which the last record has been found within top 5 *MLT* entries.

The topical diversity and homogeneity of a session for publication and dataset search is even more evident when we consider the similarity scores provided by the *MLT* module ($\texttt{sim-score}(r_f, r_l) > 0$). On average, a dataset search retrieved a similarity score of $\text{Top100} = 325.02, \text{Top5} = 475.0$ while the similarity score for publications was only $\text{Top100} = 70.8$ and $\text{Top5} = 117.9$. From this analysis, we can conclude that dataset retrieval sessions are much more focused than publication search sessions, and the searched datasets in a single session are more densely coupled than the searched publications.

4.3 Interaction Sequences

In this section, we study differences between dataset and document search on the basis of interaction sequences. We present this using *Sankey* diagrams in Fig. 2. The diagrams represent the transitions of the first eight interactions of users when searching for publications (Fig. 2a) and datasets (Fig. 2b)[6]. In the ISS, it is possible to switch between object types (e.g. from searching for research data to publication search). Hence, we extracted only those sessions from the log having a focus either on publications or on datasets without switching the type in between. Each logged interaction is associated with an action label which describes the type of action a user has performed ("view record", "search" etc.). An in-depth explanation of this analysis technique can be found in [7].

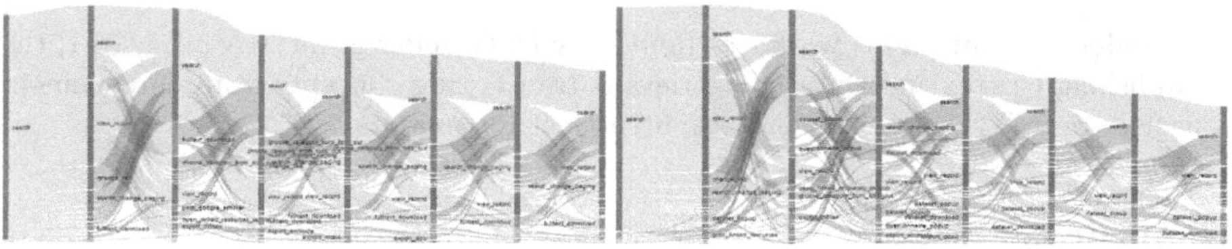

(a) Publications (b) Datasets

Fig. 2. First eight interaction transitions for publication and dataset search. The interactions are color-coded: green accounts for searching, blue for record view, orange for download (i.e. an implicit relevance signals) and grey for other interactions. Implicit relevance signals indicate a higher degree of relevance suggested by an interaction such as "export citation" immediately after a search. (Color figure online)

The analysis of the interaction sequence (see Fig. 2) shows no substantial differences between datasets and publications in terms of interaction paths. For

[6] A high-resolution figure is available at: https://arxiv.org/abs/2006.02770.

both types, the most frequent interactions after an initial search (green) were either a *view_record* (blue) or another *search*. Differences, however, can be found in two aspects: *a*) the frequency of consequent searches (green) is higher for publications; *b*) the number of implicit relevance signals is notably higher for dataset search. One can observe that a large fraction of dataset searches contain interactions related to the download of a record which is especially visible in the third interaction for datasets. Further query reformulations are less frequent for dataset searches (flow into green from any other). A possible explanation for this can be that a major portion of dataset searches appear to be known-item based. This observation is in line with our earlier observations on session diversity analysis (see Sect. 4.2).

5 Conclusion and Future Work

In this study, we presented an analysis of search logs from an integrated search system containing both, documents and datasets as repositories. In contrast to a similar study [9], we experimented with real-life queries issued by social scientists with a defined information need. Further, we argue that the reported analysis is more factual in accordance with the observations made in [8]. From our study, we observe that the queries addressing a publication are more frequent and less repetitive in comparison to dataset searches. Also, the average number of record views during dataset search is substantially lower compared to publication searches. In terms of segregating search intents between a dataset and a publication search, we note that there are barely any distinctive features to characterize a query. As part of future work, we would like to utilise the session information to personalise retrieval sessions which can further be used to construct a specialised recommender system for dataset retrieval.

Acknowledgement. This work was funded by DFG under grant MA 3964/10-1, the "Establishing Contextual Dataset Retrieval - transferring concepts from document to dataset retrieval" (ConDATA) project, http://bit.ly/Condata.

References

1. Angel, A., Koudas, N.: Efficient diversity-aware search. In: Proceedings of ACM SIGMOD, pp. 781–792 (2011)
2. Brickley, D., Burgess, M., Noy, N.: Google dataset search: building a search engine for datasets in an open web ecosystem. In: WWW, WWW 2019, pp. 1365–1375 (2019)
3. Cafarella, M.J., Halevy, A., Madhavan, J.: Structured data on the web. Commun. ACM **54**(2), 72–79 (2011)
4. Chapman, A., et al.: Dataset search: a survey. VLDB J. **29**(1), 251–272 (2019). https://doi.org/10.1007/s00778-019-00564-x
5. Chen, J., Wang, X., Cheng, G., Kharlamov, E., Qu, Y.: Towards more usable dataset search: from query characterization to snippet generation. In: Proceedings of the 28th CIKM 2019, pp. 2445–2448 (2019)

6. Hienert, D., Kern, D., Boland, K., Zapilko, B., Mutschke, P.: A digital library for research data and related information in the social sciences. In: 2019 ACM/IEEE Joint Conference on Digital Libraries (JCDL), pp. 148–157 (2019)
7. Hienert, D., Mutschke, P.: A usefulness-based approach for measuring the local and global effect of IIR services. In: Proceedings of 2016 ACM CHIIR, pp. 153–162 (2016)
8. Jansen, B.J., Spink, A.: How are we searching the world wide web? A comparison of nine search engine transaction logs. Inf. Process. Manag. **42**(1), 248–263 (2006)
9. Kacprzak, E., Koesten, L., Tennison, J., Simperl, E.: Characterising dataset search queries. In: Companion of WWW 2018, pp. 1485–1488. ACM Press (2018)
10. Kern, D., Mathiak, B.: Are there any differences in data set retrieval compared to well-known literature retrieval? In: Research and Advanced Technology for Digital Libraries, pp. 197–208 (2015)
11. Koesten, L., Mayr, P., Groth, P., Simperl, E., de Rijke, M.: Report on the DATA:SEARCH'18 workshop - searching data on the web. In: SIGIR Forum, vol. 52, no. 2, pp. 117–124 (2018)

Research Data Management and Discovery

Context-Driven Discoverability of Research Data

Miriam Baglioni(✉), Paolo Manghi(✉), and Andrea Mannocci(✉)

CNR-ISTI, Pisa, Italy
{miriam.baglioni,paolo.manghi,andrea.mannocci}@isti.cnr.it

Abstract. Research data sharing has been proved to be key for accelerating scientific progress and fostering interdisciplinary research; hence, the ability to search, discover and reuse data items is nowadays vital in doing science. However, research data discovery is yet an open challenge. In many cases, descriptive metadata exhibit poor quality, and the ability to automatically enrich metadata with semantic information is limited by the data files format, which is typically not textual and hard to mine. More generally, however, researchers would like to find data used across different research experiments or even disciplines. Such needs are not met by traditional metadata description schemata, which are designed to freeze research data features at deposition time.

In this paper, we propose a methodology that enables "context-driven discovery" for research data thanks to their proven usage across research activities that might differ from the original one, potentially across diverse disciplines. The methodology exploits the collection of publication–dataset and dataset–dataset links provided by OpenAIRE Scholexplorer data citation index so to propagate articles metadata into related research datasets by leveraging semantic relatedness. Such "context propagation" process enables the construction of "context-enriched" metadata of datasets, which enables "context-driven" discoverability of research data. To this end, we provide a real-case evaluation of this technique applied to Scholexplorer. Due to the broad coverage of Scholexplorer, the evaluation documents the effectiveness of this technique at improving data discovery on a variety of research data repositories and databases.

1 Introduction

Over the last few years, research data have gained unprecedented importance and are now considered as central as traditional publications. Being able to search, find, access, and reuse such research products helps to accelerate scientific progress [3,11], and cross-pollinate research by potentially fostering multidisciplinarity [10]. However, despite the extensive literature in the field of metadata-driven discovery technologies for scholarly communication, research data discovery still remains an open field of research. We can attribute these nonachievements to two main factors related to the yet immature positioning of research data in science.

M. Hall et al. (Eds.): TPDL 2020, LNCS 12246, pp. 197–211, 2020.
https://doi.org/10.1007/978-3-030-54956-5_15

Firstly, in many circumstances (e.g. "long-tail of data" scenarios), the absence of community practices, mandates, and incentives makes metadata description of research data unsatisfactory. Data is often perceived as supplementary material of an article and obtaining a persistent identifier (e.g. DOI) is the ultimate (and primary) aim of its deposition in a repository. To this end, research data metadata often do not undergo a curation and validation process as it occurs for libraries or publishers when research articles are submitted. Although the challenges hindering research data discovery seem in many ways similar to the ones arising for research articles and, more broadly, literature, the same solutions can hardly be applied. For example, the non-textual nature of data makes particularly hard the application of automated metadata enrichment techniques commonly in place when dealing with publications, such as natural language processing (NLP), full-text mining and topic extraction.

Secondly, research data discoverability is driven by user requirements that cannot be intrinsically satisfied by traditional metadata schemata/formats. While the discovery of research papers is motivated by the need of a researcher to find and read about the results of other scientists, the discovery of research data is driven by the need of finding data that can be reused to perform different analyses, in the same or even in different disciplines. Hence, even when research data are accurately deposited, and metadata is validated by data curators (e.g. thematic databases, repositories, archives), metadata structures cannot capture the variety of research applications the data may serve (or have subsequently served), and therefore fail in addressing such key discovery requirements. The semantic limits of metadata formats and, more broadly, the limits of the research data life-cycle, which disregards metadata enrichment based on further reuse, can be accounted as one of the main issues jeopardising data reuse practices and, ultimately, the enactment of open science.

In this work, as a solution to the problems above, we introduce the notion of *context-driven discoverability* of research data. The underlying intuition is that research data citation indexes, which populate an up-to-date graph of semantic relationships between research data and publications objects, can be exploited to propagate "research context", represented as a set of metadata properties of an object, to another related object. For example, the "abstract" and the "keywords" of an article metadata can be propagated and attached to the metadata description of research data being linked to the article via a relationship of type "cites". As a result of this process, the target research data, generated as an outcome of a given research activity and reused later to serve a different one, is also described by metadata that can leverage discovery by at least two distinct "research contexts".

To prove the effectiveness of context-driven discoverability, we *i)* present a *context propagation* technique for automated augmentation of bibliographic metadata of research data based on the semantic correlation between publications and data, and *ii)* perform an experimental study and validation of this technique using the OpenAIRE Scholexplorer's research data citation index.[1]

[1] Scholexplorer, https://scholexplorer.openaire.eu.

Table 1. Scholexplorer entities and relationships.

Measure	Quantity
# of publications	21,288,342
# of datasets	51,946,754
# of relations publication-dataset	159,796,162
# of relations dataset-dataset (no loops)	141,403,762

Scholexplorer [4] aggregates and redistributes, free of charge, over 270 million bidirectional Scholix [5] links among research literature and datasets, and thus constitutes a fertile ground for our experimentation. Our experiment applies context propagation to the Scholexplorer citation graph showing how the resulting index can complete research data metadata and enable cross-context discovery of research data, across different research applications and across disciplines.

The remainder of the paper is structured as follows. Section 2 reviews Scholexplorer as primary data source for our experimentation, Sect. 3 describes our methodology to solve the problem, while Sect. 4 points out implementation details. Then, in Sect. 5 we evaluate our approach and discuss the results obtained, while Sect. 6 briefly reviews related work. Finally, in Sect. 7, we conclude and indicate possible extensions of our approach.

2 Data and Resources

Having an up-to-date research data (also "dataset" in the following) citation index at disposal is a key enabling factor for this research. For our experiments we have relied on Scholexplorer, the OpenAIRE[2] service that provides over 270 million bidirectional Scholix [5] links among over 21 million research literature objects and 51 million datasets from 13,000 publishers, 10 data centres, CrossRef[3], Datacite[4], EMBL-EBI[5], and OpenAIRE. The whole collection is available, free of charge, via periodic dumps [7] and via API[6]. Table 1 shows the number of articles, datasets, and relationships in the dump used to perform our experiment.

The concept of *context* is flexible and may potentially include any relevant metadata field pertaining to publication entities, such as abstract, title, topics, keywords. The optimal setup might vary from dataset to dataset; indeed, a fine-tuning of the context to propagate can largely affect discoverability. In our experiment, we opted to propagate publication abstracts as they occur more frequently than topics and keywords, and therefore are a richer feed for full-text search. Besides, since relevant terms present in the title are generally present in the abstract too, we ruled out titles propagation.

[2] OpenAIRE, https://www.openaire.eu.
[3] Crossref, https://www.crossref.org.
[4] DataCite, https://www.datacite.org.
[5] EMBL-EBI, https://www.ebi.ac.uk.
[6] Scholexplorer API, https://scholexplorer.openaire.eu/#/api.

Table 2. Potential impact of propagating abstract as context.

Measure	Quantity
# publications with abstracts	9,346,875
# datasets with abstracts	7,847,271
# rels between pubs with abst and dats	151,224,353
# rels between pubs with abst and dats with abst	5,288,025
# rels between pubs with abst and dats without abst	145,936,328

Table 3. Analysis of Scholexplorer subset of providers providing datasets. For each provider, the number of datasets is shown together with the relative percentage of datasets with abstract.

Provider	Datasets (% w/abs)	
3TU.DC	164	(96.95%)
ANDS	29	(00.00%)
CCDC	716,009	(100.00%)
DataCite	8,470,681	(82.67%)
ENA	1,349,123	(42.36%)
ICPSR	6,823	(73.18%)
IEDA	488	(90.98%)
Pangaea	309,904	(38.53%)
RCSB	98,200	(00.00%)

To give a flavour of the impact of this choice, Table 2 reports on the total number of publications and datasets with abstracts and the number of relations from publications with abstract to datasets with or without an abstract. As can be noted, there is a significant number of relations (145,936,328) from publications with an abstract to datasets that could potentially benefit from context propagation. Table 3 completes this picture by reporting the number of datasets aggregated by Scholexplorer from each provider. It also highlights the percentage of datasets with a provided abstract, thus giving an indication on how "complete" are the potential targets of context propagation. Please notice, that a dataset (or a publication) in Scholexplorer can be potentially collected from several providers, hence, in this case, it would be counted multiple times.

The propagation process is driven by the semantics of the relationships between publication and data, and between dataset and dataset. Scholexplorer includes relationships whose semantics cannot be used for propagation, such as "hasMetadata", which is not relevant to the research context; Table 4 provides a breakdown of the selected semantic relationships. Finally, given the selected subset of relationships, Table 5 reports the number of publications, datasets, and relationships (with and without abstracts) that are consequently involved in the propagation process.

3 Methodology

In this section, we introduce the terminology used in the paper and describe the chosen propagation strategy based on semantics. We define as:

Table 4. Breakdown of Scholexplorer selected semantics for context propagation.

	Semantics	Quantity
pubs–data	reviews	1,785
	references	1,949,635
	documents	258,513
	cites	169,397
	issourceof	30,052
	issupplementedby	1,238,320
	isderivedfrom	267

	Semantics	Quantity
data–data	isreferencedby	67,526,737
	isvariantformof	20,115
	references	67,526,737
	isdocumentedby	5,982
	continues	139,374
	documents	5,982
	haspart	1,178,496
	iscitedby	19,529
	issupplementedby	308,884
	isnewversionof	384,570
	cites	19,529
	issupplementto	308,884
	ispartof	1,178,496
	iscontinuedby	139,374

Table 5. Analysis of Scholexplorer subgraph according to the selected semantics.

Measure	Quantity
# of publications	1,065,121
# of datasets	4,886,298
# of relations (publication-dataset)	3,647,969
# of relations (dataset-dataset, no loops)	138,762,689
# publications with abstracts	574,209
# datasets with abstracts	3,392,081
# rels between pubs with abst and dats with abst	640,864
# rels between pubs with abst and dats without abst	1,788,183

Definition 1 (Context-driven discoverability). *The ability to discover a dataset based on information present in descriptive metadata of publications related to it, either directly (i.e. a publication refers this dataset) or indirectly (i.e. a publication refers a dataset that, in turn, refers this dataset, e.g. an earlier version of the same).*

Defined as such, context-driven discoverability essentially subsumes three possible scenarios of interest: *latent*, *reuse*, and *multidisciplinary* discoverability.

Definition 2 (Latent discoverability). *The ability to discover a dataset with incomplete metadata thanks to context propagated from another related object.*

Definition 3 (Reuse discoverability). *The ability to discover a dataset used for a research activity different from the one it has been created by, within the scope of the same disciplinary domain.*

Definition 4 (Multidisciplinary discoverability). *The ability to discover a dataset used for a research activity different from the one it has been created by, within the scope of a different disciplinary domain.*

All three scenarios covered by context-driven discoverability can be enabled by context propagation, which is defined as follows:

Definition 5 (Context propagation). *The process enabling context-driven discoverability. All the relevant semantic relations are followed in order to propagate context from publications so to form richer research data metadata records, which in turn propagate to other related research datasets. The process is limited by a threshold, defined by a termination function.*

The proposed methodology for context propagation relies on the fact that scholarly knowledge and research products (i.e. publications, research data, etc.) and their underlying relations can be represented as a graph. A *graph* is an ordered pair $G = (V, E)$ of nodes V and edges E. A *node* in the graph represents the abstraction of an entity in the modelled domain – in our case, a kind of research product (i.e. publications or research data) – while an *edge* represents a relationship between two nodes (e.g. a publication *reusing* a dataset). Nodes and edges can have labels that characterise them with attributes and specify their semantics. A source node u is said to be connected to a destination node v, indicated as $u \prec v$, when it exists an edge or an ordered set of edges (i.e. a *path*) connecting them.

The context propagation method here described relies on the existence of a path connecting two nodes, and on the chain of semantics connecting them, which reveals the reason for two nodes to be connected. For example, a publication could be connected to a dataset *directly* because the dataset *supplements* the publication (i.e. via an edge), or *indirectly* (i.e. through a path), e.g. because a newer version of a dataset *supersedes* the version originally *cited by* a publication (i.e. a path of length 2 exists from the publication to the newer dataset). The fact that two nodes are connected via a path allows us to propagate the context of a publication to relevant datasets. As already mentioned, the contextual information we chose to propagate to test our approach is the abstract.

The effect of context propagation depends on the "quality" of the path propagating the information from one node to another, which may depend on the semantics of the edges in the path or the length of the path. For this reason, our process associates a measure of *trust* to the propagated context that reflects the level of direct or indirect relatedness of the two nodes: the one propagating context and the one receiving it. Trust is key as it allows to filter out propagations with lower quality (i.e. a *cutoff threshold*), chose the most suitable propagation among many, or even set a termination function for the propagation process. Trust can be computed according to two strategies:

- Path-length driven: trust is inversely proportional to the length n of the path connecting two nodes, i.e. the shorter the path, the higher the quality. A trust function could be $1/n$. This case is trivial, and it is not an object of study in this paper.
- Semantic-driven: trust is mapped into a numerical weight characterising the edges of a path. The combination of such weights defines the trust of the relation between source and destination nodes. In this case, the trust can be a number in the range $[0, 1]$ where 0 means no relatedness, and 1 means the maximum relatedness.

When the semantics of the relation is used to weight the edge connecting two nodes, the graph becomes a multi-graph, i.e. there could be multiple edges connecting two adjacent nodes. As edge semantics is a measure of the relatedness between two nodes, the higher the weight, the stronger the relation. Hence, the propagation strategy has to prefer paths that maximise the total weight. Given these premises, we define the propagation function as follows:

Definition 6 (Propagation function). *Given $G = (V, E)$ a multi-graph whose nodes belongs to two sets P (publications) and D (datasets), given $p \in P$ and $d \in D$ so that $p \prec d$, let w_{pd} be the maximum cumulative weight among all possible paths connecting the generic p at the generic d, and let $f_P(d) = PS_d = \{(p_i, w_{p_i d}) | p_i \in P \wedge p_i \prec d\}$ be the propagation function, which associates to d its propagation set (PS), where the generic weight $w_{p_i d}$ is such that:*

$$w_{p_i d} = \begin{cases} w_{d' d} * w_{p_i d'}, & (p_i, w_{p_i d}) \notin PS_d, \\ & (p_i, w_{p_i d'}) \in PS_{d'}, \\ & (d', d) \in E \\ & \\ max(w_{p_i d}, (w_{d' d} * w_{p_i d'})), & (p_i, w_{p_i d}) \in PS_d, \\ & (p_i, w_{p_i d'}) \in PS_{d'}, \\ & (d', d) \in E \\ & \\ w_{p_i d}, & (p_i, d) \in E \end{cases}$$

The propagation function depends on the product of the semantic relatedness weights in the path, and always prefers the edges with the highest weight among those at its disposal in the chosen path. Among all the computed paths connecting a couple of nodes, it chooses the path maximising the overall weight independently from its length. In this way, a low semantics relatedness along a path plays an important role as a discount factor and helps to filter unsatisfactory propagations out. At the same time, it does not penalise long paths with strong semantic relatedness.

Figure 1 shows an example of the propagation process over a sample graph. On the left-hand side, Fig. 1a shows the graph in its starting condition before propagation takes place: blue nodes refer to publications, red ones to datasets, and the edge associated to the semantics with maximum weight between each

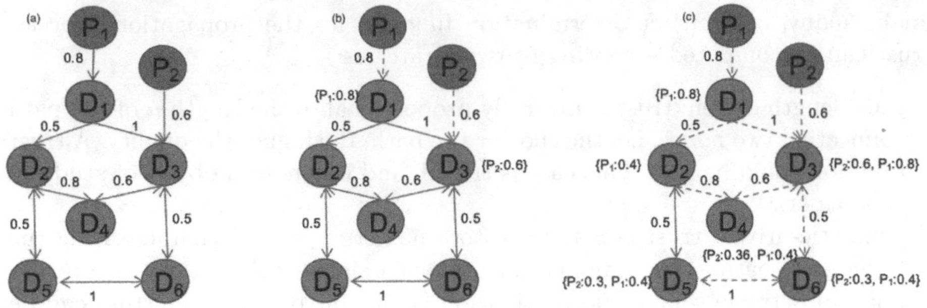

Fig. 1. Context propagation example. (Color figure online)

couple of nodes is shown. For simplicity, we assume a semantic relation and its inverse have the same weight. We also fix the trust cutoff threshold to 0.3. In each iteration, all the nodes with available context for propagation are considered and try to affect all their neighbours. In the first step, only publications have a context at disposal for propagation, so all the edges connecting them to datasets are considered (represented as dashed in the figure). This is shown in Fig. 1b: both D_1 and D_3 receive context respectively by P_1 and P_2. Each propagated context has the same weight as the edge involved since it is a direct connection. In any step other than the first one, the context is propagated among datasets. Each dataset having received a previously propagated context tries to pass it along to all its neighbouring datasets. However, this time the weight of the association is not equal to the weight of the edge connecting the dataset with its neighbours. In fact, the context has been "inherited" from a publication, and thus the indirect connection has to be taken into account. Each time a context is further propagated between two datasets d' and d, its weight is computed by multiplying the weight for the context seen at d' and the weight of the edge connecting d' and d. A context is propagated to a dataset only if it does not already belong to the dataset's PS. In case the PS already contains information about the publication whose context is being passed, its weight is computed as the maximum among the weights computed on the paths that have reached the node so far. Figure 1c shows the graph after the propagation process has terminated. D_1 receives context only from P_1, D_3 receives context from P_2 directly, and from P_1 through D_1. The weight for the context of P_1 is the same for both the dataset, since the edge that binds them weights 1. D_2 receives context of P_1 through D_1 and the strength of the correlation is multiplied by 0.5 (i.e. the edge weight). It does not receive context from P_2 because it could propagate only through D_4 or D_5, but the strength of the relation would be below the cutoff threshold in both cases, and thus they are discarded. D_4 receives propagation information from both P_1 and P_2, and both of them through D_3: the propagation weight of P_1 through D_1 would have been 0.32, which is less than the 0.4 got from D_3. D_6 also receives propagation information for both P_1 and P_2 through D_3, and the correlation strength is multiplies by 0.5 for both the publications. D_6 receives propagation information from P_1 and P_2 through D_5 with the same weight of D_5.

4 Implementation

As Scholexplorer dump occupies over 40 GB compressed on disk, it was unfeasible to treat the problem with an in-memory approach. We opted for the utilisation of our Hadoop[7] cluster and implemented the propagation algorithm as a sequence of Spark jobs in PySpark. The code is publicly accessible here[8].

Running context propagation takes about 6 h on our cluster with 20 virtual machines (VMs) for Apache HDFS DataNodes and Spark workers, each VM with 16 cores, 32 GB of RAM, and 250 GB of space on disk; plus 3 dedicated virtual machines for HDFS Name Nodes, each one with 8 cores, 16 GB of RAM, and 40 GB of space on disk. Please notice that our termination function on the Scholexplorer graph makes the process terminate after three steps of propagation, that is one direct propagation from publications to datasets, and just two steps of propagation between datasets. We do believe this is acceptable for the sake of computational feasibility as the number of nodes reachable by context propagation after three steps covers about 97% of the nodes reachable via paths originating from publications with context (evaluated through an iterative graph exploration converging at 2,266,269 nodes).

In order to make the evaluation of the proposed approach easier, we provide two full-text indexes on Elasticsearch[9]. A first index (*propagation-before*) contains metadata records from Scholexplorer before context propagation has run, while a second one (*propagation-after*) provides the same records after context propagation is performed. The former contains metadata of publications and datasets consisting mainly of *identifier*, *pid*, *type* (i.e. publication or dataset), *title*, *abstract*. The latter contains the same metadata descriptions plus one more field (*propagated abstracts*) for datasets in order to amass the abstracts coming from publications via context propagation. In order to evaluate the results, the user can play with a simple search interface[10] and explore the saved queries as examples (refer to Sect. 5.2), or query the indexes from scratch.

5 Evaluation

In this section, we present the results obtained by applying the methodology proposed in Sect. 3 and characterise them both from a quantitative and qualitative standpoint.

---

[7] Hadoop, https://hadoop.apache.org.
[8] Code repository, https://code-repo.d4science.org/miriam.baglioni/context-propagation.
[9] Elasticsearch, https://www.elastic.co/elasticsearch.
[10] Evaluation interface: https://propagation-demo.infrascience.isti.cnr.it.

5.1 Quantitative Analysis

As a mean of comparison, Table 6 reports on the number of datasets and relative percentage of datasets with abstract for each provider involved in the analysis. Table 7 instead reports the results obtained by the application of the context propagation. For each provider, the table shows the number of datasets affected by context propagation both directly from a paper ("Publication–Data" column) and indirectly from another dataset ("Data–Data" column). For each provider it shows *i)* the total number of datasets receiving an abstract ("Propagated contexts") and the percentage relative to the total reported in Table 6,

Table 6. Analysis of Scholexplorer subset of providers providing datasets in the subgraph selected according to the valid semantics. For each provider, the number of datasets is shown together with the relative percentage of datasets with abstract.

Provider	Datasets (% w/abs)	
3TU.DC	62	(93.55%)
ANDS	2	(00.00%)
CCDC	713,350	(100.00%)
DataCite	3,796,690	(88.52%)
ENA	339,868	(00.00%)
ICPSR	6,823	(73.18%)
IEDA	443	(99.32%)
Pangaea	150,759	(45.88%)
RCSB	70,557	(00.00%)

Table 7. Quantitative evaluation of context propagation. For each provider, the number of datasets touched by propagation is reported together with an estimation of latent and reuse discoverability.

Provider	Publication–Data				Data–Data			
	Propagated contexts (% tot)		Latent	Reuse	Propagated context (% tot)		Latent	Reuse
3TU.DC	27	(43.55%)	0	15	12	(19.35%)	0	8
ANDS	1	(50.00%)	1	0	–		–	–
CCDC	130,317	(18.27%)	0	333	546	(0.08%)	0	225
DataCite	405,088	(10.67%)	4,921	28,619	849,260	(22.37%)	24,859	656,862
ENA	337,814	(99.40%)	337,814	60,888	–		–	–
ICPSR	3,691	(54.10%)	743	3,303	130	(1.91%)	4	78
IEDA	41	(9.26%)	1	7	16	(3.61%)	0	6
Pangea	2,951	(1.96%)	200	600	35,770	(23.73%)	12,571	10,200
RCSB	70,398	(99.77%)	70,398	46,133	–		–	–

ii) an estimation of latent discoverability ("Latent" column), and iii) an estimation of reuse discoverability ("Reuse" column). Latent discoverability is evaluated by counting the number of datasets without own abstract that have been targeted by context propagation, while reuse is evaluated by counting the number of datasets receiving at least two propagated contexts. Please note that the reuse estimation computed as such incurs in an underestimation of the potential reuse. In fact, as an example, it does not account for datasets whose only semantic relation available is the one connecting the dataset to the publication reusing it (i.e. it should be accounted for reuse, but in this case only one context is propagated, and thus it is not counted). From the reported results, we can notice that the margin of improvement varies largely across providers: from a cumulative (i.e. for all propagation steps) 12.87% for IEDA to almost the totality for ENA and RCSB (99.40% and 99.77% respectively). We believe that focusing on absolute numbers does not deliver the right key to interpret the results as a seemingly marginal improvement can still be significant in terms of discoverability for users.

Moreover, providing a quantitative estimation of multidisciplinary discoverability is extremely hard as there are no objective tests to identify such cases. For most of them, only a domain expert has the in-depth knowledge to judge whether it is truly multidisciplinary or not; for this reason, we study this aspect from a qualitative standpoint only.

Finally, it is worth mentioning, that a few providers do not participate in data–data propagation as their datasets are not related with the selected semantics for our experimentation. For example, nucleotides provided by ENA do not have relations among them, but only towards publications mentioning them, thus they do not participate in data–data propagation.

5.2 Qualitative Analysis

In this section, we present a collection of a few chosen examples that, to the best of our knowledge, better describe from a qualitative standpoint the results achieved through our approach and advocate for its application. The reader can find them via the evaluation interface provided.

Example 1 (Latent discoverability). *The query term "SHC014" is the name of a coronavirus spike protein that has recently resonated in the media worldwide; resulted from a 2015 lab experiment, it has been wrongly associated to the current SARS-CoV-2 outbreak. The query term in the original index matches only the publication relative to the original experiment, while after the propagation the dataset "Structure of SARS coronavirus spike receptor-binding domain complexed with its receptor" emerges, despite being originally deprived of any further metadata, but the title. Moreover, as can be seen, several other relevant publication abstracts are included as dataset context, hence improving its discoverability dramatically.*

Example 2 (Reuse discoverability). *The YfdE gene from the bacteria E. Coli receives the abstracts of two publications thanks to context propagation: the* *first is a 2013 publication describing gene's function and x-ray crystal structure, while the second one is a 2018 paper referring the protein acetyl-CoA:oxalate CoA-transferase, which the gene synthesise.*

Example 3 (Multidisciplinary discoverability). *We managed to isolate the "PRIMAP-hist Socio-Eco dataset" which is used relevant to both assess anthropogenic land-use estimates and for the creation of a consistent historical time series of GDPs for 195 countries in the last 150 years. As anticipated, pinpointing true multidisciplinary examples is rather difficult without prior domain knowledge. However, we believe this example can still be a good candidate that shows how two disciplines within Earth System Science can benefit from context-driven discoverability.*

6 Related Work

The approach described in this paper and the problems it addresses share a few peculiarities with other research problems from other research applications.

A first similar application is Automated Query Expansion (AQE), whose major contributions across over 50 years of research are reviewed and summarised in [1,6]. In AQE, the terms composing the user query are expanded by adding a new set of features at query time by means of different techniques (e.g. stemming, dictionary and ontology-based augmentation, language modelling, query rewrite) in order to capture a broader set of potentially relevant documents (i.e. improve recall, generally, at the expense of decreasing precision). However, this is seldom effective in our case, as there is often little to be matched in research data descriptions. Indeed, research data metadata are often largely incomplete, and so, even if the user query is automatically-expanded consistently, the search seldom can retrieve further results potentially relevant for the user. To some extent, our approach can be still categorised as an augmentation task as in AQE. In fact, rather than augmenting the terms contained in the user query thanks to language models, we augment the metadata descriptions in research data by propagating information following their semantic relations towards relevant literature and other research data. Unlike AQE techniques, where the user might be puzzled when trying to understand why certain documents have been returned with high saliency despite being very different from the expressed query terms, our method can always provide the user with the information needed to explain why a given result has been returned as potentially relevant. In a similar way to AQE, an early work from Mannocci et al. addressed research data discoverability by providing a user interface enabling the composition of on-the-fly queries against research data archives starting from a literature record of interest [9].

A second similarity is shared with Label Propagation (LP) [14–16]. Within the research field of complex networks, LP is a specific task that aims at labelling a large quantity of unlabelled nodes across the network starting from the little knowledge present in a much smaller group of labelled nodes. Such labelling is in practice performed by propagating a finite set of labels across the network by means of nodes properties and their semantic relations (i.e. network topology). Such algorithms are originally devised to detect communities in networks, but nonetheless, they share to some extent common properties with the class of problems introduced in this work. A typical case study for such class of algorithms is the propagation of political affiliation in Fiend-of-a-friend (FOAF) networks (i.e. identify communities or clusters of right-wing and left-wing nodes). Like LP, our context of applications deals with nodes rich in information (i.e. labelled) and nodes poorer in information (i.e. unlabelled); however, in our case, the split among the two classes is far more balanced than the one noticeable in typical LP applications. Similarly, LP indeed tries to spread information (i.e. the labels) from one node to another; however, unlike in our task, the set of candidate labels is finite and known *a priori* (e.g. in the case of political orientation: "right-wing" or "left-wing"). In our application instead, the amount of information the algorithm can potentially propagate across the network is not known *a priori* and, in general, grows with the size of the network (i.e. one unique abstract for each publication joining the network). Indeed, any publication node could offer its own "label value" as a propagation candidate; however, we cannot talk about community detection in our case study as there is no real community to be discovered.

7 Conclusions and Future Work

In this paper, we described a sound methodology enabling context-driven discoverability for research data thanks to their proven usage across research activities that might differ from the original one, potentially across diverse disciplines. We showed how publication–dataset semantic relations can be leveraged in order to propagate research context (e.g. abstracts) from publication to dataset, and thus form richer metadata description. By providing a real-case evaluation on Scholexplorer, we showed how a large number of datasets across all Scholexplorer providers can benefit from the context propagated from related literature, and showcased a few selected representative examples.

The context propagation methodology here proposed can be improved and refined in several different directions. During our experiments, we observed that some semantics can be more conducive for a type of discoverability (i.e. latent, reuse, multidisciplinary) than for the others. For example, semantics as *isSupplementedBy*, *documents* or *reviews* between publication and dataset strongly suggest a potential case of latent discoverability within the scope of the same research application, while *cites* or *references* can indicate most probably a reuse. To this end, semantics could be tightly associated with the three different types of discoverability by providing a different weight for each one of them.

Moreover, in order to assess further the capabilities in multidisciplinary research, and isolate better candidates that are difficult to retrieve otherwise (especially without in-domain knowledge), we could leverage topics and keywords along with abstracts. This would enable us to match topics with known ontologies such as MeSH [8] for Life Sciences, PhySH [13] in Physics, CSO [12] for Computer Science, and therefore gain a better view on whether a dataset effectively lies on the border of two (or more) disciplines. More sophisticated NLP techniques, such as Latent Dirichlet Allocation [2], could be applied in order to let latent structure emerge from abstract plain-texts and characterise further the nodes alongside topics and keywords.

Furthermore, it is in our plans to study the feasibility of an extensive search-based user evaluation by providing access to the propagated index so to log user queries and interactions with the results (e.g. relevant, not relevant). Such knowledge can be used as ground truth in order to accurately assess the improvement achieved by context propagation by rerunning the same queries under the hood against the other index and measure the differences.

Finally, in order not to disperse the added value, propagated information could be fed back to content providers, so that it can be integrated into the original data catalogues so to deliver context-driven discoverability out-of-the-box right where it belongs and can be more effective.

Acknowledgements. This work was co-funded by the EU H2020 project OpenAIRE-Advance (Grant agreement ID: 777541).

References

1. Bhogal, J., MacFarlane, A., Smith, P.: A review of ontology based query expansion. Inf. Process. Manag. **43**(4), 866–886 (2007). https://doi.org/10.1016/j.ipm.2006.09.003
2. Blei, D.M., Ng, A.Y., Jordan, M.I.: Latent dirichlet allocation. J. Mach. Learn. Res. **3**(Jan), 993–1022 (2003). https://dl.acm.org/doi/10.5555/944919.944937
3. Borgman, C.L.: Big Data, Little Data. No Data. The MIT Press (2015). https://doi.org/10.7551/mitpress/9963.001.0001
4. Burton, A., et al.: The data-literature interlinking service: towards a common infrastructure for sharing data-article links. Program **51**(1), null (2017). https://doi.org/10.1108/PROG-06-2016-0048
5. Burton, A., et al.: The scholix framework for interoperability in data-literature information exchange. D-Lib Mag. **23**(1/2) (2017). https://doi.org/10.1045/january2017-burton
6. Carpineto, C., Romano, G.: A survey of automatic query expansion in information retrieval. ACM Comput. Surv. (CSUR) **44**(1), 1–50 (2012). http://doi.acm.org/10.1145/2071389.2071390
7. La Bruzzo, S., Manghi, P.: Openaire scholexplorer service: scholix json dump (2019). https://doi.org/10.5281/zenodo.3541646
8. Lipscomb, C.E.: Medical subject headings (MESH). Bull. Med. Libr. Assoc. **88**(3), 265 (2000)
9. Mannocci, A., Manghi, P.: Preliminary analysis of data sources interlinking. In: Bolikowski, Ł., Casarosa, V., Goodale, P., Houssos, N., Manghi, P., Schirrwagen, J. (eds.) TPDL 2013. CCIS, vol. 416, pp. 53–64. Springer, Cham (2014). https://doi.org/10.1007/978-3-319-08425-1_6
10. Pasquetto, I.V., Borgman, C.L., Wofford, M.F.: Uses and reuses of scientific data: the data creators' advantage. Harv. Data Sci. Rev. **1**(2) (2019). https://doi.org/10.1162/99608f92.fc14bf2d

11. Pasquetto, I.V., Randles, B.M., Borgman, C.L.: On the reuse of scientific data. Data Sci. J. **16**(Borgman 2015), 1–9 (2017). https://doi.org/10.5334/dsj-2017-008
12. Salatino, A.A., Thanapalasingam, T., Mannocci, A., Osborne, F., Motta, E.: The computer science ontology: a large-scale taxonomy of research areas. In: Vrandečić, D., Bontcheva, K., Suárez-Figueroa, M.C., Presutti, V., Celino, I., Sabou, M., Kaffee, L.-A., Simperl, E. (eds.) ISWC 2018. LNCS, vol. 11137, pp. 187–205. Springer, Cham (2018). https://doi.org/10.1007/978-3-030-00668-6_12
13. Smith, A.: Physics subject headings (physh). ISKO Encyclopedia of Knowledge Organization (2019)
14. Wang, F., Zhang, C.: Label propagation through linear neighborhoods. IEEE Trans. Knowl. Data Eng. **20**(1), 55–67 (2007). https://doi.org/10.1109/TKDE.2007.19067
15. Zhou, D., Bousquet, O., Lal, T.N., Weston, J., Schölkopf, B.: Learning with local and global consistency. In: Advances in Neural Information Processing Systems, pp. 321–328 (2004)
16. Zhu, X., Ghahramani, Z., Lafferty, J.D.: Semi-supervised learning using gaussian fields and harmonic functions. In: Proceedings of the 20th International Conference on Machine Learning (ICML-03), pp. 912–919 (2003)

Management of Research Data in Image Format: An Exploratory Study on Current Practices

Miguel Fernandes[1(✉)], Joana Rodrigues[1,2(✉)], and Carla Teixeira Lopes[1,2(✉)]

[1] Faculty of Engineering of the University of Porto, Rua Dr. Roberto Frias, 4200-465 Porto, Portugal
miguelfernandes197@gmail.com, joanasousarodrigues.14@gmail.com, ctl@fe.up.pt
[2] INESC TEC, Rua Dr. Roberto Frias, 4200-465 Porto, Portugal

Abstract. Research data management is the basis for making data more Findable, Accessible, Interoperable and Reusable. In this context, little attention is given to research data in image format. This article presents the preliminary results of a study on the habits related to the management of images in research. We collected 107 answers from researchers using a questionnaire. These researchers were PhD students, fellows and university professors from Life and Health Sciences, Exact Sciences and Engineering, Natural and Environmental Sciences and Social Sciences and Humanities. This study shows that 83.2% of researcher use images as research data, however, its use is generally not accompanied by a guidance document such as a research data management plan. These results provide valuable insights into the processes and habits regarding the production and use of images in the research context.

Keywords: Research data management · Image management · Image as research data.

1 Introduction

Recent technological and scientific developments gave rise to the appearance of new methods, instruments, and research tools. These changes led to an increase in the volume, complexity and importance of research data. Combined with the increase in computing and digital storage capacity, data collection, dissemination and analysis are increasingly intensive. This new feature of science has led to data-intensive science [4,5]. This paradigm shift has caused changes and challenges in the way data are stored, preserved, accessed, and shared in the context of scientific activity [15].

The rapid development of processing capacity, image management and the ease of replication and dissemination increased the access and value of image collections [9]. In the context of research, various image capture devices have

M. Hall et al. (Eds.): TPDL 2020, LNCS 12246, pp. 212–226, 2020.
https://doi.org/10.1007/978-3-030-54956-5_16

emerged. With the increased use and volume of image collections, new challenges and opportunities have arisen in image research data management. Vejvoda, Burpee and Lackie [21] give preliminary recommendations for image management in the research context through recommendations established for numerical data sets. In our search for related works, we didn't find other studies focused on image management in the research context.

This study is motivated by the lack of knowledge concerning the production processes, use, and management of images in the research context. As images constitute a valuable informational element for research, it becomes necessary to include them in research data management processes. Therefore, it is essential to know the processes and habits in the production and use of images in research to produce recommendations for appropriate management. This work does not focus only on digital images as research data, although the importance of the technological development of capture devices is mentioned here. Analog images are also included, as they are also used (albeit in smaller numbers) and are equally important in research projects.

This article presents the preliminary results of a study on the habits related to the management of images in research that will later lead to guidelines on how researchers should manage their images.

2 Literature Review

Research data management involves a set of practices that include planning, documentation, organization, storage, dissemination, and preservation of research data [11]. It aims to prolong the life of the data during and after the end of the investigation, as well as to encourage data sharing and reuse [6]. Data management forms the basis for applying the Findable, Accessible, Interoperable, and Reusable (FAIR) and open science principles, which are often required by funding agencies [11]. Several models allow the creation of abstractions, the definition of concepts, key moments, and activities of the research data lifecycle to guide the planning and implementation of research data management.

The research data lifecycle consists of a simple, understandable, and organic way of visualizing the different phases of research data management through a descriptive model [7]. These key concepts depend on the scientific area, the type of data, among other factors [10].

Research data can be defined as the factual records used as primary sources in scientific research, accepted by the scientific community, and indispensable for validating research results. These records can be textual, numeric, images, or sound records [14]. Research data is collected and produced in various formats, from digital spreadsheets to compilations of questionnaires, images, and objects [13]. Research data is considered the input of the investigation and not the output. Thus, the figures produced for articles and other publications are not the focus of this article.

An image conveys information or meaning differently from text. While text transmits information through conventional and arbitrary symbols, the image carries information through the representation and similarity of the objects as they are. The fact that the image is used in conjunction with text suggests that the image itself carries information different from the text, managing to transmit things that the text cannot [12]. It can be understood as something that depicts, it consists of a form of representation of which photography, video, drawing and painting are part, among many others [1]. The scientific community currently accepts the use of photographs, videos, and other similar resources. It is a common practice in several areas of research, such as Astronomy, Anthropology, Geography, History, Social Sciences, and Health Sciences [3,16,17].

3 Methodology

We used a questionnaire to study the practices and habits in the management of research data in image format. The structure of the questionnaire and the elaboration of the questions were informed by the research data lifecycle from Data Documentation Initiative [18], DataONE [2] and UK Data Archive [20]. Questions were grouped by stages of the research data lifecycle: planning, creation/compilation, quality assurance, processing/analysis, description, storage and sharing.

The questionnaire underwent several revisions by the authors where the adequacy and formulation of the questions were discussed and reflected. Before dissemination, we tested our questionnaire with an external researcher to analyze how each item question was interpreted. The objective was to assure that the questions were well understood by researchers not specialized in the subject.

The questionnaire opened on 20 February 2020 and accepted answers until 26 March 2020. The questionnaire was distributed by email at the University of Porto research community[1], namely i3S and INESC-TEC, and in research units outside the University of Porto funded in 2019 by the Foundation for Science and Technology[2]. Namely, Centre for Informatics and Systems of the University of Coimbra, Cardiovascular Centre of the University of Lisbon, Centre for Philosophical and Humanistic Studies of Universidade Católica Portuguesa and Center for Mathematics and Applications of Universidade Nova de Lisboa. An email was sent to the coordinators of each group, asking the dissemination of the questionnaire among their members.

Respondents were people with research experience, namely PhD students, fellows, and university professors. Answers were given anonymously, not allowing the identification of the participants.

We used quantitative methods to analyze closed-ended questions and content analysis for open-ended questions. There were two types of closed-ended questions. A kind of question collected answers on a 5-point Likert scale (Never, Rarely, Occasionally, Often and Always), generating ordinal variables. The other type, involved the selection, or not, of provided answer options, creating nominal variables.

---

[1] https://www.i3s.up.pt/; https://www.inesctec.pt/en.

[2] https://www.cisuc.uc.pt/; http://ccul.pt/; https://cefh.braga.ucp.pt/; https://www.cma.fct.unl.pt/.

For each question, we analyzed the general tendency in the overall set of answers and conducted comparisons between 4 scientific areas (Life and Health Sciences - LHS; Exact Sciences and Engineering - ESE; Natural and Environmental Sciences - NES; Social Sciences and Humanities - SSH) and between 3 rates of image use in research (low - less than 25% of the projects; moderate - about 50% of the projects; high - more than 75% of the projects). For ordinal variables, we used Kruskal-Wallis to detect if there were differences among the groups. In cases where differences were found, we have used the Pairwise Test Mann-Whitney with Bonferroni correction to identify the location of the differences. For nominal variables, we used a Chi-square test for equality of proportions. When reporting our results, we use * to indicate results significant at $\alpha = .05$ and ** to indicate results significant at $\alpha = .01$.

4 Results

We collected answers from 107 researchers. The questionnaire, answer data and detailed statistical results are available at a data repository (https://doi.org/10.25747/7ma9-9132).

From the respondents, 41 (38.3%) work in the Life and Health Sciences, 30 (28%) in the Exact Sciences and Engineering, 12 (11.2%) in the Natural and Environmental Sciences, and 24 (22.4%) in the Social Sciences and Humanities field. Figure 1 relates the use of images as data with the research domain. We can observe a greater tendency to use images as research data in the Life and Health Sciences domain.

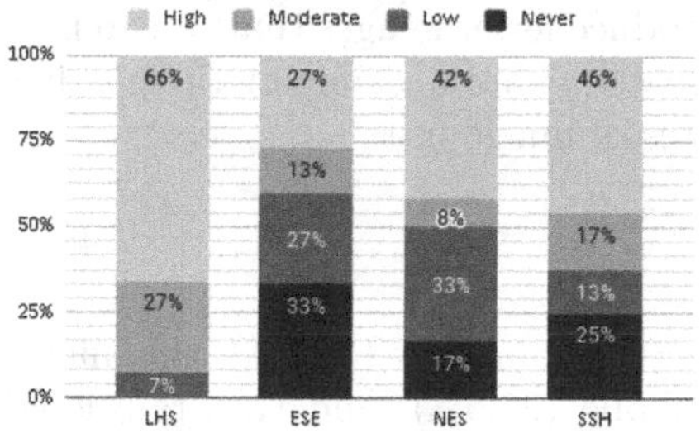

Fig. 1. Image use by domains

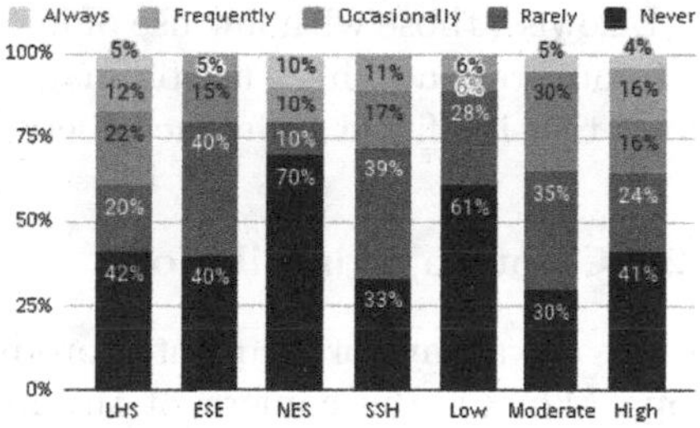

Fig. 2. Guide by area and frequency

Results are presented according to the stages of the research data lifecycle.

4.1 Planning

When asked about the existence of a document to guide the use and production of images during the research, 69.7% answered never or rarely, 16.9% occasionally and only 13.5% replied frequently or always. Even the researchers more accustomed to using images (High group) rarely make a document to guide the production and use of images, as can be seen in Fig. 2.

We did not find significant differences between scientific areas or rates of image use.

Regarding the way and frequency in which researchers acquire and produce images, most of them produce images (73%) always or frequently, although about 59.5% of the researchers also consider that they occasionally or frequently use images from past projects. It should be noted that 89.9% of the respondents state that they never buy images from others and 61.8% of them say that they rarely or never acquire images from third parties, even images with no associated cost.

We found that the Life and Health Sciences domain is associated with a significantly higher production of images in the research context when compared with the Natural and Environmental Sciences and the Social Sciences and Humanities fields. This is visible in Table 1 that shows the significant differences between scientific areas.

Table 1. Significant comparisons in planning

Description	LHS>	H>	M>
Images produced in the research	NES* SSH*	L**	L**
Images come from past research		L**	

Likewise, those with low use of images, produce fewer images that researchers with moderate and high use of images in research. This is visible in Table 1 that shows the significant differences between rates of image use.

4.2 Creation/Compilation

Images are always or frequently produced by the computer (51.7%), the microscope (42.7%), the camera of the mobile phone (31.5%), and the traditional photo camera (21.3%). In Figs. 3 and 4, we can see the percentage of use of these instruments by scientific area and frequency of use.

Regarding significant differences between scientific areas (Table 2), Social Sciences and Humanities researchers use the traditional camera significantly more than researchers from Exact Science and Engineering and Life and Health Science. The latter researchers also use this instrument significantly less than Natural and Environment Sciences ones. Similarly, Life and Health Sciences researchers are the ones who mostly use the microscope in comparison with the other scientific areas.

In Table 2, we can see that those who use images less often, use microscope images less often.

Regarding image edition/manipulation, 65.2% of the researchers say they always or frequently use image clipping, 47.2% always or frequently use simple adjustments to properties such as contrast, brightness and saturation, and 49.4% change the dimensions of the image, always or frequently. About 59.6% of researchers say that they rarely or never combine objects from different images to create a new one and 53.9% say they rarely or never use filters to improve image quality.

Table 2. Significant comparisons in creation/compilation

Description	LHS>	NES>	SSH>	H>	M>
Image capture via traditional camera		LHS*	LHS** ESE**		
Image capture via microscope	NES** SSH** ESE**			L**	L*
Perform simple editions to the image	NES*			L**	L**

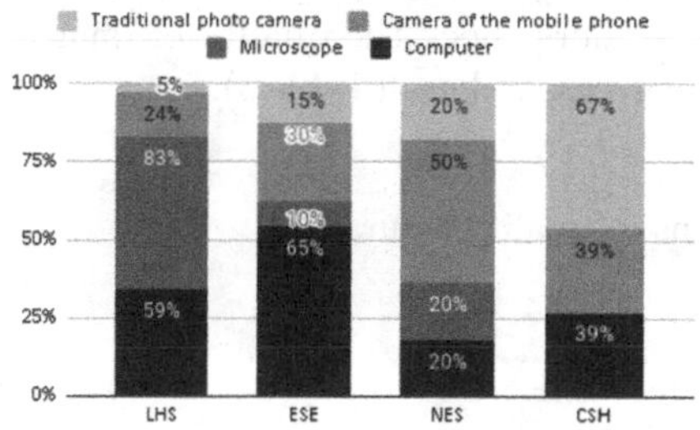

Fig. 3. Instrument of capture by scientific area

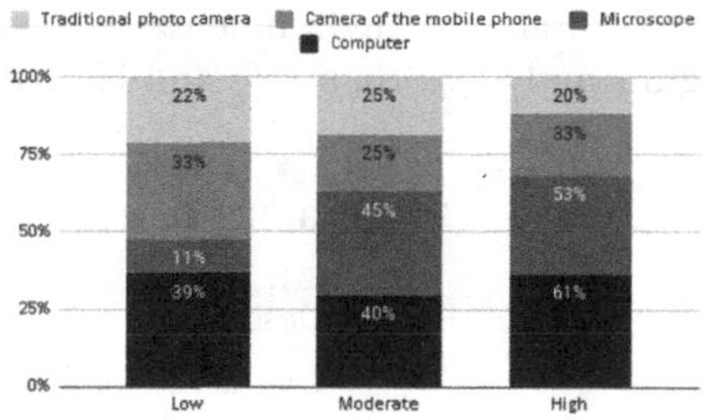

Fig. 4. Instrument of capture by frequency of use

Figure 5 relates the use of images as data with the research domain. In terms of significant differences, Natural and Environmental Sciences researchers perform significantly less simple adjustments to images comparatively to Life and Health Sciences researchers (Table 2).

Figure 6 relates the use of images as data with the frequency of use. Researchers that use images less often perform simple editions significantly less than the others (Table 2).

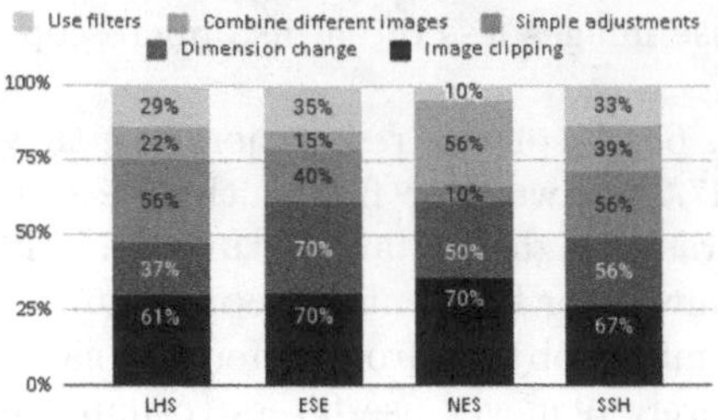

Fig. 5. Image edition by domains

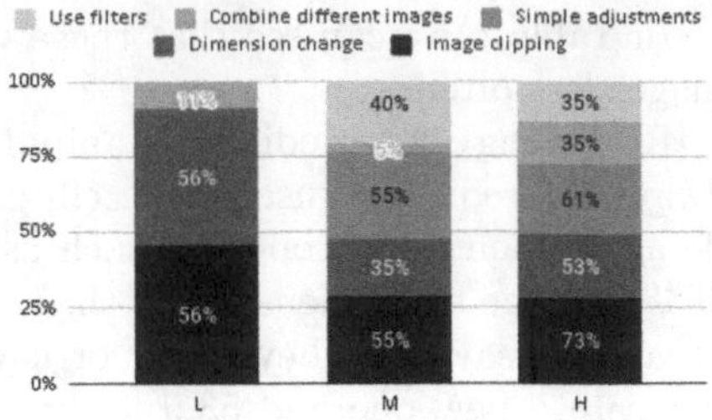

Fig. 6. Image edition by use

Of the respondents who edit the images, 57.6% indicated that they always preserve the original image, and 23.5% frequently preserves it. Only 2.4% of the researchers never keep the original image. We did not find significant differences between scientific areas or rates of image use.

In turn, documentation of editions is always or frequently done by 34.1% of respondents, and 47.1% rarely or never document. We did not find significant differences regarding research domains and rates of image use.

4.3 Quality Assurance

Of the respondents, 53.9% answered that they always or frequently check the quality of their images. Only 7.9% of the researchers say they never do it, and 14.6% rarely check the quality.

Natural and Environmental Sciences researchers check the quality of images significantly less than Life and Health Sciences researchers (Table 3).

Table 3. Significant comparisons in quality assurance

Description	LHS>	H>
Check the quality of images	ESE*	L*

The same happens in researchers that use images less often. These researchers check the quality of the images significantly less than researchers accustomed to using images (High use group) (Table 3).

As for the processes mentioned by the researchers to ensure the quality of the images, these are varied. However, the following stand out: a review of images and their properties (36%), calibration of instruments (23.3%), and disposal of inappropriate ones (9%). We did not find significant differences regarding scientific areas and rates of image use.

4.4 Processing/Analysis

When asked about the most used computer programs in image processing and analysis, the researchers mostly mentioned ImageJ (33.7%), Photoshop (19.7%), Paint (10.1%), Cell Profiler (9%) and programming languages (7.9%). About a quarter (24.7%) of the researchers do not use any computer program.

It can be said that images are the object of different types of analysis. Those that stand out the most are content analysis (37.1%), mathematical calculations (18%), quantifications (11.2%), and measurements (5.6%). Of the respondents, 20.2% do not analyze images.

Finally, we noticed that researchers tend to combine manual and automatic analysis of images. There is a balance between manual mode (38.2% answered always or frequently) and automatic mode (42.7% answered always or frequently). In Table 4 we can see that automated analysis is significantly higher in the Life and Health Sciences and in the Exact Science and Engineering domains. On the other hand, Social Sciences and Humanities researchers are the ones who use manual analysis less in contrast with Life and Health Sciences.

Researchers that rarely use images use significantly less automatic and manual modes to analyze images in comparison with those who highly use images (Table 4).

Table 4. Significant comparisons in processing/analysis

Description	LHS>	ESE>	H>	M>
Manual image analysis	ESE*		L*	
Automatic image analysis	SSH** NES**	SSH** NES*	L*	
Document the conducted analysis	NES* SSH** SSH**		L**	L**

We found that 46% of the researchers said that they never or rarely document their analysis of the images. Life and Health Sciences researchers are the ones that document more frequently the steps taken in the analysis of images in comparison with the other scientific areas (Table 4). The vast majority of researchers who do not use images often, document their analysis significantly less that researchers who do a more intensive use of images (moderate and high use groups), as can be seen in Table 4.

4.5 Description

There is a slight tendency to associate annotations with individual images (44.9% always or frequently), instead of annotations in the set of images (37.1% always or frequently). We did not find significant differences between scientific areas. Researchers with low image use, do not annotate sets of images as often as those who highly use images do (Table 5).

Regarding the support where the annotations are made, the use of documents other than the image stands out. 32 (35.9%) of the respondents said that they always or frequently write it down on a paper document, about 36 researchers annotate (40.5%) on a digital document. Only 16 (18%) of the researchers write in the image, always or frequently. Exact Sciences and Engineering researchers are the least likely to take notes on a paper document other than the image in comparison mainly with Life and Health Sciences but also with Social Sciences and Humanities. These last two have the highest percentage of researchers that annotate on a paper document, 56.1%, and 27.8%, respectively (Table 5).

Table 5. Significant comparisons in description

Description	LHS>	NES>	SSH>	H>
Annotate sets of images				L*
Describe image on paper	ESE**		ESE*	
Use of Author as a descriptor	ESE*	ESE*		
Use of Description as a descriptor	ESE*			
Use of Capture Instrument as a descriptor	ESE** SSH**			
Use of Methodology as a descriptor	SSH**			
Use of Sample as a descriptor	ESE** SSH*			

There is no clear preference in the annotation support regarding the frequencies of images use in research.

It should be noted that 65 (83.1%) of the respondents say that they never or rarely use any application that helps them describe images. Only six researchers (6.7%) say they do use, always or frequently, an application to help them. We did not find significant differences between scientific areas and frequencies of image use.

Regarding the metadata standards for image description, it is clear that few researchers use and know the topic. Of the three options given in the questionnaire (Dublin Core, Common European Research Information Format and EXIF), none showed a percentage of use above 1.1% for "always" frequency and above 6.7% for "frequently". In turn, the average percentage for the frequency "never" is 85.7%. When posed the possibility of presenting standards options other than those of the questionnaire, only five researchers answered, showing a clear trend towards the non-use of metadata standards for the description of images. We did not find significant differences between scientific area and frequencies of image use.

When asked about the vocabulary/elements of description that researchers most use and consider relevant, the answers vary. Seen as most relevant are the elements “title” (68.5%) “author” (53.9%), “date” (57.3%) and “description” (51.7%). The following descriptors are the least seen as relevant, “rights” (39.3%), “format” (40.4%) and “capture instrument” (41.6%). Among the most used descriptors are “title” (83.1%) “author” (62.9%), “date” (62.9%) and “description” (64%). With the lowest utilization percentages are also the descriptors “rights” (24.7%), “format” (39.3%) and “capture instrument” (39.3%).

Figures 7 and 8 show the descriptors used and seen as relevant by the scientific area.

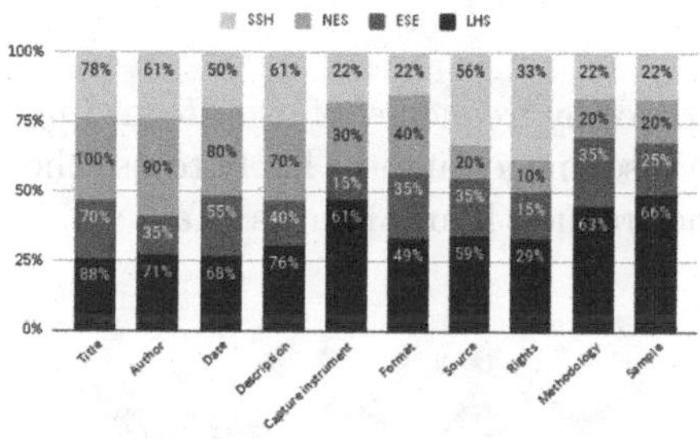

Fig. 7. Descriptors use by research domains

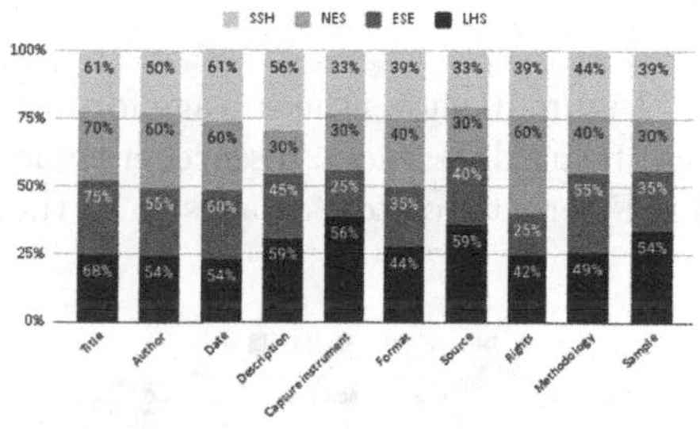

Fig. 8. Descriptors relevance by research domains

Exact and Engineering Sciences researchers are the least likely to use the *author* in comparison with Life and Health Sciences and Natural and Environmental Science as well as the *description* in comparison with Life and Health Sciences. In the opposite direction, Life and Health Sciences researchers are more likely to use the descriptor *capture instrument* and *sample* in comparison with the Exact and Engineering Sciences and the Social Sciences and Humanities domains. Life and Health Sciences are also more likely to use the descriptor *methodology* than Social Sciences and Humanities (Table 5). Regarding the relevance assigned to descriptors, we did not find significant differences between scientific areas and frequencies of use of images as research data.

4.6 Storage

Regarding storage location, the computer stands out (95.5% always or frequently), followed by external disk (73%), pen drive (41.5% always or frequently), and cloud (40.4% always or often). We did not find significant differences between scientific areas and frequencies of image use.

The most used formats to store are TIFF (74.2%), JPEG (83.1%) and PNG (61.8%). Although with very low usage percentages, RAW (13.5%), BMP (7.9%), SVG (2.2%) and PDF (3.4%) formats are also used. Figure 9 shows the storage format preference by the research domain. Regarding significant differences,

Exact and Engineering Sciences researchers are the least likely to use the TIFF format to store their images when equated to Life and Health Sciences. Similarly, Life and Health Sciences researchers are less likely to use the PNG format than Exact and Engineering Sciences researchers (Table 6).

Table 6. Significant comparisons in storage

Description	LHS>	ESE>	H>
Save images as TIFF	ESE**		L*
Save images as PNG		LHS*	

Figure 10 shows the storage format preference by frequency of use. Regarding significant differences, researchers who rarely use images are less likely to use the TIFF format to store images than those who frequently use images (Table 6).

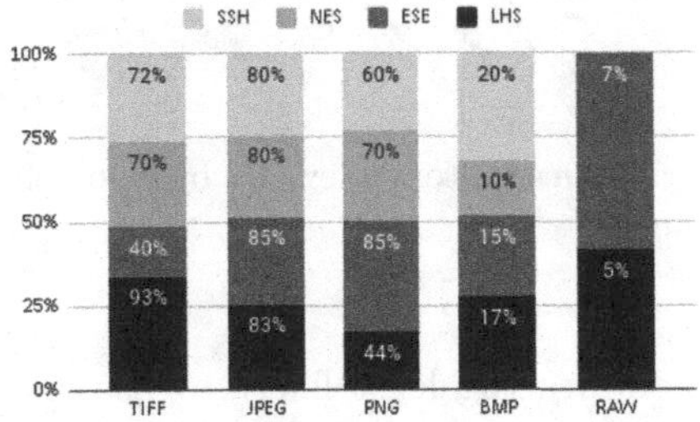

Fig. 9. Storage format by domains

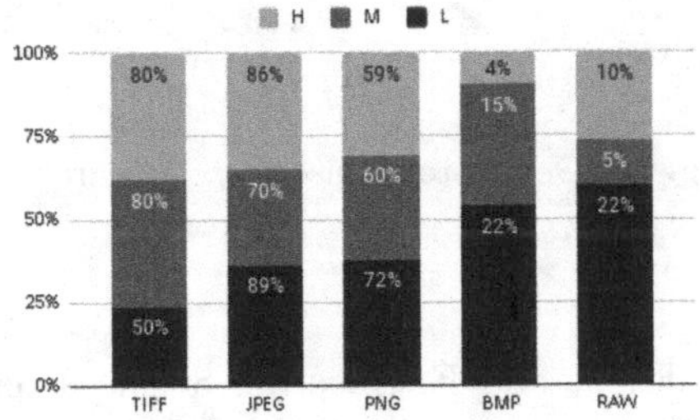

Fig. 10. Storage format by use

Regarding the volume of images stored during a research project, about 58.4% of the researchers said they were not able to quantify it. We did not find significant differences relative to the scientific areas and frequencies of image use.

When asked about the frequency with which they made backup copies, 40.4% responded monthly, 15.8% weekly, and 19.7% daily. About 18% of researchers do not regularly back up and 19.1% do not back up. When researchers make backup copies, they do it manually (65.2%), only 13.5% answered that they were done automatically. In these two questions, we did not find significant differences relatively to scientific areas and frequencies of image use.

4.7 Sharing

Image sharing occurs mainly at the end of the investigation (61.8% answered always or frequently) or during the investigation (59.5% answered always or frequently). Despite this, 41.6% of the researchers responded that they often share the images sometime after the research project is finished. In this question, we did not find significant differences between scientific areas and frequencies of image use.

To the answer about who promotes image sharing, the most frequent answer was the principal investigator (PI) (71.9%), followed by the investigator producing the image (44.9%), institution (31.5%) and funding entity (11.2%).

The PI is the one who promotes the sharing of images most significantly in the Life and Health Sciences relative to Exact Sciences and Engineering (Table 7). No significant differences were found between the frequencies of image use.

Table 7. Significant comparisons in sharing.

Description	LHS>	ESE>	SSH>	L >
Sharing promoted by PI	ESE**			
Include images location in scientific articles		LHS**	LHS*	H*

Regarding rights of use, the researchers replied more frequently that they leave the images restricted in access and use (35.4% always or frequently), followed by free to access and use (27.7% always or frequently) and free access but restricted use (20.7% always or frequently). When asked whether they shared images in archives, institutional or thematic repositories, the researchers' response was never or rarely (85%). About 4.5% replied that they shared in scientific articles. In these two questions, no statistically significant differences were found concerning the scientific areas and frequencies of use.

Most researchers (77.5% never or rarely) do not mention the location where the images are stored in scientific articles. Only 14.6% answered that they always or frequently mention the storage location in scientific articles. Life and Health Sciences researchers are less likely to mention the place where images are stored in scientific articles compared mainly to Exact Sciences and Engineering but also Social Sciences and Humanities (Table 7). Surprisingly, researchers who use images in more than 75% of their research projects are also the least likely to mention the location where the images are stored (Table 7).

Regarding who they share their images with, 67.1% of the researchers that use images said they were always or frequently shared with the research group, 40.7% with the research institute/center, 30.3% with a restricted community of researchers and 13.1% with the public in general. We did not find significant differences regarding the scientific areas and frequencies of image use.

5 Discussion

In this study, we collected information about the processes related to the use of images in research. We found that researchers often use them as research data, mainly in the Life and Health Science domain. Although they are widely produced and used in the research context, there are no guidelines that contribute to the standardization and orientation of their use. These conclusions are in agreement with a study carried out at Arab universities [8] focused on research data management in general.

In the creation process, there is a wide use of digital instruments, which may suggest that the digital revolution was an essential factor for the greater use of images as research data. The most significant use of the microscope in Life and Health Sciences and the traditional camera in Social Sciences and Humanities can be explained by the fact that this use is strictly related to the object of study and methodologies employed in each area.

The processes related to ensuring the quality of the photos are diverse and not all researchers carry out this activity. Likewise, the processing and analysis are heterogeneous, with no existence of standards. This can due to the multiple analysis options that an image may be subject of and with the existence of different methodologies in the various scientific domains.

Regarding the description, researchers do not use metadata models to assist them in this task. The same result was found in past research [8,19]. When asked about the vocabulary/elements of description that researchers most use and consider relevant, the answers are varied. Only three descriptors were used and viewed as relevant by most researchers.

Regarding the storage location, the computer is the location chosen by the majority. This can be explained by easy access, familiarity, and recurring use of the computer in research projects. Elsayed and Saleh [8] found that most of the research stored their research data on their personal devices. It should also be noted that researchers are unaware of the volume of images produced and used during their research projects.

Although researchers said that they share the images used during the investigation, it was found that they do not do it by depositing the images in repositories that would ensure their preservation and sharing. A similar result was found by Elsayed and Saleh [8] were the least preferred way to make data electronically available was open data repositories. These results are also in line with the results obtained in a study [19] that found that researchers want to share their research data, but often find the process difficult.

6 Conclusions and Future Work

With this study, we identified patterns and habits in the creation, description, storage, and sharing of images. We have also compared scientific areas in terms of pratices and analyzed if the habit of using images affected habits. The phases where there was more diversity were quality assurance and processing/analysis, due to the heterogeneity of the methodologies used by the different domains.

Since no articles are addressing this subject, the results presented are useful as they provide valuable insights into the processes and habits regarding the production and use of images in the research context. Although they are preliminary results, we were able to verify that images are used as research data across all research areas. Many practices are common to all areas and some differ by research area.

Next, we will deepen our study by conducting interviews with researchers from different research domains. With the information collected through the questionnaire and interviews, guidelines for the management of research data in image format will be developed.

Acknowledgements. Joana Rodrigues is supported by a research grant from FCT - Fundação para a Ciência e Tecnologia: PD/BD/150288/2019. Special thanks to Professor Luis Teixeira for his help in the validation of the questionnaire. Thanks also to the Master in Information Science at FEUP for supporting the registration in this conference.

References

1. Catharine, A.: The epistemic value of photographs. In: Catharine, A., Katerina, B. (eds.) Philosophical Perspectives on Depiction. Oxford University Press, pp. 82–103 (2010). ISBN: 9781351517577. https://doi.org/10.4324/9780203790762
2. Alex, B.: Review of Data Management Lifecycle Models. Tech. rep. Bath, UK, p. 15 (2012). https://purehost.bath.ac.uk/ws/files/206543/redm1rep120110ab10.pdf
3. Marcus, B.: Using visual data in qualitative research. Ed. by Uwe Flick. 1st. London: SAGE Publications, p. 161 (2007) . ISBN: 9780857020260
4. Gordon, B.: Foreword. In: The Fourth Paradigm: Data-Intensive Scientific Discovery. Microsoft Research, Chap. Foreword, pp. xi–xvii (2009). https://www.immagic.com/eLibrary/ARCHIVES/EBOOKS/M091000H.pdf
5. Christine, L.B., Wallis, J.C., Enyedy, N.: Little science confronts the data deluge: habitat ecology, embedded sensor networks, and digital libraries. Int. J. Dig. Libraries, **7**(1-2) 17–30 (2007). ISSN: 14325012. https://doi.org/10.1007/s00799-007-0022-9
6. Kristin, B.: Data management for researchers: organize, maintain and share your data for research success. Pelagic Publishing, Exeter, UK, p. 189 (2015). ISBN: 978-1-78427-030-8
7. Andrew, M.C., Winnie, W.T.T.: A critical analysis of lifecycle models of the research process and research data management. Aslib J. Inf. Manage. **70**(2), 142–157 (2018). ISSN: 20503814. https://doi.org/10.1108/AJIM-11-2017-0251
8. Amany, M.E., Emad, I.S.: Research data management and sharing among researchers in Arab universities: an exploratory study. IFLA Journal 44(4), 281–299 (2018). ISSN: 17452651. https://doi.org/10.1177/0340035218785196
9. Enser, P.: Visual image retrieval: seeking the alliance of concept-based and content-based paradigms. J. Inf. Sci. **26**(4), 199–210 (2000)
10. Filipe, F., Pedro, P., José, C.: Kit sobre dados de investigação. Tech. rep. RCAAP, 2017, pp. 1–34. http://repositorium.sdum.uminho.pt/handle/1822/46351
11. Rosie, H., Daniel, B., Sarah, J.: Three camps, one destination: the intersections of research data management, FAIR and Open. In: Insights the UKSG Journal, **32** (2019). ISSN: 2048-7754. https://doi.org/10.1629/uksg.468
12. Sara Shatford Layne: Some issues in the indexing of images. J. Am. Soc. Inf Sci. **45**(8), 583–588 (1994)
13. OECD. Making Open Science a Reality. Paris (2015). https://doi.org/10.1787/5jrs2f963zs1-en
14. OECD. OECD Principles and Guidelines for Access to Research Data from Public Funding (2007)

15. Cristina, R., et al.: Os repositórios de dados científicos: estado da arte. Tech. rep., p. 54 (2010). https://repositorio-aberto.up.pt/handle/10216/23806
16. Sandweiss, M.A.: Image and artifact: the photograph as evidence in the digital age. J. Am. History, **94**(1), 193–202 (2007). ISSN: 0021–8723. https://doi.org/10.2307/25094789
17. James, R.S.: Fotograa e ciência: a utopia da imagem objetiva e seus usos nas ciências e na medicina. In: Boletim do Museu Paraense Emilio Goeldi: Ciencias Humanas, **9**(2) 343–360 (2014). ISSN: 21782547. https://doi.org/10.1590/1981-81222014000200006
18. Structural Reform Group. "DDI Version 3.0 Conceptual Model" (2004). https://ddialliance.org/sites/default/files/Concept-Model-WD.pdf
19. Carol, T., et al.: Data sharing by scientists: practices and perceptions. PLoS ONE, **6**(6), 1–21 (2011). ISSN: 19326203. https://doi.org/10.1371/journal.pone.0021101
20. UK Data Archive. Research data lifecycle. (2019). https://www.ukdataservice.ac.uk/manage-data/lifecycle.aspx. Accessed 19 Dec 2019
21. Berenica, V.K., Jane, B., Paula, L.: Image Management as a Data Service. In: IASSIST Quarterly, vol. 40, pp. 27-34 (2016)

Digital Cultural Heritage

Layout Detection and Table Recognition – Recent Challenges in Digitizing Historical Documents and Handwritten Tabular Data

Constantin Lehenmeier[1](✉), Manuel Burghardt[2], and Bernadette Mischka[3]

[1] University Library of Regensburg, 93053 Regensburg, Germany
constantin.lehenmeier@ur.de
[2] Computational Humanities, Leipzig University, 04109 Leipzig, Germany
[3] University of Regensburg, 93053 Regensburg, Germany

Abstract. In this paper, we discuss the computer-aided processing of handwritten tabular records of historical weather data. The *observationes meteorologicae*, which are housed by the Regensburg University Library, are one of the oldest collections of weather data in Europe. Starting in 1771, meteorological data was consistently documented in a standardized form over almost 60 years by several writers. The tabular structure, as well as the unconstrained textual layout of comments and the use of historical characters, propose various challenges in layout and text recognition. We present a customized strategy to digitize tabular and handwritten data by combining various state-of-the-art methods for OCR processing to fit the collection. Since the recognition of historical documents still poses major challenges, we provide lessons learned from experimental testing during the first project stages. Our results show that deep learning methods can be used for text recognition and layout detection. However, they are less efficient for the recognition of tabular structures. Furthermore, a tailored approach had to be developed for the historical meteorological characters during the manual creation of ground truth data. The customized system achieved an accuracy rate of 82% for the text recognition of the heterogeneous handwriting and 87% accuracy for layout recognition of the tables.

Keywords: Document recognition · Handwritten text recognition · Table recognition · Historical documents

1 Introduction: Libraries and the Digital Humanities

The digital turn has a large-scale impact on both society as well as the academic community and in the process forces libraries to rethink their strategies for managing and sharing collections "in radical and possibly scary ways" [1]. The task of providing access to high-quality content remains unchanged, but the medium is increasingly shifting from printed literature toward the digital world. Therefore, libraries have to adapt their organizational and, in particular, technical expertise, steadily evolving into data centers [2]. Bookshelves give way to a digital infrastructure consisting of digitization, standardization, online accessibility, and electronic publishing [3]. Accordingly, libraries "have

M. Hall et al. (Eds.): TPDL 2020, LNCS 12246, pp. 229–242, 2020.
https://doi.org/10.1007/978-3-030-54956-5_17

developed an extensive literature and toolset" [4] to be able to make their collections of written and printed material machine-readable. This is important not only to allow for advanced information retrieval strategies but also to enable "distant reading" [5] techniques, as they have been developed recently in the Digital Humanities [6].

One reason for the success of the Digital Humanities certainly is the increasing availability of digital data, and libraries play an important role in providing this data. However, this is by no means a trivial task, and libraries themselves are becoming part of the larger Digital Humanities landscape, as they have to adopt current technologies and data formats. Along the same lines, Munoz [7] argues that research, including Digital Humanities research, should be "core to the theory and practice of librarianship".

While the Digital Humanities themselves are a rather heterogeneous community that has been called a "big tent" [8], there have been several attempts to systematize the range of existing research. In a recent taxonomy, Roth [9] suggests three branches of Digital Humanities, distinguishing the (1) "digitized humanities", (2) "numerical humanities" and (3) "humanities of the digital". The latter two categories describe the application of algorithmic and statistical methods on the one hand and the study of digital cultural phenomena on the other. Altogether, however, these two areas only account for a small proportion of the existing Digital Humanities research. The lion's share of research, according to Roth [9], takes place in the first-mentioned area, the "digitized humanities", which involves the digitization of cultural artifacts and their management. Libraries – with their numerous tasks in the area of digitizing collections – can therefore easily be classified as a central player in the Digital Humanities research landscape. The requirements and expectations for libraries in the context of digitization meanwhile go far beyond the production of static images of documents using standard scanning infrastructures. Rather, text documents are to be captured in machine-readable form and represented accordingly. The special requirements of the Digital Humanities become very clear here, as humanities documents often have a historical context, which means that oftentimes paleographic aspects must be taken into account in the digitization process. Besides, many sources are handwritten, which poses additional challenges for automatic text recognition. Finally, there is a variety of highly specific text types, e.g. document types that contain numerical data that is structured in tables.

In this article, we present an interdisciplinary project at the Regensburg University Library, which deals with the digitization of one of those highly specific document types, namely the *observationes meteorologicae*, a collection of historical weather data. This very project poses many challenges in the area of OCR (optical character recognition), especially the recognition of handwritten text and the creation of appropriate training data as well as the layout recognition of table structures. In the following, we provide an overview of the main challenges, our strategies for approaching these challenges, and also some lessons learned during this ongoing project, which will be helpful for comparable, future digitization projects.

2 Observationes Meteorologicae

The Regensburg University Library houses a unique collection of local historical meteorological records from the late 18th and early 19th centuries. This handwritten collection spans nearly 57 years, with 53 volumes and about 21,000 pages, and is among the oldest continuous weather records in Europe [10]. The records were documented by several scholars in the monastery of St. Emmeram in Regensburg and range from January 1771 to December 1827. In the 18th century, St. Emmeram – like many other monasteries in Southern Germany – was an advanced center for scientific research. The monastery was integrated into a wide network of monastic scholarship and constituted an important site of contemporary research [11].

Coelestin Steiglehner, professor of mathematics and sciences, started the documentation in 1771 and continued the records for seven years. Since the records were already established nine years before the foundation of the Meteorological Society in Mannheim, the monastery became one of their data suppliers for weather quantities. In 1784, Steiglehner became the first German professor to hold lectures on meteorology at a German university, which is why he is also considered the "father of meteorology". From 1778, Placidus Heinrich and his students took over the task of creating the records. Heinrich was also an acknowledged scientist of his time and was a professor of natural science, astronomy, and meteorology in Ingolstadt between 1791 and 1798. Under his leadership, the standardized instruments of the Academy of Sciences were established, which integrated the observations from St. Emmeram into a national measurement network. Up to thirteen times a day, temperature, air pressure, humidity, wind force and wind direction were recorded and from 1782 onwards, further information on cloudiness, fog, rain, floods, moon phases, and sunspots was added. In 1797 Heinrich published the "Münchener Ephemeriden", the oldest meteorological representation of Germany, and proved his precise, scientific work. After his death in 1825, scientist Ferdinand von Schmöger, then director of the Emmeram observatory, continued the records until December 31, 1827 [12] (Fig. 1).

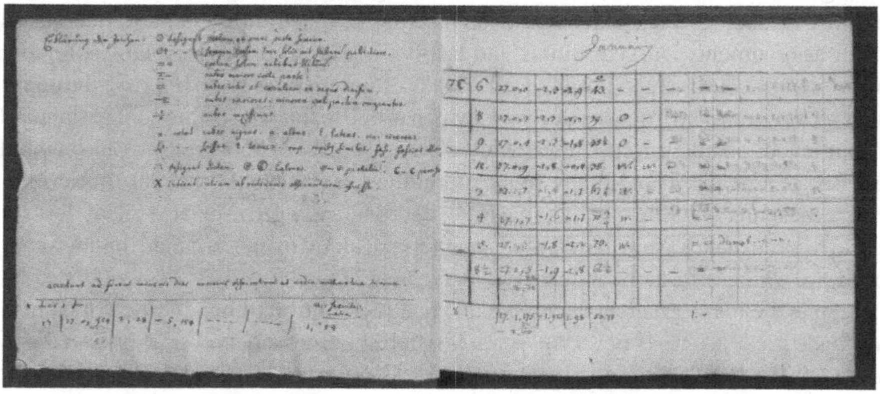

Fig. 1. Two example pages of the weather records from 1782 (left) and 1793 (right).

Due to the high degree of homogeneity and continuity, the *observationes meteorologicae* are particularly well-suited for systematic, computer-aided analysis [13]. By using this historical weather data, meteorological snapshots can be reconstructed to identify the social, political, and economic impacts and consequences of climate change. Regional archives can be used to complement and classify the weather quantities to analyze local historical developments and events.

The collection can therefore not only be worked on by various disciplines but is also closely linked to the history of the city of Regensburg. In 2017, the Regensburg University Library began to digitize the inventory and started working on the indexing of the historical documents.

Early in this process, it became clear that existing off-the-shelf software was not suitable to automate the process of data extraction. Firstly, the tabular layouts were not located and recognized sufficiently. Secondly, the number of different writers, as well as the unconstrained text layout of notes and comments, hinder automatic text recognition. Consequently, a customized developed solution to document recognition is required.

3 Document Recognition

With the rise of affordable data acquisition devices since the 1980s, libraries, in particular, are responsible for the extraction of structured data from physical documents to enable indexing and retrieval. OCR is used to extract information from documents and to convert them from their analog paper form to an adequate digital representation [14]. The process can be divided into four subtasks, namely preprocessing, layout analysis (including text line segmentation), recognition of segmented lines, and postprocessing [15]. While the recognition of modern, machine-printed text can currently be carried out almost flawlessly [14], handwritten text in historical documents of poor quality still poses a major challenge. In contrast to a machine-printed text, which can be easily segmented into single characters and matched to characters within the used font, handwritten text is much more diverse and harder to distinguish. Historical documents often show damaged and fragmented characters as well as show-through and shining effects, marks, or ink dropouts. Further inconsistent page design, graphic illustrations, artistic decorations as well as ornaments, curved initials and last but not least, the individuality of human writing, complicate the recognition itself. A lack of linguistic tools to improve the quality of text recognition also impedes the work, which is due to missing orthographic standards and continuous changes in spelling as well as the ambiguity of abbreviations and symbols [16]. Because of these and many more difficulties, a traditional manual transcription seems almost unavoidable. At the same time, the constantly growing amount of digitized archive records makes them hardly manageable, especially in the so-called double keying procedure, which is done by at least two persons [17].

Despite the many challenges, layout and text recognition of handwritten documents have made great progress in recent years through the use of neural networks and deep learning. In the 1990s, the United States Postal service successfully used neural networks to classify handwritten digits to automate the reading of zip codes [18]. More powerful hardware and larger datasets made neural networks also suitable for handwriting recognition, replacing rule-based systems [19]. It successfully solved Sayre's paradox of handwritten letter-recognition by recognizing complete text lines, obviating the need for pre-segmented data [20]. In the same way, neural networks can be applied to analyze the layout of heterogeneous document layouts. Layout recognition also benefited from the ongoing development of algorithms and their training capabilities [21].

In our project, we present an approach for the layout recognition of tables in historical documents, as the localization and recognition of tables have not been a focus of OCR research so far. This becomes apparent when existing OCR software is used to automatically recognize tables in the *observationes meteorologicae*. In a preliminary pilot study with the open-source tools Transkribus [22], Tesseract 4 [22], and OCRopy [24], none of the tested tools was able to localize tables and extract the structure in a sample set of 38 example pages. The commercial software Abbyy FineReader [25] was able to recognize five of those tables correctly after all. Besides the layout recognition of tables, we also tried to find an efficient approach for the recognition of unconstrained handwriting.

3.1 Layout Analysis and Table Detection

Figure 2 demonstrates the overall architecture of the document recognition system which is described in detail in the upcoming passages.

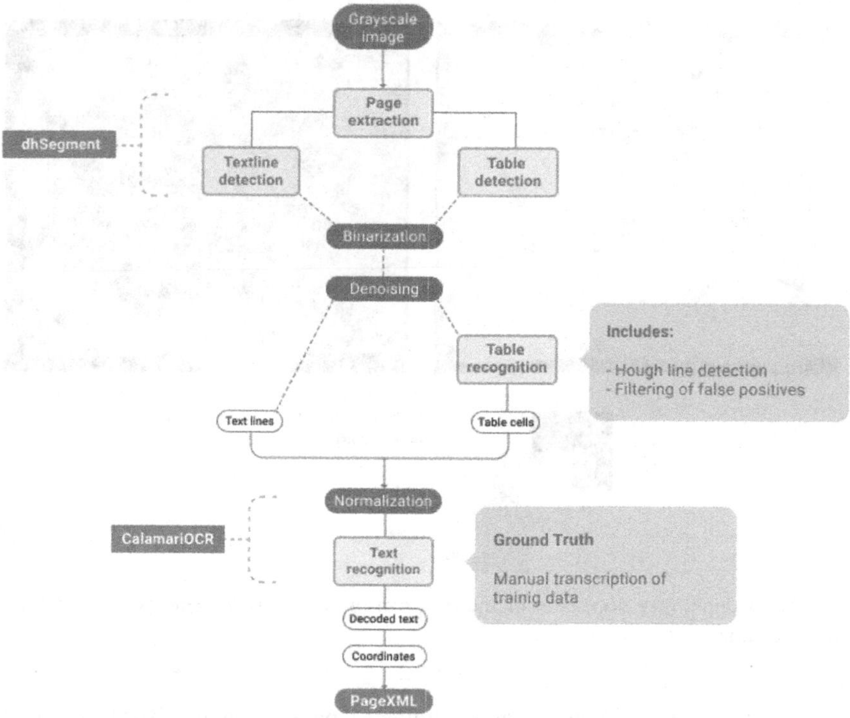

Fig. 2. The complete document recognition workflow.

As already mentioned, the first step in an OCR process is the optimization of the image material. This involves adjusting the contrast to remove artifacts and noise. First, the colored images are converted to greyscale.

Then, the image contrast is enhanced using CLAHE, an efficient approach of adaptive histogram equalization [26]. These preprocessed versions of the original images are used in the layout segmentation process as an input for the layout recognition framework dhSegment [27]. At a later stage, the images are further binarized by using the Otsu method, which is a frequently used global thresholding method [28]. Afterward, small connected components that often resemble noise are removed. These images are then used in the recognition of the table structure as well as the text line recognition.

After enhancing the image quality, dhSegment is used to extract text lines and locate tables. It uses Convolutional Neural Networks (CNN) for the pixel-wise prediction of layout elements in historical documents [21]. The engine can be trained by color-coding segments of interest. The colored images and a text file containing a unique label as well as the RGB color value of each layout segment form the input to train a model. Because of the relative ease of training the system as well as its extensive documentation, dhSegment was chosen as a suitable framework for page segmentation for our application scenario. To extract a page and localize tables, 40 scans of the *observationes meteorologicae* were annotated (see Fig. 3).

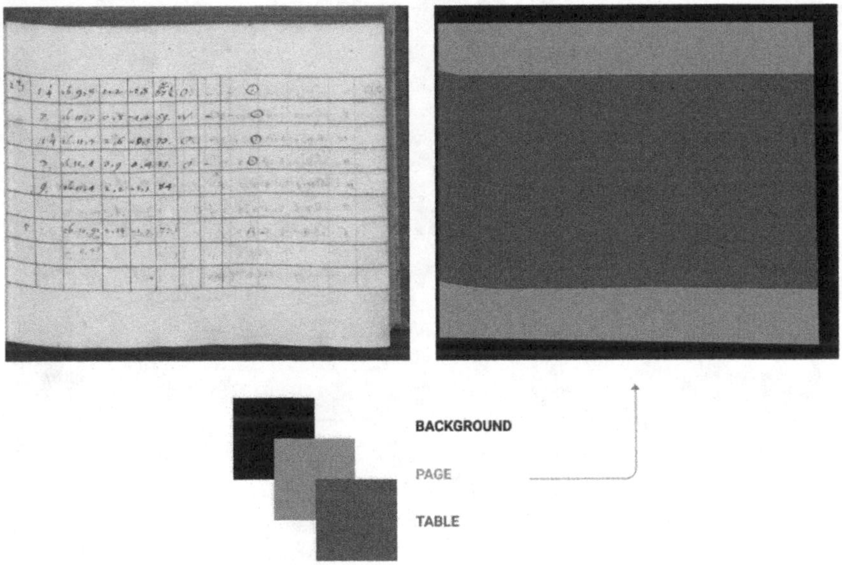

Fig. 3. An example of a document of the *observationes meteorologicae* used for training the layout segmentation models.

The model for baseline detection was trained separately on the cBAD database [29], which contains 2,035 annotated documents (see Fig. 4).

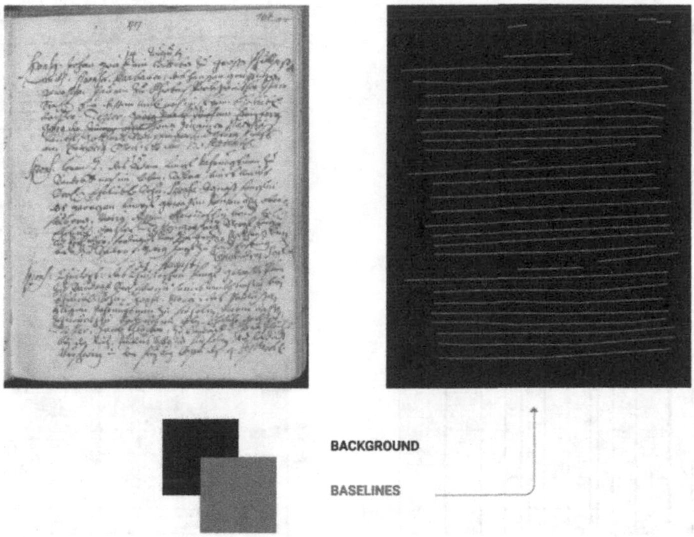

Fig. 4. An example document of the cBAD database for training a baseline detection model.

Although tables can be localized faultlessly with the trained segmentation model, generic machine learning approaches show shortcomings in the structural recognition of tables. The biggest problem is the enormous number of objects in a very confined space. Therefore, the network overlooks important visual features that could help in detecting and recognizing tables [30]. To recognize the table structures, intersections of horizontal and vertical lines are computed, as physical rulings are present. The application of the Hough transform is a popular technique in computer vision and helps to identify lines in document scans [31]. Figure 5a shows computed Hough lines on a localized table. To filter out false positives the length, rotation, and average blackness of a line are used to determine if the line is, in fact, a table line [32]. After filtering the Hough lines, the intersections of the remaining horizontal (see Fig. 5b) and vertical (see Fig. 5c) lines are computed. Based on the intersections, table cells are constructed.

As part of a pilot study, 38 pages of a volume with 381 were used as a sample set. 100% of the tables could be localized by the trained dhSegment model and 87% of the table structure, more precisely the order of rows and columns could be recognized correctly. The Jaccard index is used to compare the localization of the ground truth table against the predicted table [33]. To compare the structural similarity, the layout of the ground truth table as well as of the predicted table is represented as an HTML string. The difference between these two strings is then computed by means of the BLEU metric [34]. Better contrast adjustment to prevent show-through, as well as noise reduction, can further help to improve structural recognition (see Fig. 5d).

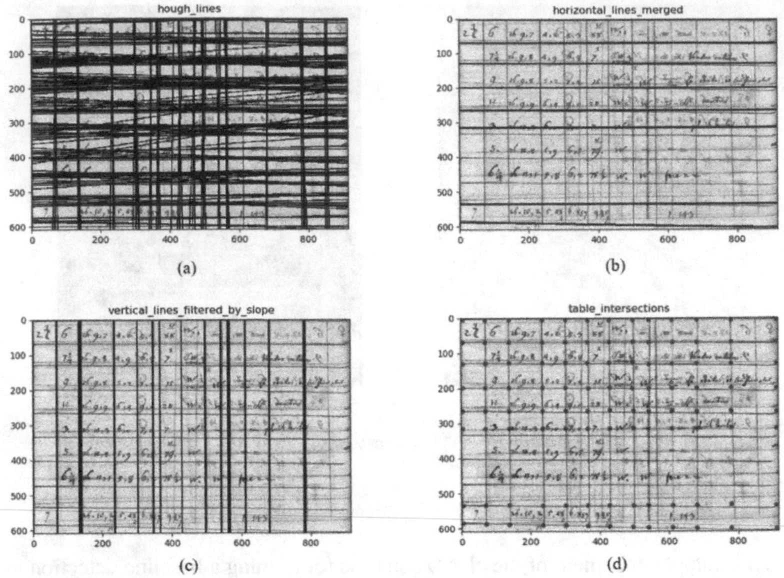

Fig. 5. The computed Hough lines (a) are filtered based on their average blackness and are grouped into horizontal (b) and vertical lines (c). Lastly, the intersections between horizontal and vertical lines are computed (d) and used to construct table cells.

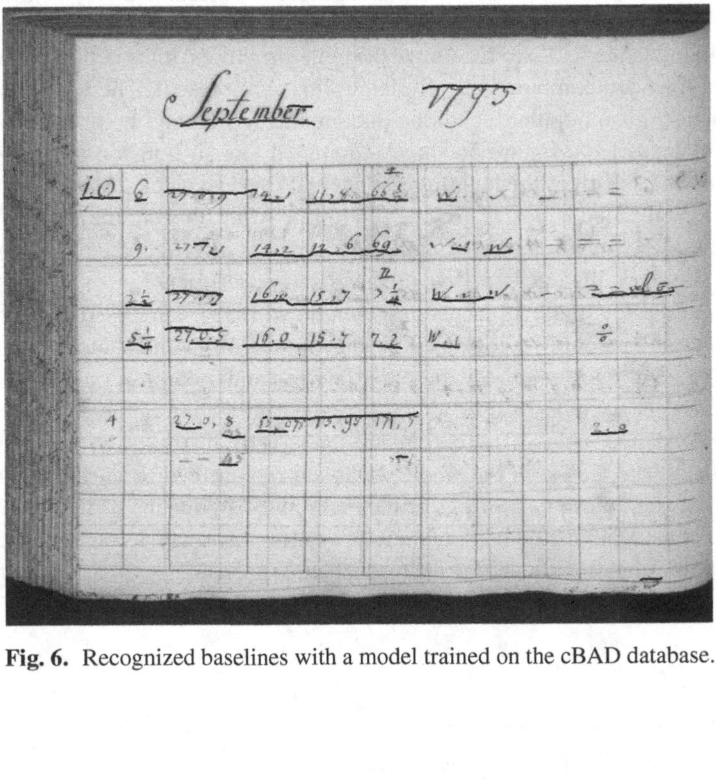

Fig. 6. Recognized baselines with a model trained on the cBAD database.

The results of the baseline detection model, which was trained on the cBAD database, were less sufficient, as some baselines are either not recognized, falsely recognized or baselines of adjacent cells are not separated (see Fig. 6).

In this case, table recognition methods that propose that the alignment of words can be used to deduce the table structure are not applicable yet [35, 36]. Consequently, training on annotated baselines of the *observationes meteorologicae* in addition to the cBAD database is necessary and currently in progress to obtain more accurate data which can help to improve the structural recognition process.

3.2 Text Recognition

The last step in the document recognition process is the automated text recognition of extracted text lines and table cells. Labeled training data is used to create a model that can make predictions about the further text of the collection. To create a set of ground truth data for training and evaluation, text images are manually extracted from the scanned documents using Transkribus [22]. The free-to-use GUI application can export the transcribed data in the PageXML format. This XML structure facilitates the extraction of the annotated text lines as they are necessary to train the text recognition framework.

A volume with multiple writers and different writing scenarios (i.e. deletions, overwriting) was a source for the training data. 36 representative pages of the 381 in the volume were transcribed, which corresponds to a total of 2,285 text lines. This amounts to approx. 10% of the dataset excluding empty pages which is our minimum of ground truth data for the training. The training data included both, the Latin text of the title pages of the volume as well as almost two complete months of tabular notes. To ensure a high-quality dataset, three experts contributed to the creation of the ground truth. For methodological principles, various established guidelines for historical transcriptions and ground truth creation were consulted. Since the collection contains mainly numbers and special characters, not all transcribing norms and guidelines were applicable [37]. In an interdisciplinary dialog, it was agreed to aim for a close transliteration of the original text images reserving all significant characteristics of the original manuscript. In addition to replacing the *long-s* with a *round-s*, *j* with *i* and *ß* with *ss*, words that were overwritten and therefore difficult to read were eliminated from the set, while crossed-out notes were marked accordingly [38].

Special characters used for meteorological terminology and the abbreviations of standardized terms required further attention. Abbreviations were represented similar to the original but were often difficult to read. In the case of historical meteorological symbols, however, directives came into conflict, since various guidelines propose to avoid mixed spellings of Unicode [39]. The historical meteorological symbols differ greatly from the modern Unicode symbols of meteorology or astrology, and some of them are not represented at all. Consequently, a customized index containing various Unicode spellings was created to visually represent the characters of the collection (see Fig. 7) [40].

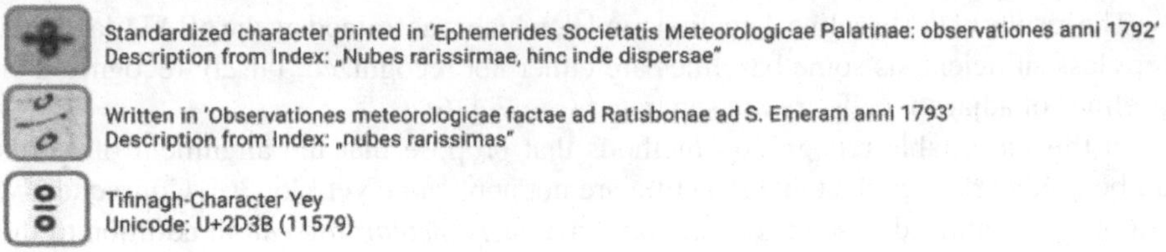
Standardized character printed in 'Ephemerides Societatis Meteorologicae Palatinae: observationes anni 1792'
Description from Index: „Nubes rarissirmae, hinc inde dispersae"
Written in 'Observationes meteorologicae factae ad Ratisbonae ad S. Emeram anni 1793'
Description from Index: „nubes rarissimas"
Tifinagh-Character Yey
Unicode: U+2D3B (11579)

Fig. 7. Example of unicode decoding using different spellings.

The ground truth data is used to train recognition models with CalamariOCR [41], an established text recognition framework. It uses a combination of CNNs and Long-Short Term Memory (LSTM) networks, which "provides access to long-range context" [20], to recognize text lines. CalamariOCR achieves state-of-the-art recognition results when compared to other open-source text recognition software [42]. Although it was originally evaluated on historical, printed books, the framework is also applicable for handwritten text due to the line-based recognition system. The used network consists of two pairs of convolutional and pooling layers, followed by a bidirectional LSTM layer with a dropout of 0.5. The network has been trained by using k-fold cross-training. The data is split into k partitions, where k-1 folds are used for the model training, and one fold is used for performance evaluation [18]. A good starting value for k is 10, as it offers the best trade-off between bias and variance [43]. 32 of the 36 pages were used for the 10-fold cross-training, and the overall accuracy of the text recognition is 82%, which implies a character error rate of 18%. The model was then tested on the remaining four pages, achieving a mean normalized error rate of 25,86%, which means that 355 errors occurred within 1373 total characters. The most common errors occur with missing dots as well as with the number "1". A pre-trained model, for example on the IAM dataset [44], could further increase the accuracy and improve computation time. An estimation of the number of required training data to achieve acceptable error rates is hardly possible, due to the enormous heterogeneity of handwritten text. For example, the user manual of the transcription software Transkribus recommends a vague number of 5,000–15,000 words [45].

In order to deal with a small training set that might be inappropriate for training a neural network, Martínek et al. [46] recommend the combination of real data with artificially generated data. Although considering the printed text, handwritten data can be generated from existing samples [47]. CalamariOCR offers the augmentation of existing data by applying distortion and blur to generate additional data. Evaluating further practical methods for synthetic data generation to enrich the training set is an upcoming task in this project.

The results of the layout and text recognition of a page document are stored using the previously mentioned PageXML format. The format allows for storing various region types, such as text, image, drawing, table, and more. Text regions can contain lines, words, and glyphs, whereas tables can contain rows, columns, and cells. PageXML is a widely used standard for data representation in OCR workflows, as it can be easily integrated into existing infrastructures and as it is extensible by creating new sub-formats [48].

4 Conclusions and Future Directions

The interdisciplinary value of the historical weather data for climate researchers, meteorologists, science historians, economic historians, etc. can be greatly increased by turning it into a machine-readable form, which allows for easy access and information retrieval, but also interactive ways of data visualization and quantitative studies. The heterogeneity and uniqueness of handwritten documents like the discussed dataset still pose a big challenge to libraries.

As we have shown, the combination of state-of-the-art methods to achieve high-quality OCR results cannot be performed in a straightforward process. The evaluation of existing methods needs a lot of experimental testing from computer scientists and humanities scholars. Specific recognition tasks, like table recognition in document images, cannot be performed with deep learning yet. In this case, a customized solution using established computer vision algorithms is less laborious than building and testing a machine learning system. Especially as OCR engines do not perform optimally out-of-the-box and training becomes a very crucial point.

The amount of required training data is difficult to create with a small corpus or collections with various handwritings, like the *observationes meteorologicae*. In the first phase of the project, the transcription of 10% of one volume with different writers achieved a satisfactory result. It represents a success for the processing of the historical data, as computer-aided annotation and transcription can facilitate the creation of training data. However, the generation of ground truth data can only be automated to a certain extent. Words that are jammed in, above or below a line, as well as special characters, abbreviations, and paratexts, are still obstacles, impossible to transcribe without human effort. Therefore, scholarly expertise and the manual transcription of a paleographer are absolutely necessary. With the further digitalization of the collection, the performance of the original training data must be evaluated.

An important upcoming task in the described project will be the creation of additional ground-truth data to improve text recognition results. We aim for a character error rate below 20% to support further computer-aided text analysis [50]. Another upcoming step will be the optimization of the table recognition process. It will be evaluated on multiple volumes of the *observationes meteorologicae* and compared to other existing algorithms. Moreover, extending the baseline detection model with annotated data of the *observationes meteorologicae* could help to further increase the structural recognition process. This will likely improve the detection of paratext and notes as well. To ease the computer-aided indexing of the *observationes meteorologicae* as well as the creation of training data, the workflow will be integrated into a user-friendly and easy-to-use tool that allows for automatic layout and text recognition of handwritten tabular documents for laypersons with various backgrounds. Ideally, this will also enable the transcription and processing of further tabular collections beyond the collection of the *observationes meteorologicae.*

References

1. Anderson, R.: Collections 2021: the future of the library collection is not a collection. https://serials.uksg.org/articles/10.1629/24211/. Accessed 5 June 2020
2. Novy, L.: Bibliotheken zwischen tradition und Fortschritt: Bewahren und Bewegen. https://www.goethe.de/ins/fr/de/kul/sup/nlc/21296095.html. Accessed 5 June 2020
3. Neuroth, H.: Bibliothek, Archiv, Museum. In: Digital Humanities: Eine Einführung, pp. 123–213. J.B. Metzler, Stuttgart (2017)
4. Webster, J.W.: Digital collaborations: a survey analysis of digital humanities partnerships between librarians and other academics. Digit. Hum. Q. **13**(4) (2020)
5. Moretti, F.: Distant Reading. Verso, London (2013)
6. Horstmann, W.: Are academic libraries changing fast enough? Bibliothek – Forschung und Praxis **42**(3), 433–440 (2018)
7. Munoz, T.: Recovering a humanist librarianship through digital humanities. In: White, J., Gilbert, H. (eds.) Laying the Foundation: Digital Humanities in Academic Libraries, pp. 3–14. Purdue University Press (2016)
8. Terras, M.: Peering Inside the Big Tent. Ashgate Publishing, Farnham (2013)
9. Roth, C.: Digital, digitized, and numerical humanities. Digit. Scholarsh. Hum. **34**(3), 616–632 (2019)
10. Universitätsbibliothek Regensburg: Observationes meteorologicae: Placidus Heinrich und seine Wetteraufzeichnungen. http://bibliothek.uni-regensburg.de/meteorologie/. Accessed 5 June 2020
11. Eimern, J.: Zur Geschichte des Wetterdienstes in Bayern. Annalen der Meteorologie (14), 7–17. Selbstverlag des Deutschen Wetterdienstes (1979)
12. Lorenz, M.: Naturforschung in St. Emmeram. In: Im Turm, im Kabinett, im Labor. Streifzüge durch die Regensburger Wissenschaftsgeschichte, pp. 12–29. Universitätsverlag Regensburg (1995)
13. Lehenmeier, C., Burghardt, M.: Historische Wetterdaten im Spannungsfeld zwischen OCR und User-Centered Design. In: Burghardt, M., Müller-Birn, C. (eds) INF-DH-2018, Gesellschaft für Informatik e.V. (2018)
14. Doermann, D., Tombre, K.: Handbook of Document Image Processing and Recognition. Springer, London (2014). https://doi.org/10.1007/978-0-85729-859-1
15. Reul, C., et al.: OCR4all – an open-source tool providing a (semi-)automatic OCR workflow for historical printings (2019)
16. Piotrowski, M.: Natural Language Processing for Historical Texts. Morgan & Claypool Publishers, New York (2012)
17. Rehbein, M.: Digitalisierung. In: Digital Humanities: Eine Einführung, pp. 179–199. J.B. Metzler, Stuttgart (2017)
18. Chollet, F.: Deep Learning with Python. Manning Publications Co., New York (2017)
19. LeCun, Y., Bengio, Y., Hinton, G.: Deep learning. Nature **521**, 436–444 (2015)
20. Graves, A., Liwicki, M., Fernández, S., Bertolami, R., Bunke, H., Schmidhuber, J.: A novel connectionist system for unconstrained handwriting recognition. IEEE Trans. Pattern Anal. Mach. Intell. **31**(5), 855–868 (2009)
21. Oliveira, S.F., Seguin, B., Kaplan, F.: dhSegment: a generic deep-learning approach for document segmentation (2018)
22. Transkribus. https://transkribus.eu/Transkribus/. Accessed 5 June 2020
23. Tesseract 4. https://github.com/tesseract-ocr/tesseract. Accessed 5 June 2020
24. OCRopus. https://github.com/tmbarchive/ocropy. Accessed 5 June 2020
25. ABBYY FineReader. https://www.abbyy.com/de-de/finereader/. Accessed 5 June 2020

26. Boudraa, O., Hidouci W. K., Michelucci, D.: Degraded Historical Documents Images Binarization Using a Combination of Enhanced Techniques (2019)
27. dhSegment. https://github.com/dhlab-epfl/dhSegment. Accessed 5 June 2020
28. Gatos, B.G.: Imaging techniques in document analysis processes. In: Doermann, D., Tombre, K. (eds.) Handbook of Document Image Processing and Recognition. LNCS, pp. 73–131. Springer, London (2014). https://doi.org/10.1007/978-0-85729-859-1_4
29. ScriptNet: ICDAR 2017 Competition on Baseline Detection in Archival Documents (cBAD). https://zenodo.org/record/835441. Accessed 5 June 2020
30. Schreiber, S., Agne, S., Wolf, I., Dengel, A., Ahmed, S.: Deepdesrt: deep learning for detection and structure recognition of tables in document images. In: 14th IAPR International Conference on Document Analysis and Recognition (ICDAR), pp. 1162–1167 (2017)
31. Szeliski, R.: Computer Vision: Algorithms and Applications. Springer, London (2011). https://doi.org/10.1007/978-1-84882-935-0
32. Lee, B.C.G.: Line detection in binary document scans: a case study with the international tracing service archives. In: IEEE International Conference on Big Data (Big Data), pp. 2256–2261. IEEE Computer Society (2017)
33. Kleber, F., Dejean, H., Lang, E.: Matching table structures of historical register books using association graphs. In: 16th International Conference on Frontiers in Handwriting Recognition, pp. 217–222. IEEE Computer Society (2018)
34. Li, M., Cui, L., Huang, S., Wei, F., Zhou, M., Li, Z.: TableBank: table benchmark for image-based table detection and recognition (2019)
35. Rashid, S.F., Akmal, A., Adnan, M., Aslam, A.A., Dengel, A.: Table recognition in heterogeneous documents using machine learning. In: 14th IAPR International Conference on Document Analysis and Recognition (ICDAR). pp. 777–782 (2017)
36. Clinchant, S., Déjean, H., Meunier, JL., Lang, E., Kleber, F.: Comparing machine learning approaches for table recognition in historical register books. In: Proceedings of the 13th IAPR International Workshop on Document Analysis Systems (2018)
37. The distinctive format and the partly standardized Latin terminology made negotiation processes of spelling variations less important
38. Mundt, L.: Empfehlungen zur Edition neulateinischer Texte. In: Mundt, L., Roloff, H.-G., Seelbach, U. (eds.) Probleme der Edition von Texten der Frühen Neuzeit. Beihefte zu editio Bd., vol. 3, pp. 186–190, Tübingen (1992)
39. Transcription guidelines for ground truth. https://ocr-d.de/gt//trans_documentation/trSchreibweisen.html. Accessed 5 June 2020
40. The selection of the different Unicode characters was chosen with a Unicode Shapecatcher regardless of the unicode spelling. https://shapecatcher.com/. Accessed 5 June 2020
41. CalamariOCR. https://github.com/Calamari-OCR/calamari. Accessed 5 June 2020
42. Wick, C., Reul, C., Puppe, F.: Calamari – a high-performance tensorflow-based deep learning package for optical character recognition (2018)
43. Raschka, S., Mirjalil, V.: Python Machine Learning, 2nd edn. Packt Publishng, Birmingham (2017)
44. IAM Handwriting Database. http://www.fki.inf.unibe.ch/databases/iam-handwriting-database. Accessed 5 June 2020
45. Transkribus in 10 (oder weniger) Schritten. https://transkribus.eu/wiki/images/c/cf/Transkribus_in_10_Schritten.pdf. Accessed 5 June 2020
46. Martínek, J., Lenc, L., Král, P.: Training strategies for OCR systems for historical documents. In: MacIntyre, J., Maglogiannis, I., Iliadis, L., Pimenidis, E. (eds.) AIAI 2019. IAICT, vol. 559, pp. 362–373. Springer, Cham (2019). https://doi.org/10.1007/978-3-030-19823-7_30
47. Jayasundara, V., Jayasekara, S., Jayasekara, S., Rajasegaran, J., Seneviratne, S., Rodrigo, R.: TextCaps: handwritten character recognition with very small datasets (2019)

48. Pletschacher, S., Antonacopoulos, A.: The PAGE (Page Analysis and Ground-truth Elements) format framework. In: Proceedings of the 2010 20th International Conference on Pattern Recognition, pp. 257–260. IEEE Computer Society (2010)
49. van Lit, L.W.: C: Among Digitized Manuscripts: Philology, Codicology, Paleography in a Digital World. Brill, Boston (2020)
50. Hill, M., Hengchen, S.: Quantifying the impact of dirty OCR on historical text analysis: eighteenth century collections online as a case study. Digit. Scholarsh. Hum. **34**(4), 825–843 (2019)

Online News Monitoring for Enhanced Reuse of Audiovisual Archives

Rasa Bocyte[1](✉), Johan Oomen[1], Lyndon Nixon[2], and Arno Scharl[3]

[1] Netherlands Institute for Sound and Vision, Hilversum, The Netherlands
{rbocyte,joomen}@beeldengeluid.nl
[2] MODUL Technology GmbH, Vienna, Austria
nixon@modultech.eu
[3] webLyzard Technology GmbH, Vienna, Austria
scharl@weblyzard.com

Abstract. Digital publication platforms and social media have opened possibilities for cultural heritage institutions to share their content online, in particular favouring audiovisual content. To better valorise large-scale digital collections and increase their visibility and societal impact in this digital landscape, archives and libraries need to find optimal opportunities to re-publish this audiovisual content and reuse it in relevant contexts. This demo presents the *Topics Compass*, a tool for monitoring online news and discussions on social media and predicting topics that will be popular in the near future. The tool assists heritage professionals in identifying current and future stories in the media that present opportunities to reuse and publish archival collections with the aim to contextualise these stories and inform and entertain the general public. We present a use case where Topics Compass is configured to support the distribution of broadcaster collections on social media.

Keywords: Data visualisation · Content reuse · Trend monitoring

1 Reuse: Opportunities and Challenges

The recent growth of video-on-demand services and social media have propelled the consumption of video content online [1]. For cultural heritage institutions (CHIs), this presents an opportunity to promote their audiovisual collections. This particularly benefits organisations hosting broadcaster collections where significant resources are dedicated to content production, archiving and preservation, even if the content has been broadcasted only once. Online distribution platforms serve as routes to gain more value from these collections by reusing them in new context to inform and contextualise contemporary topics [2].

However, given the increasingly growing digital collections and the plethora of platforms at their disposal, CHIs are faced with the challenge of how to manage and reuse these large-scale resources in meaningful and effective ways. Curators and editorial teams need to have a comprehensive overview of stories and topics covered in their

M. Hall et al. (Eds.): TPDL 2020, LNCS 12246, pp. 243–248, 2020.
https://doi.org/10.1007/978-3-030-54956-5_18

collections and at the same time, continuously monitor societal discussions to identify opportunities for creating online exhibitions, blogs and social media posts that reuse archival content in response to these discussions. The exponentially growing number of online publication platforms, and content creators, including professionals and amateurs, in combination with the 24/7 news cycle renders this a particularly demanding task that requires data mining tools to identify meaningful stories and patterns and monitor them as they develop in real time [3].

Responding to this, ReTV[1] is a pan-European research action funded by the EU's Horizon 2020 scheme that aims to increase the reuse of audiovisual content in media archives and broadcaster organisations. The project consortium is building a modular technical infrastructure that provides solutions for audiovisual content repurposing, adaptation and publication on digital platforms. This demo paper presents an application enabled by one part of that infrastructure - *Topics Compass* visual analytics dashboard that assists CHIs in making well-informed decisions and identifying opportunities for the reuse of their collections. The tool provides three main advances compared to systems currently in use: (i) real-time analysis and visualisation of stories from cross-platform, multilingual data, (ii) capability to foresee topics that will be relevant in the future, and (iii) ability to compare contemporary online news sources with metadata from archival collections.

2 Topics Compass

ReTV's *Topics Compass* (see Fig. 1) is a visual data exploration and analytics tool that allows users to monitor topics in online data sources across platforms and channels and track their development over time, including their forecasted popularity at a given future point in time. Utilising various data visualisations along multiple context dimensions, the user can analyse evolving topics in online media, inspect how different sources report on them and see how audiences react. With these insights, the user can make well-informed decisions about what archival content would be relevant to audiences at a particular moment in time and how it could complement discussions happening online. The dashboard is based on the Web intelligence platform developed by project partner *webLyzard technology*. The highly customisable dashboard [4] goes beyond simple statistical representations.[2] It supports different types of information-seeking behaviour, including browsing, searching and trend monitoring. Real-time synchronisation mechanisms based on multiple coordinated view technology [5] help to analyse and organise the extracted knowledge, both factual and affective (e.g., the co-occurrence of keywords with a topic, sentiment of social media posts), through trend charts and other visual analytics components.

Figure 1 shows the results of a query on cultural events for the month of June 2020, including (at the time of writing) future dates. The user can select preferred keywords from the list of semantic associations on the top left and visualise their popularity throughout the month using the trend chart in the middle. The visualisations in the right

[1] www.retv-project.eu.
[2] See www.weblyzard.com/showcases for public versions of the dashboard from previous projects.

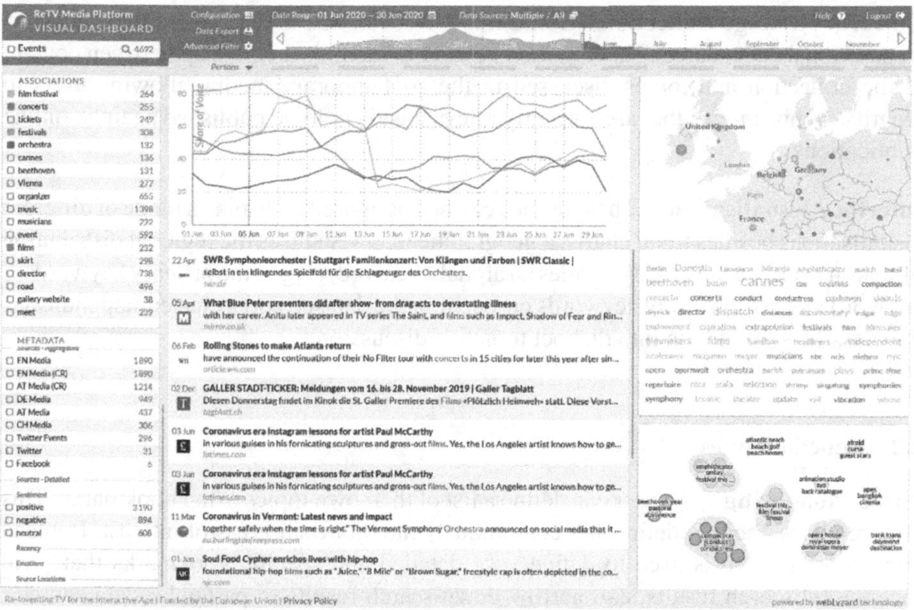

Fig. 1. Topics Compass interface showing visualisations for the query on cultural events.

sidebar show their geographic distribution, a tag cloud with the top associations and a cluster map with the top stories (=groups of similar documents).

2.1 Configuration

The dashboard is configurable to support specific use cases in various domains including fake news monitoring [6] and tourism [7]. For the application in the cultural heritage domain, it is adapted to support the type of content and topics users would be interested in tracking and provide visualisations that allow curators and editorial teams to work with this information.

Online Data Sources. For each use case, a list of data sources is collected. This includes URLs of specific web pages, usernames of social media accounts (Twitter, YouTube, public Facebook accounts) that can be crawled or accessed via APIs. An additional list of terms and phrases determine what content is crawled from various social media platforms and what content should be disregarded entirely. For the purposes of ReTV use cases, the dashboard supports content analysis in English, Dutch, French and German, and could be extended to include Spanish and Italian. This analysis refers to a NLP, NER and NEL pipeline which performs keyword and entity extraction from text, links entities identified inside our own Semantic Knowledge Base (SKB) with resources on DBPedia and WikiData [8], and supports sentiment and emotion detection for documents and sentences.[3]

[3] https://www.weblyzard.com/sentiment/.

Cultural Heritage Collections Metadata. CHIs can add their collection metadata as an additional data source. This can then be used to identify the overlap between content in the collection and topics discussed in the contemporary media, allowing users to identify archival items that are currently relevant and could be published again in online publications.

Interface Visualisations. The interface can be configured to display a range of different visualisations besides trend charts: a geographic map visualises the regional distribution of search results, a tag cloud provides an alphabetical ordering of the primary keywords, a keyword graph shows how keywords co-occur in the dataset, and a cluster map indicates the classification of data into distinct topics of discussion.

2.2 Functionalities

Topic Monitoring. The user can define a list of their own topics using bookmarks. This feature allows them to define and continuously monitor their areas of interest. Boolean query construction is used to define very detailed and specific bookmarks that yield meaningful search results, e.g. narrow down search results to particular data sources, languages, sentiment or impact of the publication. Phrase lists can use regular expression syntax to capture common variations in words in textual documents, e.g. singular/plural. The user can also set up alerts to receive email notifications about the development of their selected topics.

Topic Detection. The large number of documents matching a query can be better understood when clustering them using unsupervised techniques. Based on co-occurrence of keywords across documents, each cluster represents a specific topic of discussion within the dataset [9]. The emergence, growth and disappearance of topics may be tracked over time. For example, an overview of topics of discussion in the news related to cultural heritage during the last week of March 2020 (see Fig. 2) at the end of the week is dominated by the keywords "Vincent Van Gogh, Museum Director, Rijksmuseum" (highlighted in red) - relating to the theft of a Van Gogh painting from a closed Dutch museum.

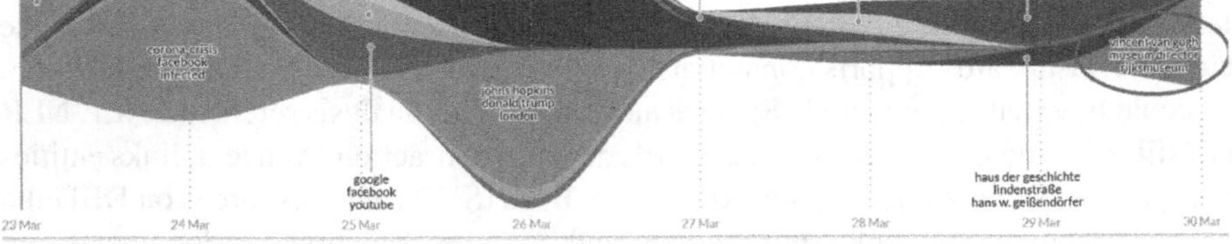

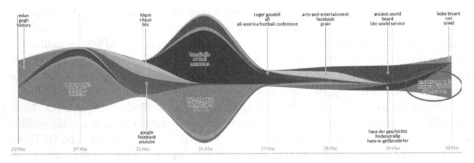

Fig. 2. Story flow for the topic of "cultural heritage" in international news

Prediction Mode. Complementing the analytics and visualisations available for data collected up to the present moment (going back several years), ReTV has developed a hybrid prediction model for topics that may be more popular at a future date. The prediction results can be explored through the dashboard's Prediction Mode where the user may switch to a future date range and view predicted values for any topic. The predictions are based on three approaches: (1) time-series forecasting from past quantitative data using regression models [10], (2) extended using event knowledge from an Event Knowledge Base as an additional feature in machine learning with these models and (3) the use of future dates detected in documents to create an aggregation of keywords associated with that date which, combined with the previous two approaches, will lead us to a hybrid prediction model.

Embeddable Visualisations. Individual dashboard visualisations are embeddable in third-party applications to provide contextual insights for various workflows. In ReTV, the dashboard's visualisations are embedded in other applications in order to provide lexical, stylistic and contextual suggestions for text accompanying content postings, and to assist users in selecting media items stored in their content management applications based on a visual overview of trending news stories.

3 Use Case: EUscreen Broadcast Collection

To demonstrate the application of the tool to enhance the reuse of audiovisual archives, we build a use case around the EUscreen collection[4], a network of broadcasters and media archives that promotes Europe's audiovisual cultural heritage. EUscreen's collection portal includes over 60,000 videos that cover content from across Europe over the last century. The Topics Compass assists in identifying topical content from the collection to be shared on EUscreen's social media accounts by analysing current and future stories in the media and comparing them to content available in the collection. EUscreen collection metadata available via the Europeana API is integrated in the tool and is used to visualise the topics covered in the collection. These can be compared to topics discussed in contemporary data sources defined for the use case - news articles on the Web, blogs about European history, social media accounts of European CHIs. Bookmarks can be used to monitor the emergence of stories about topics documented in the collection. The prediction feature in particular aids the user by highlighting relevant topics for future social media posts and indicating when it would be the most relevant to publish them. The ability to review an array of distributed data sources via a single dashboard interface allows the users to identify more diverse news stories that can be used as an opportunity to reuse a wider range of content from the collection.

4 Conclusions and Future Work

This paper presented the Topics Compass, a visual analytics dashboard that offers a novel proposition on how to enhance the reuse and relevance of archival content using

4 http://euscreen.eu/.

insights from the analysis of contemporary digital data sources. We demonstrated how the dashboard can be employed to increase the online publication of large-scale audiovisual collections but equally, it could be set up to support any other cultural heritage collection. Our future work lies in evaluating the impact of publications guided by the analytical and predictive capabilities of the tool and further tailoring it to the needs of users from the cultural heritage domain.

Acknowledgements. This work was supported by the EUs Horizon 2020 research and innovation programme under grant agreement H2020-780656 ReTV. The authors would like to thank Alexander Hubmann-Haidvogel, Daniel Fischl and Max Göbel from webLyzard for their work on the *ReTV Topics Compass*.

References

1. Kalogeropoulos, A.: Online news video consumption: a comparison of six countries. Dig. J. **6**(5), 651–665 (2018)
2. Bocyte, R., Oomen, J.: Content adaptation, personalisation and fine-grained retrieval: applying AI to support engagement with and reuse of archival content at scale. In: Proceedings of the 12th International Conference on Agents and Artificial Intelligence, vol. 1., pp. 506–511 (2020)
3. Karlsson, M., Sjøvaag, H.: Content analysis and online news: epistemologies of analysing the ephemeral web. Dig. J. **4**(1), 177–192 (2016)
4. Scharl, A., Hubmann-Haidvogel, A., Sabou, M., et al.: From web intelligence to knowledge co-creation - a platform to analyze and support stakeholder communication. IEEE Internet Comp. **17**(5), 21–29 (2013)
5. Hubmann-Haidvogel, A., Scharl, A., Weichselbraun, A.: Multiple coordinated views for searching and navigating web content repositories. Inf. Sci. **179**(12), 1813–1821 (2009)
6. Scharl, A., Hubmann-Haidvogel, A., Göbel, M., Schäfer, T., Fischl, D., Nixon, L.: Multimodal analytics dashboard for story detection and visualization. In: Mezaris, V., Nixon, L., Papadopoulos, S., Teyssou, D. (eds.) Video Verification in the Fake News Era, pp. 281–299. Springer, Cham (2019). https://doi.org/10.1007/978-3-030-26752-0_10
7. Scharl, A., Lalicic, L., Önder, I.: Tourism intelligence and visual media analytics for destination management organizations. In: Xiang, Z., Fesenmaier, D.R. (eds.) Analytics in Smart Tourism Design. TV, pp. 165–178. Springer, Cham (2017). https://doi.org/10.1007/978-3-319-44263-1_10
8. Weichselbraun, A., Brasoveanu, A., Kuntschik, P., Nixon, L.: Improving named entity linking corpora quality. In: Poster at RANLP 2019, Varna, Bulgaria (2019)
9. Nixon, L., Fischl, D., Scharl, A.: Finding the story and eyewitness video of it inside social media. In: The Book "Video Verification in the Fake News Era". Springer (2019)
10. Nixon, L.J.B.: Predicting your future audience: experiments in picking the best topic for future content. In: ACM International Conference on Interactive Media Experiences (IMX 2020), online (2020)

Author Index

Printed in the United States
By Bookmasters

Printed in the United States
By Bookmasters